REALIGNING ACTORS IN AN URBANIZING WORLD

Realigning Actors in an Urbanizing World

Governance and Institutions from a Development Perspective

Edited by
I.S.A. BAUD and J. POST
Department of Geography and Planning
University of Amsterdam

LONDON AND NEW YORK

First published 2002 by Ashgate Publishing

Reissued 2018 by Routledge
2 Park Square, Milton Park, Abingdon, Oxon OX14 4RN
711 Third Avenue, New York, NY 10017, USA

Routledge is an imprint of the Taylor & Francis Group, an informa business

Copyright © I.S.A. Baud and J. Post 2002

The editors have asserted their moral right under the Copyright, Designs and Patents Act, 1988, to be identified as the authors of this work.

All rights reserved. No part of this book may be reprinted or reproduced or utilised in any form or by any electronic, mechanical, or other means, now known or hereafter invented, including photocopying and recording, or in any information storage or retrieval system, without permission in writing from the publishers.

Notice:
Product or corporate names may be trademarks or registered trademarks, and are used only for identification and explanation without intent to infringe.

Publisher's Note
The publisher has gone to great lengths to ensure the quality of this reprint but points out that some imperfections in the original copies may be apparent.

Disclaimer
The publisher has made every effort to trace copyright holders and welcomes correspondence from those they have been unable to contact.

A Library of Congress record exists under LC control number: 2002026180

ISBN 13: 978-1-138-74299-4 (hbk)
ISBN 13: 978-1-138-74297-0 (pbk)
ISBN 13: 978-1-315-18197-4 (ebk)

Contents

Foreword ... ix

1 Evolving Views in Urban and Regional Development Debates in Africa, Asia and Latin America: Introducing the Key Themes ... 1
Johan Post and Isa Baud

PART I
Urban Economies and the Local-Global Interface

2 Firms, Regions and Resources in a Globalizing Economy: A Relational View ... 25
Jan Lambooy

3 Embeddedness: The Role of Local Factors in Economic Development ... 43
Guus van Westen

4 Urban Cluster Trajectories in Developing Countries: Beyond the Industrial District Model ... 63
Peter Knorringa

5 Partnerships, Meso-Institutions and Learning: New Local and Regional Economic Development Initiatives in Latin America ... 79
Bert Helmsing

6 Earning More or Less: Income, Micro-Production and Women's Status in Lima's Poor Neighborhoods ... 101
Annelou Ypeij

7 Urban Fringes in Asia: Markets versus Plans ... 119
Hans Schenk

PART II
Local Governance, Partnerships and Urban Development

8 Healthy Cities and Urban Governance ... 139
Ton van Naerssen

9 Popular Participation and Urban Poverty Alleviation in Bolivia 157
Aart Schalkwijk

10 Popular Participation and the Participatory Planning Practice in Latin America: Some Evidence from Bolivia and Brazil 175
Paul van Lindert and Gery Nijenhuis

11 Combining Capitals: The Assets of Community-Based Organizations and Local Government for Neighborhood Environmental Management in Lima 197
Michaela Hordijk

12 New Partnerships in Urban Solid Waste Management and their Contribution to Sustainable Development: Experiences in Accra (Ghana) and Chennai (India) 219
Isa Baud and Johan Post

PART III
Livelihoods, Rural-Urban Linkages and Regional Development

13 About Trade and Trust: The Question of Livelihood and Social Capital in Rural-Urban Interactions 243
Leo de Haan and Paul Quarles van Ufford

14 The Provisioning of African Cities, with Ouagadougou as a Case Study 265
Ton Dietz and Fred Zaal

15 Economic Networks and the Importance of Rural-Urban Linkages, with the Focus on Sub-Saharan Africa 287
Sjoukje Volbeda

16 Resource Flows and Urban Governance: Approaching Environmental Transitions in Cities and their Hinterland 313
Isa Baud and Michaela Hordijk

17 Regional Development Planning in Latin America: Towards a More Sustainable Use of Space 329
Annelies Zoomers

PART IV
Urban Poverty Reduction: Mapping the Policy Arena

18 Urban Poverty Reduction Options at Local Level
  in a Globalizing World   349
  Emiel Wegelin

19 Reducing Urban Poverty: Constraints on the Effectiveness
  of Aid Agencies and Development Banks
  and some Suggestions for Change   373
  David Satterthwaite

20 The Rise and Decline of an Urban Poverty Unit
  in the Dutch Ministry of Development Cooperation   403
  Joop de Wit

  Index   423

Maps: UvA Kaartenmakers, Amsterdam

Foreword

The contributions to this book have been collected on the occasion of the farewell lecture of Ad de Bruijne, who has held the chair of Human Geography of Developing Countries at the University of Amsterdam since 1985, and before that, at the Free University in the same city. During the period in which he has held the chair, there have been major shifts in the international development debate. One the major turns has been the revaluing of the relative importance of the state, the private sector, and civil society organizations as development actors. The emerging neo-liberal paradigm in the 1980s led to the view that the private sector should be the main actor in development and a lessening of interest in the possible exclusionary effects of such a form of economic growth. In the 1990s, there has been a further shift in recognizing the importance of state and public sector organizations as enablers and standard-setting organizations in their own right, and the role of civil society organizations in promoting alternative forms of development that reflect the wishes of ordinary citizens more clearly.

De Bruijne has primarily focussed his attention in research and teaching on issues of poverty and development in urban areas, including their connections to regional and global transformations. Throughout his work, he has paid attention to the notion of the city both as a place of residence and as a center of economic growth and development, recognizing the diversity of regions throughout the world. Several years ago, he lamented the lack of a volume bringing together some of the insights from urban and regional development research, which would be useful for MA students and development practitioners. With this volume, the editors have brought together the results of recent studies by a large number of Dutch academics in this area, in an attempt to combine such contributions into one volume. This volume reflects the combination of issues in which De Bruijne is interested. He has pursued a wide range of thematic issues, and continues to do so. He has always tried to ground the scientific – as well as the political – debate firmly in the lives of people and their communities.

In the geographical discourse a major issue includes the way in which institutions operating at different levels of scale influence initiatives by local actors to produce economic prosperity. Global-local linkages are a central theme throughout De Bruijne's academic work. An anecdote from De Bruijne's classroom experience nicely illustrates this point. He shows a group of Surinamese geography teacher trainees a video about slums in Latin

America. The students pity these Latinos, but feel no connection with them. Their reference point is the Netherlands, and that shapes the way they reflect on and go about their lives. The message is that in this case, and as a result of a long process of globalization, the lives of people in Surinam are greatly influenced by the lifestyle of people thousands of miles away. Life in Surinam is part of a wider, interdependent structure in which large players, such as the USA, and increasingly, Brazil, mold the daily activities of the Surinamese. Making people aware of these linkages and enabling them to respond is one of the challenges Ad de Bruijne takes up in his work.

Cities as places of residence in the developing world are often associated with endless slums and huge numbers of people living in hazardous, unhealthy environments. Naturally, their 'habitats' have received a great deal of attention from international development specialists. One central discussion centers on the re-alignment of the actors responsible for urban planning and management. In the 1960s and 1970s, the government was seen as the main actor in providing social housing and neighborhood improvements. Bulldozing squatter settlements and replacing them with large building schemes was seen as an effective strategy to create clean and healthy living environments. Governments soon proved to be unsuccessful in realizing these ideals. Mainly based on Latin American experience, the insight grew that the creativity and resourcefulness of the urban population should be given far more attention than hitherto had been the case. It became evident that, with the help of from community-based organisations, local people were capable of improving their own houses and neighborhoods. In a Surinamese newspaper of 1968, De Bruijne already stated that the poor were not passive victims and that research increasingly had uncovered the many ways urban dwellers managed to create assets and procure their livelihoods.

Government and donor agencies accepted this notion of so-called self-help and shifted their efforts to providing the urban poor with tools to enhance their capacities, e.g. through sites and services projects with security of tenure and credit schemes. From the early 1990s on, this approach evolved into a more post-modern view in which urban development is conceptualized as a common challenge to governments, the private sector, and civil society. The government's role has changed from direct provider to a coordinator and enabler of urban action. De Bruijne sees the multi-partner cooperation as a crucial process in human development. He believes that empowering the urban poor is essential to achieve meaningful outcomes. At the same time, he warns against an overemphasis on bottom-up approaches as this could easily deteriorate into escapist behavior by those in power. He therefore strongly advocates that local governments show more responsibility, accountability, and determination in decision-making and in allocating budgets. He has put this focus into practice, advising the Dutch and Surinamese governments over a long period of time; by being member of the Dutch Advisory Council on Development Cooperation (NAD), by co-founding the Habitat Platform and by being Director of the Indo-Dutch Program on Alternatives to Development (IDPAD). This interest is reflected in the final section of the book, which links research to policy and practice from a number of perspectives.

Cities are also nodes in regional development. This role has regained new emphasis in the context of globalization. Globalization of production, commerce, and finance capital requires a new geography of cities, urban networks, and urban-rural linkages. In competing for global investment, cities try to enhance their comparative advantages in terms of both physical assets and social infrastructure. Networking and the facilitation of innovation systems have become key issues in the analysis of cities and their role in regional development. At the same time it has become increasingly difficult to make meaningful distinctions between urban and rural life within regional settings. Livelihoods in many regions have become multi-local. This means that they are produced through networks spanning different localities both rural and (distant) urban. De Bruijne has consistently placed his research on urban areas in the context of the city as an open system in the regional setting. He linked his research on cities with their local and global surroundings.

Ad de Bruijne was, and continues to be, a dedicated, inspired and inspiring researcher, teacher, colleague and friend. This book marks only the end of De Bruijne's formal career, not the end of his engagement or his willingness to contribute, influence and advise on issues of poverty and development. Poverty and inequality, issues that have dominated Ad de Bruijne's work for over forty years, have become even more pressing today. These interrelated problems still call for attention from, the commitment of, and action by researchers, in particular development geographers. There is no justification for a diminishing interest. Because of de Bruijne's ability to bridge the gap between research and policy, he has left clear footprints on the field of Dutch development policy and development cooperation. He will undoubtedly continue working on research projects in the coming years. Thus, we are sure that his colleagues and friends will bump into him again one day, in the heat of Surinam, or on the crowded streets of India.

Isa Baud, Hebe Verrest
January 2002

1 Evolving Views in Urban and Regional Development Debates in Africa, Asia and Latin America: Introducing the Key Themes

JOHAN POST AND ISA BAUD

Since the beginning of the 1990s, the development market place has been swept by new concepts and strategies – participatory governance, partnerships, social capital, synergetic development, and collective learning, to name just a few – suggesting that the crisis of development is long passed. Despite radical attacks on the idea of development by post-development scholars such as Sachs and Escobar, mainstream development thinking currently stands firm. This is probably because it is finally trying to come to terms with the complexity and diversity of development, and with the idea that development is about human beings. As a result, many elements and practices stemming from alternative development have gradually found their way into mainstream development (Nederveen Pieterse, 1998).

In this book an attempt is made to critically assess some of the new ideas that have gained prominence in the development discourse. The focus of the book is on urban and regional development, i.e., on those spatial levels where the direct interface between global forces and national, regional, and local forces occurs. The local level has also gained importance, because decentralization processes have increased government responsibilities at the local and regional level, and thus their influence on future development paths.

The increasingly complex pattern of global interaction in many domains during the last quarter of the 20th century provides the context for studying urban and regional development processes. Since the late 1970s, a new international economic order has gradually evolved, dominated by financial centers, global markets, and transnational corporations (TNCs). Major transformations in patterns of production and distribution have occurred. Companies organize commodity chains globally, albeit with localized production plants. Capital moves freely to those locations where profits can be maximized. Such TNCs have become the primary shapers of the contemporary global economy. Technological advances, particularly in information and communication technologies, have enabled TNCs to maintain centralized control over dispersed production locations. Their increased flexibility in production and the mobility of capital has resulted in national governments losing control over key sectors of their economies. Currently they primarily seem to act as the facilitators of international capital, rather than as the caretakers of social equity and wellbeing (Hobsbawn, 1996; Hoogvelt, 1997; Dicken, 1998; Held et al., 1999; Mittelman, 2000).

This new phase in the development of capitalism – which is called flexible production, lean production, or post-Fordism – is accompanied by a restructuring in the governance of economies. The Keynesian logic that supported the expansion of mass production (1947-1976) was discredited and replaced by the neo-liberal logic of the market. The shift towards market-led economic strategies was prompted by the conservative wave in many key Western countries in the 1980s, the collapse of the Soviet Union, and the partial shift to a market economy in China. Structural adjustment policies, based on the logic of the Washington Consensus, were foisted on many developing countries by the IMF and the World Bank in order to revitalize their economies, which were regarded as deadlocked. Even though neo-liberalism is already past its peak and its negative externalities are increasingly becoming clear – financial instability, 'jobless' growth, environmental degradation, tensions between democracy and the market (Nederveen Pieterse, 2000, p. 10) – it has profoundly affected, and continues to shape, the policy environment.

The new global political economy has produced a new type of inequality, one that is primarily social (rather than geographical) and cuts across nations. There is talk of social exclusion and the rise of a so-called Fourth World, including those areas of the former First, Second and Third Worlds that are no longer relevant to the working of the capitalist system (Hoogvelt, 1997, p. 89). Large segments of society no longer perform a 'useful' function either as producers or consumers in the global market, and suffer the consequences. Such inequalities are also apparent in the international urban system. Many major cities have managed to reassert their importance, and others have adapted to the new challenges. Despite the hyper-mobility of capital, there is a continued, perhaps even increased, need for strategic sites with vast concentrations of resources and infrastructure. These so-called 'global cities' function as command nodes in the organization of the world economy, and as sites where the leading financial and specialized service institutions are located. They are closely connected to each other through financial markets, flows of services, and investment. At the same time, many other urban centers – notably port towns and manufacturing towns (not only in the developing world, but also in advanced economies) – are in decline (Harris, 1997; Sassen, 1998).

Another trend that has profoundly affected the policy arena of urban and regional development, is the global spread of parliamentary democracy since the end of the Cold War. The drive towards democratization can partly be seen as a response to domestic pressures stemming from popular dissatisfaction with the economic mismanagement, lack of representation, and corruption characteristic of many states in Africa, Asia, Latin America, and Eastern Europe. Equally important, however, is the rise to prominence of the liberal-democratic ethic since the fall of the Berlin Wall. The new wisdom is that 'democratic' policies and a slim, efficient, and accountable public bureaucracy are not simply desirable, but are necessary for a thriving free-market economy (Leftwich, 1994, p. 69). Donor agencies have increasingly made their development assistance conditional on the adoption of democratization, decentralization, and popular participation policies. Decentralization, for example, is considered not only vital in the campaign of rolling back the central state, but also a necessary condition for bringing government closer to the people. Furthermore, it gave governments an opportunity to regain some of the legitimacy they had lost in the crisis years (Helmsing, 2000).

In the 1990s, the concept of 'good governance' entered the development industry as a convenient tool to criticize both the technical shortcomings of public administration (lack of efficiency, transparency, accountability, and rule of law) and the weakness of democracy. Through the governance debate, the state came back into focus, albeit not as the pioneer of development, but as an enabler, a coordinating agency able to work together with a variety of other organizations. Although the discourse is often severely biased towards the adoption of Western norms and standards, the concept can also be used in a more empirical way to discuss the various ways in which people regulate public goods provision (Kaul et al., 1999). This does not imply a denial of the importance of democratic principles, but rather the need to look for locally grounded forms of popular engagement in planning and decision-making with respect to public matters, as well as a focus on collaborative actions across the public-private divide. This interest is reflected in very promising research on such themes as co-production, partnership arrangements, and participatory governance (Evans, 1996; Ostrom, 1996; Stoker, 1998, Baud, 2000; Nederveen Pieterse, 2000).

Undoubtedly, the forces of global markets and politics are profound and affect livelihoods across the globe. However, the inherent selectivity of globalization leads not only to homogenization, but also to increased diversity, and the growing importance of regionalism, community, and 'local' identities (Haan, 2000a: p. 32). Global processes produce different outcomes in different settings. This statement fits well with the conventional wisdom in today's social sciences that social realities are constructed. Both structure and agency play a part in this process of construction.[1] The importance of individual agency is apparent in the diversity of responses to globalization processes. The numerous ways in which the poor deploy their assets or capitals in order to secure and enhance their livelihoods is an expanding area of research (Chambers, 1995; Moser, 1998). In many cities, poor households collectively undertook initiatives with a variety of NGOs in order to counter poverty and promote community and neighborhood development (Baud, 2000).

Similarly, in the debate on international competitiveness, the abilities of local actors to create a favorable climate are gaining priority. Increasing attention is given to the importance of external economies, collective learning, and the quality of governance in enhancing local economic development (Helmsing, 2001). Finally, the numerous forms of collective resistance to globalization – ranging from attempts to articulate traditional cultural identities in the face of invasive Western values, to battles against environmental degradation and the abuse of child labor – are also being increasingly documented (Mittelman, 2000). These examples attest to the renegotiation processes being carried on, and to people's resilience and ingenuity in turning threats into opportunities.

The contributors to this book describe the variety of responses to global transformation processes, with special emphasis on the realignment between market, state, and civil society in the African, Asian, and Latin American context. The question of realignment is considered from three main perspectives: urban areas as motors of economic development and their interface with globalization processes (Part 1); governance and collective action issues at the local level (Part 2); and urban areas as the nodes of political and economic development in their regions (Part 3). These perspectives are complementary and provide an insight on how development processes are currently shaped by a variety of institutional arrangements. The last section of the book (Part 4), raises the question of urban poverty reduction within

---

1. Agency refers to the ability of people to accommodate, transform, or resist.

the context of shifting policy paradigms and new forms of co-operation between public and private actors.

Urban Economies and the Local-Global Interface

The first part of the book focuses on cities as motors of economic development by looking at the external relations of such urban economies, particularly those resulting from globalization processes as well as the diversity of urban economies within the spatial confines of the city. A major question addressed is how urban economies position themselves within globalization processes, and the consequent unevenness in local economic development. Some authors have suggested that only a small number of cities will be able to maintain their competitiveness in a global context and that the rest will fall by the wayside (Castells, 1996). Although many cities are competing for world city status it is extremely difficult to become a major control, command and management center and equally difficult to defend this position. Obviously, most cities in the developing world cannot hope to aspire such a status; this is probably why contemporary work on world cities virtually ignores the plight of large cities in less developed economies (Short and Kim, 1999).

A city's attractiveness to global capital is not entirely dependent on market forces. Many authors believe competitiveness can be constructed, at least partly, through public policy. While technological advances have reduced the role of 'space' (distance) in the organization of economic activity, 'place' – location-specific conditions – is back on the map with a vengeance (Storper, 1997; Krugman 1997; Sassen, 1998; Helmsing, 2001). By investing in the material and social infrastructure that constitutes the place-bounded conditions of production, national and local governments can try to promote their cities (Sassen 1998; Devas, 2001). The World Development Report (World Bank, 2000), for example, sketches the agglomeration advantages of cities, in terms of human capital, financial capital, and infrastructure and communication systems. It suggests that supporting these location advantages by improving institutional support and increased integration with globalized markets can work to the advantage of local and regional development. However, the challenge to create a favorable environment for transnational corporations has to be matched with the need to secure a livable habitat and livelihoods for local residents. The desire to join the league of world cities can entail considerable social and environmental costs as the situation in many Pacific Asian cities painfully exemplifies (Douglas, 2000).

The governance agenda of global cities, therefore, is much wider than much of the literature on local economic development in the era of globalization would have us believe. These issues are taken up particularly in Part 2 and 3 of this book.

The majority of chapters in this part of the book deal with the dynamism of urban agglomerations as spatial nodes of socio-economic development. In the literature on economic globalization increasing attention is paid to the importance of local factors in shaping the development path of a city and its region. Research on these issues starts from firms, and the factors that affect their competitiveness at local and higher scale levels. The focus in much research has been on various sets of factors; primarily on firms and their forward and backward linkages, but also on spatial and organizational clustering, and meso-level institutional arrangements that shape the way collective learning takes place. In the chapters by Lambooy, van Westen, Knorringa, and Helmsing, these factors are taken up from different perspectives, in an attempt to provide answers to what policies, institutional arrangements between government and private sector, and collective action by the private sector contribute to economic prosperity.

Lambooy takes up the issue of urban and regional development in relation to the ways firms organize the use of a variety of resources. He emphasizes the role of regional or national 'resource systems' and institutional structures in the process of differentiation. Firms and workers develop specific kinds of tacit or codified knowledge, which can increase their competitiveness. He suggests that firms are increasingly open systems, connected through networks with other firms and other actors. Although firms primarily need to develop a specific set of distinguishing attributes, they also need a certain flexibility to adjust to changing environments, in which fierce competition exists with other firms. One result of flexibility is that firms, especially transnational corporations, can benefit from opportunities both in the world market and in regional specialization. Another result of flexibility is that many firms can use new technologies or develop new markets. Regional embeddedness and innovation systems facilitate the access to resources. He concludes by suggesting that strong regional and local networks can reduce the threats of globalization, and enhance its beneficial aspects in promoting changes.

Westen follows on from this discussion by examining the role of 'local' factors in the regional 'embeddedness' of firms. The concept of embeddedness implies that economic decisions reflect not only market rationality, but also the social context of economic actors. Traditionally, embeddedness through local supply linkages has been emphasized, as an indication of the degree in which global business is integrated in the urban economy. With intensified globalization, interest in the interaction between local and external factors has drawn attention to other ties linking activity with locality. A variety of economic actors – entrepreneurs, workers, trade groups – may organize themselves in ways that facilitate exchange of information and mutual understanding ('trust'). The local state may, directly and through partnership with private parties, enhance conditions for local growth. And less tangible social and cultural institutions may create specific types of 'social capital' to enable successful cooperation in economic life, most notably through technological learning. Contrasting the development experience of a number of urban regions in Southeast Asia and Mexico, Westen concludes, interestingly, that moderate political embedding of the economy where the state – in partnerships with the private sector and civil society organizations – creates a framework conducive to growth, may well be the most effective way of promoting local economic development.

Knorringa in turn takes up the issue of how the 'clustering' of firms and the trajectories followed by such clusters can lead to important differences in their competitiveness. Clusters in developing countries differ significantly from those in Europe in the extent to which they depend on outside actors for implementing incremental process innovations. The chapter compares the capability of specific types of clusters to do so. For the large group of industrial clusters at survival level found in developing countries, the industrial district model is not a suitable frame of reference. For more mature and export-oriented clusters operating in buyer-driven commodity chains, endogenous upgrading capability is important because it makes them more attractive to global buyers in quality-driven market segments (Gereffi, 1999; Schmitz and Knorringa, 2000). The trajectory towards a so-called Italianate district (a competitive, closely networked geographic and industrial district), which offers the greatest potential for endogenous upgrading, is very rare in developing countries. The lack of endogenous technological innovative capabilities and resources, and institutional settings in which social inequalities are often strengthened because of extreme differences in bargaining power between actors, are contributing factors to this situation. In contrast, the trajectory towards a satellite district, which appears to offer the least potential for endogenous upgrading, is most commonly found. Knorringa concludes, therefore, that the role of the national and local state remains crucial in giving outside support to local enterprises to promote local development.

Helmsing follows this up by examining a set of twelve case studies from Latin America, concerning changing forms of local private and public governance, and the way they shape the institutional context for 'collective learning' by local firms and employees. The main question is whether improving partnerships leads to 'bottom-up' growth processes, and strategies required from firms, households, as well as at the meso-level of business organizations and regions for such a process. Rather than focussing the discussion on joint action by the private sector only, the question is also raised how the public and private sector can work together towards more effective local institutional arrangements. The case studies show that public-private cooperation centers on the creation of meso-institutions at the level of territory and industry. Although a variety of processes of learning occur, they remain rather restricted in some cases, and only rarely reach the stage of an 'innovative milieu'. Concrete initiatives focus predominantly on enterprise or business development and in some cases on the physical redevelopment of cities.

Within the concern for local economic development another important line of research relates to the ways in which identities, resources, and institutional arrangements influence initiatives by local actors to produce economic prosperity at the local and regional level. Ypeij shows that gender hierarchies limit the opportunities of female micro-entrepreneurs to build up capital and expand their business. She also shows that male and female entrepreneurs have different forms of social capital, which privileges men in attracting labor and capital. However, female entrepreneurs seek solutions by separating their economic activities from household economies, and by actively using neighborhood networks to expand production. As subcontracting units, they are drawn into globalized production processes, creating new dependencies locally. However, the meanings women attach to their economic activities include resistance to existing inequalities, and as such, have a value in contributing to social transformations.

A final concern included in this section on the global-local interface concerns the changing spatial formation of economic activities as cities grow – the urban fringe discussion. This discussion has been related to the question of whether centralized planning by governments for economic expansion is still realistic, in the more liberalized environment now prevalent. In the context of previously state-led countries, these questions are urgent because they result in a complete turnabout in the way that local (and national) government operate. It has also been related to the changing character of the urban fringe, with its mixed rural and urban way of life as one of the most dynamic areas of growing cities (desakota discussion in McGee, 1991).

Schenk has looked at changing practices on the ground, comparing the effects of structural adjustments in the political economy of two Asian countries on the way cities grow. In both India and Vietnam, planned regional development, including the promotion of secondary towns and economic growth centers, is fading away. The prospect of directing economic development and migration to such centers, and of curtailing the growth of major metropolitan cities, has become more and more irrelevant. Instead, urban fringes have emerged as an important spatial component of economic growth. Secondary growth centers do not offer jobs, while the urban inner cities do not offer social and physical space. Hence, the urban fringe becomes an area where more and more migrants settle and try to survive. Schenk suggests that Hanoi can learn from the experiences of Bangalore and other cities to effectively promote local economic development.

Local Governance, Partnerships and Urban Development

Devas distinguishes two major areas in recent work on urban development in the South. Studies on urban government and management tend to have a technocratic, top-down, and prescriptive orientation (the public management perspective), and analyses of urban poverty and livelihoods usually adopt a more bottom-up approach, are more actor (agency) oriented and empirically grounded (the people-centered view) (Devas, 1999, p. 2). While the former tend to assume that the state is in a position of control, the latter conceive of the state as either oppressive or irrelevant.

The public management perspective on urban development gained popularity in the context of the developing world in the 1980s. At the time, the anti-urban mood that had characterized mainstream development thinking in the previous decade, started to give way to a more positive attitude toward the role of cities in the development process. In view of the disappointing experiences with previous strategies to confront the urbanization process, a new approach was desperately needed, one that would be able to bring together issues of the urban economy and the city as a living environment. The United Nations Centre on Human Settlements (UNCHS) was a major actor molding these new directions in thinking on urban development. The so-called urban management approach was heavily influenced by prevailing neo-liberal beliefs in market-led development and a minimal role of the state. It is basically a question of how to use the capacities of the public sector (at different levels), the business community, and civil society organization to bring about urban development. The new approach is based on the concept of enablement, referring to a situation in which the government moves away from direct intervention, and concentrates on creating favorable conditions for other actors to undertake economic and social activities (UNCHS, 1996). It may be further unraveled by distinguishing between enablement of the market, the local state, and communities (Burgess *et al.*, 1997). While market enablement is closely linked to the neo-liberal policy framework (including policies of privatization and deregulation), enablement of the local state involves both a restructuring of central-local relations (decentralization policies), and a reform of local management practices. Finally, community enablement refers to a government strategy to coordinate and facilitate the efforts of community-based organizations (CBOs) to initiate, plan, and implement their own projects (policies of participation and empowerment).

At first the prevailing idea was that good urban management required the establishment of a more effective, accountable, and transparent local administrative and governmental framework. Capacity- and institution-building programs put considerable efforts into improving the performance of government institutions, both nationally and locally. The latter could conceive of these reforms as basically internal reorganizations that did not challenge their authority. In the course of the 1990s, however, the emphasis shifted from a predominantly technocratic-managerial and inward orientation, to a more encompassing governance perspective. This new style of governing looks at the interplay between the actors in decision-making and action for development. The concept implicitly recognizes the enormous contribution by non-government actors – private enterprises, CBOs, and NGOs – in delivering public goods (Stoker, 1998; Helmsing, 2000). Although most international agencies will be reluctant to admit it, the urban management debate has gradually become more political, dealing with issues of power (Devas, 1999). In essence the concept of enablement involves a shift in the existing balance of power – from central to local governments, and from governments to the private sector and local communities – which is why the implementation of policies of privatization, decentralization, and participation is so often fraught with difficulties (Post, 1997).

The studies on urban development from the bottom-up perspective often follow the alternative development discourse. Although encompassing a wide variety of views and strategies, the alternative development 'school' constitutes something of a counterpoint to mainstream development emphasizing the human (and environmental) dimensions of development (Nederveen Pieterse, 1998). The re-emergence of poverty as a central development priority in the 1990s not only attracted attention from macroeconomists and development planners, but also stimulated research that took the ideas, strategies, and goals of the poor themselves as a starting point (Chambers, 1995; Moser, 1998). A very promising avenue of research is that on collective action by poor households in urban areas to organize shelter, basic services, security, etc. In these activities, CBOs usually play a prominent role by helping residents to enter into partnerships with external actors, notably private enterprises, local governments, and NGOs (Hordijk, 2000). Such contacts are needed in order to scale up their activities. To improve service levels requires legal recognition, permits, connections to trunk networks, and/or financial and technical support. Such partnerships, co-management, or co-production arrangements, have become key elements in new forms of local governance (Baud, 2000). In fact, this is the debate where the public management perspective and the people-centered perspective in urban development studies meet. Investigations into the dynamics of partnership arrangements show that they have great potential in improving the production of public goods and services or in problem-solving activities. However, synergetic development does not arise automatically from attempts to cross the public-private divide. Ostrom (1996) and Evans (1996) have clearly pointed out that complementarities may be great but that other conditions have to be fulfilled as well before the advantages of collaboration will materialize. A great deal depends on the existence of trust and accountability between actors (also labeled 'embeddedness') as well as a fair distribution of inputs and outcomes. Furthermore, one does well to remember that social differences and unequal power relations between stakeholders cannot be wished away, and that inclusion of the weakest sections of society continues to be an awkward issue (Johnson and Wilson, 2000; Mitlin, 2001).

In the second part of the book we will try to show what actually takes place in various settings in the area of urban management and local governance. The cases presented illustrate the difficulties of switching from government to governance. The first three chapters in this section start from a public management perspective by taking a critical look at reforms and interventions initiated from above. In the chapter by van Naerssen, the vicissitudes of the World Health Organisation's Healthy Cities Programme are investigated. Despite the common framework, the actual design and implementation of such programs differ considerably depending on the social and political circumstances. In Dar es Salaam, for example, the WHO field office was the major driving force behind the program activities. However, it prioritized collaboration with government bodies over participation by CBOs. Consequently, its activities remained largely confined to the traditional health agenda, rather than encompassing broader environmental health concerns. In Managua, there was a much higher level of civil society involvement and, therefore, much more public support (ownership) of the program. The major problem here was political cleavage, with the local government finally opting out of the program. Van Naerssen distinguishes two basic orientations within the concern with Healthy Cities, one that emphasizes improved cooperation between the health sector and local governments regarding health promotion and improvement of the urban environment, and another that focuses on the urban poor and community participation in the design and implementation of programs. The author thinks the latter have a greater chance of meeting people's own health needs and of encouraging them to solve their own health problems.

Two chapters in this part of the book deal with decentralization and participation in Bolivia. The one by Schalkwijk looks at the situation in major urban centers, while the contribution by van Lindert and Nijenhuis focuses on experiences in six smaller municipalities. According to Schalkwijk, participation is still largely a paper tiger. Although participatory structures have been put in place, they do not generate the beneficial effects anticipated by the national Law on Popular Participation. Local communities seem trapped in their customary, non-effective strategies of demand making cultivated by the political system of patronage. The reform has not been accompanied by restructuring and reorientation of the local government machinery, which is still largely unaccountable and non-transparent. Schalkwijk urges that more pressure be put on authorities to take participation processes more seriously. Outside donors should not only try to strengthen new governmental institutions (the public management approach) but also support civic associations. CBOs, in turn, should endeavor to unite in order to strengthen their bargaining power, but should also try looking beyond the municipality for support.

Van Lindert and Nijenhuis' account of the impact of decentralization and participation in Bolivia is more optimistic. A new law has ensured local democracy in the rural areas for the first time ever, enabling peasants and indigenous people to present their views in the political arena. According to the authors, a process of democratization has been set in motion that will prove difficult to stop, as any attempt to modify the current legal and regulatory framework will meet with fierce political opposition. However, the reality of local governance is somewhat different. The commitment of local administrators to the principles of participation is still rather weak because the idea came down from above, which is why the priorities of local government spending do not always reflect the needs of the population. However, the authors describe the situation in a growing number of Brazilian municipalities where genuine participatory planning approaches demonstrate what may be achieved if supportive political conditions exist. Impressive improvements in urban infrastructure and services have been realized as a result of the collaboration between informed citizens and dedicated officials. They constitute promising examples of collaboration across the public-private divide.

Collaborative efforts to improve urban habitats are also the subject of the contributions by Hordijk, and by Baud and Post. In both chapters the authors adopt a combined governance and collective action perspective, acknowledging the variety of actors (public and private) that have taken on roles in decision-making and action with regard to public affairs. In an innovative way, Hordijk links discussions on household assets/capitals to the functioning of neighborhood organizations in Lima (Peru). She shows how various capitals are utilized in collective actions directed at neighborhood improvement. Collaboration between CBOs and local governments produces only limited results on the ground because of a mismatch of capitals. Successful partnering requires complementary resources, but this is difficult to achieve for partners that are equally short in certain essential capitals, notably financial and physical. This is why Hordijk thinks the collaboration does not qualify as a genuine partnership. However, although collaboration does not always produce concrete outcomes, in the process new types of capital are created, notably political, organizational, and intellectual capital. It also helps to build up norms and loyalties between citizens and the administration (embeddedness) that can be fruitfully deployed under the new political conditions the recently installed Toledo government is seeking to establish.

Baud and Post take the partnership concept as the start of their investigation into solid waste management practices in Accra (Ghana) and Chennai (India). They provide a concise analytical framework for studying partnership arrangements, but confine their analysis largely to the outcomes of more or less institutionalized forms of collaboration. The originality of the paper lies in the attempt to assess the contributions partnerships in solid waste management made to sustainable development goals. For that purpose, the authors present a series of indicators tailored to this specific sector and subsequently use that system to assess the performance of concrete partnerships. Among the conclusions they arrive at are the official disregard (or worse) of small-scale, indigenous solutions to solid waste management problems, the lack of concern for community involvement in solid waste management (which can lead to mismatches in provision), and the lack of integration between the various domains within solid waste management.

Livelihoods, Rural-Urban Linkages and Regional Development

The present speed and scale of integration of the world's production and consumption – or, to use another focal concept of this book, 'livelihood' – is without precedent. The massive exchange of people, goods, services, finance, information, and ideas leads to globalizing markets and social relations. Actors in different places on the globe are easily connected to one another, but may, at the same time, be disconnected from places in their immediate surroundings (Castells, 1996). With respect to the spatial processes pertaining to the theme of this part of the book, globalization has three overriding repercussions. First, in regional development, attention shifts from city-hinterland interactions to the integration of localities in global networks. Secondly, the new patterns of mobility of actors, capital, and information reshape urban-rural linkages and blur the old urban-rural dichotomy. Thirdly, as a result of globalization, which places a premium on flexibility and adaptability, livelihood is increasingly attained through networks spanning many different localities.

Two qualifying remarks have to be made here. On the one hand, globalization provokes not only global homogenization but also local differentiation. This is the so-called global-local nexus (Robertson, 1995). On the other hand, one has to bear in mind that often a biased image of globalization is created, i.e., as a new round of chances. One should not forget that globalization is also accompanied by the exclusion of people and localities, i.e., those least able to respond to change, and that it is no guarantee against marginalization (Gore, 1994).

Underlying rural-urban linkages are the livelihood of actors. Increasingly, livelihood is no longer confined to one place – not even to a town and its hinterland or the countryside and a central place. Livelihood now includes a variety of places, i.e., it has become multi-local and exploits a number of resources, resulting in a combination of strategies, making it more multi-dimensional. This means that livelihood is attained through networks, taken as a set of relations between actors. Urban centers remain the nodes in this network, and therefore these livelihood networks shape rural-urban linkages (Haan, 2000b). However, at present the result is perceived less as a nested hierarchy of urban-rural linkages, but rather as a patchy network, connecting some actors and localities while excluding others. Although those excluded can be part of other networks, they may be excluded altogether.

Though networks are becoming increasingly global, space (as distance) is still a factor that counts, although some have proclaimed the end of distance and the end of geography. Even in globally integrated production systems, proximity, distance, and the characteristics of localities (as place) remain important factors. Especially large cities – or perhaps better, mega-cities – act as hubs in global networks. Gradually, the negative image of urban primacy (surplus extraction from rural areas, regional disparities) has become a positive one: A specific environment for production and consumption that enables the fruits of globalization to be plucked (Knox and Taylor, 1995). Notwithstanding this reassessment of the role of mega-cities, small and intermediate centers often continue to be regarded as bridging the rural-urban divide, although sometimes small centers fade away when rural-urban symbiosis and the blurring of the rural-urban gap are discussed.

Rural-urban linkages are mostly discussed in terms of social and economic relations. Since Rees (1992) introduced the 'ecological footprint', increasingly ecological relations are taken into account too, analyzing flows of resources and waste. Finally, the question arises whether there is still a role for policy to play in rural-urban relations and regional development. Instead of a top-down and directive approach, an enabling role and sometimes even a decentralized and participatory approach is advocated.

The third part of the book starts with a chapter by Haan and Quarles van Ufford focusing on rural-urban linkages in sub-Saharan Africa. It starts from the premise that economic actions can only be understood if looked upon as embedded in social structure. Therefore, the concept of livelihood/sustainable livelihood is elaborated. Livelihood is taken to emanate from the interactions of actors with vital capitals. These are embedded in a wider natural and politico-socio-economic context. The authors argue that in the era of globalization, livelihood increasingly becomes more multidimensional and multi-local, spanning rural and urban areas at the same time. Moreover, it is argued that exactly because of the social embeddedness of economic activities, it is necessary to pay special attention to the importance of social capital for livelihood. Changing rural-urban linkages are considered in this chapter, focussing in particular on trade in food, i.e., in maize, yams, and cattle. Expanding flows between rural areas and urban outlets are analyzed against the background of the livelihood strategies of traders, paying special attention to trade organization, networks, entry modes, and accumulations paths. Herein, the role of social capital is highlighted. Social capital is considered as a historical prerequisite in linking the rural and the urban, which still holds to a certain extent in the globalization era.

The next chapter, by Dietz and Zaal, also deals with sub-Saharan Africa, especially the provisioning of cities with particular attention for Ouagadougou. The provisioning of the rapidly growing cities with such basics as food, water, and energy by rural producers depends very much on characteristics of the hinterland, i.e., the agro-ecological situation, population densities, the existence and quality of investments in skills, and on means of transport and communication. The organizational skills of entrepreneurs who bring together supply and demand are also a crucial element. The public sector has undertaken these entrepreneurial roles in the past, too, but presently this is strongly discouraged by donors. Even if governments are not directly active as traders, government performance is important in maintaining law and order, in providing a legal framework for entrepreneurial activities, in improving and maintaining infrastructure, in taxation behavior, and in cushioning or aggravating the impact of natural disasters on supply and demand.

Volbeda's contribution to the book is on economic networks and rural-urban linkages. She argues that these networks and their linkages are crucial to the development of a region. The chapter focuses on sub-Sahara Africa, a macro-region where urbanization has not been accompanied by economic growth. This is caused by the malfunctioning of linkages between economic networks. It is argued that investments in rural-urban linkages (such as infrastructure and transport) and in institutional assets (such as governance) are needed to generate economic growth. The chapter shows that regions that are more integrated in urban networks, experience more rapid economic growth. It is argued that regions without good urban-rural linkages will become more marginalized. A plea is made for development interventions to be focused on so-called catalysts for economic interactions, i.e., infrastructure and transport, information, and education to improve those linkages.

Improving sustainable development in cities by reducing environmental impacts is the explicit focus of the chapter by Baud and Hordijk, who take water and solid waste management as their main examples. By looking at issues of ecological sustainability at the level of cities and their hinterlands, the authors develop a research framework that may contribute to effectively tackling urban environmental problems in a larger eco-regional context, defined as the area of resource extraction and the area of environmental impact caused by urban activities. It is concluded that in such a research framework, the role of the natural environment within and surrounding urban areas in its own right should be recognized. Moreover, such an analysis should include the way in which natural resources are transformed into products used in human activities. In addition, competing demands made on resources by different groups of urban and rural inhabitants, the conflicts concerning resource use, and the possibilities to reduce such conflicts should be taken into account. Finally, the authors argue that the framework should include an analysis of how more participatory styles of governance influence the direction of demand on resource use, the equitability of the resource use socially, spatially, and over time, and how partnerships can contribute to solving existing conflicts.

In fact, Zoomers combines a number of policy considerations discussed by the authors of the previous chapters in her plea for a renewed and contemporary conceptualization of regional development planning. She argues that current trends in regional development are not always in line with the goal of sustainable development, nor do they automatically contribute to efficient, equitable, or sustainable space. In the past, regional planning was aimed at reducing urban primacy and regional disparities, i.e., at creating a physically integrated system of urban and rural centers. Though spatial disparities have declined in cases where it was successful, we are now faced with a new set of spatial problems often neglected in the development debate. Dispersed urbanization and increased mobility are too easily mentioned as a positive result of current spatial trends, and as a motive for nullifying the need for regional planning. Practice shows that these processes also have a problematic side, such as spatial fragmentation, mobility problems, and unsustainable land use. Sustainable development requires that space provides opportunities to lead a stable life. At present, urbanization is too dispersed and mobility is too high to provide people with a sufficient basis for a sustainable livelihood. Decentralized and participatory regional planning should therefore aim at regulating peri-urban development rather than accepting dispersed urbanization, and bringing infrastructure into line with modern patterns of mobility.

Urban Poverty Reduction: Mapping the Policy Arena

The final part of the book looks at the policy domain, particularly at policy and action regarding urban poverty. Here one can also observe a proliferation of actors. The central state is no longer the only, or even the leading, agent in public policy development in general and poverty alleviation campaigns in particular. Its role has been redefined to creating favorable macro-economic conditions and facilitating other actors to make more effective contributions in reducing poverty and promoting development. This new role requires different skills, less technocratic and hierarchical management by large bureaucratic departments, and more strategic planning, selective intervention, and negotiation and dialogue with private and community organizations to achieve commonly agreed goals (Helmsing, 2000). In numerous national, urban, and regional development arenas, a new negotiation culture is developing in which public actors (central governments, local governments, and pseudo-government companies) work together with private actors, both from the commercial and from the non-profit sectors. In some cases this results in uneasy confrontations, in many others in a network of new partnerships, sometimes initiated by state agencies, often initiated by civil society and/or market actors. In a number of cases, the new alliances leave out the state agencies altogether and form 'bottom-up' semi-public agencies, based on community-based initiatives (for a study about the African situation see e.g., Dietz and Foeken, 2001).

Turning to anti-poverty policy as such, an important shift in orientation is apparent. Whereas the conventional approach primarily looks at what can be done for the poor (the poor as objects), the contemporary approach takes poor households' own perspectives as its starting point and recognizes their strength and creativity in the fight against poverty (the poor as subjects and agents (Chambers, 1995; Moser, 1998; Bebbington, 1999). People call upon various assets or capitals – human, natural, physical, financial, social and political- to secure and enhance livelihood. Some of these assets are directly available to individuals, households or social groups, while access to others is circumscribed by institutions. The 'poverty inspired' debates on endowments and entitlements to natural resources (e.g. Dietz, 1996; Fine, 1999; Leach et al., 1999; Haan, 2000) as well as on social exclusion (Haan, 1998; Kabeer, 2001) both emphasize the importance of institutional arrangements in determining access. These institutions operate in a setting of power differentials and emerge from underlying sets of rules that are constantly made and remade through people's practices. As institutions are man-made constructions they are also available for reform, and, hence, for policy targeting.

Another major development in anti-poverty policies relates to the move away from more or less standardized solutions – e.g. the World Bank's focus on utilization of the poor's labor potential and enhancing their labor productivity in combination with safety net provisions to protect vulnerable groups and the very poor – towards more flexible, diversified approaches tailored to expressed needs of the poor in their particular context. Poverty is more than a lack of income, and consists of multiple deprivations ranging from economic to psychological. However, the exact nature and magnitude of poverty differs between individuals, households and social groups as well as in time and place. There is growing awareness, for instance, of substantial differences between rural and urban poverty, which require selective policy responses (Satterthwaite, 1997). In the urban setting, many aspects of deprivation can be mitigated through secure housing, better infrastructure and services rather than through measures directly related to employment and income. On the other hand one should probably not be too preoccupied with the peculiarities of the urban or rural context as it obscures the underlying causes of poverty (Wratten, 1995).

The chapters by Wegelin and Satterthwaite each look at urban poverty alleviation from a different angle. Wegelin's approach fits well into the mainstream of public management thinking with respect to urban development. He argues that the world has become an urban place and that the urban poor will soon outnumber the rural poor. This situation is increasingly threatening political stability, at both national and global levels. The author subsequently outlines the diversity of options available to local governments in their efforts to combat urban poverty. He emphasizes the importance of strengthening the so-called informal sector and improving access to urban services and land for the urban poor and their businesses. In the fields of water provisioning, sanitation and solid waste, primary health care, education and training, urban transportation, and slum upgrading, Wegelin provides a range of issues that local authorities can/should take up, preferably by linking up with private and community actors. He also emphasizes the current attention given to problems of vulnerability and social exclusion on the local political agenda. Supporting the institutional capacities of local-level actors in the urban arena (local governments, CBOs, and NGOs) should be the core of 21st century development cooperation.

Satterthwaite's main concern is the constraints aid agencies and development banks face in addressing urban poverty. These include their limited capacity to support local institutions that respond to the needs and priorities of low-income groups and that are accountable to them. It describes the distance between decision-making processes of most international agencies and the urban poor, and the very limited possibilities for the urban poor to influence what gets funded and by whom. The chapter also discusses the political constraints that have inhibited donor agencies from being more effective and suggests how support for locally-based community initiatives could help overcome these. It ends by describing the low priority given by donor agencies to urban poverty reduction and suggests some changes that would help development assistance to meet its targets for reducing urban poverty. In fact, Satterthwaite advocates institutional reforms that enable donor agencies to link up more successfully with the established practices of people in their fight for a secure livelihood and habitat.

The relative neglect of urban poverty is well illustrated by de Wit's account of the ill-fated history of this policy domain within Dutch development cooperation during the last decade. He regrets the lack of attention given to the global urbanization processes and the continuing dominance of conventional interests within the Ministry, following recent reorganizations. Things seemed to be improving in the late 1980s, when a specific unit was established in the Ministry to deal with urban poverty. It became a think-tank with a varied agenda. However, after a promising start it withered away. Especially after 1998, when the new minister Herfkens introduced the 'sector approach', urban poverty alleviation virtually disappeared. Instead of institution building, the institutions were destroyed and with them the possibilities to form promising alliances within the Netherlands itself.

References

Batley, R. (1996), 'Public-Private Relationships and Performance in Service Delivery', *Urban Studies*, Vol. 33(4-5), pp. 723-51.

Baud, I.S.A. (2000), *Collective Action, Enablement and Partnerships, Issues in Urban Development*, inaugural address, Free University, 27 October 2000.

Bebbington, A. (1999) 'Capital and Capabilities: A Framework for Analyzing Peasant Viability, Rural Livelihoods and Poverty' *World Development*, Vol. 27 (12), pp. 2021-2044.

Burgess, R., Carmona, M. and Kolstee, T. (1997), *The Challenge of Sustainable Cities, Neoliberalism and Urban Strategies in Developing Countries*, Zed Books, London.

Castells, M. (1996), *The Rise of the Network Society*, Blackwell Oxford, Massachusetts.

Chambers, R. (1995), 'Poverty and Livelihoods: Whose Reality Counts?', *Environment and Urbanization*, Vol. 7(1), pp. 173-204.

Devas, N. (1999), *Who Runs Cities? The Relationship between Urban Governance, Service Delivery and the Urban Poor*, Theme paper 4 of the Urban Governance, Partnerships and Poverty Programme, University of Birmingham.

Devas, N. (2001), *Urban Governance and Poverty, Lessons from a Study of Ten Cities in the South*, University of Birmingham and DFID.

Dicken, P. (1998), *Global Shift, Transforming the World Economy*, Paul Chapman Publishing Ltd., London.

Dietz, T., and Foeken, D. (2001), 'The Crumbling of the African State System', in G. Dijkink and H. Knippenberg, *The Territorial Factor. Political Geography in a Globalising World*. Vossius Pers, Amsterdam, pp. 177-200.

Douglas, M. (2000) Mega-Urban Regions and World City Formation: Globalization, the Economic Crisis and Urban Policy Issues in Pacific Asia, *Urban Studies* Vol. 37 (12), pp. 2315-2335.

Evans, D. (1996), 'Government Action, Social Capital and Development: Evidence on Synergy', *World Development*, Vol. 24 (6):, pp. 1119-32.
Fine, B. (1999) 'Entitlement Failure?' *Development and Change*, Vol 28 (4), pp. 617-647.
Gereffi, G. (1999), 'International Trade and Industrial Upgrading in the Apparel Commodity Chain', *Journal of International Economcs*, Vol. 48(1), pp. 37-70.
Gore, C. (1994), *Social Exclusion and Africa South of the Sahara: A Review of the Literature*, International Institute for Labor Studies, Labor Institutions and Development Programme DP 62, ILO, Geneva.
Haan, A. (1998) '"Social Exclusion": An Alternative Concept for the Study of Deprivation' *IDS Bulletin*, Vol. 29 (1), pp. 10-19.
Haan, L.J. de (2000a), *Livelihood, Locality and Globalization*, Inaugural Address, 17 March 2000, Nijmegen University Press, pp. 5-39.
Haan, L.J. de (2000b), 'Globalization, Localization and Sustainable Livelihood', *Sociologia Ruralis*, Vol. 40(3), pp. 339-65.
Harris, N. (1997), 'Cities in a Global Economy: Structural Change and Policy Reaction', *Urban Studies*, Vol. 34 (10), pp. 1693-703.
Held, D., McGrew, A., Goldblatt, D. and Perraton, J. (1999),*Global Transformations, Introduction*, Polity Press, Cambridge, pp. 1-28.
Helmsing, A.H.J. (2000), *Decentralization and Enablement, Issues in the Local Governance Debate*, inaugural address, Faculteit Ruimtelijke Wetenschappen, Universiteit Utrecht.
Helmsing, A.H.J. (2001), 'Externalities, Learning and Governance: New Perspectives on Local Economic Development', *Development and Change*, Vol. 32, pp. 277-308.
Hobsbawm, E.J. (1996), 'The Future of the State', *Development and Change*, Vol. 27, pp. 267-78.
Hoogvelt, Ankie (1997), *Globalization and the Postcolonial World: The New Political Economy of Development*, MacMillan Press, London, Chapters 6 and 7, pp.114-49.
Hordijk, M. (2001), *Of Dreams and Deeds, the Role of Local Initiatives for Community Based Environmental Management in Lima, Peru*, Thela Thesis, Amsterdam.
Johnson, H. and Wilson, G. (2000) 'Biting the Bullet: Civil Society, Social Learning and the Transformation of Local Governance' *World Development*, Vol. 28 (11), pp. 1891-1906.
Kabeer, N. (2001) Social Exclusion, Poverty and Discrimination, Towards an Analytical Framework, *IDS Bulletin*, Vol. 31 (4), pp. 83-97.
Kaul, I., Grunberg, I. and Stern, M. (1999), *Global Public Goods, International Cooperation in the 21st Century*, UNDP, Oxford University Press, Oxford.
Knox, P. and P. Taylor (eds), *World Cities in a World System*, Cambridge University Press, Cambridge.
Krugman, P. (1997), *Development, Geography, and Economic Theory*, The MIT Press, Cambridge Massachusetts.
Leach, M., Means, R. and Scoones, I. (1999) 'Environmental Entitlements; Dynamics and Institutions in Community-Based Natural Resource Management' *World Development*, Vol. 27 (2), pp. 225-247.
Leftwich, A. (1994), 'Governance, the State and the Politics of Development', *Development and Change*, Vol. 25, pp. 363-86.
McGee, T.G. (1991) 'The Emergence of Desakota Regions: Expanding a Hypothesis', in N. Ginsberg, B. Koppel and T.G. McGee (eds), *The Extended Metropolis – Settlement Transition in Asia*, University of Hawaii Press, Honolulu.

Mitlin, D. (2001) 'Civil Society and Urban Poverty: Examining Complexity' *Environment and Urbanization*, Vol. 13 (2), pp. 151-173.

Mittelman, J.H. (2000), *The Globalization Syndrome, Transformation and Resistance*, Princeton University Press, Princeton, New Jersey.

Moser, C.O.N. (1998), 'The Asset Vulnerability Framework: Reassessing Urban Poverty Reduction Strategies', *World Development*, Vol. 26(1), pp. 1-19.

Nederveen Pieterse, J. (1998), 'My Paradigm or Yours? Alternative Development, Post-Development, Reflexive Development', *Development and Change*, Vol. 29(2), pp. 343-73.

Nederveen Pieterse, J. (2000), 'Trends in Development Theory', in J. Nederveen Pieterse, *Development Theory Deconstructions/Reconstructions*, Sage, London, pp. 1-17.

Ostrom, E. (1996), 'Crossing the Great Divide: Co-production, Synergy, and Development', *World Development*, Vol. 24(6): pp. 1073-87.

Post, J. (1997), 'Urban Management in an Unruly Setting: the African Case', *Third World Planning Review*, Vol. 19 (4), pp. 347-66.

Rees, W. (1992), 'Ecological Footprints and Appropriated Carrying Capacity: What Urban Economics Leaves Out', *Environment and Urbanization*, Vol. 4(2), pp. 121-30.

Robertson (1995), 'Glocalisation: Time-space and Homogeneity-heterogeneity, in M. Featherstone, S. Lash and R. Robertson (eds), *Global Modernities*, Sage, London, pp. 25-44.

Sassen, S. (1998), 'The State and the Global City: Notes Towards a Conception of Place-Centred Governance', in S. Sassen, *Globalization and its Discontents, Essays on the New Mobility of People and Money*, The New Press, New York, pp. 195-218.

Satterthwaite, D. (1997), 'Urban Poverty: Reconsidering its Scale and Nature' *IDS Bulletin*, Vol. 28 (2), pp. 9-23.

Schmitz, H. and Knorringa, P. (2000), 'Learning from Global Buyers', *Journal of Development Studies*, Vol. 37(2), pp. 177-205.

Short, J.R. and Kim, Y.H. (1999) '*Globalization and the City*' Addison Wesley Longman, New York.

Stoker, G (1998), 'Governance as Theory: Five Propositions', *ISSJ*, Vol. 50(155), pp. 17-28.

Storper, M. (1997), *The Regional World*, Guilford Press, New York.

UNCHS (1996), *An Urbanizing World: Global Report on Human Settlements* 1996, Oxford University Press, Oxford and New York.

World Bank (2000), *World Development Report* 2000/2001, Oxford University Press, Oxford.

Wratten, E. (1995) 'Conceptualizing Urban Poverty' *Environment and Urbanization*, Vol. 7, (1), pp. 11-36.

PART I

Urban Economies and the Local-Global Interface

2 Firms, Regions and Resources in a Globalizing Economy: A Relational View

JAN LAMBOOY

Introduction: A World of Relations

Regions are characterized not only by their physical attributes, but also by the economic and cultural attributes of people, firms, and cities. The process of differentiation of economic activities can lead either to a cumulative attraction of cities and regions – due to the spatial clustering of economic activities in certain regions – or to advantages of agglomeration (Jacobs, 1984). Agglomeration advantages, in turn, result in a stronger attractiveness of certain city regions. However, in many regions, the economic system is not well developed due to the region's specific economic or institutional attributes and its location (e.g. regions with anti-business cultures, or those located in poor rural or woodland areas). Urban and regional development has to be connected with the development of a variety of resources, both from within the regional system and from other regions. Those cities and regions where firms and other organizations are located that are the best in getting and combining the resources in the most productive manner, can be expected to be successful. Enterprises are the most important organizers of the use of resources, but they are embedded in regional or national resource systems and in institutional structures. Cities and regions depend strongly on enterprises and entrepreneurs for their development. In the process of differentiation, firms and workers develop specific attributes, more in particular certain kinds of tacit or codified knowledge (Lambooy, 2000). Adam Smith already posited that the growth of an urban economy depends on the actual level of the division of labor, and on the level of specialization in certain activities or tasks. He argued that the size of cities and regions is a function of both specialization and the division of labor, inside the region as well as with other regions by means of trade relations. Urban and regional development is for an important part dependent on the economic development of related external urban and regional systems. The own resource system, the set of relations with other regions (or the connectivity), and the configuration of economic activities (or the production structure), determine for a large part the capacity of economic growth. The relations consist of trade and the geographical transmission of people, information, and knowledge (Lambooy, 2000). The carriers of these relations and knowledge are often concentrated in such organizations as universities and firms, but are also personified in workers and other individuals who transmit ideas on how to do and how to think, and in urban systems.

A city derives its importance from three factors. First, its position as a nodal point in a region. This position is based on the forces connected with the set of relations within a region; the interactions of consumers and firms with each other and with centrally located public facilities. Second, the process of cumulative attraction over time, which tends to result in favoring the urban center that has the best accessibility for the functions most frequently used in the region. Third, the external trade relations, which connect the region with the rest of the world, but primarily with the neighboring regions.

Ideas and attitudes are often institutionalized in the behavioral rules in organizations or countries. Institutions have a strong impact on economic subjects, providing them with rules and guidelines for dealing with exchange relations, market relations, and non-market relations. Institutions also define the structure of incentives that influence the driving forces of work attitudes.

In a context of globalization, many values and rules need to be adjusted in order to accommodate new economic conditions. This process requires the input of human resources, more in particular the input of new knowledge of technology and on the organization of firms and markets. A consequence is that companies, cities, and regions have to be connected in worldwide networks of relations, consisting of more kinds of relations than market relations alone. The development of regional resources is a principal issue in development policy and in the evaluation of the impacts of globalization.

In this paper we will focus on the impact of the increasing openness of enterprises in an internationalizing economy, and on the opportunities this offers for the resource development of cities, regions, and countries as an evolutionary process of economic growth (Boschma and Lambooy, 1999). A relational view will be developed, meaning that companies will be analyzed with an emphasis on the structure of their relations with their environments on various spatial scales. Enterprises are seen as open systems with many kinds of relations. The development of firms depends on the innovativeness of entrepreneurs and on the impacts of the three kinds of selection environments. Not only economic effects but also social effects will be taken into consideration, because a strong current of critical reviewers regard globalization as potentially dangerous for the social cohesion of regions and nations.

In Section 2 we will consider the openness of firms and the relational view as important issues for understanding regional economic growth opportunities. This is related to the evolution of firms, networks, institutions, and innovation. Section 3 will focus on the concept of resource in relation to regional economic growth. Section 4 will emphasize the impact of globalization on firms that are embedded in their regions. Section 5 will deal with regional policy, and some conclusions will be presented in Section 6.

The Development of a Relational System of Firms

Firms are the basic economic units for urban and regional development. Through their production, they provide the income and the employment for the population. The regional resources have to be used and transformed into products and services for the consumers within the region or elsewhere.

Firms are increasingly open systems, connected in networks of relations with other firms and other actors. However, firms are heterogeneous with regard to their composition of resources. They have to defend their imitable assets and to fully exploit their unique set of resources in order to benefit from or survive the competition.

According to many textbooks, economic growth is primarily the result of investments in capital, labor, and technology. This reduced view has come under attack, however. Other variables – such as institutions, learning processes, resource development, and organization – have been added to explain economic growth (Nelson 1996; Hunt 2000; Lambooy, 2000). Here, countries and regions can also be considered relevant. Economic development is further associated with such processes as globalization and innovation. More recently, institutional factors are stressed, like good governance (the management and control sides of organizational structures). The existence of efficient institutions of a private and of a public nature, and relations with stakeholders and management. Part of the emphasis has shifted from the neo-classical production function to the organizational and social aspects of both enterprises and entrepreneurs, as conditions for economic development. Such concepts as institutional structure, transaction costs, networking, flexible specialization, innovativeness, and embeddedness (a concept first introduced by Polanyi in 1944, and reintroduced by Granovetter in 1985) are important in these new approaches to economic development. The general picture is that knowledge of how such factors as technology, governance, and other institutional aspects influence economic growth and regional development is essential for understanding the position of firms in the modern economy and, concomitantly, for understanding the contribution of firms to regional economic development.

Knowledge cannot easily be contained within one firm; it is the ultimate proof of the open character of modern production in manufacturing and service industries, because it is tied to people. Knowledge can be acquired from various sources, but sometimes it is a specific asset of a particular firm. Knowledge as a resource is difficult to confine to one production unit or firm for a long time, because it is related to human experience and interaction, and thus involves a collective process (Lambooy 1997; 2000).

The process of production is becoming more and more fragmented by an increasingly extensive division of labor and a division of responsibilities and controls. This increases the complexity of coordination. In the governance structure of larger enterprises, there are many stakeholders. The division of labor can be organized within companies or between companies, within regions or between regions, or even on a global scale. In order to optimize their corporate results (profits and market shares), transnational corporations have the market power to organize the entire production chain. However, even these powerful organizations are dependent on governments, labor unions, shareholders, environmentalist groups, and consumers. Hence, even their boundaries are not completely controlled, although they are more controlled than those of small and medium-sized enterprises (SMEs).

Firms are much more than the isolated black box of production functions as depicted in neo-classical economics. Entrepreneurs and employees have their distinct goals and are part of various groups, networks, and cultures. The coordination of economic activities leads to many contacts, which are not necessarily limited to market relations.

Enterprises consist of tangible and non-tangible resources, as a set of core attributes and routines that can be organized either as a separate firm, or as a technical unit of a larger enterprise (establishments in various locations). This creates a certain fuzziness in the boundaries of the production units or firms. In this openness, we can distinguish economic and non-economic relations. The latter kind is associated with ties with governments and other institutions, as well as with personal ties based on ethnic or religious belonging. Economic relations exist mainly through market relations, often within the supply chain or the production chain (vertical relations), but also with other economic subjects (horizontal relations), which may be competitors or entrepreneurs in a cooperative association. It is not always clear where one enterprise ends and other enterprises begin. The wave of mergers and acquisitions, and the creation of new firms by spinning-off, do not help to make it any clearer. Also, the acquisition of such inputs as knowledge is not a clear matter in this respect. Nevertheless, firms attempt to develop their specific assets in order to strengthen their position in bargaining and in the market processes.

In general, we can conclude that the relational structure of firms is becoming very important. Firms are involved in a constant interactive flow of relations with their environments. But, what do we mean when using the concept of environment? This concept is used in a wide variety of meanings. We distinguish three different approaches to environment:

- A 'place to live', the concept of human geography. In this broader concept of environment, it indicates the area in which people live and invest, where they share ideas and spaces. Here they meet other people and receive information, act in political arenas, send their children to school, and meet entrepreneurs at parties and seminars, in restaurants and on sporting grounds. People, entrepreneurs included, are embedded in these environments.
- A 'selection environment', where it is decided which initiatives, new ideas, or new firms will be sustained or preferred.
- A 'locus of opportunities'. These opportunities can be connected with, for instance, a new technology or a new market. Here, resource development is possible. In certain areas, these new elements will be realized, whereas in other regions they may be looked upon as strange and unrealistic ideas. Boschma and Lambooy (1999) showed that, in a historical perspective, it is impossible to predict which region will become the right location for the future development of new technologies and new firms.

There are three kinds of selection environments:

- The market, which is the most important as far as economists are concerned;
- The institutional context, with values and rules to regulate the behavior of the market parties; and

- The physical environment or locational setting (including buildings and infrastructure).

In economic theory the concept of environment is diffuse, but here it can be used in a relational perspective, to indicate a location in a region where the three kinds of selection environments are acting simultaneously. Economic actors are influenced by a set of relations with other market participants, as well as by the institutional rules of the game and by physical structures.

Firms respond to these various environments in different ways. An important strategy is to create forms of organization that match the challenges of the environment. Networks are developed as one way of reorganizing sets of relations.

Williamson (Williamson and Winter 1990, p. 12) defined networks as a hybrid form of coordination, a hybrid of market and hierarchy. Networks are the focus of the relational approach to firms. Networks can be investigated from different angles (Lambooy 1987; Lambooy 1994). First of all, a network can be seen as a solution to the problem of insufficiently functioning market relations, where information can be asymmetric and incomplete. Secondly, it can be perceived as the result of the rational behavior of market parties, by creating a hybrid structure between the market and the hierarchy (Williamson 1985; Williamson and Winter, 1990). This may be the case when the market is turbulent and technology is changing rapidly. As a third approach, a network can be seen as the purposeful behavior of entrepreneurs, based on attitudes of trust-building (investment in social capital) or power-building, or on the development of associations and trust.

There is yet another view on network configurations (Lambooy, 1987). Networks can be based on socio-cultural and political criteria, or on economic criteria. In economic theory they are based on market transactions and on linkages between goods, services, and information. We will mention only the three sub-types.

The first category is based on vertical relations, for instance in the production chain. The second category exists when companies develop horizontal relations, as in the case of industrial districts. The third category can be observed when both kinds of relations exist, possibly combined with lateral relations, like in *filières* and clusters. These networks are all based on the principle of the division of labor, on the minimization of transaction costs, and on strategic responses to turbulent environments and uncertainty.

The most well-known category is that connected with the production chain or commodity chain. The increasing complexity of production chains, associated with globalization, rapid technological developments, and the growing division of labor, has made it necessary to continuously adjust the activities, the technology, the information requirements, and the organization of firms. Mergers and takeovers, licensing and outsourcing, relocation, and changing technologies are more or less daily phenomena. It shows that a firm often has to change and adjust to new conditions, but still needs to keep some core capability of its own. Adjusting to these external forces enables the firm to change its position within the production chain or within other network configurations, by shifting to other products and other suppliers and customers. Sometimes even relocating to another region or country may be necessary to survive. This is why companies (or their constituent technical units) can be conceived as building blocks of the economy, or as modules in the complex networks. Hence, modules can be perceived as firms or as technical units with a certain independence within companies.

Technical units can be reconfigured within an enterprise, or they can themselves be established as firms, or they can even be sold to other firms. These are not the only strategic responses possible. Units or even entire firms can relocate as well.

What matters to the success of both regions and firms, is the entire production chain and the *filière*, because the value added is not created in a single technical unit or firm (Porter, 1998). Even large companies rely heavily on outsourcing. Well-known examples are cars and computers, which are assembled from a multitude of different parts, sometimes purchased from hundreds of suppliers, business services included. Not all of these suppliers are small and dependent. The larger supplier firms, with strong specific knowledge bases (e.g., Bosch, Philips, Canon, etc.), are often specialists in a certain technology, which provides them with a strong countervailing power.

Cooperation can be a basic factor for success in turbulent environments (Nooteboom, 2000). But this view can be one-sided. In many publications, networking is praised for being beneficial only to the constituent firms. But that is a narrow view of how networks can be used. That effect only exists in situations with complementary or equal opportunity structures. In certain cases an asymmetric relation exists, often caused by an unequal access to knowledge or to markets. Cooperation can also be used in a different way, that is, it can be used by large monopolists as a tool to exploit smaller firms, for instance in Third World countries. When networks are created by entrepreneurs, they can be perceived as tools to achieve certain goals which cannot be realized without certain forms of cooperation, or as a result of trust in structures of symmetrical information.

Firms primarily need a specific set of distinguishing attributes, but they also need a certain flexibility to adjust to the changing environment, in which fierce competition exists with other firms, which are also developing strategies to adjust to new technologies, products, and locations. One result of flexibility is that firms, especially multinationals, can benefit from opportunities both in the world market and in regional specialization. Another result of flexibility is that many firms can use new technologies or develop new markets.

The concepts of flexibility and flexible specialization have often been used to denote a fundamental change from past standardized methods of production – frequently called Fordism – to modern, more flexible processes of production and new forms of organization, based on networks. However, increasing flexibility also needs organizational adjustments. This can result in networks of cooperation among firms, more in particular among SMEs. One of the main concepts which can be used in this context is that of the cluster, which sometimes can be used as a synonym for industrial district (Visser, 1996: Ch 1). A cluster is a set of locationally interlinked firms, which also encompasses connections with institutions such as governments and universities. Companies that are intensively cooperating in networks can end up in regional clusters (Porter, 1998, p. 207-8), in which firms are embedded by linkages, by common pool resources, by trust, and by institutional structures.

Firms, Resources, and Regional Development

Economic studies show that regions differ considerably, due not only to their physical attributes (Parker, 2000) but also to their configuration of resources. Resources can be defined as possible inputs, both tangible and intangible, that are essential to production and consumption. In traditional economic theory, resources were limited to the so-called production factors; capital (capital goods like seeds or machines, and financial capital), quantities of labor, and land (or products of nature). In our approach, we suggest considering a perspective which encompasses more kinds of resources, like knowledge, organizations, institutions, social capital (or a network of social relations), time, and space, to name but a few. Knowledge is an extension of labor, but it is no longer possible to accept labor as an homogeneous input. Organization is an essential ingredient for the efficiency of production. Institutions are a decisive resource, because they define the rules, the opportunities, and the incentive structure that can also influence the effectiveness of the production process. The access to resources is strongly dependent on the kinds and the structures of the institutions involved. This access is unequally divided over the individuals and the firms in a country. Space (location) can also influence the access. For an individual to be born in a slum or a backward region determines to a large extent whether she or he will have access to schools and universities. Time can be important as well. Poor people in cities have time to go to distant street markets to find the cheapest goods.

In the following scheme, the framework for the access to resources is presented. At the level of the general institutional environment, the values are formed and institutionalized. Here the entitlement rules are defined, for instance, those concerning property rights. At the micro level, individuals, workers, or entrepreneurs can make arrangements as to how their relations will be, but the freedom to do so is constrained by the general level. Of course, individual competencies are very important. Even seemingly equal individuals can differ in this respect, and may display special gifts to learn or to produce. Firms also are basically heterogeneous in their characteristics and competencies, which is an important basis for acquiring a better competitive position. Spatial configurations can also be relevant for the costs involved in getting access to resources.

Table 2.1   Framework for access to resources

Level I (Macro level)
General institutional environment
The determination of values, norms;
Expressed in laws and regulations
Level II (Micro level)
1)   The rules of economic behavior and institutional arrangements
2)   Location
3)   Individual competencies
Resulting in:
Access to resources

Cities, regions, and countries differ as to both the level of institutional context and the composition of competencies. One of the most important issues with regard to the full exploitation of competencies is the institutionalization of innovation and the resource system in a regional (or national) innovation system (Boschma, 1998, p. 1). Innovation is the competence of entrepreneurs to develop new opportunities (products, technologies, markets). Aside from individual risk-taking in uncertain environments, knowledge is an important resource to innovate efficiently. The cognitive abilities of entrepreneurs, workers, and government officials are essential for this process. The structuring of relations between economically active persons and organizations producing knowledge is very important. Agglomerations with a strong differentiation of economic and cultural activities are good breeding grounds for innovation and the development of knowledge (Lambooy, 1997). Nations and regions can develop and institutionalize innovation systems to promote economic growth. Lundvall (1988) argued that knowledge is the most important resource and learning the most important process for economic development.

The resource endowments and the control of resources are different for firms and regions. There are systematic differences across firms and regions, which are relatively stable and difficult to change. Knowledge and knowledge development are central to change, but change always needs a certain institutional support. It is known that institutions do not change very easily. It takes a lot of time to acquire a new institutional structure. Some firms can develop by changing their location, in order to benefit from the resource system of other regions and countries.

A region or country is increasingly dependent on external relations. Firms can develop into multi-locational companies that can use the resource systems of more locations than just those of their home base. Countries and regions can improve their competitive position by focusing on a certain group of activities related to the strengths of their resource base. In certain regions, industrial districts and clusters are the locational configurations in which specializations have developed. In these districts and clusters, a learning process can lead to a regional advantage in international markets (Porter, 1990).

Regional Embeddedness and Global Markets

Globalization is a phenomenon with many dimensions. The main focus is on the international company with locations in more than one country. But other dimensions – like the loss of regional cultures, the corrosion of national identities, and a loss of control by national states – are also important. Transnational companies have to organize their production in various environments as well as in different economic and institutional regimes. They have many kinds of relations; market relations, relations with governments and labor unions, and with many other groups, such as consumer organizations. Hence, their governance structure has to be flexible in order to be able to respond to these different contexts. Firms have a multitude of relations. Governance is a useful concept to help understand the set of relations and their influence on decision-making.

Ever since Williamson (1985) introduced the concept of governance structure to indicate the way in which the coordination of decisions on transactions inside companies or via markets is structured, this concept has received much attention. Williamson (Williamson and Winter, 1991, p. 12) distinguished three basic forms of coordination; the market, the hierarchy (or the organization of an enterprise), and hybrid forms such as networks. Firms can produce commodities or services within an organization (the enterprise), or they can contract out the production or parts of it to other firms via the market. The hybrid forms can be indicated by the concept of network, which is a combination of elements of both market and hierarchy, depending on the nature of contacts and contracts.

The governance structure also relates to the distribution of power (control) within a company and to the relations with other firms and institutions. The organization (the enterprise) is basically hierarchical, but even the entrepreneur and the management have to deal with other forces (shareholders, labor unions, governments, and environmental groups, to mention but a few of the outside relations which can influence the decisions). Williamson argued that the decision on how to produce (inside the firm, or via the market by contracting out, or else by buying from other producers), depends on the transaction costs, the costs of getting information and knowledge (the costs of contact), of getting in touch with suppliers and buyers (the costs of making contracts), and the costs of execution and control (the costs of control) of these contracts. In many cases, buying from other suppliers means lower transaction costs than those involved in producing everything within the own firm. In the case of buying from other firms, these other firms have opportunities to develop. Scott (1988: Ch 1) argued that in these cases it can be an explanation of why, in large agglomerations such as Los Angeles, vertical disintegration enables the existence of many smaller firms. Due to lower transaction costs, the supply chain can be organized more cheaply in a market situation with many large and small firms than in a situation with only one large company.

Governance structures are important for the analysis of globalization, because they can be used to show the effects of increasing internationalization on the sovereignty of states, which is one of the principal issues in the debate on globalization (Lambooy, 1986). Governments are by definition constrained by their territorial boundaries, whereas companies are not. More in particular, the fiscal and labor laws are important to firms when considering locations in other countries. The tax levels vary strongly from country to country. Also, the institutional differences between countries like the USA and many European nations as to labor-related laws are striking.

Apart from the economic structure, the institutional structure of countries and regions also differs. For many internationally active companies, this is an important reason to choose the most efficient locational structure for their activities. The normal reaction of governments would be to suggest possible other locations, sometimes sustained by subsidies and tax reductions. In some cases, governments do not agree with a company's decisions regarding location or takeovers. The strategic response of firms can be to relocate elsewhere, with the concomitant loss of income, employment, and knowledge.

However, firms are not completely free to relocate. In many cases they are dependent on certain kinds of labor (often knowledge workers), on their input-output structure in clusters, and on the consumer markets, which are largely located within the rich countries. Companies that do not 'behave correctly' can be punished by governments and the general public for their negative attitudes. The power of Internet information, daily newspapers, television, and other media is increasingly important to influence the decision makers within large companies. Famous examples are the Brent Star (Shell) and the Exxon Valdez oil spill off the coast of Canada and Alaska, respectively.

Firms, even the larger ones, are not fully closed systems. They are inherently sensitive to the judgment of the market. Due to the power of consumers and the media, companies have become more sensitive to other people's opinions. Their reputation is a strong factor in their market position. Even large companies have to be open to influences they do not always want. This is one reason why, to a certain extent, firms are dependent on their environment. They are intricately interwoven in networks and institutions. However, for governments a different dimension is more important, viz. the impact of the locational and the investment behavior of transnational companies on economic growth.

The concept of *embeddedness* has been used in many ways. In the original contribution by Polanyi (1944), it was meant to denote the various ways in which economic actors in primitive societies were engaged in socially and culturally determined decisions. He argued that this would diminish in modern societies, where economic decision-making would be less determined by this kind of 'embeddedness' (Jacob et Vérin, 1995, p. 18). Granovetter (1985) emphasized, however, that the influence of social and cultural values continued to be important even in modern Western economies. He argued that economic relations are also social relations, and that embeddedness is as important now as it was before. But he also warned that this concept can easily become an empty box and a concept to explain anything. He further argued that this concept may help to focus attention on the way in which people organize their resources and create networks to sustain the changes in which they are involved (Granovetter, 1995, pp. 20-1).

In geography, this concept has various uses. Oinas (1998) elaborated this point – more in particular, the relations between firms and their environments – in her book *The Embedded Firm*. In economic geography, the central issue is the effect of embeddedness on the behavior of entrepreneurs and firms in particular environments or regions. In this paper, we focus on the effect on regional economic development.

Economic development can be considered the result of an evolution of economic activities, in the sense of the creation of new opportunities or new attitudes toward economic and institutional change. Embeddedness as such does not clarify the processes of adjustment of entrepreneurs to the dynamic aspects of the economy. It only points to the fact that economic actors use more variables in their decisions than prices and quantities alone. Admittedly, the pure neo-classical equilibrium theory is under-socialized, but other economic theories – such as evolutionary economics and, more in particular, institutional economics – have more to offer in that respect.

In an economy with modular firms, both localized and non-localized networks exist. As Perroux (1955, pp. 307-8) argued, it is possible to conceive of firms as acting in two kinds of space; the topological economic space (the strictly relational space of input-output relations, or market relations, without geographic dimensions), and the geographical or technical space (where the real location matters). In the first case, proximity means intensive relations within the topological network, wherever the geographic location of the actors, while in the second case it means the physical situation close to other partners in the network. Neo-classical market relations are to be seen as topological. They are a-spatial (or Utopian: Without space), atemporal, and under-socialized. Perroux stressed that the development of economies can be influenced by governments if the cores of the topological structures (or networks) are stimulated. The so-called growth poles. Major investments in these growth poles could affect all related firms, wherever the locations of the connected firms. Empirical research (for instance, in the Mezzogiorno of Italy) has shown that major projects based on the growth pole theory have often failed, due to the fact that no supporting and related industries emerged within the region. The large investment projects then became cathedrals in the desert. They did not develop networks of related SMEs, and they remained isolated in many senses. These large enterprises remained relatively closed entities, without intra-regional economic relations; their markets were exclusively interregional or even international. It shows that, for economic development, 'geography does matter'.

More recently, the concept of the cluster has been receiving more attention than the growth-pole approach. A cluster denotes a set of firms with a shared history, with direct or indirect interrelations, and with relations with the regional institutions. Porter (1998, pp.77-8) argued that: 'Paradoxically, the enduring competitive advantages in a global economy lie increasingly in local things – knowledge, relationships, and motivation that distant rivals cannot match'. He further argued that spatial proximity has certain advantages, and that a positive influence exists when firms cooperate in local networks. He then defined the concept of cluster as follows: ' Clusters are geographic concentrations of interconnected companies and institutions in a particular field'. It is important to note that, here, Porter acknowledges the relevance of governments and institutions in the development process, because in his well-known publication *The Competitive Advantages of Nations* (Porter, 1990) such acknowledgement was still lacking.

The cluster concept is related to the concept of the industrial complex (Chardonnet, 1953) and that of the industrial district (Marshall 1890; 1966). These concepts share the emphasis on spatial proximity, intensive relations, externalities, and contacts other than market relations (Visser, 1996). The concept is also related to that of advantages of agglomeration, which emphasizes that locational proximity can create advantages of scale, scope, and learning (Lambooy, 1997; 2000).

Regional Policy and Regional Resource Development

Regional policy is a distinct kind of policy, first developed in the 1930s in the US (e.g. the Tennessee Valley Authority) and in the UK (often associated with town and country planning). The basic idea was that markets did not produce the neo-classical equilibrium with inter-regional convergence, so that governments, as part of the New Deal, intervened with special programs to develop regional resources. One option was to subsidize enterprises located in peripheral areas, another was to enhance the basic attractiveness of such regions by heavily investing in infrastructure, public utilities, and large manufacturing industries with many linkages, like the steel industry, oil refineries, and the automotive industry.

Many approaches were used in regional policy. One of the earlier and very influential theories is the so-called growth pole theory (Lambooy, 1969), based on the ideas of the French economist Perroux (1955). This theory focuses on the idea that economic development occurs through the expansion of networks of connected firms, wherever their location (*l'espace économique*, as Perroux called it), with nodes or growth poles, consisting of the principal firms, the driving forces of economic growth, as the focal points in the networks. These economic relations were dependent not only on location, but also – and more decisively so – on the nature of market relations in economic space, not in geographical space. Nevertheless, governments could decide to invest in heavy industry (which they considered as growth poles) in peripheral locations, which then could develop their own networks of related firms, by outsourcing and subcontracting. In that case, part of the multiplier effects of these investments were expected to develop in these peripheral regions, which consecutively should start a cumulative regional development process.

A related approach can also be found in the theory of Gunnar Myrdal (1957). In contrast to the neo-classical theory of inter-regional convergence via the market mechanism, Myrdal (1957: Ch 2) used the idea of cumulative development, a process in which a virtuous cycle of investment and increased attraction creates a spatial disparity of regions. Metropolitan regions, or other regions with an initial advantage, would develop even more, while peripheral regions, even with low wages, would decline instead of grow. The theoretical end-product of neo-classical theory should be equilibrium and convergence towards equalized wage and profit levels, not increased differences in growth as predicted by Myrdal's approach.

Many regions, even those with an acceptable level of economic growth, are developing new strategic plans, aimed at keeping up in the rat race of inter-regional competition to attract the best investments. This competition may be seen as the result of an increasing variety of production opportunities in a growing number of regions across the world. New variety has evolved by the development of new technologies and new organizational structures. Many regions feel the threat of being outperformed by other areas. The regional authorities, the labor unions, and other institutions are well aware that many economic activities are no longer locationally fixed. Capital is, more than ever, free to move to other locations. Many regions have dreams of becoming a New Silicon Valley, a Technopolis, or The Major Gateway, and others have similar highly speculative goals.

Regional policy presupposes the possibility to intervene in the process of development of the regional resource base and of the inter-regional spatial matrix of economic development. Policy means that intervention should lead to a self-defined path of development, different from that which is perceived as the current one. Policies are often focused on short-term problems, such as reducing unemployment, although quite often a changing structure can only be influenced over a longer period, more in particular if the resource base is improved. The choice of a theory by politicians can influence the design of the policy. Keynes's much quoted remark that 'we will be all dead in the long run' has had a negative effect on the interest in structural issues and the supply side of the economy. His theory was focused on intervention in the business cycle via the demand side. The perspective of intervention via the supply side – which is very important for regional policy – is sustained by several economic theories. In the USA and in many other countries, the present focus is on rationalization (mainly by deregulation and a stronger focus on the market mechanism) and on the supply side, that is, first, strengthening the motivation to seek higher rewards, and, second, improving the quality of the factors of production, e.g., physical infrastructure and knowledge. For regional policy, this has resulted in abandoning the emphasis on subsidies for unfavorably developing regions, and shifting attention to the strengthening of structures, mainly infrastructure. In national economic policy – more in particular, in technology policy and industrial policy – a strategy of picking the winners (often the new sectors with increasing returns, e.g., electronics and biotechnology) is pursued. The same often happens in regional policy, but – as is also true for countries – most regions tend to attract the same winners, which results in hefty competition.

In our perspective, regional policy does not take into account the relational view of firms and the fundamental issue of resource development in the broad meaning of resources. Also, it does not consider either the building of a knowledge base or other non-classical production factors. Regional policy should focus more consistently on the development of all possible resources. It should also develop a more integral view on resource development. Regional economic structures are entities that are not easily changed. They display a certain path-dependency, which means that the initial conditions determine for a large part the achievement of possible development initiatives, but also that seemingly small changes in resources can have unexpected results later. Anyway, providing access to resources for the entire population should be a primary goal.

Conclusions

The relations of firms with other firms, wherever their location, are an important driver for the development of new opportunities to use available resources or to introduce new ones. Knowledge and institutional structures are increasingly important to gain a competitive edge. Countries and regions can have a strong influence on the firms located within their territories if they are prepared to construct an innovation system based on cooperation and institutional evolution. Building agglomeration advantages and clusters within an urban system may favor such a development.

References

Boschma, R.A. (1998), *The Industrial Rise of Third Italy; Open Window or Locational Opportunity*, Paper presented at the RSA conference in Vienna.
Boschma, R.A. and Lambooy, J.G. (1999), 'Evolutionary Economics and Economic Geography', *Journal of Evolutionary Economics*, Vol. 9, pp. 411-29.
Boschma, R.A. and Lambooy, J.G. (2000), 'The Prospects of an Adjustment Policy Based on Collective Learning in Old Industrial Regions', *Geojournal*, Vol. 49, pp. 391-99 (Kluwer Academic Publishers).
Chardonnet, R. (1953), *Les Complexes Industriels*, PUF, Paris.
Granovetter, M. (1985), 'Economic Action and Social Structure: the Problem of Embeddedness', *American Journal of Sociology*, Vol. 91(3), pp. 481-510.
Granovetter, M. (1995), 'La Notion 'd'Embeddedness'', in A. Jacob et H. Vérin (eds), *L'Inscription Sociale du Marché*, L' Harmattan, Paris, pp. 9-20.
Hunt, S.D. (2000), *A General Theory of Competition; Resources, Competencies, Productivity, Economic Growth*, Sage, London.
Jacob. A. and H. Vérin (eds.) (1995), *L'Inscription Sociale du Marché*, L'Harmattan, Paris.
Jacobs, J. (1984), *The Wealth of Cities*, Penguin, London.
Lambooy, J.G. (1969), *Het Geografisch Systeem en de Groeipool Theorie*. Oratie Vrije Universiteit Amsterdam, Van Gorcum, Assen.
Lambooy, J.G. (1986), 'Locational Decisions and Regional Structure', in J.H.P. Paelinck (ed.), *Human Behavior in Geographical Space*, pp. 149-65, Gower, London.
Lambooy, J.G. (1987), 'Information and Internationalization', *Revue d'Economie Régionale et Urbaine*, Vol. 5, pp. 719-31.
Lambooy, J.G. (1994), *Network and Proximity: Transactions and Knowledge*, Paper presented at the International RSA conference, Groningen.
Lambooy, J.G. (1997), 'Knowledge Production, Organization and Agglomeration Economies', *GeoJournal*, Vol. 41(4), pp. 293-300.
Lambooy, J.G. (2000), 'Learning and Agglomeration Economies: Adapting to Differentiating Economic Structures', in F. Boekema, K. Morgan, S. Bakkers and R. Rutten (eds), *Knowledge, Innovation and Economic Growth. The Theory and Practice of Learning Regions*, pp. 17-37, Edward Elgar, Cheltenham, etc.
Lundvall, B.A. (1988), 'Innovation as an Interactive Process', in G. Dosi et al. (eds), *Technology and Economic Theory*, Pinter, London, pp. 349-69.
Marshall, A. (1890;1966), *Principles of Economics*, Macmillan, London.
Myrdal, G. (1957), *Economic Theory and Underdeveloped Regions*, Duckworth, London.

Nelson, R.R. (1996), *The Sources of Economic Growth*, Harvard University Press, Cambridge Massachusetts.

Nooteboom, B. (2000), *Learning and Innovation in Organizations and Economies*, Oxford University Press, Oxford.

Oinas, P. (1998), *The Embedded Firm? Prelude for a Revised Geography of Enterprise*, Helsinki School of Economics and Business Administration, Helsinki.

Parker, Ph. (2000), *Physioeconomics; the Basis for Long-run Economic Growth*, MIT Press, Cambridge Massachusetts.

Perroux, F. (1955), 'Note sur la Notion Pôle de Croissance', *Economie Appliquée*, Série D, Vol. 8(1-2), pp. 307-20.

Polanyi, K. (1944), *The Great Transformation*, Beacon Press, Boston.

Porter, M. (1990), *The Competitive Advantage of Nations*, Free Press, New York.

Porter, M. (1998), *On Competition*, Harvard University Press, Cambridge, Massachusetts.

Scott, A. (1988), *Metropolis: from the Division of Labor to Urban Form*, University of California, Los Angeles.

Visser, E.J. (1996), *Local Sources of Competitiveness. Spatial Clustering and Organizational Dynamics in Small-Scale Clothing in Lima, Peru*, Thesis Publishers Amsterdam.

Williamson, O.E. (1985), *The Institutions of Capitalism*, Free Press, New York.

Williamson, O.E. and Winter, S.G. (1991), *The Nature of the Firm*, Oxford University Press, Oxford.

3 Embeddedness: The Role of Local Factors in Economic Development

GUUS VAN WESTEN

Introduction

The past few decades witnessed two paradigmatic shifts in the approach to urban and regional development. Traditionally, geographers tended to focus on local factors in explaining economic conditions – the physical, social, and cultural characteristics of place. Since the 1960s, more critical generations of scholars have challenged the role of such horizontal factors in explaining development, or its absence. In the wake of the *dependencia* school, they stressed the importance of vertical forces in explaining underdevelopment, such as the subservient position imposed on communities in the South within a hierarchic world system. The neo-liberal counter-revolution of the 1980s produced yet another shift in thinking. Not so much perhaps in theoretical insights – essentially these comprised refinements of existing approaches – as in the globalization that ensued. Globalization was first considered as a phenomenon, i.e., the acceleration of economic and social integration processes spanning substantial parts of the globe, driven by technological innovation on the one hand, and by the liberalization of the policy framework on the other. In the 1990s, globalization also emerged as a new discourse in world affairs, not least in development studies. I will not purport to define the globalization paradigm here, but as an approach it challenges the separation of the various spheres of life (as between the economic and the cultural), is preoccupied with interaction patterns between actors (perceiving networks and clusters everywhere), and it raises the issue of scale levels. This last factor means that, instead of implicitly adopting a horizontal (as the traditional regionalists did) or a vertical approach (as the structuralists did), the globalization approach focused on the questions what different scale levels mean in the development process, and how vertical and horizontal forces interact with one another.

This chapter attempts to shed some light on the role of local factors in economic development. To what extent is economic growth embedded in the specific characteristics of a town, a region, or even a country? What local conditions are favorable for progress? In the quest for a preliminary answer, the next section will explore the conceptual roots of the local in local development, i.e., the embeddedness of economic activity. This will identify a few spheres of embeddedness, which will be discussed in the subsequent sections of the chapter.

Conceptual Background: Embedded Economic Activities and Social Capital

Although the notion that economic activity is embedded in specific social settings that are likely to influence its performance is not new, the fact that it has been in use for over half a century has not yielded much conceptual clarity. For economists, embeddedness stands for the fact that 'economic (market) relations coexist with a set of social attributes' (Boschma et al., 2001). In other words, economic decisions are not only based on market forces, such as prices and quantities, but are also influenced by social attributes, such as cultural values, personal relationships, etc. i.e., who you are, what you know, and – not least – who you know. According to Leyshon (1996, p. 67), the concept of embeddedness was first introduced in an attempt 'to chart an analytical course between the traditional interpretations of 'the economic' developed by neo-classical economists on the one hand, and Marxism on the other'. In other words, the notion that economic behavior is embedded in social relations serves to bridge the gap between the neoclassical preoccupation with market forces, and the political economy approach of the structuralists and others. Karl Polanyi (1944) is credited with having been the first to use the term. His purpose differed somewhat from our concern with variations in local economic development. Polanyi criticized the assumption that economic interests have always dominated other considerations in steering human behavior. He argued that this had not generally been the case before the 'great transformation', the first industrial revolution and related changes in Western societies since the late 18th century. Economic self-interest may have become the dominant principle of social life since the 19th century – at least in the more advanced market economies – Polanyi argued, but before, economic life was typically embedded in social relations, even to the point of being subordinated to, for instance, religious and political interests.

A similar argument can presumably be extended to non-Western societies that have as yet been incompletely integrated into the world economy. It is at this point that embeddedness assumes a specific meaning for development studies. In its original sense (as used by Polanyi), embeddedness essentially stands for pre-capitalist remnants in the organization of the economy. One may surmise that the more developed an economy becomes, the less embedded its economic actors will be – in the sense that they will be able to free themselves from restrictions imposed by their social environment. Seen from this perspective, both globalization and development are processes of disembedding economic actors from their regional (local, national) context. This is, indeed, an argument advanced by Giddens (1990), in a context not restricted to the economic, as Polanyi would have noted with approval. Giddens sees globalization as the spread of disembedding institutions and practices, steadily displacing location-specific social mechanisms, and resulting in a certain homogenization of economic space. To a certain extent, this disembedding can be welcomed as a move towards a more rational allocation of resources, free from customary obligations. Think, for instance, of the familiar complaints of African entrepreneurs who are expected to meet the needs of an extensive kin group. On the other hand, delinking economic activity and local environment, risks eventually resulting in a dislocated enclave, where activity and environment have no meaning for each other.

The concept was reintroduced in a different context by Mark Granovetter (1985), who gave it a somewhat different meaning. Granovetter was less concerned with societies or 'superstructure', but focused on the social groups in which people are embedded – the families, clubs, neighborhood communities, etc. to which they belong and whose interests they take to heart. These networks of personal relationships inspire loyalties as well as communality of purpose and understanding. Two important conclusions result from this. One is that economic actors are inclined to consider other interests in addition to their own, because their sense of well-being is not uniquely defined in individual terms. The other is that membership of such social groups actually makes cooperation easier, thus enhancing economic efficiency beyond the level reached by the atomic actors of neo-classical economics. This quality is called social capital (Coleman, 1988; Putnam, 1993). Since a lot of social interaction is contained within a distinct geographical setting, places with a rich tapestry of such affinity networks among economic actors may benefit from more social capital than others, and prosper.

Meanwhile, many geographers and regional planners have favored a much more restricted interpretation of embeddedness, viewing it essentially as the degree to which businesses are integrated into the local economy in terms of backward and forward linkages; 'Probably the most important single indicator of local embeddedness ... relates to supplier relationships' (Dicken *et al.*, quoted in Pavlínek and Smith, 1998, p. 621). This view, while conceptually eclectic, reflects the practitioner's concern with the impact of activities on regional economic development. This especially applies to the local economic impact of foreign investment. Studies in this tradition typically focus on the localization of sources of inputs on the one hand, and the local processing of raw materials and semi-finished products on the other hand.

In sum, the literature on local factors in economic performance has yielded several versions of embeddedness. Jessop (1997) identified three main uses of the concept. The first is Polanyi's original sense of the societal embeddedness of economic operators; the second is Granovetter's social embeddedness in interpersonal relations, usually focusing on key decision takers within firms; and the third is the embeddedness of firms in networks of organizations, including inter-firm supply linkages. The following sections will loosely follow Jessop's distinction in three notions of embedding by presenting them as different scale levels. First the macro-level of society and culture will be discussed, with the nation-state as the corresponding spatial entity. Then, the meso-level of networks of firms and organizations will be taken up, essentially at the regional level. And finally we will turn to the micro-level of individual firms and their supply linkages. Note, however, that this classification is somewhat arbitrary. Scale levels are closely linked and their boundaries are fuzzy. Post-modernist complexity has caught up with economic geography.

The Macro View: Society, Culture, and Economic Performance

The idea that some societies are better at generating economic progress than others has been with us for centuries. After all, the evidence seems to support this view, as reflected in the annual reports of the World Bank, United Nations, and others. How exactly these differences are produced is a rather more contentious subject. Much of the literature on the subject is notoriously vague, eclectic, and lacking in empirical underpinning. Among historians, the debate centers on the issue of European exceptionalism. Is the fact that European societies were the first to experience development, due to uniquely Western characteristics? In other words, is there a qualitative difference that sets European societies and historical experiences apart from others? Or is it partly a matter of coincidence, and were European societies simply the first to breach a certain threshold beyond which a cumulative process of capitalist expansion was triggered; something that in principle could have happened elsewhere? Some claim evidence in support of the first view, that of European exceptionalism, albeit on a bewildering range of arguments that run from culturally-embedded institutions favoring adaptation and innovation (Landes, 1998) to germs (Diamond, 1997). The second interpretation would be rather more welcome, however, among both structuralists ('Just get rid of nasty Western capitalism') and neo-positivists ('Just get the basics right').

Hofstede (1980), made a notable attempt to tackle the link between culture and economic performance on an empirical basis. He compared the attitudes of employees of a single corporation (IBM) in over 50 countries, in an attempt to find basic differences between national cultures. His interpretations of the survey material led him to identify a few differences, i.e., the role of social inequality and authority within society, the position of the individual vis-à-vis the collective, the relative emphasis on gender relations, and the issue of how to cope with uncertainty and conflict. Later, the time horizon of human activity (essentially Western 'short-termism' versus the predominantly Eastern long-term orientation) was added as a fifth dimension of cultural difference (Knippenberg, 1995, p. 49). Some of these cultural variations display a measure of covariance with economic performance indicators. For instance, individualism was much more pronounced among IBM workers in the more developed countries, as against a more collective orientation in less advanced countries. Few would argue with this general finding. However, it is far from clear how the surmised link between individualism and economic progress operates. For instance, rather successful Asian economies (such as South Korea and Taiwan) stand out as collectivist cultures. Sometimes a particular cultural characteristic is presented as a source of stagnation in one context, and used to explain economic success in another. This is the case with the Confucianist value system of the Chinese. Long accused of stifling initiative among younger generations, it is now often credited with inspiring discipline, dedication, and mutual trust. For all we know, both may be true, but then it should be concluded that culture can have different economic outcomes in different contexts. The same applies to Weber's idea of the Protestant work ethic, which has not prevented Catholic areas such as the 'Third Italy' or Bavaria from outperforming other parts of Europe in our own age. If culture matters in economic performance, then how does the link work?

Fukuyama (1995), among many others, attempted to take up the challenge by asserting that trust is a crucial variable in economic success. It is the glue that makes social capital possible. Social capital is 'the ability of people to work together for common purposes in groups and organizations' (Fukuyama, 1995, p. 10). When specific characteristics of a local (or national) setting encourage trust among economic actors, this makes it easier for them to do business, i.e., it allows them to cut back on transaction costs. Again, what exactly inspires this trust or causes social capital to flourish is less clear. Different things in different contexts may add to social capital, and some of them may well belong to the realm of culture. Fukuyama distinguishes between high-trust societies – where voluntary associations in multiple forms thrive, easing economic activity – and low-trust societies, with less social capital between the key institutions of the family on the one hand, and the state on the other. The way he defines these two categories of societies is arbitrary. They are presented as such, rather than shown to differ on the basis of empirical research. The dividing line between high- and low-trust societies runs right through the Western and Eastern world, which is rather convenient for an author catering to race-sensitive American audiences. Fukuyama does not claim that low-trust societies are destined to remain poor. Family-based firms may well thrive (as in Italy and in Chinese communities), and the public sector can intervene and provide the institutional support mechanisms that voluntary initiatives offer in high-trust societies. Nevertheless, following his arguments, it would take concerted efforts by the state to overcome the lack of social capital in low-trust societies. This finding echoes Gerschenkron's observation that cases of catch-up industrialization tend to be state-led. It points to the importance of political embedding, a subject that, although a macro-issue, is more conveniently taken up later in this chapter.

There is enough in Fukuyama to take aim at, but the idea of trust as a crucial component of social capital is a useful one. Both Hofstede and Fukuyama considered culture as characteristics of the national level – a higher scale level than we have in mind here. However, there is reason to postulate that factors at Polanyi's societal level have some relevance at more local levels as well. An anecdotal observation may illustrate this. A visible difference between the two neighboring Pacific island states of Yap and Chuuk in Micronesia is the state of the local roads. Roads on Chuuk are full of potholes, so that after a heavy rainfall, Weno – the main island – looks like a disaster zone. Yap's roads are well maintained and often carefully landscaped. Asked about this lack of maintenance, the Chuukese official in charge of public works explained that the island has no asphalt production facility; road repairs have to wait until external contractors ship in a temporary facility. His Yapese counterpart remarked that conditions there were not different, 'but we fill potholes with cement for as long as needed'. A range of similar examples can be quoted, showing Yap to be a more cohesive, better-organized entity than Chuuk (although this is not often put down in writing). The root difference is not so much one of capabilities or funding, as both communities share similar access to funding under their Compact of Free Association with the United States. Rather, they reflect different perceptions of responsibility between the officials in both communities. It is tempting to link this difference with the historical trajectories of both island groups. Between the two world wars, Chuuk served as a major Japanese naval base. Japanese settlers outnumbered the indigenous population and the traditional Chuukese social structure (the authority of chiefs, the mechanisms defining a person's position in society) to a large extent collapsed, resulting in social dislocation. Yap, although not free from such problems, had a far less important role under Japanese occupation. Its society changed under external pressure, but survived as a functioning social system. Traditional values and social relations, including chiefly authority, continue to count for something (Hezel, 1995). This relative survival of social cohesion in one community and its destruction in the other can help to explain the differences in responsiveness of government. Yet it would be difficult to substantiate these impressions with solid proof.

Meso-Views: Networks of Firms and Regional Institutions

A better understanding of how trust-based social capital can work requires us to take the analysis to the level of the networks linking people and organizations with one another, i.e., to Granovetter's notion of social embeddedness. This brings us closer to the local level, which is our main concern. As mentioned, in reality the dividing lines between scale levels are not so clear-cut. Cultural factors (macro) and social networks (meso) are often closely linked. Think, for example, of the 'bamboo network' of ethnic Chinese businesses that generates much of the economic activity across Southeast Asia. These networks are as much defined in cultural terms (embedded in Chinese family values) as they are defined as social networks (linking individuals and their businesses). Similarly, minority entrepreneurial groups are found in different parts of the world, from Jews in pre-war Europe to the Syrian traders in West Africa and South Asian businesses in East Africa. In each of these cases, substantial social capital is generated in social groups that in varying degrees are seen as disembedded from the local context. The perceived distance from local societies is likely to contribute to social capital within the minority groups.

However artificial it may be to separate meso-level institutions (networks, regions) from their macro- and micro-contexts, there are still good reasons to make an attempt. To explain this we have to take a bird's eye view of changes in the organization of the world economy in the last two decades or so. Whether these changes amount to a new 'great transformation' (Castells, 1996) or not (Harris, 2000), they have marked the rise of an economy based on networks. Two reasons account for this. One is the restructuring of economic activity in response to the demise of the Fordist mode of regulation, and its replacement by flexible accumulation. To detail the reasons behind this restructuring would be going beyond the scope of this chapter. However, it is clear that technological advances (especially in ICT) and the widespread liberalization of national economies since the late 1970s have changed the context in which firms operate. Competition has intensified and former certainties evaporated. The vertically integrated corporations and the conglomerates of the Fordist era have usually responded by shifting the firm boundary inward, i.e., by reducing the extent and variety of in-house activities and refocusing on what they do best, or rather on the more profitable sections of the value chain. Other activities are assigned to other firms. The result is a network society in which businesses, government agencies, and other organizations are linked to one another in extensive functional webs.

The second (and related) reason why economic networks have emerged as a key subject of interest lies in the increased importance of technological innovation as a source of competitive strength. Intensifying competitive pressures compel firms (and local economies) to either tighten their belt, or to escape this low road by opting for the high road strategy of becoming more efficient through innovation. In industrial networks composed of many firms, this learning is no longer a matter of individual firms alone, but assumes collective features. After all, a company's efficiency is partly derived from the performance of its network partners. Hence, principal firms encourage innovation within their supplier families, while smaller companies often rely on teaming up with others in order to make innovation possible. As the capacity for innovation in part depends on tacit knowledge embodied in people and local institutions, it follows that local factors play a key role in the ability of (especially small) firms to embark upon a technological upgrading strategy. The scope for technological learning within local economies depends in part on their networking characteristics. This has spawned a body of literature on local (national) innovation systems and 'learning regions' (Lundvall, 1988; Asheim, 1996; Morgan, 1997). Hence, innovation becomes embedded in new institutional arrangements, involving cooperation across the firm boundary and partnerships – or rather alliances (Baud, 2000, p. 4) between large corporations, local family-based businesses communities, and public sector agencies.

What, then, does embeddedness mean for innovation? At first sight, embeddedness would encourage innovation thanks to enhanced cooperation. Boschma, Lambooy, and Schutjens (2001) postulate that there actually is an inverse U-shaped relationship between degree of embeddedness and a firm's innovative performance. At first, cooperation, mutual understanding, common institutions, and enhanced communications facilitate the performance. However, higher degrees of embeddedness start to jeopardize competition, isolate local firms from external influences, and steer the local economy towards a lock-in dictated by a collusion of dominant interests. Thus, Boschma *et al.* argue, innovation will tend to decrease again beyond a certain optimal point. This hypothesis echoes the point often made with respect to the competitive strengths of industrial districts of clusters of small firms specialized in a particular industry. The advantages of such clusters are considered to derive from an optimal mix between cooperation and competition among its members. The industrial district loses its edge once the balance between the two is disturbed.

Most of the literature on innovation in embedded clusters is based on examples from advanced economies. We should now consider the question to what extent local economic networks in developing countries offer such moderately embedded conditions. A finding common to several studies of clusters of enterprises in developing countries is that firms that increased cooperation showed greater improvement in performance (Humphrey and Schmitz, 2000, pp. 8-9). In a summary overview of collective learning in the South, Helmsing (2000, pp. 36-38) states that conditions in many countries do not appear very conducive. In many developing countries, often a few large firms dominate markets. The middle segment of medium-sized firms is often weak, while the remainder consists of a large number of undifferentiated small firms. This industrial structure does not encourage cooperation and collective learning processes. Moreover, turbulent economic environments seem to stand in the way of a more competitive restructuring of companies. Many prefer to stick to vertical integration, and avoid becoming dependent on a large number of suppliers. Instead, competitive pressures are more typically countered by cutting costs and margins rather than by innovation (Helmsing, 2000, p. 37). Despite liberalization programs, important business groups in the South are more notably embedded in their country's political apparatus than in regional economic networks (Tsai, 2000; Hamilton and Waters, 1995). Often, major enterprises are persistently concentrated in national core areas around the capital.

The above is a sweeping generalization, as Helmsing warns us (2000, p. 36). The emerging export-oriented industrial economies of East Asia show very different patterns of development, and there are dynamic industrial districts reported from places ranging from rural China (Christerson and Lever-Tracy, 1997) to Brazil's Sinos Valley footwear cluster (Schmitz, 1999). Yet in general, local economic environments in many developing countries appear to have little in terms of the 'stocks of relational assets', in Storper's words, that have become a strength of flourishing regional economies elsewhere.

This begs the question how acknowledged centers of economic activity have managed to succeed, especially in the case of regional economic centers away from national core areas deriving substantial advantages from being the locus of political power. In a collection of studies on the emergence of secondary industrial centers in several Latin American and southern European countries, Cerruti and Vellinga (1989) focus on the role of local business elites. Especially in Antioquia (Colombia), Monterrey (Mexico), and Arequipa (Peru), industrialization occurred along remarkably similar lines. In each of these cities, a relatively homogeneous group of local entrepreneurs, closely related in terms of economic transactions as well as family ties, spearheaded the industrial development process. In most cases, capital was initially derived from trade, which gradually diversified into family-owned industrial groups, each perceived as a *gran familia*. The importance of kinship ties in the organization of economic activity was matched by a generally high degree of regional embeddedness in the areas studied. It is true that industrial growth depended on the integration of national markets in order to attain the necessary economies of scale, but apart from that the entrepreneurs formed typical regional elites, often combining economic and political power in their home areas and showing characteristic local pride, often expressed in embellishment programs in their home town. Hence, a degree of political and economic autonomy with respect to the national economy (interests based in the respective capital cities) was a further factor in secondary city industrial success (Cerruti and Vellinga, 1989, pp. 284-87). This was often enhanced by their physical distance from the respective core regions. The continued existence of such locally-embedded industrial systems cannot be taken for granted, however. The restructuring of Peru's economy along neo-liberal lines in the 1990s led to the acquisition of several of Arequipa's family businesses by Lima-based corporations. This apparently ended much of the regionally-embedded nature of the city's major industries (Menno Vellinga, personal communication).

Here an issue presents itself that is too often overlooked in much of the cluster literature, the role of vertical links between the local economy on the one hand, and national and global economies on the other. An example illustrates this well. Take the province of Surat Thani in southern Thailand. The economy of Surat Thani, like that of much of provincial Thailand, revolves around the production of raw materials for external markets. Close to two-thirds of the agricultural land is planted with rubber trees, from which rubber sheets and parawood for distant markets are produced. Recently, intensive, industrialized shrimp cultivation has taken over in some coastal areas, servicing markets from Singapore to Japan and the USA. Oil palm plantations have emerged in sparsely populated areas, catering to rising national demand. Each of these leading sectors is a typical agro-export industry, with Surat Thani specialized in producing the raw material, as well as in processing activities that make the raw materials more suitable for transportation (cleaning and freezing shrimps, treating and grading rubber mats and liquid latex, etc). Downstream manufacturing activity remains limited, although there is some production of rubber gloves.

Surat Thani may have a relatively subordinated position in the Thai as well as international division of labor, but this does not mean that it lacks a local economic elite (Goewie, 2001). Five local tycoons dominate the provincial economy, each of them a descendent of ethnically Chinese business people who settled there one or more generations ago. Each of these *Pi Jai* ('Big Brothers', as they are called) has a diversified portfolio of local business interests, although they differ in sectoral emphasis. One is more focused on the construction industry, another more on palm oil. Each of these business leaders is the center of a close-knit group of substantial business people, independent entrepreneurs or managers of the local establishments of larger concerns, as well as officials. Social interaction within these groups is often intense; some meet daily in a restaurant that belongs to a group member. While primarily a circle of friends, the composition strongly suggests that members are partly selected for their ability to support each other. This is clear from the fact that ranking officers from the powerful armed forces, police, and customs department, as well as local administrators are typically among the membership. Relations between the five tycoons, while not necessarily hostile, are far more distant. Local business associations exist, but such impersonal institutions tend to be weak. The five tycoons and their friends display a considerable level of local embeddedness. They invest in local assets, show themselves concerned with Surat Thani's standing in the world, and their families have developed roots there. However, they are not provincial in the sense that they are unfamiliar with the way things are done in Bangkok. Most have had a good education abroad or in Bangkok, and all have frequent business in the Thai capital.

The example of Surat Thani shows that the impact of trust-based social capital depends a great deal on the context. Surat Thani's business people show a high degree of local embeddedness; they tend to be well-informed and influential, thanks to the close contacts they maintain with a circle of peers and other useful people. Yet this has little effect in terms of regional economic development. Presumably, Surat Thani's insertion into international commodity chains as a low-end producer of selected raw materials makes all the difference. Functional links are with external suppliers and markets, and the local economy does not offer the economies of scale that allow other activities to grow beyond local servicing. Although the local business elite does not lack resources or skills, their own interests to a large extent are vested in the same limited range of activities. With the exception of the tourist industry, they see little point in promoting a high road upgrading strategy that would make things more difficult for existing activities.

Thus, the case of local economies such as Surat Thani reminds us that horizontal networks of people and institutions are not the only generators of social capital within a locality. We also have to consider the vertical question of how a local economic network is incorporated into a larger (national, global) economic system. As Humphrey and Schmitz have pointed out (2000, p. 3), developing economies tend to be engaged in precisely those mature commodity industries that are traded in global commodity chains orchestrated by transnational global buyers. The development perspectives of local enterprise clusters can be greatly influenced by the governance structure in which they are contained. According to Humphrey and Schmitz, local small firms may benefit from their insertion into global value chains organized and dominated by buying TNCs, generally operating from advanced countries. The benefit derived from this type of integration is that the formidable challenges of securing access to major markets, and learning of design and product specifications are taken care of by the buyers – leaving local firms to concentrate on what they do best, namely performing cost-effective physical production activities. This comes at a cost, however. Producers have to maintain low margins due to the threat of the arrival of new, lower-cost producers. It also implies restricted opportunities for upgrading to more rewarding activities within the value chain, as this would entail a confrontation with the external buyers on which they depend. 'Global chain governance can create barriers to local upgrading' (Humphrey and Schmitz,

2000, p. 13). Even when growth creates upgrading opportunities for local firms, it is doubtful whether the buyers will allow them to move into their core competencies of designing, marketing, and branding goods – in other words, in assuming control of the organization of the value chain. Once lock-in into a dependent position has occurred, significant investments and effort by both private and public sectors are required to overcome such blockades. It is difficult to see such how such effort could take place without forceful government intervention – which is not likely to take place in the context of a local or regional economy, but might conceivably be undertaken if the national economy is at stake. An important conclusion here is that the scope for autonomous policy in local clusters may be expected to be far lower than is the case in industries or regional economies engaged in more sophisticated product lines.

Micro-Views: Supply Linkages of Firms

The focus in the previous section was on the network of firms and supporting organizations as a meso-level institution in their own right, on the assumption that the whole of the cluster is more than the sum of its components, thanks to the 'relational assets' (Storper, 1997) in the regional economy. This final section discusses the degree to which the supply linkages of firms are contained within the regional economy. Supplier linkages are also networks, but the reason for viewing this as a micro-level issue is that the supply decisions are taken within the firm, and not in the realm of meso-level institutions.

As stated above, the backward and forward linkages of production units are classical subjects in regional development. They obviously matter when considering the developmental impact of foreign investment, one of the key issues in the debate on globalization and local development. As Castells has emphasized (1996, p. 129), since around 1980, the performance of developing economies increasingly depends on their export performance and their ability to attract foreign direct investment (FDI). For over two decades, two opposite schools of thought have vied with one another when considering the local impact of foreign plants. The neoclassical view assumes that supply linkages will increase over time. Branch plants will learn more about their environment, and start using local sources of supply in view of the obvious advantages. Hence learning (by branch plants as well as by local entrepreneurs) will yield increasing locally embedded linkages over time (e.g., ILO, 1981). Over time, upgrading towards more attractive activities will take place.

This view was challenged by researchers with a structuralist view (e.g., Fröbel et al., 1976). They stressed the fact that parts of the production process were only moved to developing countries in order to benefit from low labor costs. Sourcing decisions are taken within the global corporate strategy, and the operation of branch plants is not concerned with the local economy. Moreover, 'footloose' production facilities will be moved as soon as cost considerations show this to be attractive. This obstructs any significant move towards localization and upgrading of the host economy.

The last two decades have produced evidence in support of both views, but vindicated neither. Foreign branch plants in the Dominican Republic and several other Caribbean islands have largely remained enclaves, locked into the role of a low-cost performer of simple labor-intensive activities. In contrast, foreign investment in several East Asian countries, such as in the electronics industry in Singapore and Malaysia, has contributed to successful local industrial development, including partial localization and industrial upgrading. Hence, FDI can have remarkably different outcomes in different contexts.

Broadly speaking, local linkage creation depends on the characteristics of the firm and the industry on the one hand, and on the characteristics of the region on the other. Both will be briefly considered. First, some types of industry inherently have a much higher propensity for creating local linkages than others. Obviously, car production, which requires thousands of parts and components, is more conducive to the creation of supply linkages than the production of T-shirts. On the other hand, mature industries using standardized technology (including garment production) tend to establish more local linkages than advanced industries with complicated technology and demanding product specifications, such as the optical instruments industry (Dicken, 1998). Local producers are less likely to be able to meet product specifications and performance standards in high-tech industries, thus reducing the scope of local linkage creation.

Second, regional characteristics determine the extent of linkage formation in two broad ways (Egeraat, 1995, pp. 28-30). The complexity of the region's economic structure has much to do with the opportunities for local linkages. Hence, foreign branch plants in developed industrial regions are much more likely to source a great deal of their inputs locally, than are 'screwdriver plants' in low-cost locations with a shallow industrial profile. This is obvious, but it is not always understood that the same establishment may yield different outcomes in different localities. This is demonstrated by Pavlínek and Smith (1998) in the context of the privatization and acquisition by a single foreign corporation of both the Czech and the Slovak car industry. Volkswagen's acquisition of Škoda in the Czech Republic led to the rationalization of operations, but most local linkages were retained, and the well-developed Czech automotive cluster survived as a comprehensive industrial complex. In contrast, Volkswagen's acquisition of BAZ – Slovakia's van producer with a far less developed local supplier system – turned the Slovak plant into a locally disembedded supplier of a narrow range of parts for Volkswagen factories elsewhere, competing essentially on costs. Hence, globalization in the shape of foreign investment within a well-developed regional industrial economy may foster localized economic growth through a web of local linkages. On the other hand, industrial FDI in a largely virgin industrial economy is less likely to impact the regional economic structure by encouraging the emergence of a local supplier base.

Similarly, it should be noted that the geographical sourcing patterns of branch plants do not inevitably move in the direction of more localization. An example is the shift in the geographical origins of material inputs used by Philips Audio's production facility in Penang, Malaysia, in the 1990s, which at the time was Philip's largest production site for mass-production audio sets (Grotjohann, Sterkenburg, and Grunsven, 1996). Initially, a global sourcing strategy was applied. Procurement decisions were taken at headquarters, favoring the best supply option worldwide. Once the Penang branch was well established, sourcing decisions were decentralized to the plant management, which by then was well aware of local opportunities. This encouraged a considerable localization of inputs, except for the most advanced components. In 1991, 65 per cent of total material input value was purchased in Malaysia. By 1994, however, Malaysia's share of the input value had dropped again to 49 per cent as a result of a re-globalization strategy. Pressure to cut costs across the board within Philips during Operation Centurion, transferred sourcing responsibilities back to a higher level in the organization, and reintroduced a global sourcing outlook. Scale economies are achieved by using no more than three suppliers for each item, selected for quality as well as their commitment to Philips. Reducing the number of suppliers also allows for stricter quality monitoring. Philips showed a certain loyalty to local suppliers, in the sense that orders for a given product line were not normally withdrawn. This loyalty, however, did not necessarily extend beyond the lifecycle of a particular model of audio equipment (i.e., a few years).

From Micro back to Macro: A Tentative Conclusion

Are we then to conclude that only established industrial economies are able to benefit from locally embedded supply linkages? The emergence of new industrial economies, especially in East Asia, suggests otherwise. For possible explanations we have to return to the institutional and policy environment, i.e., to the macro-level. There is compelling evidence that some countries are much more effective in using foreign investment as a tool in national economic upgrading than others. In the late 1980s, the divergence between selected Asian and Latin American newly industrializing countries, for instance, was widely noted (e.g., Gereffi and Wyman, 1990; Stallings, 1995). While countries such as Mexico and Brazil had embarked upon industrialization programs well before East Asia (other than Japan), and for years had received similar inflows of FDI, their results paled in comparison with the 'Tigers' of the East. Even if the latter have lost some of their luster since the 1997 financial crisis, this has not invalidated the differences.

Explanations tend to focus on the role of the state in economic development. In brief, several but not all East Asian states are considered to benefit from relatively professional government bureaucracies, commanding sufficient political autonomy with respect to various interest groups to pursue a genuine development policy. Latin American states, in contrast, are supposedly less independent of vested interest groups, and this compromises the ability of their bureaucracies to withstand pressures for policies that do not serve the national development agenda. Although the precise mechanisms behind the political embeddedness of economic development are not necessarily well understood, a parallel may be proposed with the 'moderate embeddedness' thesis advanced by Boschma *et al.* (2001). Political disembedding – in this case, neo-classical laissez-faire policies – has in most cases produced disappointing results in terms of creating linkages as well as upgrading local economies. At the other extreme, collusion between holders of political power and economic interests leads to rent seeking and ineffective distortions in the policy environment. Somewhere in between the two, there is an area of moderate political embedding of the economy, where the state, in partnerships with the private sector and civil society organizations, can create a framework conducive to growth.

Two caveats, however, have to be mentioned. The first is that significant economic policies are the privilege of national governments. Local authorities can do a lot in the provision of infrastructure, training, and cooperative action in order to stimulate local social capital, but they cannot pursue the policies that Asian countries used to engineer localization and upgrading (e.g., regulations on local content and technology transfer). The second caveat relates to the regulation of the international economy. WTO rules since the Uruguay Round no longer allow host economies to impose such rules on local content, technology transfer, and export quota. The development trajectories used by countries such as Malaysia are no longer open to others. New ways will surely be found, but the type of policy-embedding used by the more successful developing countries in the last few decades is fading away.

References

Asheim, B.T. (1996), 'Industrial Districts as 'Learning Regions': a Condition for Prosperity', *European Planning Studies*, Vol. 4, pp. 379-400.

Baud, Isa (2000), *Collective Action, Enablement and Partnerships: Issues in Urban Development*, Inaugural address, Vrije Universiteit, Amsterdam.

Boschma, R., Lambooy, J. and Schutjens, V. (2001), 'Social Capital, (regional) Embeddedness and Innovation', in M. Taylor and S. Leonard (eds), *Social Capital and the Embedded Enterprise: International Perspectives*, Chapter 2, Ashgate, Aldershot.

Castells, Manuel (1996), *The Rise of the Network Society*, Part 1 of The Information Age: Economy, Society and Culture, Blackwell, Oxford.

Cerruti, Mario and Menno Vellinga (eds)(1989), *Burguesias e Industria en America Latina y Europa Meridional*, Alianza Editorial, Madrid.

Christerson, Brad and Constance Lever-Tracy (1997), *The Third China? Emerging Industrial Districts in Rural China*, Blackwell, Oxford.

Coleman, J.S. (1988), 'Social Capital in the Creation of Human Capital', *American Journal of Sociology*, Vol. 94 supplement pages s95-s120.

Diamond, Jared M. (1997), *Guns, Germs and Steel: the Fates of Human Societies*, Cape, London.

Dicken, Peter (1998), *Global Shift. Transforming the World Economy*, 3rd edition, Chapman, London.

Egeraat, Chris van (1995), *Nieuwe Industrie-vestigingen en Regionale Economie in Johor, Maleisie. Een Onderzoek naar Directe Productie Linkages*, Unpublished MA thesis, Utrecht.

Fröbel, F., Heinrichs, J. and Kreye, O. (1976), 'Tendency Towards a New International Division of Labor, Worldwide Utilization of Labor Force for World Oriented Manufacturing', *Economic and Political Weekly*, Vol. 11, pp. 159-70.

Fukuyama, Francis (1995), *Trust. The Social Virtues and the Creation of Prosperity*, Free Press, New York.

Gereffi, Gary and Wyman Donald (1990), *Manufacturing Miracles. Paths of Industrialization in Latin America and East Asia*, Harvard University Press, Princeton.

Giddens, A. (1990), *The Consequences of Modernity*, Polity, Cambridge.

Goewie, Jamy (2001), *Industriële Ondernemingen: Van de Regio of in de Regio? Studie naar de Economische en Sociale Inbedding van Industriële Ondernemingen in Surat Thani, Thailand*, Unpublished M.A. Thesis, Utrecht University, Utrecht.

Granovetter, Mark (1985), 'Economic Action and Social Structure: The Problem of Embeddedness', *American Journal of Sociology*, Vol. 91(3), pp. 481-510.

Grotjohann, J., Sterkenburg, T and Grunsven, L. van (1996), *Sourcing Strategies and Local Embeddedness of MNCs in the Asian Pacific Rim: the Case of Philips Electronics in Malaysia*, Geographical Studies of Development and Resource Use, Utrecht University, Utrecht.

Hamilton, Gary G. and Waters Tony (1995), 'Chinese Capitalism in Thailand: Embedded Networks and Industrial Structure', in Chen, Edward K.Y. and Peter Drysdale (eds) *Corporate Links and Foreign Direct Investment in Asia and the Pacific*, Harper, Pymble (NSW), pp. 87-111.

Harris, John (2000), 'The Second 'Great Transformation'? Capitalism at the End of the Twentieth Century', in Tim Allen and Thomas Alan (eds), *Poverty and Development into the 21st Century*, Open University/Oxford University Press, Oxford pp. 325-41.

Helmsing, Bert (2000), *Externalities, Learning and Governance. Perspectives on Local Economic Development*, Inaugural address, Institute of Social Studies, The Hague.

Hezel, Francis X. (1995), *Strangers in Their Own Land. A Century of Colonial Rule in the Caroline and Marshall Islands*, University of Hawaii Press, Honolulu.

Hofstede, Geert (1980), *Culture's Consequences: International Differences in Work-Related Values*, Sage, Beverly Hills.

Humphrey, John and Schmitz, Hubert (2000), *Governance and Upgrading: Linking Industrial Cluster and Global Value Chain Analysis*, IDS Working paper, No. 120, Institute of Development Studies, Brighton.

ILO (1981), *Employment Effects of Multinational Enterprises in Developing Countries*, ILO, Geneva.

Jessop, B. (1997), 'The Governance of Complexity and the Complexity of Governance: Preliminary Remarks on Some Problems and Limits of Economic Guidance', in A. Amin and J. Hausner (eds), *Beyond Market and Hierarchy*, Edward Elgar, Cheltenham, pp. 95-128.

Knippenberg, Hans (1995), 'Wereldwijde Integratie en de Kracht van Regionale Cultuurverschillen', in Ben de Pater, (ed.), *Eenwording en Verbrokkeling. Paradox van de Regionale Dynamiek*, Van Gorcum, Assen, pp. 19-56.

Landes, David S. (1998), *The Wealth and Poverty of Nations. Why Some Are So Rich and Some So Poor*, Norton, New York.

Leyshon, Andrew (1996), 'Dissolving Difference? Money, Disembedding and the Creation 'Global Financial Space'', in P.W. Daniels and W.F. Lever (eds), *The Global Economy in Transition*, Longman, pp. 62-80.

Lundvall, B.A. (1988), 'Innovation as an Interactive Process: From User-producer Interaction to the National System of Innovation', in G. Dosi et al. (eds), *Technical Change and Economic Theory*, Pinter, London, pp. 349-69.

Morgan, K. (1997), 'The Learning Region: Institutions, Innovation and Regional Renewal, *Regional Studies*, Vol. 5, pp. 491-503.

Pavlínek, P. and Smith, A. (1998), 'Internationalization and Embeddedness in East-Central European Transition: The Contrasting Geographies of Inward Investment in the Czech and Slovak Republics', *Regional Studies*, Vol. 7, pp. 619-38.

Polanyi, Karl (1944), *The Great Transformation*, Beacon Press, Boston.

Putnam, Robert D. (1993), 'The Prosperous Community,' *American Prospect*, pp. 35-42.

Schmitz, H. (1999), 'Global Competition and Local Cooperation: Success and Failure in the Sinos Valley, Brazil', *World Development*, Vol. 9, pp. 1627-50.

Stallings, Barbara (ed.) (1996), *Global Change, Regional Response. The New International Context of Development*, Cambridge University Press, Cambridge.

Storper, Michael (1997), *The Regional World. Territorial Development in a Global Economy*, Guilford Press, New York/London.

Tsai, Ming-Chang (2000), 'State Power, State Embeddedness, and National Development in Less-developed Countries: a Cross-national Analysis', *Studies in Comparative International Development*, Winter 1999/2000, pp. 66-88.

4 Urban Cluster Trajectories in Developing Countries: Beyond the Industrial District Model

PETER KNORRINGA

Introduction

At first sight, the recent European industrial district success stories from especially the Third Italy seem very relevant as an example for clusters in developing countries.[1] These European industrial districts by and large share the following characteristics (Schmitz and Musyck, 1994; Rabellotti 1995). First, they tend to specialize in labor-intensive artisanal sectors, such as footwear or garments, in which less developed countries are often thought to enjoy a comparative advantage. Secondly, the Italianate industrial districts are built on local firms, mainly of small and medium size. Most clusters in developing countries also consist overwhelmingly of small and very small firms. Moreover, local and regional policy makers in developing countries are desperately looking for ways to stimulate a more endogenous industrialization process. Thirdly, the Italian industrial districts are situated in regions that were rooted in small-scale agriculture and which industrialized relatively late. This means that these success stories were part of an industrial 'periphery'. Similarly, most clusters in developing countries are also located in the peripheral areas of their respective countries. In short, at first glance the Italianate industrial district experience appears to show that a successful industrialization process built on locally owned firms is possible after all, even in peripheral areas.

---

1. This chapter builds on a paper presented at a European Management and Organisation in Transition (EMOT) workshop, at the ISTUD, in Stresa, Italy, 11-14 September 1997 and an EADI workshop on the importance of innovation for small enterprises development in the Third World at the Institute of Social Studies (ISS), The Hague, 18-19 September 1998. I thank participants in these workshops for their constructive comments.

However, a fundamentally different institutional setting, with widespread poverty, a labor surplus and more extreme differences in bargaining power between cluster actors, may well lead to very different outcomes in developing countries. Besides, apart from being different from the Italian setting, the diversity of institutional settings within the developing world is also mind-boggling. Nevertheless, even though each cluster may have a unique story to tell and direct transferability of experiences may be absurd, it is important not to become mentally imprisoned by history (Schmitz and Musyck, 1994). Therefore, without glossing over the fundamental differences in institutional settings, I feel it is useful to take the industrial district literature as a frame of reference for an analysis of cluster trajectories in developing countries. Moreover, the extent of transferability of experiences appears to be much higher within a framework that focuses on trajectories rather than static models (Humphrey, 1995). While it is now commonplace in cluster studies from developing countries to refer to the Third Italy, only few studies have so far tried to incorporate the idea of trajectories. A notable early exception is Swaminathan and Jeyaranjan (1994) who have tried to analyze the Tiruppur knitwear cluster through a trajectory from artisan to dependent subcontractor to Mark I and to Mark II stages, as coined by Brusco (1990). This chapter identifies various possible trajectories that clusters in developing countries may follow, and discusses their relative potential for endogenous upgrading.

While clusters in developing countries as a rule do not initiate radical innovations, they appear to differ significantly in the extent to which they depend on outside actors for implementing incremental (process) innovations. In this chapter, the capability of constellations of local actors in specific clusters to implement and build on incremental innovations – leaving aside the origin of these innovations – denotes their potential for endogenous technological and organizational upgrading. For the more mature and export-oriented clusters operating in buyer-driven commodity chains, such endogenous upgrading capability is important because it makes them more attractive to the more demanding but also better paying global buyers in the more quality-driven market segments (Gereffi, 1999; Schmitz and Knorringa, 2000).

This chapter first looks briefly at the large group of survival clusters for which the industrial district model is not a suitable frame of reference. Section 3 positions a wide variety of case studies on three different stylized cluster trajectories, and discusses the extent to which examples of endogenous upgrading can be found. The next section aims to identify to what extent policy lessons from the Third Italy may be useful to local and regional policy makers in developing countries. The last section contains the conclusion.

The Case Against a Meaningful Comparison: Survival Clusters

Probably the most common type of manufacturing cluster to be found in developing countries is the survival cluster (see, for example, Pedersen, 1997). Such clusters are based on horizontal specialization and not (or at least not primarily) on inter-firm division of labor within the commodity chain. However, relatively lower transaction costs may be achieved because of lower search costs for potential customers (consumers as well as traders) and the presence of a local specialized labor pool. Because such transaction costs are often extremely high, especially in the least developed areas of the developing world, they often provide clustered enterprises with a crucial competitive edge over isolated firms. In comparison to other clusters, perhaps the main feature of survival clusters is that they face very unstable conditions and are usually not the only, and sometimes not even the main, activity of participating actors. Heinen and Weijland (1989) raised the question whether such clusters should be interpreted as a sign of poverty or progress. Micro-level studies reveal that rising incomes have in some cases led to the collapse of such clusters, while in other cases they have led to a consolidation of the participants' commitments towards cluster activities. However, without wanting to be deterministic, also consolidated survival clusters face daunting barriers to their development into more mature clusters with, for example, increasing inter-firm division of labor and the building up of upgrading capabilities. A parallel with the informal sector and small enterprise literature may be useful here. The common understanding in much of this literature appears to be that in enterprise development 'little acorns do not as a rule grow into mighty oaks' (Grosh and Somolekae, 1996), or in other words, 'graduation' from survival to micro- to small-scale is the exception rather than the rule (Farbmann and Lessik, 1989). A similar caution in assessing the opportunities of survival clusters to grow into more mature clusters seems justified.

Even though probably most of these survival clusters are found in rural areas, they also exist in metropolitan areas. The main difference is that most metropolitan clusters are built on survival-oriented self-employment, where actors have fewer local roots and operate more in modern sectors (Alam,

1994; Benjamin, 1991).[2] These sectoral specializations largely correspond with the well-known European clusters; fashion-sensitive and labor-intensive sectors with significant market niches which add surplus value to quality-competitive artisanal products, such as footwear, other leather products, clothing, wooden furniture, jewelry, glassware, some metal products, and types of toys and handicrafts. The more promising clusters in developing countries, especially in Asia and Latin America, are usually located in medium-sized towns.

In the literature, it appears as though Africa does not possess such promising clusters (for a recent overview of African case studies, see McCormick, 1999). However, this observation should not be taken at face value. First, researchers on clusters in Africa have tended to focus on the informal (*jua kali*) segment of a particular sub-sector. Second, and related to the first point, the operationalization of the cluster concept has been much stricter in terms of geography.[3] Most cluster studies deal with, for example, an area on the outskirts of a bigger town where all vehicle repair shops / garages have been concentrated (see, for example, Kinyanjui, 1997). To put it bluntly, as soon as one comes across a few printing workshops next to those garages, the cluster ends. In contrast, the Agra footwear cluster, notwithstanding concentrations in specific neighborhoods, is spread out over a city of almost two million inhabitants, and encompasses both large, modern factories and informal home-based units (Knorringa, 1996). In the African context, such variety within a sub-sector in one big city may well exist, but it would not be discussed as one cluster. For example, the garment sub-sector in Nairobi appears to encompass large, modern factories (often export-oriented and owned by white entrepreneurs), as well as a hidden medium-sized segment of workshops predominantly run by Asian entrepreneurs, and an informal survival segment run by indigenous black artisans (McCormick, 1999).

Notwithstanding such different approaches, it seems safe to say that most clusters in developing countries are survival clusters with limited potential for endogenous upgrading. The industrial-district model does not offer a particularly useful angle to approach the problematic of these survival clusters. What remains is that in terms of total employment and in terms of likely policy priorities for poverty alleviation, this large group of survival clusters may well be more important and more in need of support than the

---

2. In turn, rural clusters tend to be concentrated in traditional sectors, often with artisanal roots (Klapwijk 1997). For an in-depth longitudinal case study on the impact of technological change on cluster formation in rural Java, see Sandee 1995.
3. From a discussion with D. McCormick, W. Mitullah and M. Kinyanjui at the IDS, Sussex University, April 1997.

more mature clusters, which will be discussed in the remainder of this chapter.

The Case for Meaningful Stylized Trajectories

This section presents the three stylized trajectories that emerge from the literature, and aims to show their usefulness when systematizing experiences from more mature urban clusters in developing countries. Any typology inevitably simplifies and may give the wrong impression that clusters are homogeneous when they enter a particular trajectory. Clearly this is not the case. Clusters possess unique characteristics shaped by their respective social, cultural, political, and economic environments. Notwithstanding this path-dependent uniqueness of clusters, many of the more mature clusters appear to evolve along three distinguishable trajectories. These three trajectories are derived from Markusen (1996),[4] who came up with the labels as part of a typology of industrial districts and their description for industrial economies, and from Humphrey (1995, p. 159), who described possible cluster trajectories in developing countries without providing labels. Remarkably enough, the trajectories sketched by Humphrey can be seen as moving from a 'basic' agglomeration to one of the types of industrial districts that Markusen distinguishes. But, to start with, the first option is a stagnating cluster that does not evolve along any of the possible trajectories. Such clusters: " ...will continue to be agglomerations of firms enjoying the external economies of agglomeration but without the inter-firm linkages which are at the heart of the industrial district model." (Humphrey, 1995, p. 159). To be able to enter one of these relatively more successful trajectories requires a shift from 'static gains' to 'dynamic gains' (Rabellotti, 1995), or from competitive advantages derived 'just' from external economies to include processes of consciously pursued joint action by cluster participants (Schmitz, 1995).

In the first trajectory, a cluster evolves into the set of stylized facts that represent the Italianate industrial district. In Italy, it now appears as though at least some of its clusters are evolving into hub-and-spoke districts with a limited number of larger leading firms and many subcontractors. A second

---

4. The fourth type of industrial district identified by Markussen, the State Anchored District, is not dealt with in this paper. However, it could be a useful metaphor in a discussion on the role of the state in trying to create industrial districts from scratch. However, among researchers in the area of small enterprise development in developing countries, there is a consensus that this is impossible (Humphrey and Schmitz, 1996).

trajectory, more common in developing countries, concerns clusters that evolve from a 'basic' agglomeration into a hub-and-spoke district without an intermediate stage in which they have resembled the main features of the Italianate model. A third trajectory runs from a 'basic' agglomeration to a satellite district, in which most small and medium firms manufacture for leading firms located outside the cluster. There are indications that some satellite districts may subsequently evolve into hub-and-spoke districts. In the remainder of this section, I position a selection of case studies from developing and developed countries on one of these trajectories, and discuss their potential for endogenous upgrading. Given the scarcity of longitudinal case studies, this review necessarily relies mostly on comparing studies done in a single time period.

The First Trajectory: Towards an Italianate District

The first trajectory – towards an Italianate type of industrial district – is the most difficult to find in developing countries. In fact, only two such cases were found in the literature; the surgical instruments cluster in Sialkot (Pakistan), and the ceramic tile cluster in Criciúma (Brazil). Especially the former appears to have displayed a significant number of the Italianate features, at least in the beginning of the 1990s (Nadvi, 1996). As Humphrey wrote in his overview, the Sialkot cluster consisted of: '... large numbers of small firms engaged in extensive inter-firm exchanges of service, horizontally and vertically, active producer associations, supportive local and regional governments, and the cluster's powerful position in the world market for basic surgical instruments' (Humphrey, 1995, p. 159).

However, a few years later this cluster appears to be on a trajectory towards a hub-and-spoke district. Nadvi (1999) reports on the consequences of the crisis for Sialkot's manufacturers. In May 1994, the Food and Drug Administration of the United States, the most important export market for Sialkot, embargoed the import of Pakistani (i.e., Sialkot-made) surgical instruments for failing to meet international quality standards. By 1996, Sialkot appears to have come out of this crisis even stronger than it was before. Sales are above the 1993 level, and overall quality has improved. At the same time, while a substantial number of manufacturers are nowadays certified as conforming to international Good Manufacturing Practices (GMP) standards, only a few manufacturers are now ISO 9002 certified. In order to establish or maintain contacts abroad, such certification has become more and more a necessary but not a sufficient condition. Therefore, doing direct business with quality conscious importers becomes the exclusive domain of those larger entrepreneurs with the proper certifications. Moreover, within the associations and institutions of the Sialkot cluster, a relatively small group of entrepreneurs appears to have become more dominant.

In the case of the Criciúma cluster, local actors from firms and business associations deliberately try to build Italianate structures (Meyer-Stamer, 1997). The cluster consists of several medium- and two large-sized manufacturers of floor and wall tiles (all nationally owned) and a substantial number of suppliers (some nationally owned, some subsidiaries of leading firms from Italy and Spain). Unlike the case of Sassuolo, the worldwide leading tile cluster in Italy (Porter, 1990), there are no local equipment manufacturers in Criciúma. In the past there was fierce rivalry and little cooperation between firms. This changed after the industry entered into a deep crisis around 1990. Two presidents of local business associations succeeded in establishing cooperation; one of the important outcomes was the creation of a local technology center. Two further aspects are important to understand why cooperation started. First, there was the observation that firms in Italy and Spain were mostly located in industrial districts and did actually cooperate; this helped in overcoming business-cultural obstacles. Second, firms can cooperate in fields like technology because they do not establish a competitive advantage; heavy investment in new equipment and a strong effort to establish quality management concepts (like Kaizen and 5S) are no more than a precondition for survival in an increasingly sophisticated industry. Competitive advantages are established through innovative design, logistics, and marketing concepts, and firms are keen not to reveal their tricks in these fields.

In a way these examples already put forward what may well be two of the more general reasons why the Italianate trajectory is hardly to be found in developing countries. First, for small firms in developing countries it is even harder to be able to afford the investments in technology to keep up with rising quality standards. While Italianate industrial districts have been very successful in implementing incremental innovations, a big question is whether they can cope with more radical changes in technology requirements. Therefore, it seems fairly unrealistic to expect small firm clusters in developing countries to be able to conquer a part of the market niche now held by their more mechanized and computerized Italian counterparts who also possess much more experience with fashion-oriented high-road manufacturing. Nevertheless, the Italianate trajectory has the highest potential for creating endogenous upgrading capabilities, precisely because of its main strength in implementing incremental process (and product) innovations.

The second, more general, reason for the absence of an Italianate trajectory in developing countries has to do with social structure. To put it simply, I have not come across one developing-country case study that resembles the social boundary conditions for the Italianate trajectory. Clusters in developing countries are embedded in a fundamentally different setting from the Italian case studies. For example, social cohesion and the integrating role of local institutions – *the* pet themes in the industrial district literature – appear to be less prominent in clusters in developing countries. Instead, internal segmentation appears to reproduce and even strengthen inequalities. Because of extreme differences in bargaining power between actors in the cluster, possible benefits from collective efficiency are skewed in favor of leading actors and market agents (Smyth, 1992).

Perhaps there is one more reason not to be surprised to find so few clusters in developing countries on an Italianate trajectory. In the European and Italian debate, the Italianate features are increasingly seen as a phase in a broader restructuring process. Without suggesting that the Italianate model would be inherently unsustainable, it may well be less suitable to the present situation in the world market for many of the relevant sub-sectors. Even in Italy, it now appears as though at least some of its clusters are evolving into hub-and-spoke districts with a limited number of larger leading firms and many subcontractors.[5]

The Second Trajectory: Towards a Satellite District

A second trajectory runs towards a satellite district, in which most small and medium firms manufacture for leading firms located outside the cluster. In many of the relevant sub-sectors, the labor intensive manufacturing process has been transferred – in steps – to manufacturers in developing countries. In many cases, the leading firms of such commodity chains in European countries have transformed themselves into trading houses, keeping a firm grip on design and marketing.

Most observers consider the satellite trajectory to be least attractive, as it offers the least possibilities for building endogenous upgrading capabilities. Manufacturers who are attractive to leading international corporations for only one reason – cheap labor – are very vulnerable, as relative labor costs tend to keep changing between countries. Moreover, to be considered by global buyers for only a particular job is fatal, since jobs are constantly

---

5. On Italy see, e.g., Dei Ottati, 1996; Lazerson and Lorenzoni, 1999; Albino *et al.*, 1996; for an analogy with one of the oldest industrial districts, Rochdale (Manchester), see Penn, 1994.

changing. In contrast, in resilient and interdependent inter-firm relations, leading firms are more inclined to deal with a changing situation together with known partners. A leading firm must feel confident enough to rely on the specialized capabilities of its suppliers. Especially in fashion-sensitive industries, it is, nowadays, '... too costly and time-consuming to perfect the design of new products and translate those designs into simply executed steps. Those formerly charged with the execution of plans – technicians, blue collar workers, outside suppliers – must now elaborate indicative instructions, transforming the final design in the very act of executing it.' (Lazerson, 1993, p. 215). Evidently, this is a far cry from the 'export processing zones' type of assembly line work where predominantly young women without previous artisanal experience work long hours for low wages.

However, being incorporated into a commodity chain controlled by a buyer outside the cluster is not necessarily all bad. Especially in the short run, important benefits may accrue to local workers. To start with, the women workers usually involved may be able to learn industrial manufacturing skills, earn their own income, and as a result possibly strengthen their bargaining position at home. At a macro level, these increased income opportunities for women may well contribute to a more equal income distribution. Secondly, for a certain period, it can achieve a substantial production volume for both the domestic and export markets, and thus diversify the industrial structure. Moreover, although the conditions of this type of employment are not very promising, they are in many ways already an improvement on alternative job opportunities.

Entrepreneurs can also benefit from being part of such international commodity chains. Apart from earning large sums of money as intermediaries, they gain access to all sorts of relevant information on the international market in their specific sub-sector. In many cases local manufacturers may acquire endogenous upgrading capabilities within manufacturing. Moreover, in some cases entrepreneurs may even try to venture out on their own in a next phase by capturing the higher value-added stages in the commodity chain. This may start a process towards a hub-and-spoke trajectory, in which the leading actors in particular commodity chains are leading local entrepreneurs.

The footwear industry in and around Madras offers a successful example where a few local industrialists are slowly capturing higher-value added stages in the commodity chain (Rao 1993). Most of the currently renowned firms have entered the footwear industry from a leather-tanning background. These firms are long-standing suppliers of mainly European footwear firms. While the Indian firms previously supplied finished leathers

(1970s) and semi-finished leathers (1960s), now they also prepare uppers (1980s) and – increasingly – full shoes (1990s) for these leading actors. In turn, these foreign firms assist in setting up modern factories where badly paid and non-unionized women work with modern imported machines. One of these local hub-firms was the only company from India that had its own stall in one of the upper-market exhibition halls at the main European shoe fair in Dusseldorf (March 1997).

However, such examples are rare. On the whole, it seems that while most groups of exporters can be positioned on a satellite trajectory, this trajectory also provides the least likely environment for significant endogenous upgrading.

The Third Trajectory: Towards a Hub-and-Spoke District

The last trajectory to be discussed is a hub-and-spoke trajectory, which appears to be the most common trajectory for clusters in developing countries. According to Nadvi and Schmitz (1994, p. 12): '... most LDC clusters tend to be distinguished by internal hierarchies.' The most typical example is the case of the Korean *Chaebol*, where small firms orbit around large industrial complexes (Cho 1994). In the Brazilian Sinos valley (a shoe cluster), small firms tend to operate rather separately from a few Fordist giants (Schmitz, 1995). In many of the south Asian clusters, one tends to find a combination of the above two trends. A few leading families, who own the largest, more modern factories in the cluster (which are by international standards usually semi-mechanized medium-scale units), dominate local industry through the local business associations and mould the cluster image as it is perceived by outsiders. Other smaller units either supply them as subcontractors or supply to other, usually less attractive, market channels. Examples include garments in Tirrupur (Cawthorne 1995 and Swaminathan and Jeyaranjan 1994) and Ahmedabad (Das, 1996a); flooring tiles in Gujarat (Das, 1996b); textile printing in Jetpur (Dupont, 1994); bicycles in Ludhiana (Kattuman, 1994); and footwear in Agra (Knorringa, 1996; 1999). Moreover, this characterization also applies to examples such as the Tegalwangi rattan furniture cluster in Indonesia (Smyth, 1992), and the footwear clusters in Mexico's Leon and Guadelajara (Rabellotti, 1997).

In most of these clusters, one finds at least three tiers of firms: 'At the lowest tier of the hierarchy are households and small workshops which have limited resources, produce for local consumption and seek to survive. The medium tier is occupied by firms who are better endowed (in capital and skills), are able to generate an investable surplus and produce, either directly or on (sub)contract, for the domestic and often export markets. The third tier includes firms which maintain high levels of quality, are technically innovative, capable of entering export markets, and have growth aspirations.' (Nadvi and Schmitz, 1994, p. 12)

Perhaps the main risk in a hub-and-spoke trajectory, in terms of acquiring capabilities for endogenous upgrading, is that often a few leading families try to monopolize benefits and become a source of conservatism instead of innovation, even though they have the financial capacity to invest in upgrading. Many of the south Asian case studies tend to indicate how such 'fat cats' are often a drag on innovative behavior or at least prevent cluster-wide diffusion of the acquisition of upgrading capabilities (Cawthorne, 1995; Das 1996b; Knorringa, 1996).

Clusters not only need to acquire capabilities to implement incremental innovations. Particularly clusters in developing countries also need to be able to deal with radical changes in their environment. A main threat-cum-challenge for the manufacturing of tradables in many developing countries is the onslaught of the New Competition (Best, 1990) in export markets, combined with a general trend of economic liberalization in developing countries. The few case studies available on the impact of the New Competition and economic liberalization on the performance of clusters, tend to show that they are resilient and that they do upgrade but that, in response, the internal structure of clusters also changes.[6] Some actors lose out, power becomes more concentrated, and the hub-and-spoke trajectory appears to become more pronounced.

To summarize, the potential for endogenous upgrading is highest in the least-found Italianate trajectory, while it is lowest in the most frequently found satellite trajectory. The hub-and-spoke trajectory forms the intermediate case; it is increasingly found and does possess a potential for endogenous upgrading.

Concluding Remarks

The clearest and hardest message emerging from the European industrial district literature is that: '... none of the industrial districts are the result of planned action, of a local or regional industrial strategy. They all developed spontaneously.' (Schmitz and Musyck, 1994, p. 902) This chapter has attempted

---

6. Most of these case studies are brought together in a special issue of *World Development*, September 1999.

to show the usefulness of systematizing the wide-ranging experiences among more mature urban clusters in developing countries along three trajectories. This attempt to systematize does not include the largest category of clusters in developing countries, i.e., survival clusters.

The trajectory towards an Italianate district, which offers the greatest potential for endogenous upgrading, is very rare in developing countries. The reasons for this include the lack of technological innovative capabilities and resources in most clusters in developing countries, and the fundamentally different institutional setting in which social inequalities are often strengthened because of extreme differences in bargaining power between actors in the cluster. In contrast, the trajectory towards a satellite district, which appears to offer the least potential for endogenous upgrading, is the most commonly found among clusters in developing countries.

Alternatively, a trajectory towards a hub-and-spoke district offers an intermediate situation; it provides more potential for endogenous upgrading then the satellite trajectory, and an increasing number of clusters in developing countries seem to portray hub-and-spoke features. In terms of policy options, one might argue that a trajectory towards a hub-and-spoke district is the most feasible and potentially most useful metaphor to keep in mind, with the following qualifications. Policy makers should aim at facilitating the capture of higher-value added stages in the commodity chain, support attempts to acquire innovative technological capabilities, and especially facilitate platforms to enable internal conflicts to be solved. It should be a primary task of policy implementers to contribute to internal conflict resolving by not siding automatically with the leading entrepreneurs, but by trying to operate as a mediator in local power struggles by supporting the build-up of countervailing power. It is of crucial importance that local conflicts be addressed, and not neglected or hidden, because the Italian experience appears to indicate that periods of innovative growth tend to be preceded by such struggles.

References

Alam, G. (1994), 'Industrial Districts and Technological Change: A Study of the Garment Industry in Delhi', UNCTAD – *Technological Dynamism in Industrial Districts: An Alternative Approach to Industrialization in Developing Countries?*, pp. 257-66, UNCTAD, New York and Geneva.

Albino, V., Garavelli, A.C. and Pontrandolfo, P. (1996), *Local Factors and Global Strategies of The Leader Firm Of An Industrial District*, Paper presented at EuroMA Conference on Manufacturing Strategy, London, June.

Asheim, B.T. (1992), 'Flexible Specialization, Industrial Districts and Small Firms: A Critical Appraisal', in H. Ernste and V. Meier (eds), *Regional Development and Contemporary Industrial Response. Extending Flexible Specialization*, pp. 45-63, Belhaven Press, London.

Benjamin, S.J. (1991), *Jobs, Land and Urban Development. The Economic Success of Small Manufacturers in East Delhi, India*, Lincoln Institute of Land Policy, Cambridge, Massachusetts.

Best, M. H. (1990), *The New Competition. Institutions of Industrial Restructuring*, Polity Press, Cambridge.

Brusco, S. (1990), 'The Idea of the Industrial District: Its Genesis', in F. Pyke, G. Becattini and W. Sengenberger (eds), *Industrial Districts and Inter-Firm Co-operation in Italy*, pp. 10-9, International Institute for Labor Studies, Geneva.

Cawthorne, P.M. (1995), 'Of Networks and Markets: The Rise and Rise of a South Indian Town, the Example of Tiruppur's Cotton Knitwear Industry', *World Development*, Vol. 23(1), pp. 43-56.

Cho, M.-R. (1994), 'Weaving Flexibility: Large-Small Firm Relations, Flexibility and Regional Clusters in South Korea, in Pedersen (et al. 1994), Flexible Specialisation: The Dynamics of Small-scale Industries in the South, London: Intermediate Technology Publications, pp. 106-124.

Das, K. (1996a), 'Flexibly Together: Surviving and Growing in a Garment Cluster, Ahmedabad, India', *Journal of Entrepreneurship*, Vol. 2, pp. 26-42.

Das, K. (1996b), *Collective Dynamism and Firm Strategy: The Flooring Tile Cluster in Gujarat, India*, Gujarat Institute of Development Research, Working Paper, No. 76.

Dei Ottati, G. (1996), 'Trust, Interlinking Transactions and Credit in the Industrial District', *Cambridge Journal of Economics*, Vol. 18(6), pp. 529-46.

Dupont, V. (1994), *Facets of Industrial Clustering and Flexibility in the Textile-Printing Industry of Jetpur (West India)*, Paper presented to a workshop on Flexible Specialization in Pondicherry, India, March 25-26.

Farbman, M. and A. Lessik (1989), 'The Impact of Classification on Policy', in A. Gosses, et al. (eds), *Small Enterprises, New Approaches, Proceedings of the Workshop Small Scale Enterprise Development, In Search of New Dutch Approaches, March 6 and 7*, pp. 105-22, Ministry of Foreign Affairs, Directorate General International Cooperation, The Hague.

Gereffi, G. (1999), 'International Trade and Industrial Upgrading in the Apparel Commodity Chain', *Journal of International Economics*, Vol. 48(1), pp. 37-70.

Grosh, B. and Somolekae, G. (1996), 'Mighty Oaks from Little Acorns: Can Microenterprise Serve as the Seedbed of Industrialization?', *World Development*, Vol. 24(12), pp. 1879-90.

Heinen, E. and H. Weijland (1989) 'Rural Industry in Progress and Decline', in P. van Gelder and J. Bijlmer (eds.) About Fringes, Margins and Lucky Dips. The Informal Sector in Third World Countries. Free University Press, Amsterdam, pp. 13-34.

Humphrey, J. (1995), 'Industrial Reorganization in Developing Countries: From Models to Trajectories', *World Development*, Vol. 23(1), pp. 149-62.

Humphrey J. and Schmitz, H. (1996), 'The Triple C Approach to Local Industrial Policy', *World Development*, Vol. 24(12), pp. 1859-77.

Kattuman, P.A. (1994), *The Role of History in the Transition to an Industrial District: The Case of the Indian Bicycle Industry*, Paper prepared for a workshop on Flexible Specialization in Pondicherry, India, March 25-26.

Kinyanjui, M.N. (1997), *Tapping Opportunities in Enterprise Clusters in Kenya: The Case of Enterprises in Ziwani and Kigandaini,* Paper presented at a workshop on Collective Efficiency at the Institute of Development Studies, Sussex, UK, April 1997.

Klapwijk, M. (1997), Rural Industry Clusters in Central Java, Indonesia. An Empirical Assessment of their Role in Rural Industrialization, Thesis Publishers, Amsterdam.

Knorringa, P. (1996), *Economics of Collaboration; Indian Shoemakers Between Market and Hierarchy,* Sage Publications, New Delhi and London.

Knorringa, P. (1999), 'Agra: An Old Cluster Facing the New Competition', *World Development,* Vol. 27(9), pp. 1587-604.

Lazerson, M. (1993), 'Factory or Putting-out? Knitting Networks in Modena', in G. Grabher (ed.), *The Embedded Firm. On the Socioeconomics of Industrial Networks,* pp. 203-26, Routledge, London.

Lazerson, M. and G. Lorenzoni (1999), *The Firms that Feed Industrial Districts: A Return to the Italian Source,* Industrial and Corporate Change, vol. 8/2, pp. 235-265.

Markusen, A. (1996), 'Sticky Places in Slippery Space: A Typology of Industrial Districts', *Economic Geography,* pp. 293-313.

McCormick, D. (1994), *Industrial District or Garment Ghetto? The Case of Nairobi's Mini-Manufacturers,* Paper presented at an EADI workshop in Vienna, November 1994.

McCormick, D. (1999), 'African Enterprise Clusters and Industrialization: Theory and Reality', *World Development,* Vol. 27(9), pp. 1531-52.

Meyer-Stamer, J. (1997), *Path Dependence in Regional Development: Persistence and Change in three Industrial Clusters in Santa Catarina, Brazil,* Paper presented at a workshop on Collective Efficiency at the Institute of Development Studies, Sussex, UK, April 1997.

Nadvi, K. (1996), *Small Firm Industrial Districts in Pakistan,* Doctoral Thesis Institute of Development Studies, Sussex University.

Nadvi, K. (1999), 'Collective Efficiency and Collective Failure', *World Development,* Vol. 27(9), pp. 1605-26.

Nadvi, K. and Schmitz, H. (1994), *Industrial Clusters in Less Developed Countries: Review of Experiences and Research Agenda,* Institute of Development Studies, Discussion Paper, No. 339, Institute of Development Studies, Sussex.

Pedersen, P.O. (1997), 'Clusters of Enterprises Within Systems of Production and Distribution: Collective Efficiency and Transaction Costs', in M.P. van Dijk and R. Rabellotti (eds), *Enterprise Clusters and Networks in Developing Countries,* Frank Cass, London, pp. 11-29.

Penn, R. (1994), 'Contemporary Relationships between Firms in a Classic Industrial Locality', in J. Rubey and F. Wilkinson (eds), *Employment Strategy and the Labor Market,* Oxford University Press, Oxford.

Porter, M. E. (1990), *The Competitive Advantage of Nations,* New York, The Free Press.

Rabellotti, R. (1995), 'Is There an "Industrial District" Model? Footwear Districts in Italy and Mexico Compared', *World Development,* Vol. 23(1), pp. 29-41.

Rabellotti, R. (1997), *Devaluation Bonanza or Something More? Increasing Collective Efficiency Behind the Recovery of the Mexican Footwear Clusters,* Paper presented at a workshop on Collective Efficiency at the Institute of Development Studies, Sussex, UK, April 1997.

Rao, K.S. (1993), 'Development in the Indian Leather and Leather-Products Industry, in ISA Baud and G.A. de Bruijne (eds.), *Gender, Small-Scale Industry and Development Policy,* IT Publications, London, pp. 151-69.

Sandee, H. (1995), *Innovation Adoption in Rural Industry. Technological Change in Roof Tile Clusters in Central Java, Indonesia.* PhD Thesis, Free University, Amsterdam.

Schmitz, H. (1995), 'Collective Efficiency: Growth Path for Small-Scale Industry', *Journal of Development Studies*, Vol. 31(4), pp. 529-66.

Schmitz, H. and Musyck, B. (1994), 'Industrial Districts in Europe: Policy Lessons for Developing Countries?', *World Development*, Vol. 22(6), pp. 889-910.

Schmitz, H. and Knorringa, P. (2000), 'Learning from Global Buyers', *Journal of Development Studies*, Vol. 37(2), pp. 177-205.

Smyth, I. (1992), 'Collective Efficiency and Selective Benefits: The Growth of the Rattan Industry of Tegalwangi (Indonesia)', in J. Rasmussen, H. Schmitz and M.P. van Dijk (eds), *Flexible Specialization: A New View on Small Industry?, IDS Bulletin*, Vol. 23(3), pp. 51-6.

Swaminathan, P. and Jeyaranjan, J. (1994), 'The Knitwear Cluster in Tiruppur: An Indian Industrial District in the Making?', *Madras Institute of Development Studies*, Working Paper, No. 126.

5 Partnerships, Meso-Institutions and Learning: New Local and Regional Economic Development Initiatives in Latin America

BERT HELMSING

Introduction

Regional development policy perspectives have changed considerably in the past 25 years. One can distinguish three generations of theories informing policy practices. The first generation of regional policy emerged in the 1950s and 1960s. A fundamental point of departure was the fact that economic growth did not occur simultaneously throughout a territory, but was selective and uneven. The cumulative character of regional growth was generally accepted, but debate centered on questions concerning its internal or external origin, its structural permanence, and the processes of its reproduction. There were considerable differences in interpretation as to whether this unevenness would increase or decrease over time. Center-periphery theories argued that structural factors would reproduce and intensify inequalities. Others were more optimistic and predicted that regional inequalities would decline over time. Regional policies were mostly framed in the optimistic variant and were derived from neo-classical theories of optimal resource allocation. Policies aimed at reducing impediments to mobility and removing monopolistic elements that would keep prices from competitive level (Maillat, 1998). The national government was the central actor in first-generation policies. Through its regulatory powers and through financial incentives it could influence the location of firms. The provision of infrastructure was considered an important instrument to stimulate local demand and at the same time overcome regional disadvantage. Regional inequalities were a central issue in theories and policies of regional development. Can regional policies alter such structural patterns and reduce regional inequalities?

In the late 1970s and early 1980s, considerable skepticism emerged about the effectiveness of conventional regional policy instruments, and a debate raged about whether policies were ineffective or had never actually been put to a real test in Latin America (Boisier et al., 1982). A number of authors rejected the predominant paradigm and searched for regional development alternatives. Already in the late 1970s, several regional development analysts were looking for alternatives to the then dominant regional development paradigm. Walter Stohr advocated selective spatial closure (Stohr and Fraser Taylor, 1981) and John Friedmann the agropolitan approach (Friedmann and Douglass, 1978). Although there are considerable differences between the two, they have in common the search for endogenous development alternatives based on local actors, resources, and capacities.

Since then, the national and international context of regional policy has drastically changed. Shifts in national economic policies, the opening up of national economies, and processes of economic restructuring and internationalization of production during the 1980s, have reshaped regional economic landscapes. Existing core regions have been seriously affected by restructuring. At the same time, new growth regions emerged outside the established core areas, which became known as industrial districts, and were successfully competing internationally. These experiences gave rise to a new local and regional development alternative and demonstrated the potential strength of endogenous regional industrial development. Flexible specialization and industrial districts redefined the frame of reference for regional policies and gave rise to a *second generation* of local regional industrial policies. Research on industrial districts in Latin America – notably districts in Brazil and Mexico – has contributed to this generation of policies (cf. Schmitz, 1995). Central to these endogenous regional development policies is the notion 'to increase the developmental capacities of a region – to challenge international competition and technologies by mobilizing or developing its specific resources and its own innovative abilities' (Maillat, 1998, p. 7). An important difference from the first-generation policies is that government is no longer at the center stage of policy. Instead, endogenous development emphasizes the roles of inter-firm cooperation, business associations, unions, and government in developing, in interaction with each other, specific skills, resources, and 'rules of the game'. Public policy remains important but in a different capacity.

The 1990s brought about a substantial realignment of the relationships between state and society, which manifested itself in a wave of democratization and decentralization reforms, notably in Chile, Bolivia, Uruguay, Brazil, Colombia, Mexico and – to a lesser extent – Central America. Decentralization within the public sector gave local and regional governments more room for maneuver, and at the same time local governments, in view of their own financial and other limitations, began to involve other actors (private sector and NGOs). This contributed to the creation of favorable conditions for local and regional development initiatives.

Currently, a third generation of regional policies is emerging from practice. These policies are, on the one hand, a response to the further study and evaluation of endogenous regional development and policies; on the other hand, they result from the recognition that globalization, which increased in the 1990s, makes territorial production systems and not just firms compete with each other. This means that new policies cannot be exclusively local, but must take into account the position and the positioning of territorial production systems within a global context. Furthermore, recent experiences tell us that policies cannot be exclusively local or regional, to the point of excluding sectoral and national/international policies and contexts. Horizontal coordination of a range of actors needs to be complemented by vertical coordination between levels. The third-generation policies are premised on the recognition that new policies need not necessarily require more resources, but seek to enhance 'systemic rationality' in the use of existing local and extra-local resources and programs. Third-generation policies supersede the opposition between exogenous and endogenous development policies.

Local economic development (LED) may be defined, in this context, as a process in which partnerships between local governments, community-based groups, and the private sector are established in order to manage existing resources, create jobs, and stimulate the economy of a well-defined territory. It emphasizes local control, using the potentials of local human, institutional, and physical capabilities. Local economic development initiatives mobilize actors, organizations, and resources, and develop new institutions and local systems through dialogue and strategic actions.

Some 20 years ago, Sergio Boisier questioned the then prevailing regional development paradigm framed by polarized regional growth as a 'theory in search of a practice' in Latin America (Boisier *et al.*, 1982). When considering the current situation, I would suggest turning this question around. What theory is evolving out of the new practices of local and regional development promotion found in Latin America? A recently published series of studies allow us to begin to answer this question. In the mid-1990s, the UN Commission for Latin America and the Caribbean, in association with the German Technical Cooperation Agency (GTZ), commissioned a series of case studies on decentralization and local economic development. The late Gabriel

Aghón directed this project. In total more than 22 reports were published, most of which were case study reports. The studies are all available on the CEPAL website. From these I have selected 12 for a meta-analysis of the changing practices of local and regional development in Latin America. The case studies span the entire Spanish speaking part of the continent, as they cover regions from the south of Chile to a Mexican state bordering the USA. In view of the limited space available, I will not elaborate in detail on all 12 case studies (the reader is referred to the CEPAL website). Instead, I will examine overall trends emerging from them, and note commonalities and differences. In this analysis, I will focus on the central messages of new LED theory, namely the importance of interaction between public and private actors, the creation of new institutions for LED, and different processes of learning (Helmsing, 1999, 2000, 2001a).

New Local and Regional Development Practices in Latin America: Evidence from Case Studies

Introducing the Case Studies

The 12 case studies range from small peripheral communities in a mineral mining region/enclave in Chile, rural peripheral regions in Colombia, Chile, and Peru, and intermediate regional towns in Chile and Argentina, to large metropolitan cities/regions such as Cordoba, Argentina, Medellin, and Bucaramanga in Colombia and Guadalajara (Jalisco State) and Chihuahua (Chihuahua State) in Mexico.[1]

Guillermo Marianacci (2000) reported on local initiatives undertaken in Cordoba. The new local administration began to develop the local space for *concertación* on the direction of economic development. The changing national and international economic conditions called for a restructuring of the city's economy. At the same time, the MercoSur created new opportunities in terms of a development corridor in which Cordoba could acquire a strategic position. Pablo Costamagna (2000) studied the city of Rafaela, which has been on an historical trajectory of a regional agro- and manufacturing industry center. *Apertura* and internationalization posed new demands on the competitiveness of the regional economy. The author detailed the growth in 'institutional thickness' (Amin and Thrift, 1994) in

---

1. Unless otherwise specified, all data interpretations presented in Tables 1 through 5 are based on the 12 CEPAL case studies.

Table 5.1   Overview of case studies

Country	Location of case study	Type of region
Argentina	City of Cordoba, northern Argentina	Metropolitan regional economy
Argentina	City of Rafaela, northern Argentina	Intermediate region with industry and agriculture
Chile	Four municipalities in Araucania, southern Chile	Predominantly rural agricultural
Chile	Rural local communities in Provincia de Loa, Autofagasta, northern Chile	Copper mining region
Chile	Intermediate city south of Santiago	Intermediate urban economy
Chile	Rural communities in Ranquil, south-central region of Chile	Rural agricultural restructuring
Colombia	City of Medellin, north-western part of Colombia	Second largest metropolitan regional economy
Colombia	City of Bucaramanga, north-eastern part of Colombia	Intermediate city in a mining region
Colombia	Rural municipality Pensilvania, northern part of Caldas Department	Small town in a diversified agricultural and forestry area
Mexico	Jalisco State, west-central part of Mexico	Guadalajara metro economy in an underdeveloped regional state
Mexico	Chihuahua State, bordering the USA	Border region with a dualistic 'Maquiladora economy'
Peru	Municipality of Ilo south-western part of Peru	Peripheral border area

order to strengthen the local capabilities for key economic activities and LED policy. Osvaldo Bernales (2000) looked at the creation of a network of municipal strategic management teams as a means to increase the local capacity through cooperation and to promote local economic development in Araucania in the south of Chile. The province of de Loa in Antofagasta in the north of Chile is a quite different case of a region already firmly established in the international economy as a mineral mining enclave. The mineral exploitation was causing environmental damage and drawing on a scarce resource, water; both threatened to further undermine the livelihood of local rural people. Jorge Salinas (2000) examined this case, focussing on how the local resource conflict is handled, and outlined the initiatives to improve the livelihood of local people. Carlos Muñoz (2000) looked at the case of Rancagua, an intermediate city south of Santiago where successive mayors have stimulated local government to become more entrepreneurial. A city marketing campaign, initially designed with the limited objective of attracting private investment, induced the government to deepen the process of change. Private-sector concessions were introduced to finance urban renewal. Luis Cáceres and Noelia Figueroa (2000) elaborated a case of rural small-scale farming restructuring in Ranquil in the 8th region of Bio-Bio in

Chile. A local development fund, set up with the assistance of a national agency, became a stimulus for convergence on public and private investment priorities and initiatives.

Carlos Londoño (2000) took a new look at the region of Antioquia and the city of Medellin, Colombia. Public-private cooperation in this well-known case of regional industrialization has a much longer tradition than elsewhere. The author documented the initiatives undertaken since the mid-1990s. Cesar Vargas and Roberto Prieto (2000) examined the case of the intermediate city of Bucaramanga. The authors reported how the Industrial University of Santander and other universities and research institutes became more involved in the local economy. This increasing role of academic institutions in local development together with increasing public-private dialogue on local competitive advantage led to the emergence of an 'innovative milieu'. Alberto Maldonado (2000) examined the emergence of a new industry of small-scale manufacture of design furniture in the rural municipality of Pensilvania (Caldas, Colombia). A local NGO, which had developed into a local economic development agency, played a pivotal role in this rural diversification initiative.

Guadelajara is the center of Jalisco State in Mexico. It is an important industrial center and has attracted a considerable volume of *maquila* investment. Clemente Ruiz (2000a) elaborated the efforts of the new state government to increase the local spin-off from these external investments, and at the same time to spread new investment geographically to selected municipalities in the state. The second Mexican case, elaborated by the same author, also documented efforts by the new state government of Chihuahua to adopt a strategic approach to economic development, putting greater emphasis on strengthening local industries and geographically deconcentrating its expansion (Ruiz, 2000a). Finally, Maricela Benavides (2000) looked at how an initially narrowly defined and supply-driven project on better informal sector regulation, broadened into a broad-based local economic development initiative in the municipality of Ilo, Peru.

Conditions and Triggering Mechanisms

The overall political and macro economic conditions of the countries concerned also varied quite considerably. In terms of the political conditions, it is important to mention that Chile and Colombia had carried out important decentralization reforms in the early 1990s. The processes in these two countries were quite different, but in both cases they contributed to creating new spaces for local regional initiatives. In Mexico the coming into power of opposition parties, which followed the demise of the PRI in national elections, also gave new impulses to regional development. In contrast, Peru in the same period suffered from serious political instability. Argentina, on the other hand, found itself in an intermediate position. There was in this period relative political stability and no major decentralization reforms.

Globalization and economic restructuring were important factors triggering new initiatives, but this cannot be said for all cases. Clearly, MercoSur and NAFTA played a role in the cases of Cordoba, Chihuahua, and Jalisco. Also in Colombia, policies of *apertura* induced local actors to examine the consequences and opportunities for their local regional economies (Medellin and Bucaramanga). In other instances, however, the influence of economic restructuring and globalization is less immediate and evident (Rafaela, Auracania, and Ilo). Other particular factors, both positive and negative, can be pinpointed without these being an exclusive cause, such as disease and pests in agriculture (indigenous wines – Ranquil), local unexploited resource opportunities (Pensilvania), or the negative environmental consequences of mining (Antofagasta).

It is also important to mention that in several instances, the local regional development initiatives are characterized by far greater 'continuity with change' than is often recognized. The Medellin and Bucaramanga experiences have evolved into homegrown endogenous processes spanning more than a decade.

Creation of Meso-Institutions

One of the key features of 'third-generation' regional development policy is the central role of meso-institutions i.e., institutions at the level of sector and region (Helmsing, 1999). This comes, partly, in the wake of strategic conceptions of competitiveness (Porter, 1985, 1990 and 1998, and Best, 1990). That is to say, the competitiveness of a firm depends not only on its own efforts to continuously improve methods, processes, and products, but also on its suppliers and the local business environment in which it operates. Suppliers can be a source of innovation, and the local business environment can help or hinder firms in their efforts. With regard to the latter, one may distinguish between help or hindrances in the form of physical infrastructures or the lack of such (industrial land, ports and transport and logistic terminals, electricity, etc.), in human resource development and training, and in enterprise support systems. Firms located in places well-endowed with specialized infrastructures and institutions to assist them in their restructuring, may

Table 5.2   Meso-institutions in LED

Case	Institutions for policy and planning	Economic institutions
Cordoba	Mixed LED agency (ADEC)	LED agency (ADEC); Incubator
Rafaela	Municipal LED training and research institute (ICEDEL)	Small Enterprise Business Association (CAPIR); Technology and Innovation Center; Enterprise Development Center
Araucania	Informal inter-municipal cooperation	
Medellin, Antioquia	Strategic planning Council (ACTUAR), Competitiveness Council	Employment observatory, Technology Development Centers (4), Regional Guarantee Fund; Social Trade Promoting Agency
Bucaramanga, Santander	Mixed Metropolitan Planning and Economic Development Agency	Enterprise promotion agency (Bucaramanga Emprendedora); Productivity Centers (4); Incubator; Science and Technology Center (Technopolis of the Andes)
Prov de Loa, Autofagasta		
Rancagua	LED campaign agency (Rancagua Emprende)	Small Enterprise Municipal House; Incubator; Micro-Enterprise Support Centers
Ranquil	Mixed LED agency (Comite de Fomento Productivo Comunal)	Peasant committees for joint actions; Local Investment Promotion Fund
Pensilvania	None	Productivity Center
Chihuahua	Private LED agency (Desarrollo Economico de Chihuahua C.A.)	Supply Development Council of Ciudad Juarez; Supply Development Center of Chihuahua; R&T Transfer Centers
Jalisco		Enterprise Clusters (AGREMS); Design Institute, Quality Standards Institute
Ilo	Economic round table (informal)	Creation of a chamber of commerce and a local SME association

have a decisive edge over firms located in adverse local business environments.

The institutional and infrastructural endowments of the local business environment are created over time through inter-firm cooperation (e.g., with the help of business associations) and through public policy. In order to plan for these, public-private interaction is essential. This has given rise to the creation of a second type of meso-institutions, which facilitate such public-private interaction: Institutions for policy and planning (Helmsing, 2001b).

What institutions have been created in our case studies on new Latin American LED policy practices? Table 5.2 gives an overview.

From the above it may be concluded that in nine of the 12 cases the development of new meso-institutions has played a central role. In most cases the creation of policy and planning institutions *preceded* the development of specialized institutions for the local regional economy. The new policy and planning institutions served in most instances to facilitate public-private interaction. There was a noticeable trend towards establishing such bodies *outside* public law (as a mixed non-profit body). The latter is an important feature, as it places these institutions outside the realm of politics and parties.

The economic meso-institutions centered on supporting enterprise development through incubators, business development services (notably technological innovation), and cluster- and group-based programs, and on institutions serving the labor market. While micro enterprises received support in a number of cases, there is a general awareness that the strengthening of the local regional economy depends on small, medium, *and* large companies.

Noteworthy is also that organizational development within the respective local, regional, and state government was a crucial ingredient in the process. That is to say, new local economic development units (e.g., in Rancagua, Rafaela, and Bucaramanga), departments, or ministries (e.g., 'Gobernación' of Antioquia and of Santander, and the 'Secretaria' of economic development in the state government of Chihuahua) were created *inside* the government units. These units played a central role in initiating public-private dialogue, which in turn led to an institutionalization of public private interaction through the creation of new institutions of policy and planning. These bodies helped to identify the need for new meso-economic institutions.

Nature, Scale, and Type of LED Initiatives

In order to classify the LED initiatives I use a broad-based classification drawn from Blakely (1989) and from earlier work (cf. Helmsing, 1999, 2001b). A distinction is made between three main categories of local economic development initiatives. The first set refers to actions that may be broadly described as community-based economic development. Such development may be applied to both rural and urban settings, though a number of characteristics would necessarily be different. The essence of community economic development is to facilitate household diversification of economic activity as the principal way to improve livelihoods and reduce poverty and vulnerability. The second category refers to business or enterprise development. This broad category consists of initiatives that directly target and involve enterprises or a cluster/clusters of enterprises. In contrast to community economic development, this category is premised on specialization and overcoming obstacles to specialization in a market context. Enterprise or business development is normally closely associated with the existing economic base of the locality or region, or with developing a new industry in order to diversify the existing economic base. A number of the principles of enterprise development policies apply differentially to small, medium, and larger enterprises. Survival-based micro-enterprise activity is examined under the first mentioned category. The creation of industry-specific meso-economic and enterprise support institutions plays a central role. The third category refers to locality development. This is complementary to the previous two and refers to overall planning and management of economic and physical development of the area concerned. It includes, but is broader than, policy and planning of the local business environment.

Table 5.3 gives an overview of the types of LED initiatives in the 12 case studies.

In terms of concrete initiatives launched, there is a general tendency for enterprise/small enterprise development programs to predominate. In most instances, these programs concern business development services, especially technology and innovation. Enterprise finance is (surprisingly) much less prevalent than expected, and where it did occur it was in the form of venture capital for new technology firms (Bucaramanga and Chihuahua).

In larger economic units, cluster development programs constitute an important program component, notably in Mexico and Colombia. As one moves from large economic units (state regions and metropolitan cities) to rural and municipal initiatives, small and micro-enterprise development programs become more important.

In several instances, notably in Mexican and Colombian cases, there have been concerted efforts to create a local innovative milieu (Maillat, 1995, 1998). Capello (1999) considers an innovative milieu to be the highest form of collective learning, in which universities, public agencies, and firms undertake concerted action to actively create new local competitive advantages.

Table 5.3   Types of LED program initiatives

Case	Type of LED initiative
Cordoba	Locality development with major urban property development (telepuerto); Enterprise development (incubator and training subsidies); Community economic development through micro-enterprise support and credit.
Rafaela	Locality development (infrastructure and physical planning); Enterprise development (incubator, enterprise support services; innovation).
Araucania	Locality development and tourist promotion; Small enterprise development in agriculture.
Medellin, Antioquia	Labor market and human resource development (information, training); Enterprise development (cluster development and group-based programs in four industries (metal engineering, plastics and rubber, food processing and biotechnology); Community economic development through micro-enterprise support (support services and government purchasing program).
Bucaramanga, Santander	Innovative milieu; Small enterprise development through productivity centers in food processing, leather, textiles and clothing, and jewelry; Locality development (S&T park).
Provincia de Loa, Autofagasta	Community economic development through micro-enterprise support in agriculture (water conservation and irrigation processes and new products – fruits and dairy).
Rancagua	Labor market improvement and HRD; Community economic development through micro-enterprise support centers and incubator; Locality development (urban renewal through concessions); city marketing to attract outside investors.
Ranquil	Small enterprise development in agriculture (group-based learning for innovation in technologies and products – wine and forestry, and fruit and vegetables, respectively).
Pensilvania	Small and micro-enterprise development in design furniture based on business development services, training, and equipment
Chihuahua	Enterprise development and upgrading in strategic clusters (light industry, food processing, and services), development of supply clusters around FDI maquila in electronics, business development services.
Jalisco	Enterprise development through clusters in leather, textiles and clothing, furniture and decoration, and metal engineering and car parts, development of supply clusters around FDI maquila; State marketing to attract FDI; Locality development (strengthening capacity of municipalities)

Table 5.3 (continued) Types of LED program initiatives

Ilo	Locality development – general and economic infrastructure, industrial trade fairs. Community economic development through micro-enterprise support in training, rotating credit, machine centers.

Locality development concentrates on infrastructure and property development/redevelopment and on city marketing. It is important to note that in three cases – i.e., Cordoba (Argentina), Rancagua (Chile), and Bucaramanga (Colombia) – urban renewal and property development played an important role. The physical reshaping of cities is very much a part of new local economic development initiatives.

Improving the functioning of the local urban labor market takes place via information and intermediation. HRD is important in those instances where national policies provide incentives (Chile), though there is one case where a metropolitan authority provided training subsidies (Cordoba).

Actors, Partnerships, and Networks

As part of overall macro-economic reforms, central governments have considerably reduced their responsibility for regional development and place prosperity. Localities and regions have had to retake responsibility for their own development. Mostly by default and occasionally by design (decentralization and local government reforms), local actors have been given the leeway to develop the full range of processes to do so. Thus, one of the key features of third-generation local and regional development is the involvement of multiple local actors. The range of actors has increased, including governments, communities and their organizations, NGOs, and now also private enterprises and their associations.

Local producers and their associations are key actors in enterprise and local business development. Inter-firm cooperation and joint action plays a central role. However, local producers are very often individualistic and find it difficult to combine competition with cooperation. Several commentators have indicated that joint action and inter-firm cooperation, of the kind enumerated above, does not come easily. Some argue that such collaboration requires a kind of external catalyst or brokerage role (Meyer-Stamer, 1998, Barzelay, 1991, Helmsing, 2001a). The multiple roles of business associations in economic development are increasingly recognized and they may take a variety of forms (Levitsky, 1993). Traditionally, they represent their members in their dealings with government. They often negotiate with trade unions.

Their other traditional function is a social one. An association provides a reference group for individual entrepreneurs. More recently, the emphasis has shifted to two other functions; the provision of business development services and what some have called 'private interest governance' (e.g., establishing codes of conducts for an industry, settling disputes, etc.)

Several factors have contributed to a more prominent role for local government in local economic development. First of all, there has been a generalized and persistent trend towards decentralization in the public sector, which has complex and multiple causes. Public responsibilities have been transferred to local governments, but very often without adequate transfer of resources. The need to generate more local revenues has forced local governments to take more interest in the economic development of their area of jurisdiction. It is worth adding that the concern for local economic development not only derives from the need to raise revenues, but is also a genuine response to the local demands of people and enterprises. Secondly, in a number of countries new legislation has facilitated local governments to enter into public-private partnerships (e.g., Colombia, Chile, and Bolivia). Thirdly, changing perspectives on poverty reduction have made local government more active in pursuing local employment creation. Fourthly, in a number of countries, national or state governments have launched support programs to enable local and regional governments to become more active in local economic development (Chile's regional development fund). Finally, in some countries, there have been genuine regionalist pressures which stem from political demands in response to past neglect (Mexico), but which also may arise from the development of local initiatives in association with successful processes of local and regional specialization (Colombia).

In great contrast to past practices at national level, local governments generally realize that they are but one of many players involved in local economic development. Most local authorities spend a minor fraction of their budget on direct economic development support. More important, however, is the manner in which they discharge their main functions and realize their economic significance as a) a source of economic opportunity and b) a service enhancing or inhibiting enterprise development and competitiveness. Instead of self-contained, hierarchical bureaucratic processes, mediated by more or less democratically elected politicians, 'third-generation' local governments seek to involve other local actors in the formulation and/or implementation of government policies and programs. They actively pursue the formation of local policy and support networks. These were denominated horizontal networks and networking.

It is important to stress here that LED does not refer only to local institutions, but also to decentralized sector and national agencies. The participation of external stakeholders may be critical. First of all, specialized sector agencies can provide critical resources and services, such as training and finance. Secondly, national sector agencies mediate between the local and the global, and provide windows through which local firms can better understand global changes and participate in international markets. Especially when local institutions are weak on the ground, national agencies can play important complementary and enabling roles. Therefore, horizontal networking needs to be complemented with vertical networking in order to access national institutions and resources.

Table 5.4 gives an overview of actors and patterns of networking in the 12 case studies.

When examining our 12 case studies in terms of actors, partnerships, and networks, it is noteworthy that in all cases except one, there is horizontal cooperation between public and private actors. In most cases, the private sector takes part via representative bodies such as chambers of commerce and industry and sector business associations. In some instances, the presence and influence of large firms and enterprise groups is visible (e.g., Bucaramanga, Chihuahua).

NGOs are less frequently involved than initially expected. Notably in Chile and in Colombia, NGOs are active in community economic development through micro-enterprise and training programs. A rather exceptional example is the local Dario Maya Foundation in Pensilvania (Caldas, Colombia) which, as a 'vertically integrated' support agency, played a pivotal role in virtually all aspects of the local development initiative.[2]

In the majority of cases, there are also clear indications of vertical cooperation and networking. That is to say, sector or higher levels of government play a central role in the local development initiatives. In the case of Chile it is the regional governments, and in the case of Colombia the departmental governments. The National Vocational Training Agency (SENA) plays a supportive role in all three Colombia cases. In Chile, the FOSIS – a social fund/development agency – plays a similar role.

It should also be added that frequently national policies provide important resources and opportunities for local development initiatives. This is most clearly evidenced by the Colombian National Small Enterprise Policy

---

2. This NGO was established by a leading, very large landowner, whose family controls most forest resources in the municipality and owns two large saw mills, which provide a major source of local employment.

formulated in the mid-1980s, which put forward the creation of Centers for Productive Development (CPDs) and gave SENA a supporting role in them. Even though this policy did not have a large implementation coverage in terms of the number of CPDs created, all our cases-studies incorporated CPDs in their initiatives. Also the role of FOSIS and its regionally defined small and micro-enterprise projects have provided a window of opportunity for local development initiatives.

Learning Processes

Learning is rapidly gaining ground as a central concept in third-generation local and regional development. Learning takes place at the level of firms, at that of clusters of firms, and at that of the locality or region itself.

In the competence theory of the firm, a firm is defined as a repository of productive knowledge (rather than as a nexus of contracts). Learning is central to maintaining and renewing competencies. 'Core competencies are the collective learning in the organization, especially how to coordinate diverse production skills and integrate multiple technologies ... Core competencies do not diminish with use but are enhanced by it' (Lawson, 1999, p. 157). In this view, product market competition is merely a superficial expression of a deeper competition for competencies. Conceiving the firm as core competencies suggests that inter-firm competition, as opposed to inter-product competition, is essentially concerned with the acquisition of knowledge and skills (ibid.).

By being part of an agglomeration or cluster, a firm can greatly expand its capacity to learn. A cluster can help to reduce uncertainty. It contributes, organizes, and can facilitate exchanges of information. It provides additional signaling, articulates the needs of firms, and facilitates the coordination of actions. Learning at the level of cluster can take place via supply chain linkages (i.e., supplier and customer relations), via mobility of skilled labor between the firms in the area, and – last but not least – via spin-off activity (creation of new start-ups). It also involves imitation and reverse engineering; informal knowledge exchange via 'cafeteria effects'; and specialist services. In short, a cluster enables collective learning (Camagni, 1991; Lawson, 1999).

As markets become liberalized and firms are exposed to international and 'new' competition, firms need to develop a dynamic capability to renew, augment, or adapt their competencies in order to maintain economic performance. Innovation and learning are essential and involve combining diverse technological, organizational, and market knowledge. Firms have a

Table 5.4 Actors: horizontal and vertical cooperation and networking

Case	Vertical	Horizontal
Cordoba		Municipality, local business associations, university; broad-based civic consultations on city strategic plan;
Rafaela		Municipality, local business associations, a new small enterprise association and NGOs
Araucania	Municipality-regional government	Inter-municipal cooperation
Medellin, Antioquia	Municipality-departmental government	Municipality, local business associations (incl. chamber of commerce), universities
Bucaramanga, Santander	Municipality-departmental government	Municipality, chamber of commerce, private firms, universities
Provincia de Loa, Autofagasta	Dominant role by regional government, national mining company, sector agencies, national NGOS	Limited and informal
Rancagua		Municipality, private real estate companies, local micro-entrepreneur association
Ranquil	Social development agency (FOSIS) – agriculture line agency – municipality	Municipality, peasant groups, NGO, consultant firm
Pensilvania	Line agency (SENA) – local development foundation – Municipality – donors	Municipality, local development foundation, large local sawmills
Chihuahua	State govt. – two city governments – local development agency	State government – business associations – university
Jalisco	State government, selected municipalities, federal PYME agency	State government, chambers of industries – enterprise groups, university
Ilo	Limited between Ministry of Industry-municipality, inputs from UN agencies	Municipality, chamber of commerce, inter-municipal cooperation

limited capacity to undertake a range of activities. Choices must be made. Thus, when firms want to invest in new products or processes in response to new competition, they encounter problems because they lack the knowledge to efficiently undertake the complementary activities needed to produce and market them. Or a firm may be able to produce cheaply, but lack the competence to adapt the design of its products to the latest fads and fashions. Inter-firm cooperation becomes a key channel to address this issue. In regions where this complementary knowledge is available, firms have a better chance to learn and develop new routines and competencies. Skilled labor, specialist services, and inter-firm cooperation create a capability in a region or cluster to renew and augment the competencies of firms. This requires a social context and a common language and culture to facilitate exchange, and the region may provide these.

Local actors are best placed to assess their own situation and to learn by comparing it with other experiences. Learning at the regional level involves institutional and organizational processes. The form of learning takes place through interaction among local actors, i.e., firms, governments, NGOs, and community organizations. This is what Lawson (1999) conceptualized as a new (third-generation) local or regional competence. It requires the ability to spot signs of change, to create awareness and to communicate it to other actors so that all understand the implications; and it requires a responsiveness to mobilize resources to address emerging problems. Essentially this is a case of collective learning, but now at local governance level. A local regional innovation system (LRIS) is a system in which universities, research, training, and technology agencies interact with government and local industry. This contributes to greater systemic rationality at the level of the local regional economy, and is capable of generating substantial efficiencies in the enterprise support system, by reducing policy mismatches and by creating greater convergence in complementary investment and support programs. An LRIS, if properly structured, can contribute to collective learning, now at the level of local and regional policy-making. It can assist in a social and economic intelligence function by contributing to three feedback loops (Cooke and Morgan, 1998, p. 73): Assessing the extent to which the economic trajectory of a region is appropriate; comparing the region's performance with other and 'peer' systems; and working out the implications of changes in the system in order to prevent a lock-in (for example, in the orientation of and priorities for the enterprise support, training, and human resource development).

Based on the above, one can distinguish five different types of learning processes. The first is learning through education, i.e., knowledge transfer through HRD and training activity. A second form is organizational learning, e.g., within a firm in order to become or stay competitive, or in the relevant public bodies in order to learn about economic development of the territory. A third form of learning is what Hilhorst (1990, p. 31) calls planning as a social learning process. That is to say, developing among local actors a common understanding of the local development problems, identifying rationalized choices, and generating agreements about development priorities and strategic plan initiatives. A fourth form – collective learning – would be cluster- and group-based learning among local firms as outlined above. Lastly, there is learning through institutionalized local regional innovation systems in which universities and research institutes play an active role (innovative milieu).

Table 5.5 summarizes the different learning processes as they have been taking place in the 12 case studies. In all case studies we find instances of learning by educating, i.e., through training and transfer of knowledge as happened in Centers of Productive Development and in Technology and Innovation Centers. Existing HRD and training institutions (e.g., SENA) provide skills training programs, frequently oriented towards micro and small enterprises.

Common to almost all cases is organizational learning in the relevant public bodies about economic development and about how to engage other actors. As we saw above, new local economic development units, departments, or ministries (*secretarias*) were created *inside* key government agencies. Many case studies signal the importance of organizational learning within these new units, often associated with the employment of new young professionals. No doubt there is also organizational learning within individual firms, but this is not reported.

The most pervasive form of learning is that of social learning in policy and planning in relation to LED initiatives. The new generation of Latin American local and regional development practices is associated with a new style of planning; less government and public sector centered and more strategic planning, seeking to understand the likely direction of local economic development and seeking broad-based consensus on a long-term vision about desirable local development.

A fourth process is cluster- and group-based collective learning among firms. The creation of group- or cluster-based learning processes has been the object of local economic development initiatives in less than half the cases. These are oriented towards medium and larger enterprises and most take place in the larger territorial units (e.g., in Medellin, State of Chihuahua).

Finally, there are a few instances (notably in Bucaramanga, Colombia) where local economic development initiatives are systematically seeking to develop an innovative milieu in which universities, government, and the private sector cooperate to develop a stronger competence for LED policy and are undertaking concerted actions to develop local technological competitive advantage in selected local industries.

Concluding Observations

The 12 case studies examined in this paper cannot provide conclusive evidence about new trends in the practice of local and regional planning in Latin America. Nevertheless, they do provide indications of an emerging third-generation 'new institutionalism'. Central to this is the position and positioning of local economies in large national and international economic contexts. National economic restructuring and globalization have created the necessity to be concerned about this, and decentralization has provided the opportunity for local initiative. The new practices seek to give shape to new forms of public-private cooperation, in both horizontal and vertical networking. Public-private cooperation centers on the creation of meso-institutions at the level of territory and industry. They involve a variety of processes of learning, which in some cases is more restricted but in other cases reaches the stage of an innovative milieu. The concrete initiatives focus predominantly on enterprise or business development and in some cases on the physical redevelopment of cities.

The case studies also generate questions about the new practices of local and regional development. How inclusive are these new practices? While the broadening of the base of public decision-making on local economic development priorities certainly is a desirable feature of these new practices, do they also create a better distribution of economic opportunities or the means to take up such opportunities? Do they contribute to broadening the base of the local economy? Unfortunately, the case studies do not permit us to answer this last question. However, in one case – that of Pensilvania – the contribution is clearly very marginal.

Last but not least, a methodological question remains. Do the new practices of local and regional development promotion actually make a difference? This would require research that examines outcomes and relates them to local efforts. This could be done by selecting localities and regions that have demonstrated a dynamic economic performance, and examining to what extent, if any, this performance can be attributed to new practices of local and regional development promotion. Only a few of the 12 case studies explicitly raise this question.

Table 5.5 Learning processes

Case	Regularized knowledge transfers (training)	Organizational learning in local public agency	Social learning in policy and planning among public and private actors	Group-based and collective learning among firms	Local innovative system
Cordoba	Yes	LED unit	Strategic plan for city		
Rafaela	Yes	LED unit	Strategic plan for city		
Araucania	Yes	Municipal teams			
Medellin, Antioquia	Yes	Departmental and local governments	Competitiveness, strategic plans and LT visions for city and region	Enterprise groups	In formation
Bucaramanga, Santander	Yes	Departmental and local governments	Competitiveness, role of S&T, strategic plans and LT visions for city	Enterprise groups, research clusters	In advanced stage of development
Provincia de Loa, Autofagasta	Yes		On specific themes (such as water, environment)		
Rancagua	Yes	LED unit	City marketing campaign		
Ranquil	Yes	Limited	Yes, defining LED initiatives	Small farmer groups	
Pensilvania	Yes	Limited	Limited		
Chihuahua	Yes	LED secretariat	Strategic plan, strategic clusters	Enterprise clusters	
Jalisco	Yes	Same	Strategic and spatial decentralization plan	Enterprise clusters	
Ilo	Yes	LED unit	Yes, on strategic interventions		

References

Amin, A. (1999), 'An Institutionalist Perspective on Regional Economic Development', *International Journal of Urban and Regional Research*, Vol. 23(2), pp. 365-78.

Amin, A. and Thrift, N. (1994), *Globalization, Institutions and Regional Development in Europe*, Oxford University Press, Oxford.

Barzelay, M. (1991), 'Managing Local Development. Lessons from Spain', *Policy Sciences*, Vol. 24(3), pp. 271-90.

Benavides, M. (2000), *Estudio de Caso a Nivel Local: el Programa Municipal de Desarrollo Empresarial (PROMDE) y la Experiencia de la Municipalidad de Ilo, Peru*, CEPAL, Santiago, Chile.

Bernales Rivas, O. (2000), *El Programa Red de Equipo Municipales de Gestión Estratégica (EMGES): una Experiencia de Asociatividad para el Desarrollo de las Comunas de Angol, Renaico, Collipulli y Ercilla, IX Región de la Araucanía, Chile*, CEPAL, Santiago, Chile.

Best, M.H. (1990), *The New Competition. Institutions of Industrial Restructuring*, Polity Press, Cambridge.

Blakely, E.J. (1989), *Planning Local Economic Development. Theory and Practice*, Sage, Newbury Park.

Boisier, S., J.G.M. Hilhorst and F. Uribe-Echavarria (eds) (1982), *Experiencias de Planificación Regional en America Latina: una Teoría en Busca de una Practica*, Editorial SIAP – CEPAL, Santiago de Chile.

Cáceres, L. and Figueroa Burdiles, N. (2000), *Sistematización Ranquil, Chile: una Experiencia sobre la Generación de Condiciones para el Desarrollo Económico Local*, CEPAL, Santiago, Chile.

Camagni, R. (1991), 'Local Milieu, Uncertainty and Innovation Networks: Towards a New Dynamic Theory of Economic Space', in R. Camagni (ed.), *Innovation Networks. Spatial Perspectives*, pp. 121-45, Belhaven Press, London.

Capello, R. (1999), 'Spatial Transfer of Knowledge in High Technology Milieux: Learning Versus Collective Learning Processes', *Regional Studies*, Vol. 33(4), pp. 353-65.

Cooke, P. and Morgan, K. (1998), *The Associational Economy: Firms, Regions and Innovation*, Oxford University Press, Oxford.

Costamagna, P. (2000), *La Articulación y las Interacciones entre Instituciones: la Iniciativa de Desarrollo Económico Local de Rafaela, Argentina*, CEPAL, Santiago, Chile.

Friedmann, J. and Douglass, M. (1978), 'Agropolitan Development: towards a New Strategy for Regional Planning in Asia', in F.C. Lo and K. Salih (eds), *Growth Pole Strategy and Regional Development Policy*, Pergamon Press, Oxford, pp. 163-92.

Helmsing, A.H.J. (1999), 'Teorías de Desarrollo Industrial Regional y Políticas de Segunda y Tercera Generación', *Revista Latinoamericana de Estudios Urbano Regionales (EURE)*, Vol. 25(75) pp. 5-39.

Helmsing, A.H.J. (2001a), 'Externalities, Learning and Governance. Perspectives on Local Economic Development', *Development and Change*, Vol. 32(2), pp. 277-308.

Helmsing, A.H.J. (2001b), *Local Economic Development in Low and Middle Income Countries. New Generations of Actors, Policies and Instruments*, Paper presented at the Conference on Decentralization and Local Governance, organized by UNCDF, Cape Town, South Africa, 26-30 March, 2001.

Hilhorst, J.G.M. (1990), *Regional Studies and Rural Development*, Avebury, Aldershot.

Lawson, C. (1999), 'Towards a Competence Theory of the Region', *Cambridge Journal of Economics*, Vol. 23, pp. 151-66.
Levitsky, J. (1993), 'Private Sector Organizations and Support for Small and Micro Enterprises', in A.H.J. Helmsing and Th. Kolstee (eds), *Small Enterprises and Changing Policies*, Intermediate Technology Publications, London.
Londoño Yepes, C.A. (2000), *La Gestión del Desarrollo en Antioquia*, Colombia, CEPAL, Santiago, Chile.
Maillat, D. (1995), 'Territorial Dynamic, Innovative Milieus and Regional Policy', *Entrepreneurship and Regional Development*, Vol. 7, pp. 157-65.
Maillat, D. (1998), 'Innovative Milieux and New Generations of Regional Policies', *Entrepreneurship and Regional Development*, Vol. 10, pp. 1-16.
Maldonado, A. (2000), *La Experiencia de Desarrollo Económico Local en el Municipio de Pensilvania* (Colombia), CEPAL, Santiago, Chile.
Marianacci, G. (2000), *Descentralización y Desarrollo Económico Local: Estudio de Caso de la Ciudad de Córdoba, Argentina*, CEPAL, Santiago, Chile.
Meyer-Stamer, J. (1998), 'Path Dependence in Regional Development: Persistence and Change in Three Industrial Clusters in Santa Catarina, Brazil', *World Development*, Vol. 26(8), pp. 1495-511.
Muñoz Villalobos, C. (2000), *La Experiencia de Desarrollo Económico Local en el Municipio de Rancagua: Program Rancagua Emprende, 6ta Region, Chile*, CEPAL, Santiago, Chile.
Porter, M. (1985), *Competitive Advantage*, The Free Press, New York.
Porter, M.E. (1990), *The Competitive Advantage of Nations*, The Free Press, New York.
Raco, M. (1999), 'Competition, Collaboration and the New Industrial Districts: Examining the Institutional Turn in Local Economic Development', *Urban Studies*, Vol. 36(5/6), pp. 951-68.
Ruiz Duran, C. (2000a), *Esquema de Regionalización y Desarrollo Local en Jalisco, México: el Paradigma de una Descentralización Fundamentada en el Fortalecimiento Productivo*, CEPAL, Santiago, Chile.
Ruiz Duran, C. (2000b), *El Paradigma de Desarrollo Regional Basado en la Cooperación Público-Privado: el Caso de Chihuahua, México*, CEPAL, Santiago, Chile.
Salinas, J. (2000), *Concertación de Actores Territoriales para el Impulso del Desarrollo Productivo de la Provincia del Loa, Región de Antofagasta, Chile*, CEPAL, Santiago, Chile.
Stohr, W. and Taylor, F. (1981), *Development from Above or Below? The Dialectics of Regional Planning in Developing Countries*, Wiley, London.
Streeck, W. and Schmitter, P.C. (eds) (1985), *Private Interest Governance*, Sage, London.
Vargas Vera, C. and Prieto Ladino, R. (2000), *Alianza del Sector Público, Sector Privado y Academia para el Desarrollo Productivo y la Competitividad de Bucaramanga, Colombia*, CEPAL, Santiago, Chile.

6 Earning More or Less: Income, Micro-Production and Women's Status in Lima's Poor Neighborhoods

ANNELOU YPEIJ

Introduction

In the public areas of Lima, a large crowd of people is at work. In the daily search for an income, many inhabitants from the poor neighborhoods of the Peruvian capital go out and seek customers. They sell a wide range of products at the bus stops and in the streets, *plazas*, and other public spaces. Some are producers selling their end products, others limit their activities to street vending and buy their merchandise from wholesalers and producers. Clothes, furniture, soft drinks, toilet paper, and all kinds of foods are just some of the products that can be bought. In Lima's center, the many market stalls and small carts make walking and driving a difficult exercise. The large-scale presence of the small-scale economy impresses many visitors to the capital, and is confirmed by statistics. In 1993, more than half of the economically active population worked in the so-called informal sector of the economy (Gárate and Ferrer, 1994: Table III.2a).

If the economically active population is broken down by gender, more women than men are involved in small-scale and micro-economic activities, while men more commonly perform activities on a larger scale.[1] To explain the larger number of women working in the small-scale economy is a complex task. In comparison with men, women from poor neighborhoods have limited employment opportunities and lower levels of education. On

---

1. In 1991, 50 per cent of all economically active women worked in the informal sector of the economy, 39 per cent in the 'formal' sector, and 11 per cent in domestic service. The figures for men were 44 per cent, 55 per cent, and less than 1 per cent, respectively (based on Gárate and Ferrer, 1994: Table 111.2a.)

top of that, they encounter difficulties in organizing child care. Their responsibilities for the daily purchase of their family's food confronts them with the insufficient wages of their husbands, and their domestic and caring tasks are very time-consuming and demanding. To understand women's work in the small-scale economy, one has to understand gender relations and the division of labor within the household.

Though women work in larger numbers in the small-scale sector than men, very few can be defined as micro-entrepreneurs offering work to laborers. Statistics show that the overwhelming majority of owners of small-scale and micro-enterprises are men. Of the total number of employers (owners of an enterprise with hired laborers) in the informal sector, 84 per cent were men and only 16 per cent were women.[2] Few women own a micro-enterprise, and are unable to accumulate sufficient capital to hire laborers; instead, they work as a hired laborer, family worker, or an individual laborer.[3] This raises the question why relatively few women own an enterprise. Why do women, compared to men, accumulate less capital and, as a consequence, earn less?

In this paper, I focus on micro-production activities and compare male and female micro-producers. The analysis is based on anthropological fieldwork, carried out from October 1990 to December 1991 (Ypeij 2000).[4] I will argue that because of the manifestation of gender hierarchies, for example within the household, women as entrepreneurs encounter more hindrances than men when they attempt to accumulate capital. Therefore, many economic activities carried out by women do not grow beyond those of an individual producer. In the following sections, I comment on the gender hierarchy within poor households in Lima, and then focus on the differential access of female micro-producers to the means of production, capital, family labor, markets, and credit. In subsequent sections, I discuss the differences in capital accumulation between male and female micro-producers, then assess the alternatives for female micro-producers. The analysis shows that the social relations of production and those based on gender are intertwined in such a way that women's status as producers is related to their subordinate status within the household. Women's activities as producers even seem to reproduce gender inequalities at the household level. If this is so, does the

---

2. Based on Gárate and Ferrer, 1994: Tables III.5.b and III.6.
3. Other studies on Latin America and the Caribbean show that Peruvian women are not an exception (Menjívar and Pérez Saínz 1993, p. 79 and 84; Espinal and Grasmuck 1994, p. 7).
4. The study was subsidized by the Netherlands Foundation for the Advancement of Tropical Research (WOTRO).

income generated through their production activities have any implications for their status within the household? (Kabeer, 1997) To place the analysis in a broader theoretical framework, in the last section of this paper I go into the long-standing debate on women's economic dependence/independence and the power inequalities between women and men at the household level.

This study of micro-production in Lima is set within the context of the Peruvian economy, which is characterized by a prolonged recession and growing poverty. In the period 1980-1993, real urban minimum wages were down by almost 90 per cent (Webb and Fernandez, 1994: Tables 15.3). During my fieldwork in 1991, 44 per cent of Lima's inhabitants were defined as poor (Cuánto, 1991, p. 65). In recent years, the Peruvian economy has been recovering, but there are no indications that the poor are benefiting from this growth, nor that their daily survival struggle is becoming substantially easier (Hordijk, 2000, p. 102).

Gender Hierarchies within Poor Households

Households in poor neighborhoods in Lima show an evident hierarchical structure internally, with men in the position of authority. This hierarchy expresses itself in both the sexual division of labor and the control of intra-household cash flow. It is considered the primary responsibility of the man to provide sufficient income. In pursuit of an income, he is given complete freedom of movement. Childcare and household chores are considered to be the primary responsibility of the woman. Her possible income-generating activities are considered secondary to her domestic duties, which considerably limit her freedom of movement and the time she can invest. The extreme poverty of most households in poor neighborhoods aggravates domestic work substantially, because it affects the material conditions in which this work is carried out (Grandón, 1990, pp. 53-4). To mention a few examples: Many houses are temporary constructions and lack running water and/or a sewage connection. Cleaning the house, washing clothes, cooking meals, and attending to the children are therefore time-consuming tasks. Often there is no money to buy appliances to facilitate domestic work. In order to save money, many women keep livestock (e.g., chickens) and hunt around for the best food prices. Malnutrition and poor hygienic conditions affect children's health. At the same time, poverty forces many women to generate an income. As the study of the poor neighborhood El Agustino by Grandón (1990: Table 12) makes clear, the need to earn money does not release women from their domestic duties. Seventy percent of women who generate an income do more than 50 per cent of household chores, and 30 per cent carry out these chores completely on their own.

The second way in which male domination in the household expresses itself is through the husband's control over the intra-household cash flow. Based on Benería and Roldán (1987, pp. 113-23), the following ways in which a husband may exercise this control can be deduced. He may withhold or share information on the actual amount of his earnings or decide what portion of his earnings he keeps as personal spending or pocket money. He may choose the form in which the household allowance is given to his wife, and may exercise control afterwards. He may 'borrow' from the money meant for household maintenance and use it for personal purposes (cf. Kabeer, 1997, Roldán, 1988).

Different Points of Departure

In a climate of high unemployment, many inhabitants of Lima create their own work by setting up production activities. However, men start their production activities from a different work trajectory than women do (cf. Menjívar and Pérez Sáinz, 1993, p. 79). Labor histories of many male producers show that before they decided to produce on their own account, they worked as a trader or laborer in the larger scale or small-scale industry, often in the same line of business in which they then started their own production activities (cf. Grompone, 1986, pp. 112-13). Therefore, they posses experience, knowledge, and contacts, which helps them in their quest for more profitable purchasing and sales markets. My interviews show that male producers consider production on their own account, and possibly running an enterprise, as an improvement of their social status. They highly value the freedom to be one's own boss, despite all the sacrifices and the hard work involved.

Women, too, initiate production activities. However, in comparison with male producers, often their point of departure is less favorable. Many married women are motivated not by a desire to improve their social status, but by the fact that their husband's contribution to the household falls short of what the household needs. Therefore, their prime motive is to generate additional income. Many women start to produce garments, because they possess basic knowledge about sewing obtained during their preparation for and in the performance of their household duties. In addition, many women already have a sewing machine for domestic use. Their experience often does not go beyond operating such a simple machine. Precisely because they start producing out of economic necessity, they have no or only very little production capital. Often, it is laboriously gleaned by reducing household spending.

For many starting female and male producers, the organization of production activities is embedded in the organization of the household (cf. Wilson, 1990). Production is located in the home. Unpaid family labor is used and there is no separation between the cash flow of production activities and the household. Owners of the means of production are also the producers. Often this leads to a production rhythm continuously interrupted by the commercialization of products and an irregular income. Multi-income strategies, of which the production activities form part, frequently occur. Other characteristics of household-based production organization are simple technology, low quality, and a small variety of products.

Differential Access to Capital

As argued above, male producers tend to start their production activities with more capital than female producers do. The differentials in access to capital of female and male producers become even clearer when the control of intra-household cash flow is considered. Despite the fact that during the interviews many male producers were willing and able to mention how much working capital they had and how much profit they made, it is generally accepted that they withhold this information from their wife. In general, on a daily basis, the producers provide their wife with a small amount of money, a housekeeping allowance or so-called *diario*. This is meant for the purchase of food and possibly clothes. The men fix the amount of the *diario* themselves and usually take care of costs such as water and electricity. Male control of the cash flow can be an advantage in their production activities. The following case of a household characterized by a multi-income strategy is an example.

Eliana[5] is married to Manuel, who produces wooden furniture in their home. Every day, Manuel used to provide Eliana with money for the household, but according to her it was never enough. When she asked for more, he always told her that he could not give her more. With the support of Manuel, Eliana decided to open a shop in their home selling soft drinks and beer. Manuel used his working capital to buy Eliana a few crates of beverages. By

---

5. For reasons of privacy, I have changed the names of individuals.

staying open for far longer than most of the competition, this small business is reasonably successful. Eliana's income from the store is used for housekeeping, with 40 per cent of the housekeeping money coming from her work. For Manuel, Eliana's contribution to the household necessities means that he can spend less on them and can reinvest more in his production.

Because of their control of the intra-household cash flow, the financial margins of male producers are flexible. They use money intended for household maintenance, as well as income from other members of the household, for production purposes. At times they place more value on their production activities than on household maintenance, lowering or even completely withdrawing their contribution to the household economy (cf. Nelson, 1979, p. 297-98). Their financial flexibility is expressed in the continuous transfer between working capital and household income, and use of income from others.

In contrast to men, many female producers are not in a position to benefit from the intra-household cash flow. Their financial margins are limited to the housekeeping money and their working capital, and the transfer from one to the other. In addition, as the study of Espinal and Grasmuck (1994, p. 8) concerning the Dominican Republic shows, female micro-entrepreneurs tend to contribute a higher proportion of their income to the household than men. These scholars state that this pattern may be part of the explanation of why women's firms have accumulated lower levels of capital investment (cf. D'Amico 1993, p. 80).

Differential Access to Unpaid Family Labor

Locating production in the home makes it easier for male producers to claim their wife's labor. It is considered completely normal, and even favorable, for a woman to help her husband with his production activities. In this way, she lives up to the image of the perfect wife. Wives perform many different tasks in production, but normally those, which can be done within the household production site. Although some wives with adolescent children leave the house to purchase materials and sell the products, this is less common. The access to unpaid family labor offers the male producer two advantages: He is able to lower his production costs by lowering his labor costs; and the production rhythm is less interrupted and the income more regular. The male producer's claim on the labor of his wife, as well as his control over the intra-household cash flow, keeps his wife from appropriating more responsibility for production activities.

Despite the fact that, from a legal point of view, in the beginning many production activities belong to both wife and husband, many men interviewed showed an inclination to minimize the labor input of their wife, qualifying it as family labor and denying her equal participation in responsibilities, despite the hard work she performs.[6]

The married couple, Carmen and Luís, produce and sell wooden chairs and tables. Luís, together with their adolescent sons, makes the furniture; Carmen purchases the wood and looks for clients. By performing this task, she engages in what is considered a very unusual role. Women simply don't purchase wood, and at times her neighbors call her 'husband', thus expressing the thought that Carmen must have a lot of control, more than is considered normal or even suitable for a wife. However, although her participation in the production is crucial and the working capital is constantly passing through her hands, she has little control over the production. She doesn't accept an order without first consulting Luís, and every time they need wood, Luís gives her the exact amount of money required. The money from a sale she hands over completely to Luís and he, in his turn, provides her every day with the *diario*.

Compared to male producers, the access of female producers to unpaid family labor is far more limited. If married, it is unlikely that a female producer's husband is willing to do free work for her. Froehle (1994, p. 25) in her study on Venezuela states that 90 per cent of the wives who work in their husband's business are unpaid. However, all husbands who work in their wife's business *are* paid, and almost 90 per cent co-own the business. At best, female producers have access to the unpaid labor of their adolescent children. Because of the lack of a family worker, the production rhythm of many female producers is interrupted by the commercialization of products. For this reason, their income is irregular.

Differential Access to Markets

Every producer has to purchase materials and sell a product. Many a woman's mobility and available time are limited by her domestic duties. Therefore, female producers find themselves limited in their quest for purchasing and sales markets. Male producers, in contrast, have more opportunities to reach more favorable markets located further away from the

---

6. Many production activities are not registered and most marriages are contracted in community of property.

poor neighborhoods. Because purchasing close to the production area is often impossible, female producers are obliged to spend a considerable amount of time buying materials. They compensate for this by seeking nearby sales markets, mostly in their own neighborhoods.

Comparing two producers – Manuel and Cecilia – both of whom produce wooden furniture and have more or less the same amount of capital at their disposal, it is noticeable that several times a week Manuel leaves this neighborhood to go to the center of Lima to visit shops which give him orders. In contrast, Cecilia – a single mother of three children under the age of ten, who obtained her machinery after receiving a gift – has difficulties leaving her neighborhood, because she combines her production activities with childcare. She sells her furniture by having it in stock and exhibiting it for sale outside her workshop. Her clientele consists mainly of the residents of Pamplona Alta, the poor neighborhood where her workshop is located.

For the female producer, selling in her own neighborhood has two consequences. In the first place, her profit margins are reduced, because the potential clientele has very little purchasing power. She is also forced to lower her prices, because her relationship with her potential customer is not completely market-oriented. They are also friends, family members or neighbors. Therefore, selling in the neighborhood means selling on the basis of social networks. Many authors have pointed out the importance of these networks, (see de Lomnitz, 1991[1975]; Bohman, 1984, among others), which form the basis of emotional and material support, and in the context of severe poverty, can be characterized as a survival strategy.

The social networks of women consist mainly of other women, and the exchange of support only takes place in the context of long-time relationships and great mutual confidence. The giving party has to be sure that a future request on her part will be honored. Women will only confide in each other if they can judge each other as good friends or neighbors. The latter depends on behavior. Bohman writes:

> 'Women who are not deemed to behave in a decent way may not be accepted into any group of intensive interaction in the neighborhood. The female group keeps a close watch over the behavior of its respective members, judging each woman's way of coping with problems, especially those related to notions of decency, and exerts pressure towards conformity with the values and norms upheld in the group (...).' (1984, pp. 286-87)

My case material confirms Bohman's point of view. The female producers who depend on neighborhood networks for their sales markets make a great effort to behave as 'good' women. For them, their reputation as a 'good' mother and wife is an essential part of customer relations. To return to the case of Cecilia:

As a single mother producing furniture, she is in an exceptional position. In the past, the neighbors laughed at her, doubted the quality of her products, and treated her with great distrust. Gradually, distrust gave way to confidence, and nowadays the neighbors refer to her as *la señora carpintera* (madam carpenter). Cecilia confirms that besides producing high-quality products, her reputation as a 'good' woman has contributed to this. 'They asked themselves, what kind of a woman is she, that her husband left her. But now they respect me, because I didn't marry again.[7] I have to dress more seriously. I have to command respect.' Several times she emphasized that she is always in the company of her children, and how much effort it takes her to combine the washing and mending of their clothes ('So they'll look neat') with production. In fact, Cecilia is constantly obliged to prove to her potential customers that, despite her 'deviant activities', she is still a 'good' mother and a decent woman.

Male producers also have certain behavioral codes. For example, the noise of a carpenter's machinery may seriously annoy his neighbors. Because of the illegal status of most production activities, there is always the danger that a neighbor will inform the authorities. Like female producers, males have to compensate for this annoyance by behavior that is considered 'good'. However, the behavior margins of male producers are less narrow because of so-called *machismo*. For example, a man's adultery may be judged adversely, but his masculinity or his qualities as a producer will never be in doubt because of it. On the contrary, in the male community, he proves himself to be a 'real' man. In addition, male producers are away more often, and therefore their behavior is less under neighborhood scrutiny.

Differential Access to Credit

Because most micro– and small-scale production activities are judged to be of insufficient solvency and profitability for banks, micro-producers of both sexes have problems obtaining formal credit.[8] However, women approaching

---

7. It is judged negatively that single women with children establish a new relationship with a man, because of the danger that the stepfather could abuse the children.
8. Meanwhile Peru has several programs directed to provide small credits to micro-entrepreneurs.

a bank encounter even greater limitations such as the lack of knowledge of how such banks function; the higher degree of illiteracy among women and time-consuming banking procedures (Lynn 1988, p. 192).

Both male and female producers interviewed in Lima tended to approach informal credit/savings systems based on the neighborhood networks, of which the so-called *junta* is an important example. Several participants periodically deposit a fixed sum of money. For a certain period, one of the participants receives the total amount of money as a loan, and pays interest to the others. Because formal sanctions for a non-payer do not exist, the *juntas* are based on high levels of mutual confidence. Sexual segregation is an important characteristic. This can be explained by the relative distrust between women and men. Women, for example, do not want male participants because they fear that men will dominate the organization. Furthermore, mixed *juntas* are difficult to establish, because men and women have different goals and women, in general, have less disposable income than men. Many women organize *juntas* on behalf of the household as a supplement to the housekeeping money. Men, in general, organize *juntas* on behalf of their income-generating activities. Miriam and Hernán, a married couple engaged in shoe production, provide a good example of women's participation in *juntas* with a lesser capital potential.

Both Miriam and Hernán participate in *juntas* on a regular basis. Miriam's contributions amount to a total of US$125 over ten weeks. The participants are women who only have their housekeeping money or the limited profit from a small trading venture at their disposal. Hernan's contributions to his *junta*, however, amount to a total of US$ 500 over twenty weeks. The participants are men who have their own enterprises and who use the money as working capital.

Capital Accumulation by Female and Male Producers

Depending on the stage in the lifecycle of the household and its composition, there are considerable differences in the capital accumulating potential of female producers. Those with older children have more freedom of movement, and can deploy their children as unpaid family laborers or assign some domestic duties to them. The financial margins within which they operate are therefore usually rather more generous then those of unmarried mothers with young children.

However, my research shows that, from the very beginning the competitive position of female producers is less favorable than that of men producers, and accumulating capital is more difficult. More often than in the case of male producers, the activities of female producers do not evolve beyond those of an individual producer. Because their working capital is limited, or non-existent, many women are obliged to seek orders from micro-scale or larger scale producers. Thus, they become outworkers. Male producers have better access to working capital and markets. They have more knowledge and contacts. Because of their dominant position in the household, they can control the intra-household cash flow, claim the unpaid labor of their wife, and avoid childcare and household tasks. All of this enables men to produce on a larger scale from the very beginning and, as a consequence, they are more inclined to hire laborers. Therefore, more often than among female producers, their activities show the characteristics of a micro-enterprise.

The same conditions which give male producers a better start, help them to continue the process of capital accumulation. Of course, with the ongoing economic recession, men too encounter difficulties in trying to accumulate capital. However, for female producers it is much harder to participate in this process because of their limited time and mobility. In order to adapt to market fluctuations and to produce continuously, a producer will try to cover the periods of low demand by using what I call a diversification and flexibilization of business strategy. In Lima, this means intensifying the subcontracting relationships with other micro-producers. Micro-producers take orders from other producers to ride out periods without access to favorable sales markets. They also assign tasks to other, better-equipped enterprises, to improve the quality of the products without investing in better technology. Also, diversification of the business strategy means entering more favorable sales markets. Producers will try to obtain access to middle-class markets inside or outside Lima by visiting different markets in person, soliciting the help of middlemen or selling to chain stores. They are faced with severe competition from medium and large industries and are forced to make a better product at lower costs. This generally involves lowering the cost of materials by seeking more favorable purchasing markets, or by making individual arrangements with material providers, such as larger scale textile producers.[9]

---

9. In doing so, producers risk being subordinated to the large industry and chain stores which is a drag on their capital accumulation potential (MacEwen Scott 1979, p. 121). They prevent severe subordination by not exclusively producing on assignment for the large industry.

Alternatives for Female Producers

Although female producers have fewer opportunities to accumulate capital, and married women have difficulty in participating in the production activities of their husband on an equal basis, they do not take that situation for granted. They are very active in seeking solutions to the limitations and problems they meet. Some wives start their own independent production activities.

Hernán has been producing shoes for over twenty years. Right from the beginning, his wife Miriam has also been producing shoes, and now she has the knack of it. Nevertheless, Hernán hindered her in her efforts to achieve equal participation in responsibilities. He thought of himself as the leader and defined her as a family worker. One day, Miriam came home with some single orders, but Hernán refused to fill them, because he preferred to produce in quantity. After this had happened a few times, Miriam decided to fill her orders by herself. She asked her clients to provide her with an advance to purchase materials, and she subcontracted to a befriended micro-producer the assembly of the shoes. Now, the couple produce separately and both control their own working capital.

Another way in which female producers find solutions is by mobilizing their neighborhood networks and organizing independent production activities. For example, since the 1970s, Lima (and rural areas) has had a strong tradition of grassroots organizations focused on communal cooking in order to lower the cost of living (cf. Hordijk, 2000). Women involved in these organizations tended to try to start income-generating activities.

For female producers, the advantages of this type of production organization are evident. The women train each other in the required skills. The cash flow from the production is completely separated from the various households, and is therefore outside the control of the husbands. The women take turns purchasing materials and seeking sales markets. This means a more efficient use of their scarce time and partly solves the problem of their limited mobility. They are able to organize production in a more flexible way than they would were they producing individually, because the organization provides easy access to a large quantity of potential seamstresses.

This alternative form of production organization does have its shortcomings for the micro-producers. Many communal workshops lack the contacts to sell in favorable markets and are willing to accept assignments from large industries. Some export companies specialize in the production of mechanically and hand-knitted garments made of the internationally highly appreciated alpaca wool. These companies export jumpers, skirts, scarves, and caps to Europe, Japan, the United States, and other markets. A crucial element in the production organization of such companies is the subcontracting of the hand-knitting to the communal workshops located in the poor neighborhoods. Such subcontracting offers the company many advantages. Investments in the area of production remain limited. The same applies to the required number of permanent laborers. Managers save time and avoid problems by maintaining contacts only with the women leaders of the workshops. The training costs are reduced, because only the leaders are trained. They in turn pass their knowledge on to the other members of the workshop. Subcontracting increases the flexibility of production, because fluctuations in demand are directly translated into the number and size of the assignments given to the women. The production rhythm of the workshop is subsequently dictated by the export company. In 1991, the average payment to the women was US$ 15 for a jumper that took roughly forty hours to knit; in other words, she was paid just US$ 0.38 an hour. By working on assignments, the women lose control of the production process and are forced to accept low wages (cf. Benería and Roldán, 1987).

Women's Income and Status within the Household

The present analysis shows why women as micro-producers encounter many obstacles to accumulating capital, and consequently earn less than their male counterparts. In this section I want to take the analysis a step further and ask what the consequences of women's incomes are for their status within the household. What difference, if any, has their income made to intra-household gender dynamics (Kabeer, 1997, p. 267)? This question is the subject of a long-standing debate, which has increased considerably in significance since the explosive growth of job opportunities for women in export-oriented factory production in many parts of the Third World (Elson and Pearson, 1984). Within the debate, it is generally acknowledged that intra-household relationships are characterized by power inequalities, but scholars disagree on whether women's income can improve their status. Bhachu, for example, argues that wage work gives women a strong means for creating a power base in the household, because it enables them 'to invest and consume in their own interests and for their own benefit' (1988, p. 76 in Kabeer, 1997). Others stress that the social relations of production become bearers of gender and reproduce gender hierarchies. Because of that, the jobs generated by export-oriented production are exploitative and have little potential to improve women's status or generate a significant cultural change (Elson and Pearson, 1984, p. 30; Arizpe and Aranda, 1986, p. 191).

The present analysis confirms the theoretical insight that gender hierarchies are an integrated part of the social relations of production. The organization of micro-production is strongly embedded within the gender relations at the household level (cf. Wilson, 1990). The male control of intra-household cash flow and the gender-based division of labor are important analytical tools to understand why, and how, women's capital accumulating potential is hindered, and to shed light on the strong relations between women's limited incomes and their subordinate position within the household. In their search for an alternative production form, women organize themselves into communal workshops. As a result, they risk becoming an easy target for large industries seeking cheap outworkers. By accepting work on assignment, the women risk losing control of the production process and are forced to accept low wages. How can an income generated under conditions that only reproduces gender (and class) inequality ever improve women's status? From a scientific perspective, the observer would be inclined to think that this is impossible.

However, the women themselves have a different perspective (cf. Roldán, 1988). However small their earnings may be, it relieves some of the stress of the daily struggle to make ends meet. Often the women spend their money on food, clothes, and school items for their children. They also spend some on their own well-being, such as bus fares to visit a distant relative. One woman stated that she used her income to buy contraceptives. Furthermore their earnings give women a small but meaningful base from which to renegotiate their status with their husband.

Rosa – wife of furniture producer Juan Carlos – finally managed to set up her own business during the course of the research. Her husband had always obstructed her previous attempts. She started selling sweets and soft drinks on a very small scale from a stall in the doorway of her house. Then, her husband started borrowing and asked her to lend him money. To avoid an argument, she gave him her working capital, which he never paid back, thus ruining her business. Rosa was very angry, and was unwilling to accept this. To make her husband see that his dominant behavior was wrong, she mobilized her social network. Very openly she started asking advice from her neighbors, the nurse, and the priest, stressing that her intentions were only to help her children and husband. The general opinion was that she has the right to earn her own income. Her crusade ended when her husband implicitly admitted he was wrong and agreed to take a course on marital coaching organized by the church.

Although it would be an exaggeration to say that Rosa's status has improved considerably since this incident, for her it was a small step in the right direction: It has made the daily contact with her husband bearable and given her hope for future improvements.

Finally, I want to return to the members of the communal workshops who, through subcontracting relations, can be integrated into global markets. Though their low income is reason enough for the critical observer to think of their work as exploitative, the women themselves give multiple meanings to it. The assignments are brought to them by the leader of the workshop, which is normally located in or near one of the members' homes. For the members, this makes it easier to combine their paid work with their other duties. They work four hours a day in each other's company, caring for their children at the same time. The women consider all this as favorable working conditions that partly compensate for their low wages. Besides, the women speak highly of their organizations. Although the primary objective of the women's organizations is to support their members with their daily survival, they are also defined as a place for the women themselves. The women enjoy each other's friendship and solidarity, and learn to assume responsibility, to defend the democratic character of their organizations, and to stand up for themselves. Their self-esteem grows, as does their confidence in relations of solidarity and in joint action (Blondet, 1991; Sara-Lafosse, 1989; Villavicencio, 1989, p. 271). Last but not least, research indicates that the participation of the women in the grassroots organizations has the potential to change the gender relationships at the household level. According to Sara-Lafosse, the organizations introduce a cultural change concerning the seclusion in the house of married women and, as a result of women's increased self-esteem, provoke a better relationship between the spouses (1984, p. 90, see also Villavicencio, 1989, p. 268).

Concluding Remarks

The aim of this paper was to analyze why female micro-producers have fewer opportunities to accumulate capital than men. For many starting female and male producers, the organization of the production activities is embedded in the organization of the household. Based on their subordinate status within the household – of which the gender division of labor and male control of the intra-household cash flow are important manifestations – female producers face severe limitations. Compared to men, they start their activities with less capital, less knowledge, and fewer contacts. They are not able to benefit from the intra-household cash flow the way men do, and they have fewer opportunities to use unpaid family-worker. Though they do have access to informal credit systems, for female producers these systems represent fewer opportunities to raise capital. Finally, their domestic duties limit both the time they can invest in their production activities and their freedom of movement. Thus, many female producers use their neighborhood networks as sales markets, which decreases their profits and forces them to use 'appropriate' female behavior as part of customer relations. This last point once again emphasizes their domestic and caring duties. For many male producers, their more dominant position within the household offers them benefits regarding the process of capital accumulation, the possibility to avoid household and caring duties, and greater freedom of movement and time investment. It is clear that the poor who strive to improve their economic situation do so as gendered individuals: In Lima, gender identities and gender relations can be considered a form of social asset available to men, while for women they are a potential source of limitations and difficulties. Therefore, poor women who try to improve their economic situation simultaneously have to rebel against existing gender inequalities and struggle over meanings of femininity and masculinity.

The communal workshops offer female producers an alternative production organization, independent of male household members and outside their control (cf. Kabeer, 1997, p. 265). These workshops may solve some of the problems women encounter when producing individually. However, because the members lack the contacts to sell at favorable markets, they are willing (or forced) to accept assignments from large industries. If the women take their chances with these firms, they risk losing control of the production process and are forced to accept very low wages.

The women in this study generate an income under conditions that reproduce gender and class inequalities. This raises the question whether such an income has the potential to change existing gender hierarchies and improve women's status within the household. The women give multiple meanings to their work and income. They realize that their earnings are small and that their working conditions may be exploitative. However, they experience it as an advantage that their production activities can be organized around their household and caring duties. They spend their income on promoting the well-being of their children and of themselves, which enhances feelings of control and self-esteem. The very fact that they generate an income can already signify resistance to existing gender inequalities, and gives them a tool to renegotiate their relationship with their husbands. This tendency is intensified by their participation in grassroots organizations.

I share with the women their opinion that these are all small steps forward in the complex and slow process of social transformation. Only stressing the many ways gender inequalities are reproduced, involves the danger of denying the importance the women themselves give to their income, and denying the women recognition as vocal actors.

References

Arizpe, Lourdes and Aranda, Josefina (1986), 'Women Workers in the Strawberry Agribusiness in Mexico', in Eleanor Leacock, Helen I. Safa (eds), *Women's Work, Development and the Division of Labor by Gender*, Bergin and Garvey Publishers, Massachusetts, pp. 174-93.

Benería, Lourdes and Roldán, Martha (1987), *The Crossroads of Class and Gender, Industrial Homework, Subcontracting, and Household Dynamics in Mexico City*, Chicago, The University of Chicago Press, Chicago.

Bohman, Kristina (1984), *Women of the Barrio: Class and Gender in a Colombian City*, Stockholm Studies in Social Anthropology, Stockholm.

Blondet, Cecilia (1991), *Mujerfes y el Poder: una Historia de Villa el Salvador*, IEP, Lima.

Cuánto S.A. (1991), *Perú en Números*, Lima.

D'Amico, Deborah (1993), 'A Way Out of No Way: Female-Headed Households in Jamaica Reconsidered', in Joan P. Mencher and Anne Okonpiou (eds), *Where Did All the Men Go? Female-Headed/Female-Supported Households in Cross-Cultural Perspective*, Boulder, Westview Press Colorado, pp. 71-88.

Elson, Diana and Pearson, Ruth (1984), 'The Subordination of Women and the Internationalistion of Factory Production', in Kate Young, Carol Wolkowitz, and Roslyn McCullagh, *Of Marriage and the Market, Women's Subordination Internationally and its Lessons*, London and Routledge (1981), New York, pp. 18-40.

Espinal, Rosario and Grasmuck Sherri (1994), *Gender, Households and Informal Entrepreneurship in the Dominican Republic*, paper presented at the XVIII International Congress of the Latin American Studies Association, March 10-12, Atlanta.

Froehle, Mary C. (1994), *Women in the Popular Economy: New Directions for Macroeconomic Policy*, paper presented at the XVIII International Congress of the Latin American Studies Association, March 10-12, Atlanta.

Gárate, Werner and Ferrer, Rosa Anna (1994), *En Qué Trabajan las Mujeres, Compendio Estadístico 1980-1993*, ADEC-ATC, Lima.

Grandón G., Alicia (1990), *Discriminación y Sobrevivencia*, Pontíficia Universidad Católica del Perú Lima, Fundación Friedrich Naumann.

Grompone, Romeo (1986), *Talleristas y Vendedores Ambulantes en Lima*, Desco, Lima.

Heyzer, Noeleen (1981), 'Towards a Framework of Analysis', in Caroline Moser and Kate Young, *Women and the Informal Sector*, IDS Bulletin, Sussex, Vol. 12(3), July, pp. 3-30.

Hordijk, Michaela (2000), *Of Dreams and Deeds, The Role of Local Initiatives for Community Based Environmental Management in Lima, Peru*, Thela Publishers, Amsterdam.

Kabeer, Naila (1997), 'Women, Wages and Intra-households Power Relations in Urban Bangladesh', *Development and Change*, Vol. 28, pp. 261-302.

Lomnitz, Larissa A. de (1991), *Cómo Sobreviven los Marginados*, Siglo Veintiuno Editores [1975], Mexico City.

Lynn Reichmann, Rebecca (1988), 'Dos Programas de Crédito para Microempresas. Los Casos de República Dominicana y Perú', in Marguerite Berger and Mayra Buvinic (eds), La *Mujer en el Sector Informal, Trabajo Femenino y Microempresa en América Latina*, Nueva Sociedad, Caracas, ILDIS, Quito.

MacEwen Scott, Alison (1979), 'Who are the Self-employed?', in R. Bromley and C. Gerry (eds), *Casual Work and Poverty in Third World Cities*, John Wiley and Sons, London, pp. 105-29.

Menjívar Larín, Rafael and Juan Pablo Pérez Sáinz (coordinators) (1993), *Ni Héroes ni Villanas, Género e Informalidad Urbana en Centroamérica*, Flacso, San José.

Nelson, Nici (1979), 'How Women and Men get by: The Sexual Division of Labor in the Informal Sector of a Nairobi Squatter Settlement', in Bromley, C. and Gerry, G. (eds.), *Casual Work and Poverty in Third World Cities*, John Wiley and Sons, London, pp. 283-301.

Roldán, Martha (1988), 'Renegotiating the Marital Contract: Intrahousehold Patterns of Money Allocation and Women's Subordination Among Domestic Outworkers in Mexico City', in Daisy Dwyer and Judith Bruce (eds), *A Home Divided, Women and Income in the Third World*, Stanford University Press, Stanford, pp. 227-47.

Sara-Lafosse, Violeta (1989), *Comedores Comunales, la Mujer Frente a la Crisis*, Servicios Urbanos y Mujeres de Bajos Ingresos, Lima.

Villavicencio, Maritza (1989), 'Impacto de los Comedores en las Mujeres', in Nora Galer en Pilar Nuñez (eds), *Mujeres y Comedores Populares*, SEPADE, Lima, pp. 263-74.

Webb, Richard and Baca, Graciela Fernández (1994), *Perú en Números 1994*, Cuanto S.A., Lima.

Wilson, Fiona (1990), *De la Casa al Taller, Mujeres, Trabajo y Clase Social en la Industria Textil y del Vestido, Santiago Tangamandapio*, Colegio de Michoacán, Zamora.

Ypeij, Annelou (2000) *Producing against Poverty, Female and Male Micro-entrepreneurs in Lima, Peru*, Amsterdam University Press, Amsterdam.

7 Urban Fringes in Asia: Markets versus Plans

Cases from Bangalore and Hanoi

HANS SCHENK

Introduction: The Urban Fringe

The main argument of this contribution is that market-steered processes of urbanizing the fringes of major Asian cities are supplanting attempts to promote the planned growth of secondary cities and growth centers, in order to achieve what is called a more balanced regional development. Fringe developments, moreover, create a new socio-spatial urban order, in which the boundaries of central cities play an important role. Better-off urban citizens live within these boundaries in a relatively well-maintained environment, while the urban poor are increasingly found beyond the city limits, living in a much worse environment.

This is not the appropriate place to discuss in detail the concept of regional development, or that of city-hinterland balances. Nor will attention be paid to the policy attempts to arrest the growth of the large metropolitan Asian cities by diverting the stream of rural migrants to growth poles, growth centers, new towns, secondary and intermediate cities. With a few exceptions, attempts to disperse non-agricultural economic activities over a wider range of small and medium-sized urban places by planned interventions have not been very successful. Most of Asia's growth centers never grew.

Focusing on the fringe, it is difficult – and perhaps even futile – to demarcate this zone consistently. It is sometimes assumed that its inner boundaries are formed by the outer administrative limits of a municipality or otherwise named central urban place (for Bangalore: see Blore, 1989, pp. 559-560). The fringe of Delhi, however, covers the Rural Development Blocks within the territory of the Metropolitan Corporation of Delhi (Bentinck, 2000, p. 36). Within the urban districts of Hanoi Province (which actually form Hanoi City), villages still exist.

A pragmatic position will be taken here to demarcate the inner boundaries, taking into account physical appearances and socio-economic conditions (e.g. village-like settlements; preponderance of primary production) and/or administrative demarcations. The outer limits of urban fringes are primarily determined by changes that take place in the predominantly rural area surrounding a central urban place, as will be outlined below.

Fringes are indeed typified by processes of change (Ramachandran, 1991, pp. 310-17), and often they are extremely dynamic areas. Briefly speaking, five interrelated changes take place in the fringe. First, socio-economic changes occur. Subsistence agricultural production starts to be replaced by market-oriented primary production. Vegetables, flowers, poultry, etc. take the place of rice or wheat. Second, non-agricultural economic activities appear (industrial, commercial) taking the place of primary economic production. Third, physical changes in land use take place, corresponding to socio-economic changes. Residential and industrial areas, and roads impinge on rural land-uses. Fourth, an 'urban way of life' penetrates into the countryside, as Sharma (1985, pp. 71-2) puts it in a colorful way for the fringes of a town in Punjab (India): '... the villagers around Jallandhar at a distance of 15-20 miles started aping the urban standards of living which they adopted in the villages itself rather than shifting to the cities ...'.

Fifth, fringes become the target of new residents. Some of these are middle-class urban citizens who – illegally, and often contrary to land-use plans – manage to buy plots and arrange in due course the construction of a legalized house. This process has been described for Delhi as early as the 1960s (Bose, 1984, pp. 167-184), and recently by Bentinck (2000), and can be observed in Bangalore and Hanoi as well, as will be seen in Sections 2 and 3. Poor urban citizens also tend to settle in fringe areas, and in increasing numbers. Moreover, rural migrants tend to settle on the fringes of large cities, instead of in the inner city where they traditionally went. This trend will be discussed below.

We can distinguish several zones in the fringe. Ramachandran (1991, p. 304) makes a distinction between the rural fringe and the urban fringe. The urban fringe: '... has all the appearances of the city proper with residential and commercial centers, but it often lacks city services such as, in particular, piped water supply, sewerage and garbage disposal functions' while the rural fringe consists of villages partly affected by urbanization. The urban fringe therefore is characterized by 'urban' land-use and an urban appearance, but lacks basic 'urban' infrastructural facilities.

Fringes are dynamic as such; as said, they come and go. They appear at the outer limits of expanding metropolitan regions – their 'rural fringes' – and they disappear as they are overtaken by the expanding administrative and physical limits of the central cities themselves. The municipal corporations eat their fringes. However, like a phoenix, new fringes come to life and mature. Hence, fringe dynamics are twofold. Within a given fringe, processes of urbanization occur, while successive rings of fringes evolve around a growing city. However, fringe dynamics should not be seen as independent processes of change; they reflect change, growth, and other indicators of dynamics in the urban core they surround. A stagnant urban core implies a stagnant fringe, and a growing core city implies a twofold dynamic fringe.

Finally, fringes tend to develop in a relative vacuum of public control over land use and regulations such as environmental and labor legislation when they are located beyond administrative urban borders. The implementation of public controls and services has become institutionalized in an urban context, and rural local authorities are not capable of doing so. In a similar way, rural authorities are not geared to provide 'urban' services, such as those related to infrastructure (water, roads). Fringes tend to be frontier areas.

It is tempting at this juncture to compare the urban fringe with the desakota concept developed by McGee (1991). This concept has much in common with the fringe characteristics introduced above. McGee ascribes six main features to a desakota (1991, pp. 16-17): (i) The existence of a large population of mainly rice-growing smallholders; (ii) an increase in non-agricultural activities on erstwhile agricultural land; (iii) increased fluidity and mobility of residents, not only directed toward a core city but also within the region itself; (iv) an intense mixture of agricultural and non-agricultural land-use; (v) increased female participation in non-agricultural labor; and (vi) 'invisibility' from the point of view of the public authorities.

Especially the socio-economic and land-use changes, population mobility, and the lack of public controls over socio-economic and land-use changes are common characteristics of the urban fringe. However, McGee stresses characteristics of the desakota which are not necessarily comparable to the fringe realities in most Asian cities, such as a sizeable agrarian population and female non-agricultural labor participation. It may well be that the characteristics of the cradle of desakota (i.e. the region around Jakarta) has played a major role in typifying the generalized concept. Moreover, McGee does not mention some processes and characteristics that have been chosen here to characterize fringes. Notably the dynamism that characterizes an urban fringe is not reflected in the desakota concept. McGee emphasizes dynamic linkages between agricultural and non-agricultural functions (1991, p. 17), and hence suggests a sustainable equilibrium of socio-economic and land-use characteristics around major cities. This idea conflicts with the concept of fringe dynamics as outlined above, with rather continuous and one-way processes of squeezing out agriculture and all its related characteristics. Hence, fundamental dynamism stands central. The sustainability of desakota is also criticized by other authors, e.g., Hugo (1997) for Jakarta, Bentinck (2000) for Delhi, and Kelly (1999) for Manila. As Kelly (1999, p. 286) puts it:

> '... when social relations in the desakota are examined in more depth, it is the transience of the urban-rural mix rather than its persistence that emerges most emphatically. Evidence form Manila's extended metropolitan region suggests that agriculture and non-agriculture are indeed in a dynamic relationship as McGee suggests, but it is a dynamic which is leading to the "squeezing out" of agriculture.'

In the following sections, fringe developments in two Asian cities will be discussed and compared in some detail in view of the above. The first city is Bangalore (southern India), and the second is Hanoi (northern Vietnam). Naturally, these cities do not represent the full range of such developments in urban Asia, nor do they represent 'average' trends, if there are such averages. However, what can be observed for Bangalore's fringe seems rather familiar compared to observations for many major Asian cities. The choice of Hanoi is perhaps more surprising, given the socialist history of northern Vietnam since the 1950s. This history includes a rigid policy of regional development and the arrest of city-ward migration. Hence, fringe developments did not occur till the late 1980s. However, the changeover from a socialist economic system in Vietnam to a more market-oriented one – a process which started in the 1980s and is known as economic 'renovation' (*doi moi*) – has led to developments in Hanoi that seem to be somewhat similar to those in other Southeast and south Asian cities a few decades ago. In Sections 2 and 3, the cases of Bangalore and Hanoi will be presented in more detail, while in the final section the findings for these two cities will be compared and discussed.

It is hypothesized in this chapter that the processes of urban and fringe developments in Hanoi allow comparison with those in other Asian cities some two to three decades earlier (see Section 4). If this hypothesis is sufficiently valid, the Asian lessons seem good teaching material to put on the desks of Hanoi's policy makers and urban professionals.

The Fringe of Bangalore

Around the territory of the Bangalore Municipal Corporation, two 'rings' have been drawn on a map. These rings form together more or less the Bangalore fringe. In terms of land use, these rings are claimed to be under the exclusive control of the Bangalore Development Authority (BDA, a Karnataka State urban development authority); this authority has drawn a land-use plan, and develops land and legally controls spatial developments. The inner ring (the 'urban fringe') is meant for planned residential and other urban uses, while the outer ring (the 'rural fringe') has been named the 'Green Belt'. This ring should not be used for further residential development.

The BDA was founded in 1976, and it is useful to look at its impact on the fringe. During the first 15 years of its existence, the BDA managed to have 5,000 houses built in the inner ring, mainly for middle-class people, organized in building societies, whose members are professionals, clerical workers, and government civil servants. During the same 15 years, some 80,000 (Blore, 1989, p. 560) to 150,000 (Batley, 1989, p. 44; Gowda, 1987: n.p.) dwelling units – almost all of them huts – were built, illegally and contrary to the land-use plans of the BDA. In addition, shops, workshops, and industrial sheds have appeared at strategic locations, such as along arterial roads, thus also disregarding the land-use plans. Apparently, the BDA is unable to control the processes of socio-economic and spatial changes in the inner part of the Bangalore fringe. This is also the case in the outer ring. Instead of an envisaged green belt, it is estimated that some 20 per cent of the area of the outer ring was illegally 'developed' in the late 1980s (Blore 1989, p. 560).

Who lives in Bangalore's fringe? Obviously, the inhabitants of the numerous small villages scattered around the city. These villages used to be exclusively agrarian, but many have been gradually incorporated into the processes of fringe development, as happened decades ago to other villages, which are now located within the area of the Municipal Corporation. Names, a few crooked roads and paths, and here and there a village-type house are all that remain of their erstwhile rural and fringe past.

The present fringe of Bangalore (i.e., the domain of the BDA) is thus to a very limited extent inhabited by planned, middle-class residential colonies. In addition, many residents who have not been 'planned' live in it. This category can basically be divided into two subcategories. The first emerges when peasants sell land to private developers (see Schenk and Wit, 2001). Subsequently, these developers make a very modest layout of a residential colony. The modesty is expressed by their basic action; demarcation of corners of plots to be sold and, sometimes, the reservation of some land for minor roads. The focus is clearly on the sale of plots.

The sale of land is not against the law, but the change of its usage is. Moreover, the layout of the colony will more often than not be contrary to the land-use plans of the BDA, and may even obstruct its implementation. So potential buyers have to be, and are, cautious. They want to be sure that, in due course, they will be able to build a house on the plot. The implied 'security of tenure' is initially not given by the local administration, and even official threats of bulldozing any illegally built house can be made. On the other hand, housing is a scarce commodity in Bangalore, also for the better-off. So, many land- and home-hungry buyers decide to take a risk and buy a plot. However, they do not start constructing a house immediately. First they secure their plot. A caretaker is asked to live free of charge on the plot for the time being and to watch it for the owner. This serves to discourage squatters from occupying the piece of land. The owners then start – either individually or together – the slow process of getting their building plans legalized. This is a delicate and more difficult affair. The first requirement is to get political support for their wish to build a house and live on their plot, which is not intended for residential usage. The arguments used to obtain this support are obvious. The non-poor also need shelter, which is hard to get. When the political pressure is sufficient, a court case starts in which the owners demand legalization of their colony and the freedom to build a home. Legal procedures are lengthy and costly, and require both patience and money. There have been several incidents of the BDA bulldozing houses illegally erected on land illegally developed by impatient builders. Following the legal procedure may take five to seven years, a good lawyer, and a lot of money, but the end result is usually rewarding. The colony becomes legalized. The care-taking watchmen are subsequently chased away, and after a couple of months a new residential colony has been born. Some plot owners will now sell their legalized – and thus more attractive – piece of land. It is said that the price of such plots increased tenfold between the early 1980s and the early 1990s. Needless to say, further action by persistent owner-occupiers leads to the provision of all publicly provided infrastructural facilities. The BDA, finally, has to redraw its land-use plans.

This type of intrusion of the fringe of Bangalore was observed for the 1960s (Rao and Tewari, 1979, pp. 270-1), and is still ongoing. Obviously, it does not cater to the needs of the urban and rural poor. Most intrusions of the fringe, however, have been made by poor squatters. A list of all squatter settlements in the greater Bangalore area shows that of the 444 counted, 150 were located in the fringe in 1990/1991 (Ramachandran and Sastry, 2001).

An analysis of this list reveals that 35 per cent of squatter settlements in the fringe were established in the 1960s, 33 per cent in the 1970s, and 13 per cent in the 1980s. Most of such settlements are hence not very recent.

The question where the inhabitants of squatted settlements come from is relevant. Though no data are available regarding all fringe settlements, a survey of selected settlements revealed that their inhabitants increasingly come from rural areas (Schenk and Wit, 2001). Most inhabitants of some fringe settlements came from central Bangalore. Their huts had been bulldozed and they had been dropped just outside the municipal border. This is a common response of local authorities when faced with high land prices and the consequent pressure to cash in on scarce land.

Such settlements can be called 'forced' settlements. Indeed, in one such settlement, 88 per cent of the interviewed households came from the city center. Other settlements have emerged from a more spontaneous process: Squatters who have settled on 'waste land'. Seventy percent of one of these settlements was populated by settlers who arrived between 1980 and 1983. Of the settlers who arrived in 1980, the large majority came from Bangalore; however, those who arrived in 1983 were equally divided between migrants from the city and migrants from the countryside. Two swelling streams seem to populate Bangalore's fringe (apart from the few better-off who settle there); the inner-city poor, including those who have been bulldozed out, and the rural poor who had been driven away (mostly landless agricultural laborers or marginal farmers). Though both streams are growing, the latter is growing more quickly.

Life is tough in the squatter settlements in Bangalore's fringe, even though *de facto* security of tenure is often secured through the interventions of local politicians. Infrastructural facilities are rare, apart from incidental support from an NGO, and most depend on local initiatives to dig a well or illegally tap electricity. Educational and health facilities are absent. Life in a fringe squatter settlement seems to depend on a footpath to an arterial road and then onwards to a nearby factory or workshop, or to a job in the urban center. At this juncture, former inner-city squatters feel the loss of proximity to work sites, and indeed many have lost their job. Especially women who formerly worked as household servants appeared to be vulnerable in this respect (Schenk and Wit, 2001).

Yet industries move out of Bangalore as well. This peripheral move is not random. It seems to be governed by two major forces; the price of land and the degree of pollution caused by industrial activities. Hence, basically two types of industrial units have disproportionately moved out of Bangalore and settled in its fringe; major land-consuming industrial units (such as the industry related to the air-force, which is concentrated in this city) and polluting industries. The case of the former category seems obvious from all points of view, the more so since residential quarters were built to accommodate the staff of these nearby factories. The situation of polluting industries is quite different. Most industrial units in Bangalore are small or medium sized, and have many of the characteristics of 'informal' industrial employment. A sizeable proportion is engaged in polluting activities such as tanning, electroplating, etc. and has not taken sufficient control measures to prevent environmental pollution (see Kerkum, 2001 for details). Within the limits of the Bangalore Municipal Corporation, some checks on environmental pollution – based on the appropriate laws and regulations – are made, even though they are not very effective. However, outside the municipal borders, there are no controls whatsoever, and hence there is an outward movement of polluting industries. The BDA land-use plans for the fringe do not seem to be of any relevance in choosing a site. Access to arterial roads and perhaps the vicinity of a reservoir of cheap labor seem relevant factors for site selection.

Hence, the twain meet; cheap laborers meet exploiting entrepreneurs in Bangalore's fringe, where new and uncontrolled working and living conditions emerge. In the urban frontier, the laws of bosses and patrons prevail.

Hanoi's Fringe

Vietnam's policies aimed at curtailing the growth of its major cities, and promoting the growth and industrial base of provincial areas, have been rather successful in the northern part ever since the establishment of its socialist regime in 1954, which included amongst others the nationalization or collectivization of industry and trade. These policies stand in contrast to similar attempts in most south and Southeast Asian countries (Thrift and Forbes, 1986; Anderson and Sjoberg, 1996). These regional development policies were, ironically enough, also promoted by the American bombing of North Vietnam's major cities – the capital Hanoi and the major port city, Haiphong – during the 1960s and early 1970s. A sizeable part of the industrial capacity of the North was consequently dispersed from the major cities to the countryside and to minor urban centers, often together with the workers. Vu Huy Phuc (1997) states that 30 per cent of the factories and 50 per cent of the population of Hanoi was relocated to elsewhere in North Vietnam between 1965 and 1970. In the 1970s, large numbers of urban residents of and peasants from the densely populated Red River Delta were resettled in sparsely populated areas, while district headquarters with a population of say 10,000 inhabitants were to become spiders in the webs of decentralized regional development (Forbes and Thrift, 1987, pp. 119-121).

In addition, the North Vietnamese authorities introduced a barrier to rural-urban migration; the urban household registration system (*ho khau*). The corresponding card gave access to basic amenities such as housing, jobs, food, education, medical care, all provided by the state. As private alternatives to these state provisions were non-existent, the urban resident card proved to be effective against migration to the city. Hence, the growth of Hanoi's population was slow.

From the mid-1980s onwards, Vietnam's economy was 'renovated' (*Doi Moi*) and private enterprises were allowed to start business alongside the state and collective enterprises, which formerly completely controlled economic affairs. These developments led to a number of changes with regard to the spatial structure of Hanoi and its fringe.

First, the location of industrial enterprises started to change. Following the introduction of the 'renovated', more market-oriented economy, many state-sector industries found it difficult to survive. Managers of industrial units had problems in meeting new standards of profitability, market-orientation, and – perhaps more importantly – the Comecon system of international trade within the socialist world collapsed in the late 1980s. Many factories depended on 'guaranteed' deliveries to the Soviet Union or its allies, and could not easily find new markets. Relatively many of these state units were decentralized, and their fate has affected the viability of district and other towns.

On the other hand, the establishment of new industrial units financed by private capital was allowed in Vietnam. Many of these units were the results of joint ventures with foreign enterprises, originating from, e.g., South Korea, Taiwan, and – to a more limited extent – Western Europe. New industrial locations were invariably within the major cities, such as Hanoi, or in the immediate fringes of these cities. For Hanoi, this process is highly visible, e.g., in the fringe areas along the arterial road to Haiphong, where planned industrial estates and informally built workshops have sprung up. In conclusion: existing jobs in the decentralized 'state' economy seem to be in danger, while new jobs in market-oriented industries can be found in and around Hanoi.

In the second place, residents got access to land and construction materials, and started to build houses. It is estimated that in the early 1990s, some 75-80 per cent of house construction was undertaken by individual households. By far the most important reason was to improve the housing stock.

Quantitatively, in 1989 the existing average per capita dwelling space was 5.8 square meters, while 39 per cent of the population had only 4 square meters or less (Vietnam Population Census 1989, 1990). In terms of quality, most of the existing housing stock (older houses, apartments) was – and still is – in bad shape.

It is opportune here to remark that access to land formally means access to land-use rights only, since all land in Vietnam is '… the property of the people, and is subject to exclusive administration by the state' (Government of Vietnam, 1993). However, buying and selling of land-use rights is generally considered a foolproof alternative. 'Buying' land and building a house officially requires lengthy procedures at the level of one of Hanoi's seven urban districts (*quan*). However, illegal or irregular (though widely known) shortcuts are possible by paying a small fee at the lower administrative level of the ward (*phuong*).

Initially, most housing was built on available pockets of land in the city and by replacing existing dwellings. However, a gradual move to the urban outskirts is now occurring, and for a very obvious reason: the lack of available land closer to the urban core. This movement may be within the urban districts or to the adjacent rural ones. It is hard to make a distinction between these two types of districts of Hanoi Province: In the last four years, the number of urban districts has increased in two steps from four to seven, occupying tracts of formerly rural districts within the province. Relevant here are such questions as who moves to this ill-defined urban periphery, and what socio-economic changes take place there? Hence the nature of processes of 'urbanization' on the outskirts is at stake.

Most evidence points in the same direction. Hanoi's new better-off form the bulk of the urban population that seek housing in the urban fringe. Tam Pham (1997, pp. 11-12) reports on developments in a peripheral ward of Hanoi:

> 'Buoi Ward is located on the periphery of the built-up city close to the suburban district of Tu Liem. It is made up of five traditional handicraft villages which were annexed to the city as a result of the process of urbanization. Since 1990, the ward has undergone some transformation, namely rapid densification and some physical upgrading as well as development construction… After 1990, as land became scarce and increasingly more expensive elsewhere in Hanoi, the relatively inexpensive and large reserve of undeveloped land in Buoi Ward began to attract new and wealthier residents… The ward became the permanent residence of important national government institutions and agencies such as the National

Assembly, offices of the Ministry of Culture and the Army. Private and exclusive residences belonging to the Party also eventually emerged in the vicinity.'

Trinh Duy Luan and Nguyen Quang Vinh (1998) report in a similar way about developments in Vi Hau hamlet, a fringe (suburban) settlement in Dich Vong ward of Cau Giay district, west of Central Hanoi. In the early 1990s, 85 of the 105 plots sold were bought by people living in the central city, who tend to be well-off. The state-owned Housing and Development Corporation (HUD) has since its establishment in 1989 been actively involved in developing residential estates on the periphery of Hanoi's urban districts and in the adjoining suburban districts. Its first estate – at Giap Bat, on the southern perimeter of Hanoi's urban districts – is clearly upper/upper-middle class oriented, as are today's (2000) planned suburban districts, and its second project, which is under development at Lhin Dam (HUD n.d., and personal communication with its Deputy Director, December 13, 1999; see also Pandolfi, 2001).

The above-mentioned developments conform to Hanoi's Master Plan and are officially scrutinized. Other fringe developments follow more informal paths. In the same Giap Bhat area, just north of the area where HUD developed a well-planned upper-middle-class estate, farmers and fishermen informally sold part of their reclaimed plots of land to urban newcomers, ignoring Master Plan controls. Also these new settlers have a middle-class background in terms of income (Pandolfi, 2001).

Apart from changes in the composition of the population in peripheral areas in Hanoi, also socio-economic and land-use changes are taking place. The Hanoi-based Institute of Sociology studied three villages in Phu Thuong which were incorporated into an urban district of the city in 1996 (IoS, 1998; see also Leaf, 1998). In these villages, the processes of socio-economic change and corresponding changes of land use were in full swing. Traditionally, the inhabitants of the three villages grew rice as a subsistence crop as well as flowers for the Hanoi market (Ngo Vuong Anh, 1998). In 1996 these activities were an exclusive source of household income for only 15 per cent of all households, while over 60 per cent of the households draw an additional or main income from non-agricultural economic activities such as 'production', 'trade and service', and 'staff in public and private sectors', while 22 per cent of the households had become totally 'disconnected' from agricultural sources of income (IoS, 1998, p. 4). What is striking, moreover, is that in the processes of making a livelihood in fringe areas, households put their money on all available horses. The transfer from agricultural to non-agricultural sources of income is hence a gradual process at household level, during which more and more household members turn to 'urban' jobs, and in this way contribute to household incomes.

Since the Phu Thuong villages were incorporated into urban Hanoi, the inhabitants have been provided with urban services, e.g., concrete roads, drainage, and solid waste collection (Ngo Vuong Anh, 1998, p. 4). Moreover, there are plans to build a luxurious, privately financed urban complex adjacent to the villages. Also in other respects, urbanization is ongoing. Almost 50 per cent of the inhabitants have built a house during the last ten years which can characterized as a 'new type' house (as compared to the traditional 'rural type' house), and many better-off villagers have bought new electric and other appliances (IoS, 1998, p. 20). This indicates that urban lifestyles have appeared in these villages. Yet, it is observed that traditional social relations are largely maintained. According to Trinh Duy Luan (2000, p. 93): 'It would be unimaginable when Phu Thuong, adjacent to a modern metropolitan area, the very 'last' flower-growing village in Hanoi is replaced by a wildcat 'civic village', an odd brocaded robe that fails to match with its native inhabitant community.'

Recently (2000), the Institute of Sociology studied more remote villages in Hanoi's northeastern fringe. In these villages, some socio-economic changes have taken place, as has a change of lifestyle. Houses started to be built according to an urban style, and modern household equipment had made an entry into the houses, (basic tabulations and oral information from the research director, Dr. Nguyen Huu Minh).

Interpretations: Bangalore versus Hanoi

The question is how to gauge and compare the developments in the fringes of Bangalore and Hanoi. Let us look first at the fringe of Bangalore. The scattered available information shows that newcomers enter the Bangalore fringe. Some are rich, but most are poor; some come from the inner city, others come straight from the countryside, knowing that inner-city shelter is hard to find. Even though most jobs that are accessible to these poor groups are located in the inner city, more and more jobs are available in the fringe as well, as polluting and other types of industries tend to move out.

Hence, what actually happens in Bangalore – and for that matter, in many cities in India and elsewhere in Asia – is in some respects a market answer to the intentions of regional planners who focused in vain on the development of growth centers, growth poles, in order to curtail the growth of major cities. Neither work nor workers showed up at these artificial settlements blueprinted at planning offices. However, in the fringes of Bangalore, workers and work do meet – or are at least starting to meet each other – largely in an informal manner. In this way, fringes seem to be the market equivalent of planned regional development. This is a cynical statement, as fringe conditions – in terms of the local population's working and living conditions – as governed by market forces, are far removed from the ideals of a welfare state that inspired Indian leaders to engage in regional planning for many decades after Independence in 1947. It seems as though Darwin has beaten Keynes also in urban and regional development.

The fringe of Bangalore is characterized by another phenomenon. It is increasingly becoming a dumping ground for the urban poor – a dumping ground without any infrastructural provisions at all – and a refuge for polluting industries. Ironically enough, the Municipal Corporation illegally dumps its solid waste there as well (Huysman and Velu, 1994). A new environment of working and living conditions far beyond minimum standards is emerging. The central city, on the other hand, tends to become 'cleansed' of its poor and can literally afford to clean its streets. This calls for a new spatial model of the new metropolis of Bangalore, and perhaps of many other Asian cities: Similar processes can be observed in Delhi and Jakarta. A socio-economic and environmental watershed emerges, formed by the inner boundaries of the urban fringe – in the case of Bangalore, by the outer limits of the municipal corporation. Within these boundaries, relatively well-to-do citizens live in relatively comfortable environmental conditions, while the poor live on the other side of the boundary amidst 'exported' and other pollution, and otherwise with much less comfort.

At first sight it does not seem possible to compare fringe conditions in Bangalore with those in Hanoi in the 1990s. However, such a comparison would not be fair, and perhaps not even valid. Bangalore's position in the 1990s had been conditioned by half a century of development policies, without any dramatic ruptures. Hanoi's position cannot be understood without taking into account the economic 'renovation' and the introduction of a market economy in the mid-1980s. Hence, we have to enter a time capsule if we want to make a more relevant comparison.

Let us take a step back in time and give an impression of relevant characteristics of Bangalore in the period 1965-1975, using mainly the classic study of Bangalore by Rao and Tewari (1979), which was based on extensive fieldwork carried out in this city in 1973. At the time, the municipality had about a million and a half inhabitants (1971 census); 20 years later, this figure was four million. This rapid growth was partly induced by a number of large-scale 'modern sector' industrial undertakings such as Hindu Aeronautics

(HAL), which settled in the northern and eastern fringes of the city. Upper-and middle-class households followed in the factories' wake and settled in planned residential colonies.

The number of squatters in Bangalore was extremely low in the early 1970s (132,000 or 9 per cent of the urban population, as compared to 25-30 per cent in most major Indian cities), but rose to over 20 per cent in the early 1990s. A sizeable number of the squatters lived in the urban periphery, either within or beyond the municipal border. Yet, the pressure to squeeze squatters out of costly urban land hardly existed at the time, and the picture of an outward movement of the middle classes towards 'modern' residential colonies is dominant.

At this time junction, comparisons with Hanoi could be drawn. As in Bangalore in the period 1965-1975, the better-off in Hanoi moved outward from the early 1990s onwards, as has been seen above. Moreover, as in Bangalore in the past, squatters did not play a significant role in Hanoi's urban settlement pattern of the 1990s, nor in its dynamics. There are migrants from the countryside living in Hanoi, despite the still existing barriers (see Section 3). A large number of, often single, migrants live in boarding houses or on construction sites, and return home periodically (see Schenk-Sandbergen, 1997). A few others live more permanently in Hanoi, in three to four pockets where their position is 'tolerated' (Trinh Duy Luan and Nguyen Quang Vinh, 1998; Harnois, 2000). Though Trinh Duy Luan and Nguyen Quang Vinh are of the opinion that the problem posed by illegal migrants squatting is not yet a pressing one in Hanoi, they do conclude that: 'It can be forecast that the rural-urban population movements will uninterruptedly increase. The problem of illegal or irregular settlements will then be increasingly more pressing' (op. cit. p. 268).

Between 1972 and 1992, approximately 800,000 rural migrants settled in Bangalore, mostly inside the municipal border, but a growing minority in its fringe. Most of them will not have considered migrating to a secondary city or planned growth center, as knowledge about the best 'survival locations' travels far, and Bangalore holds an unbeaten position in this respect among the poor in most of southern India. It can be expected that large numbers of rural migrants from the northern Vietnamese countryside (mainly from the densely populated Red River Delta) loose their rural livelihood and are seeking to survive in Hanoi. Since *Doi Moi* and the collapse of Comecon, regional urban centers have declined in importance, and since Hanoi has gained weight in the 'new industrial economy' not many other urban choices are available.

If rural migrants flock to Hanoi in the next few decades (as expected by Trinh Duy Luan and Nguyen Quang Vinh, as well as by such other authors as Anderson and Sjoberg, 1996), as they did to Bangalore from the 1970s onwards, the question is how and where they will be accommodated in the urban society. Hanoi's administrative control mechanisms (*ho khau*) can no longer effectively prevent such streams. Where will future in-migrants (and native Hanoians) seek shelter? The obvious answer is that suburban districts (the fringe) will be the prime location for settlement, whether regular or otherwise. Locations in the urban districts of Hanoi are hard to get. This will mean that in the future, poor Vietnamese individuals and households will predominantly populate the fringe of Hanoi, while – as in Bangalore – the current trend among Hanoi's better-off to move to the outskirts will be irrelevant in terms of numbers. It also seems that even under conditions of an advantaged position of the development of planned 'counter-magnets' to northern Vietnam's major cities, the current market-driven forces are starting to converge in Hanoi's fringe.

There are, however, sizeable differences between the fringe developments in Bangalore a generation ago, and those in present-day Hanoi. It appears that local authorities in Hanoi are rather quick to transfer areas with a rural status to urban areas. This is not without its effects on the living conditions of the transferred villagers. Ngo Vuong Anh (1998, p. 4), remarks that since the villages became 'urban', they have 'received the investment funds from the city to upgrade the infrastructure of any construction,' including 3 km of concrete pathways, covered drainage, and solid waste collection. It seems that the watershed between infrastructural facilities in Hanoi is the formal designation of an administrative urban unit. In Bangalore, the better-off who settle in its fringe will be served with such facilities irrespective of administrative boundaries, while the poor in its fringes are definitely worse off in this respect. Hence, class lines (or similar distinctions used to differentiate socio-economic and political elites from the rest) seem to determine the environmental quality of urban and fringe living conditions in Bangalore.

Further, Bangalore society is highly stratified. Social, economic, cultural, and political elites can easily be identified, while traditional caste distinctions are still of importance. For all practical purposes, this means that a clear category of urban poor can be identified. This is hardly the case in Hanoi. Although there is a ruling political elite, a new and growing economic elite, and a small new category of urban poor, the 'blanket' of socialism has led to egalitarianism, both in terms of living conditions and in terms of consciousness of its inhabitants. For example, it is unimaginable that, in the near future, local authorities in Hanoi will deal with relocation issues in the way their colleagues in Bangalore do. Recent expropriations in order to construct ring roads in Hanoi have shown how strongly 'ordinary' dwellers and shopkeepers can claim their 'rights'.

Thus, there are at least two possible scenarios when it comes to predicting Hanoi's urban and fringe future. The first relies on urban Asian experiences as exemplified by Bangalore, starting a few decades ago. Hanoi would then become a regular Asian metropolis, though a retarded one. In this scenario, the urban poor and the new rural poor will increasingly meet in the urban fringe, and earn a livelihood in the industrial and subsequent servicing units that have settled there. Bangalore shows the road to this option.

A second scenario depends on a broader political perspective and political goodwill, and is based on the rapid and systematic incorporation of urbanizing fringes into formal urban areas. This has happened twice in Hanoi in the 1990s. This is not an administrative measure only. It reflects at least the concern among Hanoi's policy makers for the living conditions of urban and suburban residents alike. If this policy pertains, a 'class line' could perhaps be avoided in describing and typifying urban and suburban Hanoi. This is obviously a hopeful scenario. Apart from political will, what is also needed to bring it nearer is the development of institutions that steer fringe developments, such as low-cost-housing boards, and other institutions that help to coordinate and promote a fair quality of life in Hanoi's fringe.

References

Anderson, Henny and Sjoberg, Orjan (1996), 'Underurbanization Revisited: Closed City Policies, Rural Retention and Urban-bound Migration in Vietnam', in Lang-Hung Nora Chang, Jack F. Williams and Heather L. Bednarick (eds), *Proceedings of the Fourth Asian Urbanization Conference*, Taipeh, January 1994, East Asia Occasional Paper, No. 13, Asian Studies Center, Michigan State University, East Lansing, pp. 237-66.

Batley, Richard (ed.) (1989), *The Management of Urban Land Development in Bangalore*, Papers in the Administration of Development, No. 32, University of Liverpool.

Bentinck, Johan (2000), *Unruly Urbanization on Delhi's Fringe, Changing Patterns of Land Use and Livelihood*, Netherlands Geographic Studies, No. 270. Utrecht.

Blore, Ian (1989), 'Housing and the Working Class in an Indian Metropolis', *Public Administration and Development*, Vol. 9, pp. 557-68.

Bose, Ashish (1984), *Studies in India's Urbanization 1901-1971*, Tata McGraw-Hill, New Delhi (First revised edition).

Forbes, Dean and Thrift, Nigel (1987), 'Territorial Organization, Regional Development and the City in Vietnam', in Dean Forbes and Nigel Thrift (eds), *The Socialist Third World, Urban Development and Territorial Planning*, Basil Blackwell, London, pp. 98-128.

Government of Vietnam (1993) *Land Law*, Hanoi.

Gowda, K.S. Rame (1987), 'Fringe Area Development in Metropolitan Centers – With Special Reference to Bangalore, Bangalore Development Authority', *National Symposium on Planning and Development of Metropolitan Bangalore*, BDA, Bangalore.

Harnois, Nathalie (2000), 'A Squatter Settlement in Hanoi named Chuing Duong', in Trinh Duy Luan and Hans Schenk (eds), *Shelter and Living in Hanoi* 1, Cultural Publishing House, Hanoi, pp. 104-37.

HUD (n.d.), Housing and Urban Development Corporation Leaflet of Performances and Plans (untitled).

Hugo, G. (1997), 'Population Change and Development in Indonesia', in R.F. Watters and T.G. McGee (eds), *Asia-Pacific – New Geographies of the Pacific Rim*, Hurst and Co., London.

Huysman, Marijk and Velu, Jai S. (1994), 'Solid Waste Management by the Bangalore Municipal Corporation', in Isa Baud and Hans Schenk (eds), *Solid Waste Management, Modes, Assessments and Linkages in Bangalore*, Manohar, New Delhi, pp. 6-24.

Institute of Sociology (1998), *Report on the Results of Socio-Economic Survey in Phu Thuong Ward*, Project VIE/95/050, Hanoi.

Kelly, P.F. (1999), 'The Social Dynamics of Development in Manila's Metropolitan Region', *International Journal of Urban and Regional Research*, Vol. 23(2).

Kerkum, N. (2001) 'Industrial Pollution and Slum Dwellers in Bangalore, a First Exploration', in Hans Schenk (ed.), *Living in India's Slums, the Case of Bangalore*, Manohar, New Delhi, pp. 239-61.

Leaf, Michael (1998) *Vietnam's Urban Edge: the Administration of Urban Development in Hanoi*, Paper, 40th Annual Meeting of the Association of Collegiate Schools of Planning, Pasadena, California, November.

McGee, T.G. (1991), 'The Emergence of Desakota Regions: Expanding a Hypothesis', in N. Ginsburg, B. Koppel and T.G. McGee (eds), *The Extended Metropolis – Settlement Transition in Asia*, University of Hawaii Press, Honolulu.

Ngo Vuong Anh (1998), *The Urbanization of an Agricultural Village by its Proximity to an Urban Centre*, paper, International Conference on Vietnamese Studies and the Enhancement of International Cooperation, Hanoi, July 15-17, 1998.

Pandolfi, Laurent (2001), 'The Transformation of the Built Environment on the Urban Fringes of Hanoi: the example of Giap Bat Phuong', in Hans Schenk and Trinh Duy Luan (eds), *Housing and Land in Hanoi*, Vol. 3, series Shelter and Living in Hanoi, Cultural Publishing House, Hanoi, pp. 99-114.

Ramachandran, H. and Sastri, G.S. (2001), 'An Inventory and Typology of Slums in Bangalore', in Hans Schenk (ed.), *Living in India's Slums, the Case of Bangalore*. Manohar, New Delhi, pp. 51-64.

Ramachandran, R. (1991), *Urbanization and Urban Systems in India*, Oxford University Press, Delhi.

Rao, V.L.S. and Tewari, V.K. (1979), *The Structure of an Indian Metropolis, a Study of Bangalore*, Allied Publishers, New Delhi.

Schenk, Hans and Wit, Michael de (2001), 'Habitat in the Fringe of Bangalore', in Hans Schenk (ed.), *Living in India's Slums, the Case of Bangalore*, Manohar New Delhi, pp. 113-33.

Schenk-Sandbergen, L.Ch. (1997), *Hanoi and Migrants: Causes and Changing Rural Gender Relations*, Paper, Euroviet III Conference, Amsterdam, July.

Sharma, T.R. (1985), 'Rural-Urban Migration in India: Causes and Effects', in K.V. Reddy and K. Ram Mohan Rao (eds), *Urban Crisis in India*, Hyderabad Publishers, Hyderabad, pp. 62-73.

Tam Pham (1997), *Shelter and Environmental Improvement for the Urban Poor*, Draft of Summary Report. IDRC Project 92-1303, International Development Research Center/Hanoi Architectural University, Hanoi.

Thrift, Nigel and Forbes, Dean (1986), 'The Price of War', *Urbanization in Vietnam 1954-85*, Allen and Unwin, London.

Trinh Duy Luan (2000), 'Hanoi: Some Changes in the Contemporary Urban Life and Appearance', in Trinh Duy Luan and Hans Schenk (eds) *Shelter and Living in Hanoi 1*, Cultural Publishing House, Hanoi, pp. 85-104.

Trinh Duy Luan and Nguyen Quang Vinh (1998), *Tac Dong Kinh Te-Xa Hoi Cua Doi Moi Trong Ling Vuc Nha O Do Thi*, Nha Xuat Ban Khoa Hoc Xa Hoi, Ha Noi. Usage has been made of an unpublished translation into English.

Vietnam Population Census 1989 (1990), *Sample Results of Housing Survey*, Nha Xuat Ban Thong Ke, Hanoi.

Vu Huy Phuc (1997), *Hanoi Population During Some Major Decades (1954-1994)*, Paper, Hanoi panel, Euroviet III conference, Amsterdam, July.

PART II

Local Governance, Partnerships and Urban Development

8 Healthy Cities and Urban Governance

TON VAN NAERSSEN

Introduction

Health concerns the general physical and mental well-being of individuals. It includes more than the absence of diseases and requires a proactive attitude that implies the shaping of a physical as well as socio-economic environment conducive to a good quality of life. Health promotion and addressing the underlying causes of ill-health are important, as expressed in the saying 'Prevention is better than cure.' Nevertheless, the mainstream in health sciences concerns medical interventions and, traditionally, more attention and finance are spent on health care facilities than on improving health through the promotion of a healthy environment.

The health of people is determined by four sets of factors. The influential Lalonde Report (1974) uses the concept of 'health field' composed of the four domains of biology (including genetic factors), medical services, lifestyle, and environment (Davies and Kelly, 1993, pp. 128-29). Environment consists of a number of dimensions. It goes without saying that a bad physical environment – for example, dilapidated houses or a lack of sanitary facilities – affects health. However, the role of environmental factors in the economic, social, cultural, and political realms is often overlooked or underestimated. Nevertheless, few would be surprised to hear that different political parties have different views on health matters, that rich or middle-class people have a greater range of possibilities for leading a healthy lifestyle compared to poor people, and that some religions stress the importance of hygiene and purity more than others.

Since specific environments are often territorially bounded, the impact of the environment on health is clearly a field for human geographers. By analyzing environments at several levels of scale and the way they affect human beings, geography can contribute to better health-promoting conditions. The traditional approach of geographers to health has been different, as shown by its definition as 'medical geography' and the many books, articles, and congresses dealing with the spatial distribution of diseases and health facilities. However, the Medical Geography Commission of the International Geographical Union (IGU) changed its name already in 1976, and later again to its present Commission on Health and Environment. Medical geography is evolving into a 'geography of health', and is becoming more and more concerned with broader issues around health, and with the space and place aspects of the relations between societies and health (Verhasselt, 1993, 1997). As for developing countries, Phillips and Verhasselt's *Health and Development* (1994) is an example of a book that comprises contributions focusing on the traditional theme of health care as well as on broader themes, such as the impact of economic crisis on health, the cultural factors affecting the transmission of HIV/AIDS, and the global pharmaceutical industry.

In this chapter, I will deal with the Healthy Cities (HC) movement in developing countries as an initiative to improve urban environments for the benefit of the health of their inhabitants. Major questions to be addressed are the concept of HC, the spread of the idea to cities in the South, actors that participate in the process, and the experiences with the implementation regarding inter-sectoral approaches and community involvement. This contribution is mainly based on my experiences as member of a team of consultants to the WHO's Healthy Cities project in the period 1995-1999.

What are Healthy Cities?

For a good understanding of HC, we have to go back to the Health for All conference held in Alma Ata in 1978 under the auspices of the WHO. At this conference, a major health movement was launched (*Health for All*) and six principles for the implementation of public health were formulated, and still stand today. These principles are (1) reduced inequalities in health; (2) emphasis on prevention of diseases; (3) inter-sectoral cooperation (including reduction of environmental risks); (4) community participation; (5) emphasis on primary health care; and (6) international cooperation. The first principle meant that the conference participants were well aware of the existence of a great inequality in health, caused to a substantial extent by disparities in incomes and access to economic and social provisions. The fourth principle is important, since it acknowledges that communities need to have a say in improving their health conditions.

The principle of community participation in particular received attention at the First International Conference on Promotion of Health in Ottawa in 1986. The discussions on the promotion of health included more than the role of the mass media, the distribution of pamphlets, and the need to focus on 'target groups' of unmarried mothers, deprived children, the homeless and so on; they also stressed the importance of involving the social groups to be reached. In this conference's declaration, health promotion is defined as 'the process of enabling people to increase control over, and to improve their health'. It also states: 'Health promotion works through effective community action in setting priorities, making decisions, planning strategies and implementing them to achieve better health, at the heart of this process is the empowerment of communities, and the ownership and control of their own endeavors and destiny' (Davies and Kelly, 1993, pp. 14 and 56).

The HC movement started in the wake of the Ottawa Conference when the European office of the WHO proposed a health promotion program in cities, in particular targeting deprived urban neighborhoods (Ashton, 1992). HC acknowledges the close interrelationship between urban health and urban environment. Its projects attach great value to participatory interventions at the community (neighborhood) level. Since HC is a movement, and its idea spread more or less spontaneously by networking among cities, certain flexibility will be found in what a HC comprises. The aims of a Healthy City Program (HCP) are ' ...to improve environment and health conditions by raising awareness, and by mobilizing community participation through partnerships with local (municipal) agencies and institutions, thereby helping them to deliver effective environmental and health services. A priority objective is to develop the role of local governments in public health and to encourage them to implement a Health for All policy at city level (WHO, 1995, p. 7). In this citation the improvement of services and local government involvement get special attention. Werna *et al.* also emphasize the role of local government when they refer to HC as '...a development activity that seeks to put health on the agenda of decision makers in cities, to build a strong lobby for public health at the local level, and to develop a local participatory approach to dealing with health and environmental problems ...' (1999, p. 28).

However, if one perceives HC as a movement to support the WHO Health for All strategy in urban areas, the ultimate aim is to achieve greater equity in health. And, since HC is intended to build upon the Ottawa conference, it should be stressed that community involvement is not merely an instrument to achieve the health objectives of a local government, but also to lead to community empowerment. The other features of HC, such as health promotion and inter-sectoral cooperation, are meant to serve this aim (Naerssen and Barten, 1999).

There are, of course, many programs and projects all over the world which, departing from the principle of governance, involve local governments in inter-sectoral management and community participation. The HC approach is specific in the sense that it is directed to members of the health sector, with the message that the improvement of health is a part of larger efforts to improve the quality of life and citizenship. As I will argue, in the case of the UNDP/WHO Healthy Cities program 1995-1999, precisely these ideas of community involvement and the integration of health policies in urban development planning were strongly contended in practice.

First Initiatives in the South

At the City Summit in Istanbul, HC was presented as a best practice in urban management. Although most of the roughly 1,000 cities which form the HC movement were situated in the North, the movement and its networks had also spread to cities in Africa, Asia, Latin America, and the Caribbean. The introduction of the HC idea fell on fertile soil because of its correspondence with current concepts concerning the management of large cities in the South. Given the shortage of financial and technical resources, another reason concerned the opportunities provided by programs directly related to the WHO or arising from links with cities in the North. Involvement from the outside world proved to be important to start HC initiatives in the South.

In 1991, during the 44th World Health Assembly in Geneva, discussions were held on problems accompanying the world's rapid urbanization. It was within this framework that the WHO raised interest among representatives of countries in the South for the HC project. The WHO wanted to select a number of cities to disseminate the program to developing countries. The cities of Accra and Johannesburg were among the first to initiate HC programs, both with a very active role of local governments (see Blankers, 1995 and Mathee *et al.*, forthcoming).

Akerman (forthcoming) distinguishes two phases in the development of the HC movement in Brazil. The first phase began in 1991 with an agreement on technical cooperation between the twin cities of São Paulo and Toronto. Experts from Canada attended seminars in Brazil to explain the concept and strategies of HC to representatives of Brazilian cities. There were exchange programs between the two countries, and experiences with the programs were followed up. In the second phase, which started in 1994, the contacts with Canada and the Pan-American Health Organization (PAHO) were intensified. Especially a group of consultants from the PAHO was responsible for assisting new initiatives. A Brazilian HC movement came into existence, comprising ten cities with HC ideas on their agendas.

In the cases of Accra, Johannesburg, and São Paulo, local governments were actively involved in initiating an HC program. The role of outside donors was more outspoken in the UNDP/WHO Healthy Cities program 1995-1999. The program was realized in five urban areas: Fayoum (Egypt), Cox Bazar (Bangladesh), Quetta (Pakistan), Dar es Salaam (Tanzania), and Managua (Nicaragua). They differ widely in population size, level of welfare, and socio-political system, which makes it the more interesting to compare their experiences with the program. The starting signal for the program was given in September 1993 in Geneva with a meeting of the representatives of the Environmental Division of the WHO, the UNDP-LIFE (Local Initiative Facility for Urban Environment) program, the international NGO network HEC (Health and Environment in the Cities), and the Dutch Directorate-General of International Cooperation (DGIS). HC was brought under the umbrella of the LIFE program, which is meant to support small-scale projects and programs aimed at improving the urban environment. As a matter of principle, each LIFE project should be the result of the input of the government, private business groups, and NGOs/CBOs. Outside funding is rather limited, since the projects should, as far as possible, be based on local resources (UNDP, 1997).

The WHO Guidelines

Right from the beginning in 1986, WHO has promoted and supported the creation of HC networks all over the world. Based mainly on experiences in Western countries, a booklet was published containing a strategy of stepwise institutional development in three phases.

- Phase 1: The establishment of a Local Task Force, defined as 'a nucleus of several key individuals in the city who have leadership capabilities, the desire to improve the health conditions in the city and the ability to stimulate the participation of key actors such as NGOs, community groups, municipal agencies, university and training institutions' (WHO, 1995, p. 14).
- Phase 2: The establishment of a Partnership Task Force to replace the Local Task Force. The Partnership includes all stakeholders in the HC program, and the appointment of an HC coordinator with the objective of

formulating a Municipal Health Plan (MHP). This is basically a plan of action and a tool to promote discussion and raise awareness.
- Phase 3: Implementation of the MHP.

The project document estimates the duration of the first two phases to be six months each, and the implementation of the MHP two years.

The MHP is usually considered the major tool of the programs. It contains local health information, analysis of health, policy, advocacy, and small-scale projects. Another specific tool is the so-called settings approach. It means that HC projects will preferably be implemented in territorially defined areas such as urban districts, neighborhoods, industrial estates, and schools. At conferences and meetings on health promotion, the WHO has emphasized the settings approach. It encourages actions to improve the environment in places where people live and work in order to establish 'supportive environments'. Moreover, an advantage of the settings approach is that it facilitates inter-sectoral cooperation and actions in clearly defined areas.

In the case of the Accra HC project, the program covered the whole of the metropolitan area but, as Blankers remarks, '... it is more or less a compilation of existing plans of related and involved departments and agencies' (1995, p. 28). In the Johannesburg HC Project, the potential areas indicated for intervention were high-density and low-income areas, schools, and market places (Mathee et al., forthcoming). In the project document of the UNDP/WHO program, three settings are mentioned specifically; schools, small-scale industry workplaces, and markets. Usually it is at this level that projects are implemented, since the low-income areas of cities in developing countries are too large to be conceived as an area for an HC project.

Around 1995, WHO had already obtained wide experience with Healthy Schools and Healthy Market Places programs. A Healthy School project might comprise health education, improvement of school environment (water facilities, toilets, school playgrounds, and classrooms), parental and school children participation, and school medical service emphasizing prevention. In the case of the Healthy Market Place, a project could comprise the establishment of good and sufficient storage facilities, solid waste management, and provision of public toilets. A Healthy and Safe Workplace project might include traditional occupational health services, solid waste facilities, education and training, and worker representation in industry management.

By supporting the HC movement, the WHO thus promoted ideas about the setting up and implementation of hc, and about tools that apparently could be used all over the world. It paid less attention to the specificity of local and national contexts. In other words, it did not sufficiently take into account the political, cultural, and economic constraints on developing HC in the South (see Werna *et al.*, 1998 and WHO, 2000). In the following sections, I will focus in particular on issues regarding the inter-sectoral work and community involvement of HC in the South. Two cities of the UNDP/WHO Healthy Cities project – Dar es Salaam and Managua – will serve as case studies.

The Case of Dar es Salaam

Dar es Salaam is the commercial, industrial, and administrative capital of Tanzania. Its population is estimated at about 3 million. It is increasing at an annual rate of 7 per cent; of this increase, 40 per cent is the result of immigration. There is a huge unemployment problem due to the economic weakness of Tanzania, the effects of structural adjustment programs (SAPs), and the accompanying ideology of liberalization and privatization. At the socio-political level, the country is undergoing transformation from a one-party to a multi-party system.

SAPs started in 1981 after strong international pressure. The share of the health sector in the national budget decreased from 7.2 per cent in 1977/78 to 4.6 per cent in 1989/90, and the health expenditures per capita between 1980 and 1986 decreased by more than a third. The health reform program introduced during the second half of the 1990s, is aimed at the decentralization and privatization of health services. The low wages paid to health workers and doctors has led to demotivated health professionals in public service, a drain of professionals towards the private health sector, and a diminished quality and increased costs of the health services. Health services, both public and private, are now too expensive for most of the population (Lugalla, 1995).

As for the urban physical environment, the following key figures speak for themselves:

- Only 40 per cent of the urban population has access to piped water supply;
- Only 5 per cent of households are connected to a sewer;
- At the end of 1997, there were only 4 to 15 trucks per day available for refuse collection.

Naturally, these conditions, the rampant poverty, and the bad health of the inhabitants of the Dar es Salaam shaped the setting wherein the UNDP/WHO Healthy Cities program was introduced. Following the guidelines of the

WHO, various institutionally organized stakeholders were brought together to discuss the possibilities for the creation of a Local Task Force. As such, the potential to involve a diversity of stakeholders and to compose a many-sided Task Force proved to exist (Naerssen, 1995, 1996). This can be demonstrated by a list of major stakeholders.

- The health sector was represented by the Dar es Salaam City Commission Medical Office of Health; the Tanzanian-Swiss Dar es Salaam Urban Health Project (DUHP); the Malaria Control Project; the Ministry of Health, including the Directorates of Prevention and Health Planning; the Muhimbili University Medical Faculty; and various health NGOs.
- The physical planning sector consisted of the Ministry of Land, Housing and Urban Development; the innovative World Bank/UNDP/UNCHS Sustainable Dar es Salaam Project (SDP); the Urban Sector Engineering Project (USEP, a World Bank endeavor); and the Hanna Nassif Squatter Area Project (an ILO/SDP funded project).
- Other sectors involved the Dar es Salaam UNDP-LIFE program; the Tanzanian Association of Non-Governmental Organizations (TANGO); international NGOs, such as Plan International; and the private sector, including the Rotary Club and the Lions Club.

The two weak stakeholders were the Dar es Salaam local government and the community-based organizations (CBOs) sector. In the beginning of the 1990s, the Dar es Salaam City Council (the local government of Dar es Salaam) was in disorder and notorious for its corruption. It was replaced in June 1996 by a Dar es Salaam City Commission directly under the Prime Minister's Office. The existing NGOs were mainly associations for disabled people, and charity clubs such as the Rotary Club and the Lions Club. In 1994 a directory of TANGO mentions, among others, 42 environmental NGOs, 36 women's NGOs, and 22 health NGOs in Tanzania. At the neighborhood level, the community-organizing system inherited from the days of the one-party system was still in existence, which facilitated communication at the lower levels. There were also many informal 'invisible' initiatives at the local level (Cranenburg and Sasse, 1995, p. 27). However, there were only a few CBOs that functioned as independent organizations and could raise their voice. In short, the civil society in Dar es Salaam was in its build-up phase, although progress had been made.

On the other hand, integrative approaches and inter-sectoral cooperation were well known in the field of urban environment and health. In this respect, mention should be made of the Dar es Salaam Urban Health Project

(DUHG) and the Sustainable Dar es Salaam Program (SDP). DUHG's original aim was to rehabilitate the health facilities in Dar es Salaam, but in due course the project moved from the improvement of health care services towards a more preventive and community-based approach to urban health. As such, DUHP had a lot of experience and a wealth of information useful for improving urban health. Even more important was the SDP. It offered an institutional framework to approach urban environmental priority areas, such as solid waste, coast protection, and squatter settlements. In 1995-1996, there were 30 working groups, involving more than 100 people from 12 departments of Dar es Salaam, national governmental ministries, training institutions, civil society organizations, and international agencies.

Nearly all the SDP priority areas were relevant and open to an HC settings approach, which suggested that the implementation of HC should take place in close cooperation with the urban management project. Nevertheless, the setting-up of a Local Task Force to coordinate the program at the metropolitan level, proved to be difficult. One of the reasons was the uncertainty about the future of the local government authority. Another reason was the claim laid on the program by the WHO country office. Because there was no inter-sector Local Task Force, the coordinator of HC was appointed by the WHO country office and installed on WHO premises.

After 1997, SDP lost much of its appeal. It received less international financial support and became part of the municipal bureaucracy. The question of inter-sectoral cooperation was still on the agenda, but the potential allies were not able to reconcile their different interests, and thus could not establish inter-sectoral cooperation in order to plan a Dar es Salaam HC project. The WHO country office simply wanted to pull the strings. Consequently, integrating the MHP into an all-encompassing environmental plan for Dar es Salaam proved to be impossible.

Once the new municipal government was settled, the WHO succeeded in establishing good working relationships. A 'Consultative Workshop to Formulate a City Health Plan under the Dar es Salaam HC Project' was held in Dar es Salaam in September 1997. The workshop was organized by the Dar es Salaam City Commission in collaboration with WHO and the Ministry of Health. It received high-level support from the Prime Minister's Office, and members of the Dar es Salaam City Commission took an active part in the discussions. During the three-day workshop, around 60 participants discussed the presentations, and action plans were devised in eight working groups. In this way, the basis was laid for a Municipal Health Plan. At the project level, four settings for intervention were selected: food markets, schools, small industrial areas, and unplanned settlements.

However, there were only a few representatives of the private business sector and NGOs/CBOs at the workshop. Apparently, the WHO country office valued formal cooperation with the local and national governmental agencies much higher than inter-sectoral cooperation or community involvement. Neither the WHO nor the governmental institutions had a clear overview of health-related NGOs and community-based initiatives on which environmental health projects could be built. It is also striking that the question of equity in health was not put on the agenda, and that no use was made of a recent study of the socio-economic, environmental, and health differences between the three districts of Dar es Salaam.

For these reasons, the impact of HC in Dar es Salaam was limited to conservative – pre-Ottawa – ways of health promotion and a demonstration Healthy Market project. We are well informed of this project by, among others, a study by Dik (1999) on the sanitation requirements of the market vendors concerned. The Buguruni market is one of the many markets of Dar es Salaam, where mainly food – both prepared and non-prepared – is sold. Buguruni is a legal market and every vendor has to pay a fee. More than half of the 500 market vendors are members of the Wauza Mazao Buguruni Cooperative (WAMBUCO; Vendors Association Buguruni Market), which was established as a response to post-1989 police harassment (Dik, 1999, p. 38).

The presence of a CBO – which made the market in fact not a representative one in Dar es Salaam – was one of the reasons a WHO mission selected Buguruni as a demonstration project. Another reason was the ongoing activities of two international donors. The JICA (Japan International Cooperation Agency) had built a solid waste refuse bay, and Plan International (pi) was in the process of constructing a block of flush toilets. The WHO joined pi in building the toilets and, in connection with that, improved the water supply in a joint project with the City Commission. Later, a food safety course was given to vendors to promote hygienic behavior and sanitation improvements through participatory techniques.

From the point of view of preventive activities alone, the HC program in Dar es Salaam can be judged as positive. From the point of view of the HC philosophy, however, the two crucial components – inter-sectoral cooperation and participation – were far from optimal. The Healthy Market Task Force of 15 members (all from the health sector) did not function well, and the selection of the market as well as the interventions were matters decided by the WHO. The market vendors seemed to be content, but their major concern was not waste collection or drainage improvement, but roofs to shelter customers and thus increase sales (Dik, 1999).

One doubts whether the market vendors of Buruguni obtained the feeling of ownership of the project. As such, this is rather characteristic of the HC initiative in Dar es Salaam. It used a top-down approach, organized and appropriated by the health sector. Thus it is not surprising that at the end of the program period, HC was still very much considered as 'one of the international projects of WHO'. It had not really been rooted as a municipal health approach, sustainability had not been achieved, and HC came to standstill as soon as the WHO country office stopped receiving financial support from abroad.

The Case of Managua

The HC experience in Managu (the capital of Nicaragua) differed substantially from that in Dar es Salaam. There was much active involvement of civil society, which is explained by the specific history of Nicaragua where the population was extensively mobilized by the Sandinista government in the period 1979-1990. The current government embraces the principles of neoliberalism, but the Frente Sandinistas (the opposition party) is still strong and the idea of people's participation has many adherents.

The current population of Managua is estimated at around 900,000. Due to two decades of war and instability, there has been massive urban growth accompanied by rapid growth of the urban population (from 400,000 in 1980). This is putting pressure on the provision of the most urgent services, and has contributed to the degradation of the quality of life and environment in the city. Moreover, more than half of Managua's population is unemployed or underemployed and can only survive by performing activities in the informal sector. Less than 20 per cent of the population has access to sufficient and potable water, and only 4 per cent of houses are connected to the sewage system. Only 60 per cent of the daily production of solid waste is collected, which contributes to spontaneous waste dumping throughout the city.

Through reports from Francoise Barten – the Dutch advisor to Nicaraguan civil society groups – (1995; 1996; Naerssen and Barten, forthcoming), we are well informed about the HC process in Managua. The first phase started with a workshop in July 1995. Twenty representatives of the municipal government, government agencies, NGOs, CBOs, and academic institutions attended the workshop. From the very beginning, the intention was to build the program on local experiences and ongoing activities in urban health development. Thus the relevance of the HC program was discussed in the light of existing structures and processes. Also the role of international agencies in a local HC process was discussed, and participants stressed the need to define a national counterpart as soon as possible. The question of the ownership of the HC project was made explicit in the first workshop.

The second HC workshop was held in April 1997, two months after the installment of the new local (municipal) government. Again, representatives of the local government, academic institutions, health NGOs, and CBOs met each other. During this workshop, the Initiativa Managua Municipio Saludable (IMMS; Healthy Managua Municipality Initiative) was established based on the consensus of the participating institutions and organizations. The IMMS was conceived as a local initiative with support from the LIFE/WHO Healthy Cities program. In addition to the original HC project objectives, the IMMS identified the need to both strengthen existing local (institutional and social) resources, and to obtain the support of the central government and the international donor community. At the workshop, an IMMS Assembly was constituted, comprising members of civil society and representatives of 26 organizations in the public sector.

In August 1997 an action plan was developed with the three project phases (start up, organization, implementation) as distinguished by the WHO. In accordance with the WHO guidelines, the IMMS Assembly also established a Local Task Force. The Task Force was composed by representatives of the two main community-based organizations, the local government, the Ministry of Health, five health and environmental NGOs, and three representatives from academic institutions.

The role of the local government within HC was a sensitive issue. WHO and the Pan American Health Organization (PAHO) were in favor of the HC being led by the mayor, as representative of the local government. However, various organizations rejected the proposal. The reason was that the municipality of Managua applied political criteria when deciding whether to support a spontaneous settlement. If the community organization of a spontaneous settlement did not represent the interest of the government, municipal civil services boycotted people's initiatives to address social issues such as health and education. On the other hand, some neighborhoods did not allow the municipal government to enter their area. In order to avoid polarization and party ownership of the initiative, it was decided that IMMS would not have a particular leader. Also, since it was unacceptable to some participants to have a project officer installed on the premises of the municipal government, the monthly meetings were organized on a rotational basis in the offices of each of the member organizations. According to Barten, the meetings resulted in the main actors in HC Managua – or as it is called 'Healthy Municipality Managua' – becoming more tolerant of each other. Given the context of political polarization, this might be considered the major intermediate outcome of the project.

The mayor and the president gave IMMS public recognition through an official declaration. In 1998, activities resulted in two sectoral studies, viz. a proposal for a methodology to develop a municipal health plan (MHP), and identification of 14 micro-projects at community level. The MHP was formulated during two workshops by way of a participatory process based on consensus among the actors on main strategies and activities in two workshops. The output of the first workshop was a consensus on a vision of a 'Healthy Managua', and of the second workshop the identification of strategies and activities. However, whether the MHP will be put into practice remains to be seen. There are some doubts because apparently the local government did not adopt the plan and the lack of funding impeded the development of concrete projects. The emphasis was on institution building, and less effort was put into urban health development and promoting health agendas related to planning, poverty, and empowerment (Barten and McSweeny, 1988). IMMS succeeded in creating a space for dialogue and participation, which enabled an incipient inter-institutional coordination and a consensus among the main stakeholders on how to approach health in Managua.

Several educational activities were conducted in order to stress the relevance of hc. Consequently, some NGOs have adopted the settings approach as a main strategy. For example, CISAS – one of the main health NGOs in Nicaragua, which chairs the coordination commission of NGOs created after the destruction caused by Hurricane Mitch in 1998 – decided to adopt the construction of *comunidades saludables* (healthy communities) as main strategy. Also POPOLNA – which runs a maternal and child health center at the main market place in Managua, providing health care to approximately 21,000 women – decided to reorient health care towards the promotion of health and prevention of diseases.

The case of Managua is interesting, since it provides an example where HC was further developed based on earlier experiences. It was the specific political and historical context that proved to be a significant challenge in bringing the major actors together, and it demanded significant efforts to build a representative local team. The question of ownership was on the agenda right from the start, and the active involvement of civil society actors was encouraged from the beginning. This has probably made the HC project in Managua unique as a case of bottom-up HC building.

Other Cases

The overview in the final report of WHO called *Healthy Cities in Action* (2000) shows that the experiences in the other cities were also diverse (WHO, 2000). In Quetta, the program came to a standstill after changes in the national and local government, and the project coordinator left office. In Fayoum, experiences were more positive but the process suffered from a lack of NGO and CBO involvement.

In Brazil, only a very small number of cities advanced through phases 2 and 3. Difficulties already started during phase 1, since inter-sectoral cooperation proved difficult to establish in nearly all HC projects. Although city planning should have a central position in HC initiatives – as we have discussed in the case of Dar es Salaam – health institutions often considered themselves the prime movers of hc. In this respect, Akerman (forthcoming) remarks that inter-sectoral cooperation as well as participation of civil society actors changes the power relations in the municipal organization and between the state and the population. He also remarks that programs such as HC can give power and status to the initiators, that is to say, to the health sector.

This raises a fundamental question. Once we accept the idea that an MHP should be part of a broader municipal physical and environmental plan, why should it be necessary to have a separate HC program? Mathee *et al.* (forthcoming) show how, after the introduction of the HC initiative in Johannesburg, it became part of the development of an integrated approach to environmental management, development, and health. What happened was that the principles and approaches of HC were integrated with various other initiatives, such as Agenda 21 and the Model Communities Program (MCP) of the International Council for Local Environmental Initiatives (ICLEI). Thus 1995 saw the formation of an inter-departmental environmental management committee to coordinate the Agenda 21/HC Program in Johannesburg, and integrate it into the broader environmental management structure of the Council.

As a result, a new metropolitan committee of Planning, Urbanization and Environmental Management was formed, to facilitate a more holistic and integrated approach to urban planning and the environment. The committee had to ensure that the principles and approaches of HC and of Agenda 21 would be fully integrated into broader urban development plans and incorporated into the overall urban management process. Mathee *et al.* (forthcoming) rightly suggest that we should not regret the short life HC had in Johannesburg, since the idea of HC has been adopted at the municipal level and health is considered an integral part of the planning of the city. However, it must be admitted that the political circumstances in Johannesburg were favorable for such a process. After the end of apartheid, the city started with a clean slate and had fewer vested interests to deal with.

Lessons Learnt

In their overview of HC programs in developing countries, Werna et al. (1999) pay much attention to the scarcity of financial and other resources compared to cities in the North. Therefore, they argue, the local stakeholders are less able to assimilate the project. However, the foregoing sections show that the problems HC programs have to cope with are a matter not only of few resources but, at the institutional level, also of power relations between the stakeholders.

Nowadays, two streams of thinking on HC can be distinguished. The first focuses on cooperation between local government and the health sector regarding health promotion and the improvement of the urban environment. In this view, inter-sectoral cooperation and community involvement are lower ranked priorities (Burton, 1999; Werna et al., 1999). The second stream focuses on the urban poor and attaches much value to the participation of civil society actors and the related question of ownership of the programs. The involvement of communities in problem identification, priority setting, resources allocation, and the implementation and evaluation of activities is considered a cornerstone of the HC philosophy. This view is supported by Akerman (forthcoming), Montiel and Barten (1999) and Naerssen and Barten (1999) who, among others, build on the earlier ideals of Alma Ata and Ottawa.

This is not to say that participatory approaches do not fit into the first stream of thinking. However, they are used as a tool that can facilitate program implementation and by way of this they will give the poorer sections of the urban population more access to health. One of the reasons is that the new urban management style and HC have been introduced in developing countries during a period following the implementation of SAP programs. It implies that HC had to fit into the framework of health reforms, cuts in the health budget, and cost-efficient health interventions. Thus the notion of participation became accepted as a way to consult the 'target groups' among the urban poor in order to achieve greater efficiency. In other words, their involvement in the implementation and maintenance of projects was primarily a means to an end.

Real participation, however, concerns the empowerment of deprived social groups, and requires political processes to get people involved and to improve their capacity to gain access to decision-making structures. These are preconditions for starting participatory processes at the community level. It would be politically naive to expect that this concept of participation can directly be implemented in all cities. The national, regional, and local policy contexts of cities are widely different and it would be foolish to expect the same kind of participation in Dar es Salaam, Fayoum, or Managua. But one should at least work towards empowering the poor and supporting emancipatory processes that improve their health. One of the basic constraints on real participation is that it presupposes a strong civil society with a diversity of independent NGOs and CBOs. However, where such a civil society is lacking, it could well be that HC programs should aim at supporting the creation and the strengthening of new health NGOs and community organizations.

There are different interpretations of what represents success in an HC program. The starting point for HC is the principle of health as a basic and fundamental right. I agree with those who argue that, for this reason, a major criterion for success concerns the capability of communities to meet its own health prevention needs or to solve their own health problems. Even in a setting with a desperate scarcity of financial resources and technical skills, one can work towards this – perhaps Utopian – situation. In the end, only participatory processes from the bottom up can realize sustainable health plans and healthy urban settings. Working at the institutional level is important and, for health geographers, a challenging field for research and applied geography, too.

Acknowledgements

The author would like to thank Francoise Barten of the Nijmegen Institute for International Health for her useful comments. The usual disclaimers apply.

References

Akerman, M. (forthcoming), 'Healthy Cities in Brazil', in T. van Naerssen and F. Barten (eds), *Healthy Cities in the South*, Saarbruecken: Verlag für Entwicklungspolitik. Nijmegen Studies in Development and Cultural Change.
Ashton, J. (ed.) (1992), *Healthy Cities*, Milton Keynes, Open University.

Barten, F. (1995), *Start-up phase of the Healthy Cities project in Managua-Nicaragua. Preliminary Consultancy 2-14 July 1995*, HEC secretariat University of Nijmegen, Report submitted to WHO, Geneva.

Barten, F. (1996), *Healthy City project Managua – Nicaragua. Report on behalf of WHO Healthy Cities Project Managua, April-May 1996*, HEC secretariat University of Nijmegen, Report submitted to WHO, Geneva.

Barten, F. and McSweeny, C. (1998), *Initiativa Managua Municipio Saludable. Report on behalf of UNDP-LIFE-PAHO/WHO Healthy Cities program*, August 31-September 5 1998.

Blankers, A. (1995), *Healthy Cities in the South. An Implementation Analysis of the Accra Healthy Cities Project*, University of Limburg, Maastricht, Research for Healthy Cities monograph series, No. 7.

Burton, Selma (1999), 'Evaluation of Healthy City Projects: Stakeholder Analysis of two Projects in Bangladesh', *Environment and Urbanization*, Vol. 11(1), pp. 41-52.

Cranenburg, O. van and Sasse, R. (1995), *Tanzania. NGO Country Profile 1995*, Oegstgeest: GOM (Gemeenschappelijk Overleg Medefinanciering).

Davies, J.K. and Kelly, M.P. (1993), *Healthy Cities. Research and Practice*, Routledge, London.

Dik, F. (1999), *Need for Sanitation? A Study on Desired Sanitation Facilities at a Food Market in Dar es Salaam*, Masters thesis, Groningen, University of Groningen, Faculty Spatial Sciences.

Lugalla, J.L.P. (1995), 'The Impact of Structural Adjustment Policies on Women's and Children's Health in Tanzania', *Review of African Political Economy*, No. 63, pp. 43-5.

Mathee, A., Schirnding, Y. von and Pick, W. (forthcoming), 'Johannesburg: an African Healthy City', in T. van Naerssen and F. Barten (eds), *Healthy Cities in the South*, Verlag fuer Entwicklungspolitik, Saarbruecken, Nijmegen Studies in Development and Cultural Change.

Montiel, R. and Barten, F. (1999), 'Urban Governance and Health Development in Leon, Nicaragua', *Environment and Urbanization*, Vol. 11(1), pp. 11-26.

Naerssen, T. van (1995), *Report of a Visit to Dar es Salaam April 4-20*, Report submitted to WHO Geneva.

Naerssen, T. van (1996), *Report of the Second Visit on Behalf of WHO Healthy City Project to Dar es Salaam, February 13 – March 3, 1996*, Report submitted to WHO Geneva.

Naerssen, T. van and Barten, F. (1999), 'Healthy Cities in Developing Countries: a Program of Multilateral Assistance', in D. Simon and A. Närman (eds), *Development as Theory and Practice. Current Perspectives on Development and Development Cooperation*, Addison Wesley Longman, Harlow, pp. 230-46.

Naerssen, T. van and Barten, F. (forthcoming), 'Healthy Cities in Developing Countries', in T. van Naerssen and F. Barten (eds), *Healthy Cities in the South*, Verlag fuer Entwicklungspolitik, Saarbruecken, Nijmegen Studies in Development and Cultural Change.

Phillips, D.R. and Y. Verhasselt (eds) (1994), *Health and Development*, Routledge, London.

United Nations Development Program (UNDP) (1997), *Reconceptualising Governance*, Discussion paper, No. 2, Management Development and Governance Division, Bureau for Policy and Program Support, New York.

Verhasselt, Y. (1993), 'Geography of Health: Some Trends and Perspectives', *Social Science Medicine*, Vol. 36(2), pp. 119-23.

Verhasselt, Y. (1997), 'Geography of Health in Developing Countries', in T. van Naerssen et al. (eds), *The Diversity of Development. Essays in Honour of Jan Kleinpenning*, Van Gorcum, Assen, pp. 241-46.

Werna, E., Ilona Blue and Harpham, T. (1998), *Healthy Cities in Developing Countries: an International Approach to Local Problems*, Earthscan, London.

Werna, E., Ilona Blue and Harpham, T. (1999), 'From Healthy Cities Projects to Healthy Cities', *Environment and Urbanization*, Vol. 11(1), pp. 27-39.

World Health Organization (WHO) (1993), *The Urban Health Crisis. Strategies for Health for all in the Face of Rapid Urbanization*, Geneva.

World Health Organization (WHO) (1995), *Building a Healthy City: a Practitioners' Guide*. Unit of Environmental Health, Office of Operational Support, Geneva.

World Health Organization (WHO) (2000), *Healthy Cities in Action: 5 Case-studies from Africa, Asia, Middle East and Latin America*, Department of Protection of the Human Environment, Geneva.

9 Popular Participation and Urban Poverty Alleviation in Bolivia

AART SCHALKWIJK

Introduction

Within the development debate, the central government is no longer seen as the sole agent of national development. It has been given a more modest role of facilitator, transferring its economic activities to the private sector, delegating responsibilities for local development to lower levels of government, and allowing civil society to participate in local and national planning and development. The parallel and complementary processes of privatization, decentralization, and participation seem to have created a favorable climate for the formation of partnerships between the various stakeholders in the development process; the government, the private sector, civil society, and – to some extent – international organizations.

Combating urban poverty should be one of the most central policy goals of urban administrations, as poverty is increasingly concentrated in urban areas and the urban poor are the worst affected group wherever there is a sudden decline in economic growth (Habitat Debate, 2000, p. 2). Economic growth itself does not necessarily lead to a reduction in poverty; special measures must be taken by local government to ensure participation of the poor in economic development. Effective democratic local government can, in theory, contribute to poverty alleviation through a chain of causal relationships, starting with increased participation by the urban poor which should lead to increased representation and thus to empowerment, in turn leading to the poor having increased access to resources (Blair, 2000).

The urban poverty debate is increasingly focussing on the building up of assets such as the quality of labor, human capital, housing, household relations, and social capital by the poor as a means to reduce their vulnerability and to overcome poverty (Moser, 1998; World Bank 2001). Policies, according to Moser, should be aimed at recognizing invisible, non-tangible assets such as social capital[1] and removing barriers in order to promote the accumulation of such assets.

With an increasing emphasis being placed on 'good governance', the global trend has been to relieve the inefficient, unresponsive central government of a number of its tasks and duties, and delegate these to local government. Decentralization is expected to result in higher accountability of local government as government is brought closer to the population and is elected by the people at the local level. One usually assumes decentralization is accompanied by increased participation[2] by the population. Participation, besides being an essential component of good governance, is also seen as a vital element in strategies to reduce poverty, as it enables the poor to gain better access to resources. 'Empowerment of the poor' has therefore become a popular slogan.

It is argued that partnerships can provide effective means for managing urban development by allowing other stakeholders to support local governments, which by themselves are not able to solve the problems of fast-growing cities (Baud, 2000, p. 3; see also UNCHS, 1999). Partnerships between the government, private sector, and civil society are promoted by international agencies such as the World Bank and UNCHS/Habitat as indispensable ingredients of good governance. The partnership model supposes that government acknowledges its shortcomings and is willing to accept the participation of representatives of civil society – private and social – in the formulation and/or implementation of policy. Apart from stated good intentions, expressed through the signing of covenants with other stakeholders, it must be seen whether government is indeed ready to share responsibility with the other stakeholders. As government controls the access to resources and holds final responsibility for urban administration and development, it will have a dominant position in relation to the other stakeholders in partnerships, and these partnerships will therefore by definition not be equal in nature. So far, there have not been many successful partnerships between government and civil society in terms of durable, equitable relations, except perhaps between government and the private sector in the provision of urban services. Research into the theme continues, focussing also on ways to include the urban poor in such partnerships (Baud, 2000).

---

1. Defined here as 'the trust that facilitates people working together toward a common purpose' (Blair, 2000, p. 28). CBOs can be seen as an important form of social capital.
2. The World Bank definition of participation is used here, i.e., 'a process through which stakeholders influence and share control over development initiatives and the decisions and resources which affect them.' (World Bank, 1996, p. 3)

Bolivia is an interesting case if one wishes to examine more closely the extent to which reality conforms to the policy prescriptions emerging from this debate. The country is one of the poorest in Latin America, making poverty alleviation one of the most important themes of the Bolivian government's policies. As a poor, heavily indebted country, Bolivia is very dependent on foreign financial assistance in the implementation of its development strategy. The country is undergoing a rapid and massive urbanization process, with two-thirds of the population now living in an urban center. Far-reaching reforms have been implemented to effectuate decentralization and popular participation. The case of Bolivia will be used here to address the issue of the formation of partnerships. The main question that will be taken up is to what extent national and local government enable the urban poor to participate in and meaningfully contribute to urban poverty alleviation.

Economic Development, Poverty and Urbanization

As a poor, heavily indebted country, Bolivia is very dependent on financial assistance from multilateral and bilateral donors for the financing of its national development. All of its major social and infrastructural sectors (education, health care, rural development, neighborhood improvement, road construction) are dependent on foreign financial assistance. Of total public investment in 1999, 45 per cent was financed with external resources, while for the whole decade it averaged 50 per cent (GNB, 2001). In 1999 the country had a total public debt of US$ 2,895 million, equivalent to 213 per cent of exports (IMF/IDA, 2000), most of it owed to multilateral development banks.

Economic growth in the late 1990s averaged 4.5 per cent, while inflation was reduced to 3.5 per cent in 1999 (from 8 per cent in 1996). Since 1985 Bolivia has, in close collaboration with the IMF, continuously worked at a comprehensive structural reform program to stabilize the economy and stimulate economic growth as a basis for social development. As a result, private local and foreign investments and foreign trade have expanded significantly. Exports almost doubled in eight years. International reserves have increased more than expected, while local revenue collection has improved significantly and expenditures have been contained. Social investment increased from 10 per cent of public expenditure at the beginning of the 1990s to 50 per cent in 1999.

In general, Bolivia's creditors have expressed their satisfaction with the progress the country has made in restructuring the economy, and have been willing to reschedule its debts. The World Bank concludes that Bolivia is a 'top IDA performer' (1999, p. 10). Substantial progress has also been made in the areas of institutional reform and social development, and in the promotion of participation by civil society (IMF/IDA, 2000).

However, there is one area in which little success has been achieved according to the donors; poverty reduction. This is acknowledged by the Bolivian government. Continued economic growth has not significantly affected the level of poverty. While economic growth has averaged 4 per cent in the past decade, poverty has only declined by 1.2 per cent per year. The lack of impact of economic growth on poverty is attributed to high levels of economic and social inequality, with the top 20 per cent of the, mostly urban, population earning 54 per cent of total income, while the bottom 20 per cent earns a mere 4 per cent (GNB, 2001, p. 6). At present, 63 per cent of the population lives below the poverty line, a level twice as high as the average for the whole region. The continued high incidence of poverty in the country is seen by the government as a threat to democracy, as it breeds social conflict whereby the poor demand more equality and access to opportunities (GNB, 2001, p. 9). Indeed, social unrest is very common in everyday Bolivian life, with frequent violent demonstrations in the major cities, and roadblocks across major national roads set up by angry *campesinos*. The roadblocks have caused severe economic damage, mainly to the small rural producers and poor urban consumers, interrupting for weeks on end the exchange of goods between rural and urban areas and between cities.

In 1976, Bolivia was still mainly a rural country, with only 42 per cent of the population living in urban areas. By 1992 this situation had been reversed, and for the first time in its history Bolivia had a predominantly urban population (58 per cent of the total population). It is calculated that today more than 65 per cent of the country's population lives in a city. Urban population growth between 1976 and 1992 averaged 4.2 per cent per year and is now estimated at 3.6 per cent per annum.[3] On the other hand, population growth in rural areas has been stagnant. Between 1976 and 1992, the population in the countryside diminished by 0.1 per cent per year, natural growth apparently not compensating for the loss of migrants to the city.[4] Rural-urban migration is a clear expression of differences in levels of devel-

---

3. Data are from the Bolivian Instituto Nacional de Estadística (INE) (GNB, 2001, p. 13).
4. In addition, the countryside is also losing population because of migration to other countries, especially Argentina.

opment between cities and countryside. Urban municipalities recorded an average score of 0.573 on an indicator of human development,[5] while rural municipalities scored an average of only 0.4. The major cities all scored over 0.6, with the exception of El Alto. In comparison, the rural Altiplano area of Potosí had a score of only 0.297. Ninety-five percent of the rural population was considered poor in 1992, against 53 per cent of the population of urban areas (El Alto: 73 per cent). As a result of widespread migration, poverty is now gradually being transferred to the towns and cities of Bolivia. It is estimated that today, the majority of poor in Bolivia (52 per cent) reside in urban areas (GNB, 2001, p. 5).

Participation in Urban Municipalities

The centralized, authoritarian political structure Bolivia had before the *Ley de Participación Popular* (Law on Popular Participation, LPP) of 1994 provided few opportunities for civil society to participate. This applied especially to the marginalized indigenous population living in peripheral rural areas of the country. The LPP provides legal recognition to *Organizaciones Territoriales de Base* (territorial-based organizations; OTBs) as representatives of the people; *campesino* and indigenous communities in rural areas and neighborhood councils or *juntas vecinales* (JVs) in urban areas. According to the Norm on Participatory Municipal Planning, OTBs are 'principle actors in the process of planning and administration of sustainable municipal development'.[6] The OTBs are expected to contribute to the development of their communities by identifying its needs, and to participate in and supervise the execution of projects and programs. To create an additional mechanism of social control, the law called for the installation of *comités de vigilancia* (CVs) which act as a link between the OTBs and municipal governments, and whose primary task is to supervise the spending of public funds.

Representatives of the CVs are chosen by OTBs, and CVs have the power to demand the suspension of national funds allocated to municipal government if public funds are not spent in compliance with original programming formulated in consultation with the OTBs. Furthermore, municipal govern-

---

5. An indicator combining life expectancy, level of education and income on a total scale of 1 to 10.
6. Norma de la Planificación Participativa Municipal, article 43 (Sistema Nacional de Planificación, 1997). Translation from Spanish by the author.

ments are compelled to draw up five-year municipal development plans based on demands formulated by the OTBS. To this end, the Vice-Ministry of Strategic Planning and Popular Participation (PEPP) has developed methodologies and manuals for the participatory formulation of these plans in both rural and urban municipalities.

Since the enactment of the LPP, 13,827 OTBS have received legal recognition all over the country, representing 80 per cent of all estimated existing CBOS (PEPP, 1999, p. 1). In addition to the OTBS, most communities also have a number of sectoral organizations such as women's, cultural, and sports clubs. The existence of such a large number of recognized OTBS indicates a high level of formal organization among the population, which benefits especially the poor of the country, both rural and urban, as the CBOS form important channels of demand-making on local government. In urban areas, as a result of the greater population size, there is more social distance between the OTBS and municipal government. It is very difficult for leaders of the OTBS in major cities to gain access to the mayor or to other representatives of the *alcaldía* (municipal government, town hall), and OTBS have to compete among themselves to draw attention to their problems.

With regard to representation, there are significant differences between CVs in urban and those in rural areas. The ratio of OTBS to CVs in large urban centers is 154:1, while in the smaller rural municipalities this figure is 9:1. Blanes (1998, p. 13) also notices a major gap between JVS and CVS in urban areas, as CVS are very much dependent on *alcaldías* for their financial and technical functioning, and are often silenced by being adequately 'compensated' for their work. Wils (2000, p. 5) points to the problem of co-optation of CVS by political parties who then proceed to use the CVS for their own political agenda.

In urban areas, the *Federaciones de JV* (Federations of Neighborhood Councils; FEJUVES) are seen by most JVS as their main representatives in negotiations with municipal government. The task of representing the JVS has, however, been given by the LPP to the CV[7] who are regarded by the FEJUVES as artificial parallel organizations. The relation between FEJUVES and CVS in most cities is therefore antagonistic. The effectiveness of FEJUVES in solving urban problems and contributing to the improvement of the wellbeing of their members is strongly limited, as the FEJUVES have been infiltrated by political parties and are sometimes openly affiliated to them (Blanes, 1998). Where FEJUVES and *alcaldías* belong to different political parties, there is little chance of collaboration or partnerships.

---

7. The reason for this might have been that FEJUVES do not exist in rural areas.

At the national level, urban FEJUVES are united in an umbrella organization, the *Confederacion de JV* (CONALJUVE). The CONALJUVE has signed a number of protocols with various national ministries (education, health, housing, popular participation) to collaborate in promoting social development, especially for the urban poor. In general, these agreements exist only on paper and are not implemented due to the ministries' lack of interest, which appear to regard the protocols mostly as a means to silence the CONALJUVE. The organization is one of the more manifest civil organizations receiving substantial press coverage, and has repeatedly opposed government policies by calling on JVs to take to the streets. The CONALJUVE maintains contacts with similar organizations in other Latin American countries.

A National Program for Neighborhood Improvement

At the national level, the government has created a program aimed at urban poverty alleviation; the Subprograma Mejoramiento de Barrios (Neighborhood Improvement Subprogram; SPMB). The program is in principle very important for the urban poor, as it is one of the very few national programs targeted specifically at them. The program was started by the previous administration in 1995 and is financed mainly by the Inter-American Development Bank (US$ 40 million), while the national government has contributed another US$ 10 million. The program aims at improving the living conditions of low-income households in peri-urban areas through the provision of drinking water, sanitation, and electricity, the construction of basic sanitary units (toilets and bathrooms), road improvement, drainage, the construction of social facilities (such as communal centers, playing fields, and kindergartens), the planting of trees, and the regularization of property titles. The maximum financing is set at US$ 1.6 million per neighborhood and US$ 2,800 per lot. The program is executed at the national level through the Fondo Nacional de Desarrollo Regional (FNDR), one of the three national social funds, while municipal governments are responsible for the local implementation and are expected to contribute 30 per cent of the investments. The active participation of local communities is both expected and stimulated, and it is hoped that they will not 'simply be recipients of the program's benefits.' The participation of NGOs is also sought in the implementation of community development components. The program thus provides the perfect setting for partnerships between international donors (the IADB), the government (national, regional, and local), the private sector (providers of basic services), and civil society (NGOs and CBOs). The program also provides a significant incentive for the development and consolidation of assets and social capital by the urban poor.

Inclusion in the program is determined by holding open rounds every six months, during which local governments can present the projects and documentation of eligible neighborhoods until all the funds of the program are committed. This set-up promotes competition between neighborhoods and between municipalities, and active local governments are thus rewarded with substantial financial funds for neighborhood improvement.

The program was started in 1997 with a number of pilot projects for selected neighborhoods in four municipalities. Unfortunately, three years later (in 2000), none of the pilot projects had actually been started, as municipalities were still grappling with a number of technical and financial problems. The first open round of the program in 1999 yielded a meager harvest of applications from three municipal governments (out of a list of 45) for eight neighborhoods. During the fourth round in June 2000, the total came to 82 neighborhoods, presented by 26 municipalities, thereby committing all the funds of the program. Surprisingly enough, most of the poorest urban municipalities failed to present projects, perhaps an indication of their very limited organizational and technical capacity to formulate project proposals.

Being one of the largest and poorest urban centers in the country, one would expect the municipal government of El Alto to make a special effort to enter the program with as many of its destitute neighborhoods as possible. However, because the various factions within the CONDEPA party,[8] which rules the *alcaldía*, were mired in political infighting, the local authorities apparently overlooked the need to put together a technical team to prepare and implement the program at the local level. During the first and second open rounds, El Alto presented no applications for inclusion in the program. Then the Comisión Impulsora de la Lucha Contra la Pobreza (Driving Committee for the Fight Against Poverty)[9] discovered the existence of the program, and formed a loose and ad hoc partnership with the prefecture, the Ministry of Housing and Basic Services, and the FEJUVE of El Alto to select eligible barrios, prepare the necessary documentation in close collaboration with neighborhood leaders and residents, and pressure the alcaldía to present the projects officially to the FNDR for inclusion in the program. In

---

8. A populist party with backing mainly among the indigenous of the Altiplano.
9. A semi-governmental commission installed by President Banzer to tackle the problem of poverty in El Alto and led by the charismatic Father Obermaier, a Catholic priest.

this way, and despite almost total non-participation by the municipal government, El Alto finally managed to get eight neighborhoods included in the program, thus becoming the number one urban municipality in number of barrios approved for financing by the program.

Almost five years after its conception, however, no investments have been made by the program in neighborhood improvement (not even in the pilot projects), while there is great demand from the target group. Municipal governments blame the bureaucratic nature of the FNDR, which demands a great quantity of project documentation before the financing of any neighborhood can be approved. However, it is more likely that the municipalities themselves are the main cause of the delays. The tasks and responsibilities of the *alcaldía* in the execution of the program are many; forming a special multidisciplinary technical unit within the *alcaldía*, providing information on the program to the target group, selecting eligible neighborhoods, collecting basic data on those *barrios*, formulating various project documents, having the selected neighborhoods approved by the municipal council, providing the counterpart funds (30 per cent) for the investments,[10] presenting the projects to the FNDR, contracting out the works to local contractors, and overseeing the execution of the works. The tasks seem far too complicated and demanding for the limited technical capacity of municipal governments, and their decisive role appears to be the major impediment preventing the program from being more successful. Poor neighborhoods with great needs that qualify for the program cannot apply directly to the FNDR for financing, but are totally dependent on the willingness and capacity of their local government. Although the program stressed the active participation of the community, most *alcaldías* applied the traditional technical approach to the program by contracting out all the work to consultants.

Organization and Participation of the Poor in El Alto

The city of El Alto (population 600,000) has 374 *barrios*, each with its own *junta vecinal* (neighborhood council). A non-representative sample of 58 mainly peripheral neighborhoods of El Alto, with an average age of 12 years and an average occupancy rate of 71 per cent, shows that 38 per cent of the *barrios* had no access to the electricity network, 46 per cent had no connection to the city water supply, and 86 per cent had no connection to the sewer

---

10. These funds can also be contributed by the neighborhood itself, in the form of labor.

system. Garbage was not collected in 67 per cent of the neighborhoods, and 95 per cent had only dirt roads. The economic base of most of these *barrios* is very weak with very few local economic activities. From a more detailed survey of two of such *barrios*, it was gathered that the average family income amounted to some 550 bolivianos (US$ 100) per month, with the majority of the families (60 per cent) having only one earner, as most female partners do not work, as they either cannot find employment or have to look after their small children. The main bottleneck for the residents of these *barrios* in using the opportunities of the urban labor market is their low level of education.

One of the more important productive assets for the urban poor of the peripheral neighborhoods is their ownership of their plot and house. Plots were bought at an average price of US$ 1,000. Ninety percent of the families are property owners, and a number of them sublet part of their house to tenants to earn extra income. In a few cases, the house or plot is used by the owner as a workshop for a micro-enterprise.

Practically all of the city's JVs are officially recognized as OTBS and are in possession of their official papers from the prefecture and the municipal government. The formation of JVs is an autonomous process with no involvement from NGOs or political parties as external mobilizing agents, with only organizational support from the *Federación de JV*. All JVs are members of the FEJUVE of El Alto. JVs represent on average 450 families (2,250 persons), although membership – depending on the size of the neighborhood – ranges from 50 to 3,500 families. Each family is a member of the JV by choice or by social compulsion, and is asked to contribute a small monthly fee and receives a membership card. The JVs are elected every two years by the residents, a process overseen by the FEJUVE. Each JV has its own statutes and a record is normally made of all meetings with the residents. Meetings are held at least once every month. During them, information is given on the progress of specific issues regarding the community, and residents have the opportunity to voice their concerns. Participation in meetings by residents is fairly regular and often quite a high percentage of residents turn up, at least in those *barrios* still in a process of consolidation. Residents also participate in communal activities in the neighborhood, such as improving access roads, removing garbage, planting trees, as well as in cultural activities, such as commemorating the foundation of the community.

Solidarity is aided in the neighborhoods of El Alto by the city's specific homogenous cultural character. Almost all residents have a rural Aymara background, and very often residents of a neighborhood come from the same region of the Altiplano. The migrants maintain links with their village of origin, where they keep their fields and to which they return for sowing, harvesting, cultural activities, and to visit their relatives. Neighborhoods can to some extent be seen as transplanted rural villages in a new urban setting, with *barrio* residents retaining – at least for some time – their rural-cultural customs and traditions.[11] The village perspective of the residents is also found in the way they view the use of urban services. Each *barrio* expects to have its own basic school, health care center, day care center, community hall, and playing fields, regardless of the size of the neighborhood, and facilities are not easily shared with neighboring *barrios*. The idea, promoted by some NGOs, of forming *mancomunidades de barrios* (associations of neighborhoods) so as to be more effective in collective bargaining for improvements by *barrios* with similar problems, was not very popular with leaders or residents. Apparently, solidarity does not reach beyond the limits of the *barrio*. Apart from the JV, neighborhoods have other types of formal and informal community organizations, such as *Clubes de Madres*, youth clubs, sports clubs, and churches, although in newer settlements these organizations may well not have been formed yet.

In the sample of 58 peripheral *barrios*, all had a functioning JV, 40 per cent had a sports club, 38 per cent had at least one church, while 18 per cent had or had had an NGO working in the area. Nine percent had a *Club de Madres* and 10 per cent had a youth club. The presence of these sectoral organizations is normally higher in the older, more consolidated *barrios*.

Contacts with authorities are maintained by the leaders of the JV. Each JV will have 10-16 elected members (*dirigentes*) forming the junta, of which normally 3-5 members will form an active core and act on behalf of the JV and the community. Most *dirigentes* are males in their 30s to 50s; the participation of women or youths in a junta is very rare, and where they do participate they usually occupy minor, symbolic posts. The leaders generally do not differ in profession or educational level from the rest of the residents. The neighborhood leaders are in general very active in trying to gain benefits for their community. As offices are open only on weekdays, they have to take time off from their own work to act on behalf of their community. Most time is spent knocking on doors of the *alcaldía*, the prefecture, the offices of the utility companies, NGOs, the FEJUVE, the CV and any other institution, collecting information on programs and procedures, and building up and maintaining networks of acquaintances, intermediaries who can open doors

---

11. A clear example is the frequent use of Aynis, the undertaking of collective activities such as the construction of a house, cleaning up of the neighborhood, and *Aptapis*, collectively prepared meals for special occasions such as the reception of honored guests to the *barrio*.

to decision-making and financing. Further time is spent in meetings with the JV on various aspects pertaining to the community, and on contacts with residents. These meetings take place mostly at night or at weekends, when residents and other members of the JV are at home. Apart from their work as *dirigente* of their JV, they often put in time as members of trade unions, the FEJUVE, or the CV. Their knowledge of planning procedures, of the rights and obligations assigned to OTBs by law, and of effective bargaining strategies are usually quite weak, but neighborhood leaders display a great deal of interest in participating in workshops and training sessions – usually organized by NGOs or international organizations – to enhance their knowledge of programs and procedures and to improve their leadership skills. In general, neighborhood leadership is one of the very important forms of social capital for the urban poor of El Alto.

Like all other major cities and towns in Bolivia, El Alto has a FEJUVE, uniting all the separate 374 JVs of the city and representing them in contacts with other institutions – the *alcaldía* being the most important of these. The FEJUVE has 64 functionaries working on a voluntary basis, all of whom are *dirigentes* from member *juntas* of the FEJUVE. One of the FEJUVE's main functions is to help organize the work of the affiliated JVs, e.g., overseeing their election, helping with their documentation and with their registration as legally recognized OTBs, and generally mediating in conflicts within and between JVs. Its other main function is to advance the interests of its members during contacts with the local authorities. As such, in theory the FEJUVE can be a powerful actor in the urban scene as a representative organization of civil society, as it represents the whole urban population. In reality, however, the FEJUVE is heavily politicized and is mainly engaged in power politics. Its position is defined by the political affiliation of its main leaders. Belonging to the CONDEPA party, the FEJUVE spent most of its energy fighting the *alcaldía* and the CV, both of which also belonged to the CONDEPA, but apparently to different factions. The FEJUVE is usually one of the main actors, along with the trade union COB, in organizing marches and blockades in the city. The FEJUVE showed little interest in attempts by NGOs from ElAlto to form a broad urban platform to help promote urban social development.[12] Nor did the FEJUVE mobilize its member JVs to enter the Neighborhood Improvement Subprogram or to pressure the *alcaldía* to fulfill its duties within this program.

---

12. The effort was abandoned after a few meetings due to the participating partners' lack of interest.

The CV is another potential instrument of the urban poor of El Alto to influence municipal decision-making. The CV of El Alto has seven members, one from each district, and all seven are *presidente* of one of the JVs of their district. On the positive side, this ensures that they are true representatives of the poor. All members of the CV have a humble Aymara background, a low level of education and a low-class or lower-middle-class job. However, their function as *presidente* of a JV also influences their position vis-à-vis the other JV within the district they are supposed to represent, as they try to favor their own communities in the allocation of financial means reserved for their district. This is clearly recognized by the other *presidentes* of the JV of the district, who therefore have little trust in the CV. The *presidentes* generally place more confidence in the FEJUVE as representative of their interests. Like the FEJUVE the CV was most often engaged in party political conflicts with the *alcaldía*.

Interaction Between Local Government and the Urban Poor

As all new *barrios* in El Alto start off as unauthorized subdivisions, and are delivered by private developers without any basic services, it is imperative for the residents to organize themselves into collectives in order to negotiate with the authorities for formal recognition of their area and for service delivery. Main issues around which actions are organized by the residents are thus (more or less in chronological order); legal recognition of the JV as an OTB; formal recognition of the subdivision by approval of the subdivision plan; improvement of access and secondary roads, water, electricity, and garbage collection; and – at a later stage – registration of individual plot titles, connection to the sewerage system, and the construction of community provisions such as community halls, schools, clinics, parks and playing fields. The residents are therefore very much dependent on the *alcaldía*, while the *alcaldía* seems to view the residents' demands as a nuisance, and a claim on scarce technical and financial resources of the municipality. Communities have to compete with other communities for access to the limited municipal resources, and success depends to a large extent on the effectiveness of the bargaining strategy used by the community leaders, in which access to information as well as persistence and patience are vital ingredients. Realization of the provisions takes years, and often decades. All improvements in their community depend on their own initiative and efforts, as the municipal government takes action only after pressure from the community.

The community leaders mostly use the most common method of demand-making between communities and authorities; 'personal dealings'. These are carried out directly and on behalf of the specific community only; alliances between *barrios* are very rare and the dealings are not conducted through intermediaries such as NGOs. The community leaders frequent the various offices of the municipal government to find the procedures to be followed, to undertake the necessary paperwork, and to pursue financing where necessary. Most often, community leaders leave the offices of the *alcaldía* without any results. It is not uncommon to induce municipal employees to speed up procedures by offering them coimas (bribes), especially as these are expected by the civil servants. In negotiations with employees of the *alcaldía* or where possible during audiences with the local authorities themselves such as the mayor or councilors, delegations usually adopt a subservient position, emphasizing their position as *gente humilde* (humble people) who are putting themselves at the mercy of the esteemed authorities. The authorities are often invited to visit the community to see for themselves the condition in which residents have to live. Normally these invitations are ignored and residents do not often get a chance to receive representatives from the municipality. Most often negotiations (or, more accurately, requests) by the JV do not lead to results, and the community feels frustrated by the unwillingness or inability of the municipality to attend to their needs.

These frustrations give rise to a second type of demand-making by the urban poor on the authorities; the protest march. Protests are usually organized by the trade unions and/or the FEJUVE who, through the JV, mobilize the residents of the communities. Marches are periodically organized to protest against new laws or regulations, or against price increases. Marches often lead to the blocking of busy intersections and, occasionally, to occupation of the *alcaldía*, and can be accompanied by destruction, violence, and confrontations with the riot police. The frequent use of protest marches might be linked to the militant tradition of El Alto, which results from the presence of mine workers, *campesinos*, and strong trade unions. The result of this form of demand-making is at best ambiguous. It frequently leads to interruption of economic activities, and damage to public and private property. It also does not yield much support from the rest of society for their cause; on the contrary, it might contribute to a hardening of differences between the interests of lower versus the middle and upper classes, frequently along ethnic lines. In some cases, government is forced to change its position on the issue at hand, but the negative effects appear to outweigh the positive results.

A third form of demand-making by the urban poor seen in El Alto and in other cities in Bolivia, is what can be called 'symbolic politics'. These are carefully arranged mass meetings between the poor and authorities. The venue is either the *alcaldía* or a public place in one of the communities. At these meetings, to which the press is invited in order to give the event coverage, the authorities illustrate their good intentions by performing a symbolic deed, such as publicly signing an agreement, handing out certificates or other tangible goods, or inaugurating a public facility such as a school or playground. These meetings begin with the authorities' spectacular arrival in a caravan of four-wheel drives, the singing of the national or municipal anthem, and the parading of flags; this is followed by speeches in which the authorities extol the virtues of their administration and promise more good deeds, while representatives of the target group present their demands and express their hope of benefiting from the policies of the government. The meetings are used by the authorities to give the target groups the impression that they are aware of the needs of the community and have every intention of addressing these in the very near future, thereby legitimizing their authority. The meetings lead to the poor having increased expectations that the government is willing and capable of satisfying their needs, only to be disappointed by reality.

Apart from the types of demand-making described here, there are few other channels open to the poor that might lead to a satisfaction of their demands. Gaining access to the local government's budget through the CV is almost, but not totally, impossible, as neighborhoods have to compete with a great number of other *barrios* in their district, and members of the CV are viewed as partisan, favoring their own neighborhoods. Besides, the real allocation of municipal resources by the *alcaldía* usually differs greatly from the planned allocation. Another channel – the use of political parties – offers only a temporary solution, as political representatives only show themselves in the neighborhoods around election time, bringing gifts with them in the hope of persuading residents to vote for their party.

In general, the types of demand-making used by the poor in El Alto yield very poor outcomes, as most efforts are not rewarded by concrete results. In the end, communities do gain access to some of the resources sought, but the process is extremely slow. The lack of results and the inability to influence decision-making leads to a build-up of frustration in the communities. The potential beneficial effects of popular participation by law have not yet reached the urban poor of El Alto as access to decision-making has not become a reality, hampered on the one hand by an unaccountable non-transparent municipal government, and on the other by the lack of effective strategies by OTBS to use the opportunities the law provides them with. Communities seem to be stuck in traditional, non-effective forms of demand-making cultivated by the political system, almost totally directed at the municipal government and characterized by thinking in terms of demands (i.e., 'begging') rather than solutions, placing them in a very dependent position vis-à-vis the municipal authorities. What is lacking is an effective strategy to pressure the authorities to fulfill their duties in a proper manner. A first handicap is the lack of knowledge communities have of the legal means at their disposal to influence government decision-making. Communities are furthermore insufficiently aware of their assets and their possibilities to gain access to resources through their own efforts outside of the *alcaldía*, using for instance NGOs to gain access to donor funding, and combining forces with other *barrios*.

Conclusion

The partnership model does not seem to hold for Bolivia. As stated, the model presupposes a government's interest in pursuing general developmental goals, and its willingness to share its power and responsibilities with other stakeholders in development. Although the Bolivian government has stated its support for such an approach – i.e., that it accepts civil society as being 'co-responsible' for development – not much evidence is seen of it in practice, at either the national or the local level. Representatives of civil society, both NGOs and CBOs, have often expressed their desire to participate more fully in local and national development and to cooperate with the government, but have not been given a chance to do so. The problem is that – and this might be a structural limitation of the partnership idea – the government controls access to the resources, and civil society is in a dependent position, a situation not favorable for the formation of partnerships based on equality or at least on mutual dependency. Exclusion of civil society and especially of the poor in Bolivia has led to the exact opposite of partnerships; loss of credibility for the government, confrontations, and violent, destructive actions threatening the country's still fragile democracy.

If partnerships do not work, what alternatives are there? It is evident that some way must be found to include civil society, and especially the poor, in local and national development and to use society's willingness to participate as well as its potential. One of the main assets the urban poor have in Bolivia is a high level of organization, enhanced by active community leadership. The LPP has given civil organizations legal recognition and instruments to gain access to decision-making and become involved in municipal development. Unfortunately, urban citizens have not been able to fully utilize this potential. Rather than expressing their demands via a political organization, they have been trained by the political system to express them by demanding favors from the government, thus putting themselves in a dependent position.

Where the formation of partnerships does not seem feasible, it is proposed to think more in terms of pressure. Government as an unwilling but necessary actor must be pressured to act in the general interest of the nation. In poor countries that are heavily dependent on foreign aid – like Bolivia is – the most effective pressure is that from above, i.e., from donors. As donors control access to much needed resources, they have leverage to push national and local governments in the direction of good governance. This is already being done by both multilateral and bilateral donors, but efforts are mostly directed at institutional reform and the strengthening of government, with too little attention being paid to the aspect of participation by society. Pressure must also be exerted from 'below', from CBOs that represent the interests of the poor. Strengthening of these civil organizations is needed to expand their negotiating capacity to successfully bargain with local authorities. Permanent training is necessary to build-up their knowledge, to make them better acquainted with the fundamentals of urban municipal development, and to make them more aware of the opportunities the law offers them to participate in decision-making. Part of such training has to focus on teaching CBOs to think in terms of solutions rather than demands, and to point out their own role in solving problems of urban development and urban poverty by, for instance, building up and maintaining their own assets.

References

Baud, I. (2000), 'Collective Action, Enablement and Partnerships. Issues in Urban Development', Inaugural address, Free University, Amsterdam.
Blair, H. (2000), 'Participation and Accountability at the Periphery: Democratic Local Governance in Six Countries', *World Development*, Vol. 28(1), pp. 21-39.
Blanes, J. (1998), *Juntas Vecinales y Comités de Vigilancia: Su Papel en la Planificación Urbana*, CEBEM, La Paz (paper).
Gobierno Nacional de Bolivia (2001), *Estrategia Boliviana de Reducción de la Pobreza*, Dialogo Nacional 2000, La Paz.
IMF/IDA (2000), *Bolivia. Decision Point Document for the Enhanced HIPC Initiative.* IMF, World Bank, IDB.

Moser, C.O. (1998), 'The Asset Vulnerability Framework: Reassessing Urban Poverty Reduction Strategies', *World Development*, Vol. 26(1), pp. 1-19.
PEPP – Viceministerio de Planificación Estratégica y Participación Popular (1999), *Diagnóstico de Situación de* OTBs, CVs, Acs *y Organizaciones Funcionales*, Resumen Ejecutivo.
SPMB – Ministerio de Vivienda, Fondo Nacional de Desarrollo Regional (1999), *Subprograma Mejoramiento de Barrios*, Presentación del Subprograma, La Paz.
UNCHS (1999), Habitat Debate, Vol. 5.
Wils, F. (2000), *Bolivia: Ley de Participación Popular y el Papel de Partidos Políticos en la Implementación de esa Ley en Ciudades Mayores: Notas Preliminares de una Breve Investigación*, Institute of Social Studies, The Hague (unpublished).
World Bank (1996), *The World Bank Participation Sourcebook*, Adobe Acrobat PDF Version.
World Bank (1999), *Bolivia: Implementing the Comprehensive Development Framework*, Country Management Unit, Latin America and the Caribbean Region, Report No. 19326-BO.
World Bank (2001), *World Development Report 2000/2001: Attacking Poverty*, Oxford University Press, New York.

10 Popular Participation and the Participatory Planning Practice in Latin America: Some Evidence from Bolivia and Brazil

PAUL VAN LINDERT AND GERY NIJENHUIS

Almost all Latin American countries have now introduced some form of decentralization policy. Decentralization is thought to have a favorable impact on the efficiency of government actions, on equity, and on popular participation in local decision-making processes. With respect to the last factor, decentralization is frequently mentioned as an instrument for achieving good governance, which is usually seen as the endeavor to realize greater accountability, transparency, equity, and representativeness in governing practices.

Popular participation is an important ingredient of good governance. In theory, the transfer of functions and funds to sub-national levels makes it easier for people to participate in local decision-making concerning key issues that affect their lives. However, this implies a redefinition of the concept of participation, from beneficiary to citizen and from consultation to decision-making (Gaventa and Valderrama, 1999).

This chapter focuses on decentralization and popular participation in local decision-making in the Latin American context. The objectives are:

- To provide an overview of the implementation of decentralization policies and popular participation in Latin America, and
- To analyze the factors conditioning participatory planning in Brazil and Bolivia.

The first section introduces the concept of decentralization and presents an overview of some Latin American experiences with decentralization. This is followed by seven case studies, i.e., six municipalities in Bolivia and the city of Porto Alegre in Brazil. Bolivia is an excellent example of a country in which decentralization was implemented only recently. Until 1994, the structure of local government was confined to urban areas; in rural areas (i.e., most of the country's territory, and encompassing 43 per cent of the population) there simply was no local government. Brazil, on the other hand, has a longer history of decentralization, and local governments are much more consolidated, although clientelism still is very common. In contrast to Bolivia, popular participation in Brazil is limited to a number of cities, and is not formalized by a legal framework.

The Concept of and Rationale for Decentralization

Decentralization means the transfer of authority over and responsibility for public functions from the central government to subordinate, lower government organizations or to the private sector. Generally, four types of decentralization are discerned; devolution, deconcentration, delegation, and privatization (Rondinelli et al., 1984; Smith 1985; Litvack et al., 1998; Manor 1999):

- *Devolution* transfers the authority for decision-making, finance, and management to sub-national units of government, which are substantially outside the direct control of central government.
- *Deconcentration* is the transfer of a certain amount of administrative authority or responsibility within central government ministries.
- *Delegation* means delegating the managerial responsibility for specific functions to organizations that are outside the regular bureaucratic structure and are only indirectly controlled by central government.
- *Privatization* involves transferring functions and responsibilities from the public to the private sector.

Generally, decentralization policies in Latin America are a mix of these four types (Manor 1999), as most countries have transferred a certain number of functions and a certain amount of funds to lower levels, whose authorities have been elected by the population.

The rationale for the implementation of decentralization policies varies. As Smith (1985), Litvack et al., (1998) and Manor (1999) argue, decentralization policies are usually inspired by political motives. In Latin America, for example, democratization was an important objective of decentralization policies in the 1980s, a period during which most military regimes were replaced by democratically elected governments. More recently, the implementation of structural adjustment programs based on neo-liberalism, the collapse of state communism, and the failure of the central state has been the driving force behind decentralization. Also, globalization ('think globally, act locally') is an important impetus to decentralization, as the local arena becomes more and more important (Leftwich, 1994; Schuurman, 1996).

Decentralization and Popular Participation in Latin America

Since the late 1970s, almost all Latin American countries have introduced decentralization policies involving deconcentration or delegation of functions, accompanied by some form of popular participation in local decision-making. Although these policies have many characteristics in common, they differ with respect to, for example, the share of sub-national levels in total public spending, the functions transferred to lower government levels, and the extent of electoral autonomy. Table 10.1 summarizes the main ingredients of decentralization policies in several Latin American countries. Based on these, countries can be divided into three main categories, i.e., those with a high degree of popular participation, those with a moderate degree of popular participation, and those in which popular participation is weakly developed.

Traditionally, participation of the population in government decisions is weak in most Latin American countries. Despite this, community participation in everyday life is very common, particularly in countries with a large indigenous population, such as Guatemala, Peru, and Bolivia. However, as Nickson (1995, p. 83) puts it, the presence of such a large indigenous population also contributes to the social exclusion of these generally poor segments of civil society. Popular participation in local decision-making has often been restricted by military regimes, as was the case in Guatemala, El Salvador, Paraguay, and Peru. Currently, popular participation in Latin America takes many different forms, ranging from some isolated experiments – in e.g., Buenos Aires and Montevideo – and the consultative boards in Chile, El Salvador, Honduras, and Nicaragua, to the more elaborated models in Bolivia and Porto Alegre in Brazil.

In Honduras, the Municipal Reform Law of 1990 introduced open town meetings. This law also granted citizens the right to participate in municipal planning and the right to use resources. An evaluation of this reform, however, revealed that these open town meetings were often purely ceremonial and that popular participation functioned only in municipalities where

Table 10.1 Decentralization and popular participation in Latin America: Some characteristics

Degree of popular participation (pp)/country	Year of reform (a&b)	Share of local govern-ment in total expenditures (in %) (a)	Election of authorities (a&b)	Characteristics of popular participation (a and b)
High degree of PP				
Bolivia	1994	12 (1995) (c)	Local level	Participatory planning; formal control of local government by the population.
Brazil	1988	18 (1991)	Both levels	Referenda, popular tribunal, popular initiative; participation by representative bodies.
Chile	1986	11 (1991)	Local level	Community council: advisory role.
Colombia	1983	24 (1992)	Both levels	Since 1986: *comunas/corregimientos*; JALs; Cali.
Moderate degree of PP				
Honduras	1990	8 (1984)	Local level	*Cabildos abiertos* since 1990.
Nicaragua	1988	13 (1989)	Local level	Two cabildos (budget/implementation), municipal councils.
Ecuador	1982	5 (1992)	Both levels	*Cabildo ampliado*, not directly elected.
Mexico	1977	3 (1990)	Both levels	Solidarity program 1989, participation of citizen groups in selection/implementation of projects.
El Salvador	1986	3 (1990)	Local level	*Cabildos abiertos*, popular consultations, advisory community groups.
Venezuela	1989	7 (1989)	Both levels	Parish councils, consultative role with accompanying measures.
Low degree of PP				
Argentina	1983	9 (1992) (d)	Both levels	No specific measures; some interesting initiatives; clientelism.
Costa Rica	1967	4 (1989)	Local level (by council)	Community groups, limited role local government.
Guatemala	1987	14 (1987)	Local level	Military regime, minimal citizen participation.
Panama		2 (1991)	Local level	Nation-wide, sub-municipal level, but more miniature governments than independent bodies.
Paraguay	1991	2 (1988)	Both levels	Development commissions, some interesting initiatives.
Peru	1984	8 (1987)	Local (mun.) level	Lima also PP, but Sendero/Fujimori activities limited PP.
Uruguay	1984	4 (1986)	Local (dep.) level	Departments instead of municipalities; local boards, but lack of demand; experience of Montevideo.

Sources: (a) Nickson (1995); (b) Burki *et al.* (1999); (c) Faguet (2000); (d) Wilson *et al.*, 1999.

intensive support programs were being implemented (Lippman and Pranke, 1998).

In Costa Rica and Ecuador, popular organizations tend to bypass local governments by directing their demands directly to the central government. Martinez (1996, p. 73) describes popular participation in Ecuador as institutionalized, because of the important role of the government and the limited room for those who really have an interest in planning. Another characteristic in Ecuador is that the political will to really incorporate popular demands into planning is lacking. Summarizing, although mechanisms for participation by citizens exist in many countries, in practice participation is limited to a consultative role.

Popular Participation in Bolivia

Before 1993, the Bolivian political and administrative structure was determined by a strong centralist tradition. Although a departmental level (headed by a prefect) did exist, in actual fact all decision-making and policy implementation took place at the central level. Investments were mainly directed at urban development, with the ten largest cities absorbing 94 per cent of all public funds. The remainder was invested in rural areas through Regional Development Corporations – semi-governmental entities established in the 1970s to promote economic development in Bolivia's rural provinces. These highly bureaucratic and corrupt investment entities (Galindo, 1996) were in fact the only governmental actor in rural areas.

In 1993 Gonzalo Sanchez de Lozada won the national elections with the ambitious 'Plan de Todos' campaign. In line with this plan, his government introduced several drastic reforms, such as bilingual education, privatization of state enterprises, land reforms, and pension laws. The decentralization program – currently serving as best practice for decentralization in other countries – in particular is seen as one of the major steps of Bolivia on the path towards democratization. The Bolivian decentralization model is based on two laws: The Law on Popular Participation (LPP), which took effect in July 1994, and the Law on Administrative Decentralization (LAD),[1] which came into force in January 1996. The LPP is intended to improve the living conditions of the Bolivian population. The main objectives are the better

---

1. The Law on Administrative Decentralization, wherein the structure and responsibilities of the departmental level are defined, gives more power to departmental governments and their head, the prefect. This law will not be considered here.

distribution and administration of public funds, and an increased participation of civil society in policy-making. The law encompasses three aspects: 1) restructuring municipalities, 2) popular participation, and 3) redistributing funds in favor of the population.

Municipal restructuring implies the creation of 314 new municipalities, with borders based on existing sections of provinces, and each with its own juridical status. The rural areas were also included in the municipal reform. Many responsibilities were passed on to the local level, including health and educational infrastructure, transportation, promotion of rural development, agricultural infrastructure, and services in the field of sports, recreation, and culture.

Popular participation in local government is institutionalized through the registration of already existing neighborhood committees, peasant communities, and indigenous communities, the so-called Territorial Base Organizations (TBOS). By formal registration, TBOS obtain juridical status. TBOS are supposed to formulate their demands and present them to the municipal council. The regulatory framework is intended to promote genuine participatory, bottom-up planning. However, only existing territorially based organizations are accepted for registration. Other important non territorially based organizations (e.g., clubes de madres) are excluded from participation. Another point of criticism is that the reform was designed in a top-down manner and that civil society was not involved in the elaboration of the law (Molina Monasterios, 1997, p. 206). At first, this resulted in strong resistance on the part of peasant communities (sindicatos) who considered the LPP an attempt by central government to gain control over rural areas. In later years, however, opposition waned as peasant TBOS came to realize that indeed they could profit from the potential money transfers involved.

Funds are redistributed in order to provide municipalities with adequate resources to implement their responsibilities. Some 20 per cent of all national tax revenues are distributed to the country's municipalities. The amount a municipality receives is determined by the number of persons registered in that municipality. Municipalities must invest 85 per cent of these funds in projects; the remainder can be used to cover administrative costs and salaries. Additional funds can be obtained by collecting municipal taxes, cooperating with NGOs, or applying for funds from other public entities. Municipalities must present an annual investment plan describing the projects and activities planned for the coming year. To guarantee the implementation of all this, an Oversight Committee (OC; Comités de Vigilancia) has to be established in each municipality. This OC consists of representatives of the population within a municipality.

Experiences of Six Municipalities in the Department of Chuquisaca

Popular participation is an important element of the Bolivian decentralization model. This section focuses on the main elements of popular participation, by presenting the experiences of six municipalities in the department of Chuquisaca.[2] The six municipalities range from rather small (5,040) to medium sized (30,000) and are predominantly rural, with agriculture as the main source of income. Monteagudo is an exception to this, as it serves as a regional service center. All these municipalities have relatively limited financial resources, limited opportunities to increase the municipal budget, and limited human resources capacity.

Our discussion focuses on a selected number of aspects related to popular participation, i.e., representation, actual participation, priority-setting, projects programmed, and accountability.

Representative Democracy

The LPP explicitly mentions the integration of formerly marginalized groups (e.g., peasants, indigenous people, women) into local decision-making. It also aims at voting their representatives into office. The first municipal elections after the LPP came into effect were held in December 1995. In three of the six municipalities in this case study, a peasant was elected mayor.[3] However, in 1999 – just three years after the elections – only one was still in office; the others had been removed as the result of a vote of censure (voto-censura constructivo), that is, the councils had passed a motion of distrust. The main reasons for doing so was either poor performance or financial mismanagement by the mayor. Although mayors across the country are subject to this type of punitive action, our study suggests that it is applied more often to mayors with a peasant or indigenous background.

---

2. This part of the analysis is based on PhD research in six municipalities in the southeastern department of Chuquisaca (Yotala, Poroma, Sopachuy, Presto, Monteagudo, and Huacareta) on the contribution of Bolivian decentralisation policy to good governance and local economic development; the fieldwork was done in 1997, 1998 and 2000. Structured interviews with representatives of local government, TBOs, local entrepreneurs and political parties were the main methodologies used, as well as the collection of secondary sources such as municipal financial records.
3. At the national level, 28.6 per cent of the total number of elected municipal councillors are a peasant or an indigenous person (Albo, 1997, p. 7). In 79 of the 311 municipalities, a peasant-indigenous councillor was elected mayor.

The Bolivian political system does not recognize local political parties, and allows only national parties to present candidates for municipal elections. This restricts the opportunities of peasants and indigenous people to participate in these elections, as they have to be affiliated to a national party. Generally, national parties look for strong candidates, and as peasants and indigenous people have less experience in the political arena, often the traditional political elite appears on the lists. There are few women in local government. After the 1995 election, there were even fewer women in municipal councils. In the six municipalities, men held all posts within local government (mayors and municipal council), while women held only the role of substitute councilor for these male councilors. According to a new law regulating elections, women must comprise at least 30 per cent of the listings, and every councilor should be replaced by someone of the opposite sex. This has resulted in an increase of women on the lists, but their role remains limited to that of substitute councilor.

Representativeness: Who Participates?

The LPP also entailed the introduction of participatory planning at the local level. Before 1994, planning was almost exclusively the domain of the Regional Development Corporations and – particularly in rural areas – of NGOs. However, since the implementation of the LPP, TBOs can express their priorities to local government. Each year, TBOs can file their demands for investments and call upon the funds transferred by the LPP.

First of all, it is interesting to see to what extent the claims presented are representative of the entire population. An important objective of the LPP is to increase the participation of women in local decision-making. However, in the municipalities in the valleys (Yotala, Poroma, Sopachuy, and Presto) and, to a lesser extent, the eastern lowland municipalities (Monteagudo and Huacareta), female participation in local meetings of peasant communities is very restricted. Participation in these meetings is often considered a male activity and women are only given 'voice and vote' if the male members of the household are absent (e.g., because of seasonal migration) or are considered too young to participate (female headed households). In this way, priorities often are male biased. Recently, however, this situation has begun to change, as a result of training aimed at the importance of including women. Also, in all six municipalities, it is mostly men who perform the role of dirigente (communal leader). The urban context presents a different picture, as the case of Monteagudo shows. The town of Monteagudo comprises 13 TBOs, of which seven are run by women.

According to our study the internal level of organization of neighborhood organizations is much weaker than that of the peasant communities. The latter hold meetings at least once a week, and almost everyone participates in them (attending meetings is compulsory). In contrast, participation of the population in neighborhood organizations is limited, as these are governed by a board. Meetings are held once or twice a year, and often only 10 per cent of members show up. These differences in levels of participation can be explained by the fact that most urban neighborhoods already have access to such facilities as schools, health posts, a sewage system, and paved roads, making community organization less vital. Another reason is that initially the LPP was presented as a law aimed at poverty alleviation in rural areas. Therefore, neighborhood organizations did not consider themselves a target group of this law.

In addition to the peasant communities and the neighborhood organizations, the LPP recognizes a third type of TBO; the indigenous communities. Two of the research municipalities had a number of such TBOs, notably recently established Guarani communities. The Guarani used to live and work on haciendas. However, these large properties are currently less profitable as a result of new land tenure laws and are gradually being sold to the Guarani. The organizations of indigenous communities are still rather weak as a result of the inheritance of dependence. Landowners used to suppress all kinds of organization, and participation was zero. Furthermore, knowledge about the LPP is often limited.

An example of traditional elites co-opting the system of popular participation is provided by the municipality of Huacareta, which is located in the eastern lowlands of the department of Chuquisaca. This region was almost untouched by the 1953 land reform, and large hacienda-like properties still dominate the land tenure system. Many landowners realized that the LPP provided an excellent opportunity to obtain additional facilities such as electricity, irrigation, and road improvement. They registered as a TBO, by assigning themselves the role of communal leader. According to the law, these TBOs meet all the requirements, whereas in actual fact, they only represent the landowner. The same mechanism, albeit with different actors, was observed in other municipalities; traditional elites that smoothly adopt the LPP, thereby restricting participation of the poor.

Priority-Setting

Participatory planning as introduced in Bolivia is quite a complex process, and therefore an impressive number of manuals have been developed to guide the process. Theoretically, each year TBOs are entitled to present their priorities, as defined during communal meetings, to the municipal council. The council subsequently considers the demands and, after consulting with the TBO leaders, incorporates them into the annual budget as projects. Usually the municipal meetings where the different TBOs can present their claims are rather chaotic. Very often, the meetings are closed without having reached any decisions. To make it worse, even if decisions have been taken, it is far from unusual for discussions and debates over issues on which agreement has already been reached to be restarted at the next meeting. In the end, it is usually the municipal council itself that takes the final decisions on which projects are to be incorporated into the annual investment plan.

During the first years, most municipalities operated according to these basic norms. However, over the course of time several different scenarios have been developed with regard to the process of municipal priority-setting. These adjustments generally were inspired by problems encountered with the number of TBOs in the municipality, the time-consuming character of the process, and difficulties related to aspects of equity and the development of a midterm development vision.

Many municipalities with a large number of TBOs decided to 'decentralize' participatory planning, by introducing an intermediate level for priority-setting. Monteagudo – with more than 80 TBOs – adopted this model and divided the municipality into smaller planning areas, i.e., cantons. The representative of the canton – the appointed corregidor – collects the demands within his jurisdiction and presents these to the municipal council. In contrast, the municipality of Sopachuy – with only 23 TBOs – each November invites all communal leaders to the alcaldia for a meeting to determine the contents of the plan.

A second adjustment was the introduction of five-year plans as an additional planning instrument. Most local governments contract NGOs or commercial consultants to identify the main problems and to elaborate the plans. Most municipalities (especially the rural ones) lack the experience and capacity required to design a medium-term development strategy themselves. In the preparatory phase, all TBOs are to be consulted, and for each TBO priorities for the next five years are set. This procedure simplifies priority-setting and reduces the time to be spent on preparing the annual budget. Also, the risk of TBOs presenting a 'shopping list' is reduced, as they are forced to carefully discuss their real priorities. Although all municipalities in this case study had a five-year plan, each used the instrument in a different way. Some, such as Monteagudo, used it as a starting point for their annual budgeting, so that 95 per cent of the priorities set in the five-year plan were translated into projects in the annual plan. Other municipalities, however, disregarded their five-year plans. Reasons for not making use of the plan may be a change of mayor. Most new mayors refuse to implement the plans formulated by their predecessor, especially if he was affiliated to another political party. In other cases, the five-year plans had not been formulated according the norms, and thus did not reflect the demands of the population. In contrast, other municipalities firmly stick to these five-year plans, with the result that there is sometimes little room for emergencies, such as the requests for seed after periods of droughts.

A five-year plan also facilitates the aspect of equity. Most TBOs assume that they are entitled to one project each year, corresponding to the amount of money their municipality receives each year. However, as most projects exceed this amount of money, it is not possible to award every TBO a project each year. This is difficult to explain, and therefore a five-year plan wherein the distribution of funds is determined equally facilitates this.

Selection and Implementation of Projects

Although rural TBOs usually outnumber urban TBOs, most municipalities target investments more at the towns. This may be attributed to the fact that the urban part of the municipality often functions as a service center for the rest of the municipality, with regard to schools and health care, and thus has a relatively larger share of projects. However, this does not explain a similar bias in the allocation of projects not aimed at providing communal services. Research into the factors conditioning the success of TBOs in obtaining projects revealed some interesting facts. Neighborhood committees are much more successful in getting their projects included in the annual plan than the two other types of TBOs. This is probably related to their physical proximity to the local government. Their leaders are better informed and more able to put pressure on the local administration. Furthermore, they are usually better educated than those representing the peasant and indigenous organizations.

Looking at the nature of the projects that are taken up in the six municipalities under investigation it appears that the emphasis is on investments in the social sector, i.e., education and health infrastructure. Most rural municipalities suffer from a lack of such services, in particular for the peasant and indigenous communities. The LPP was also designed with the aim of redressing spatial inequalities in social servicing. Furthermore, there is a tendency towards community-oriented projects. Within TBOs, projects that will favor the entire (or at least the majority of the) community are most popular.

However, a shift to more general projects (directed at the entire municipality) can be observed. After six years of LPP implementation, most communities enjoy such basic services as primary schools and health posts. Therefore, other projects (e.g., community strengthening, the provision of milk to primary school children, veterinary services) are now being selected. The share of productive projects – i.e., those aiming to increase agricultural productivity or rural infrastructure (irrigation, mills, warehouses) – is hardly increasing. These projects receive lower priority as they are relatively expensive and technically difficult to implement, and benefit smaller fractions of the local community.

Another trend observed was the speeding up of implementation. The ratio (i.e., the proportion of planned investments that had actually been realized before 31 December) increased from less than 40 per cent in 1995 in all municipalities, to 65-80 per cent in 1999. Especially in the early years of the LPP, many municipalities planned projects without having secured the necessary funds.

TBOs not only engage in setting priorities, but also contribute to the implementation of projects. This type of participation was introduced for both financial reasons (cost reduction) and management reasons. People feel more responsible for a project if they have been involved in its implementation. In this respect there was a noticeable difference between peasant and indigenous communities on the one hand, and neighborhood committees on the other. While rural TBOs often contributed labor or materials to projects, urban TBOs generally provided money.

Accountability: The Oversight Committees

In order to ensure the accountability of local government in Bolivia, the first Oversight Committees (OCs) were introduced in 1994. Since then, OCs have been established in all municipalities via direct elections. The main function of an OC is to oversee and assure accountability of funds allocated through the LPP. The instruments to do so, however, are limited. OCs do not receive any funds to perform their activities, and most depend on the generosity of local governments for such facilities as an office, phones, and transport. The relationship with the local government can be strained. Some local governments do not accept the interference of OCs in municipal affairs. In these cases, OCs are seriously limited in their ability to act as watchdogs. In other cases, local government exerts control over the OCs by interfering with the elections or offering members of the OCs money in exchange for their support.

A more practical bottleneck in the performance of ocs, specifically in rural municipalities, relates to the dispersion of projects that have to be monitored in combination with poor communication and accessibility. Furthermore, most members of the ocs are not familiar with controlling the financial and technical aspects of projects. A consequence is that training is an important element in strengthening the ocs. However, as the composition of the ocs changes almost every year, the training needs to be repeated annually.

Lack of capacity is also a bottleneck for local governments. Most municipalities, especially the rural ones, had to start virtually from scratch. Problems are most pronounced in the execution of several administrative and technical tasks, such as computerized systems of accounting and project management, and the elaboration of project profiles. Most rural mayors and municipal councils have problems turning official requirements regarding popular participation into practice. In our study none of the mayors or municipal councils was able to support the TBO. Of course, one should remember that participatory planning in Bolivia was implemented rather recently. Therefore, it is worthwhile looking at another more long-standing experience with participatory planning, that of Porto Alegre in Brazil.

The Participatory Budgeting Experience in Brazil[4]

Local participatory planning was introduced in the late 1970s/early 1980s in several Brazilian towns, e.g., Lajes, Boa Esperanca, Fortaleza, Diadema, Vitória, and Vila Velha. In the new (1988) constitution, ideas on administrative decentralization and popular participation were given a legislative basis. This marked the start of various experiments seeking to turn theory into practice at the municipal level. The new constitution also introduced transfers of financial resources from the central state to local government. Especially the more progressive elements of the constitution, such as the Urban Reform Chapter, had been influenced by a national movement in which the Partido dos Trabalhadores (PT) played an active role.

The case of Porto Alegre – a city with a population of 1.3 million in a metropolitan region encompassing 3.3 million people in the south of Brazil – has become renowned both in Brazil and elsewhere for having adopted an innovative method of municipal budgeting; the participatory budgeting

---

4. The Porto Alegre case study is based on interviews with key informants and visits to Brazil in 2000 and 2001.

approach. At the 1996 Habitat-II Conference, it was considered one of the forty 'best practices'. Porto Alegre is a partner in many regional and South-North networks, such as Mercocities and Red URB-AL. It maintains strong ties with cities such as Barcelona, Saint-Denis, Toronto, Brussels, and others that have expressed their intention to apply participatory planning instruments like those developed in Porto Alegre.

Porto Alegre's participatory budgeting served as an example to many other Brazilian cities. In 1988, the PT won the municipal election (or became part of a left-wing coalition) in such places as Sao Paulo, Santos, Belo Horizonte, Campinas, Goiana, Vitória, Santo André, and Betim. It introduced participatory budgeting or similar innovative experiments in each of these cities (Correa de Oliveira, 2002). By the year 2000, participatory budgeting had been adopted by 140 municipalities throughout Brazil. Because the PT consolidated its position in many cities and further expanded its influence in others[5] in the municipal elections in December 2000, it is likely that participatory budgeting will spread to more and more municipalities. Meanwhile other political parties have also embraced this principle of local governance, although there are some marked variations in methodology and instruments. More than 30 non-PT-governed municipalities in Brazil apply some form of participatory budgeting.

One of the main factors behind the success of Porto Alegre's participatory budgeting venture is the political continuity of PT administrations since 1988. The city administration was able to first experiment with and then consolidate and institutionalize popular participation in the design of its annual municipal public investment plans. Many observers also point out that Porto Alegre has a strong social movement tradition, which dates back to the 1970s and allegedly was at the base of popular participation in the 1990s. Indeed, Porto Alegre was the scene of a fierce struggle against the use of toxic substances by the expanding soy bean industry in the 1970s, and was the birthplace of Brazil's ecological movement. Also, neighborhood organizations existed in Porto Alegre already before the democratic transition. In a different vein, Alves dos Santos (2000, p. 589) points out that people in Porto Alegre have significantly more leftist sympathies and are significantly more organized into labor, civil, and political associations than the inhabitants of other major Brazilian cities. Dos Santos is particularly explicit in stating a causality between this associational activity and the success of the participatory budgeting process in Porto Alegre.

---

5. Souza (2001, p. 164) gives an account of the number of PT victories in successive Brazilian municipal (mayoral) elections: 32 in 1988, 53 in 1992, 115 in 1996 and 187 in 2000.

The implementation of the participatory budgeting process in Porto Alegre has been neither easy nor a matter of course. Particularly in the early years, the newly elected administration went to great lengths to explain its objectives and to sell its ideas and principles of popular participation to the population and to non-PT representatives.

In 1988, the new local authorities were confronted with a huge debt inherited from their predecessors. Moreover, 96 per cent of the municipal budget was absorbed by the salaries of the municipal workers and only 3.2 per cent was left for investment in public works (De Sousa Santos, 1998). In 1989, the PT government organized various meetings between municipal staff and workers on the one hand, and the population at large on the other, to discuss the financial crisis and its possible solutions. Many people from the poorer neighborhoods attended these meetings, and there was a consensus that the problem should be solved jointly. Nevertheless, it took two years to create a solid institutional base from which mass participation in the municipal budgeting process could be organized. Crucial in this respect was a major tax reform, which was first discussed with the inhabitants and subsequently — with mass popular support — forced through the conservative Camara de Vereadores (the city assembly, and thus the legislative body). The tax on urban property (both land and buildings) in particular was expected to contribute ever greater shares of total municipal revenue. Based on the principle of progressive rates, the contribution from this tax has risen from 6 per cent of municipal revenues in 1990 to 20 per cent today. Meanwhile, the share of the municipal budget (US$ 400 million) available for investment in 2001 has risen to 15-20 per cent. Here it helped also that in the period 1989-1993 increasingly more funds were transferred from the central state budget to the local administration.

The following is a brief description of the main elements of the functioning of the participatory budgeting practice in Porto Alegre. At the heart of the philosophy is the objective to break with the traditional authoritarian and clientelist model of governance, and to empower citizens by giving them a greater say in municipal decision-making with respect to the allocation of expenditure. People should be able to debate public spending and defend their neighborhood's interests against those of the more powerful pressure groups in the city. Also, citizens should become effective controllers of municipal public spending. Only then will they be convinced that it is worth investing energy and time in the priority-setting process. This permanent monitoring and control function is also a stimulus to future participation in the budgeting process.

In Porto Alegre, the participatory budgeting is a year-round activity involving assemblies, gatherings, forums, and intermediate consultations. Most of these meetings are attended – and indeed, guided – by municipal officers and officials, although there are many local settlement meetings which may also address other issues (in addition to those concerning the allocation of public expenditure) which do not need the participation of people from the Prefeitura. Over the years, many adaptations and improvements in the structuring of the budgeting process have been made, but one constant is the intense involvement of municipal officers and community organizers hired by the city administration. Thus, the role of local government has not diminished as popular participation increased. On the contrary, a continuous effort of awareness-raising, popular education, training, and dissemination of information at the neighborhood level proved to be necessary in order to bring the participatory budgeting message to the people; in general, this process has been successful.

Each year, the implementation of the previous year's investment plan is discussed and reviewed during a first round of discussion meetings. This review process, and all subsequent activities until the final priority-setting for the coming year, is done in the general assemblies of Porto Alegre's 16 districts. At the same time, assemblies and other meetings are held along the lines of six thematic clusters. During a second round of assemblies, in each district and thematic group the priorities for the coming year are discussed and two delegates for the District and Thematic Forums are elected, as are representatives for the Municipal Budget Council. In between the officially established assemblies and Forum meetings, at the settlement level frequent meetings may take place between the local inhabitants in order to decide upon their specific demands. Yet, it is striking to see how people have already learned to abstract from their own particularist interests, and to give priority to more urgent needs felt in neighboring settlements in their district. They have also learned that modesty in one year will be rewarded by their demands being given priority at some later date. According to many observers, one of the most important benefits brought about by the participatory budgeting exercise is the 'impressive learning process that occurred through the budget debates' and the development of a 'capacity to systematize their changing attitudes into general rules for how resources ought to be distributed' (Abers, 1998b). In a study of the budgeting process in three municipalities which form part of the Sao Paulo Greater Metropolitan Area (Santo André, Mauá, and Riberao Pires), Carvalho and Felgueiras note an interesting difference between the Santo André experience and that in the other two municipalities. The researchers observe a distinct learning process both among the administration and the population in Santo André, which was already in a second term of PT government at the time of study. The two adjacent municipalities were still in a first phase of participatory budgeting, and its process was characterized by a very high degree of informality which resembled the first-phase experience of Santo André (Carvalho and Felgueiras, 2000, p. 65).

Over the years, the city administration has experimented with various tools to secure a certain degree of equity in the distribution of the scarce resources through participatory budgeting. In 2001, this equity-oriented mechanism consists of three simple, objective criteria which are applied to each of the various investment sectors. These criteria are the total population of the district, the lack or shortage of infrastructure and services, and the thematic priorities established by the district population. Different weights are attached to these criteria. In this, the size of the population is less important than the shortage or lack of infrastructure and the priorities. For the year 2000, the highest city-wide priorities went to the sectors. Housing (57 grades), street paving (44), health (43), basic sanitation (39), and social welfare (31). Considerably less priority was given to education (12), economic development (6), recreational space (4), culture (3), and transport (1). The remaining sectors (sports and public lighting) were not selected as a priority area in any of the 16 urban districts (POA, 2000, p. 19). Indeed, the distributive mechanisms of the participatory budgeting instrument are such that low-income neighborhoods have profited much more than the well-off ones during all the years of PT administration.

Of course, not every project proposed by the residents of a neighborhood or district will be feasible from a technical or financial point of view. Thus, for example, the municipality rejects proposals for rainwater drainage in unpaved streets. Housing construction in hazard-prone areas is also rejected. The responsible technical departments of the municipality have to provide quick answers regarding the feasibility of proposals (including the financial implications) before the entire city budget (and the expenditure plans of each city agency) is approved by the municipal council.

As such, the participatory budgeting exercise results each year in many urgently needed and very visible infrastructure and service provision projects. The commitment of the successive local administrations to meeting the demands of the population has contributed to mobilizing ever more support for the PT. Many observers agree that the high degrees of transparency and accountability of the local government have been essential for the three successive re-elections of the PT to Porto Alegre's city hall. The participatory budgeting policies imply a breakaway from the traditional closed-door decision-making, clientelism, and favoritism of previous administrations in this city (Abers, 1998b). Some – in particular, the members of the city council – question the representativeness of those who participate in the budgeting process. Although in the year 2000 a record of 40,000 people in Porto Alegre participated in one way or another, this figure represents only three percent of the total population of the city. Joao Verle, the current vice mayor of Porto Alegre, answers to this criticism that these 40,000 people may well be a small share of the total population, but it is considerably more than the 43 members of the city council. The participatory involvement of the population thus complements representative democracy in city hall. At the same time, the budgeting process adds to local accountability, because it is widely known (and now an institutionalized procedure) that the implementation of the approved projects will be carefully monitored.

Conclusion

This contribution focus on the effects of decentralization processes on local governance in Latin America, with an emphasis on Bolivia and Brazil. These two countries have implemented highly interesting experiments involving the delegation and devolution of responsibilities to lower levels of government. In both countries, specially designed policies are intended to involve the population in democratic decision-making, in particular with respect to the quality of their living environment. As such, participatory democracy is promoted by means of some very innovative, in-house developed instruments. Decentralization has not stopped at the borders of the municipal entity, but has moved further down the administrative ladder into the districts and settlements, both urban and rural. At the same time, it has facilitated the emergence of multi-actor platforms for developing a jointly shared vision and strategy for future local development.

Thus, the experiences analyzed in this contribution are very much in line with the principles of Local Agenda 21 (a result of the Earth Summit in Rio de Janeiro, 1992), and also with those of the Habitat Agenda, which was adopted in 1996 at the City Summit in Istanbul. Similarly, the recent Urban and Local Government Strategy of the World Bank (2000) emphasizes important notions of local governance, such as transparency, accountability, ownership, and participation. Although the focus here has been on the issue of popular participation, the examples from Bolivia and Brazil demonstrate that local authorities are also trying to come to grips with the other basic elements of good governance.

Bolivia and Brazil provide cases of local governance and popular participation which, in addition to the similarities, show some marked variations as to the model of participation and the participatory planning practice. Before summing up some of the most important conclusions, it is pertinent to note that we must be cautious with easy generalizations. First, although Porto Alegre's participatory budgeting methodology is undeniably the best-known example, it is certainly not the only one in Brazil. Many other municipalities have developed instruments for participatory budgeting; although many of these were very much inspired by the Porto Alegre experience, each has its own particular characteristics. Secondly – and much more importantly – the rise of PT and other leftist municipalities over the last decade cannot conceal the fact that the majority of local governments in Brazil are still dominated by conservative politicians, who continue to govern in a traditional context of private-like feuds based on patron-client relationships. And thirdly, the Bolivian examples were taken from some essentially rural municipalities in the traditional highlands and valleys of the Chuquisaca department, which offer a quite different picture than that of indigenous lowland communities or, for that matter, the biggest cities.

Despite these qualifying remarks, this comparative overview has demonstrated some marked differences between the decentralization process in Brazil and that in Bolivia. Although the latter process is the younger in terms of age, it has matured more rapidly and spread throughout the country on a more generalized basis. Within only a few years, the Bolivian decentralization process has become fully institutionalized in the country's 314 municipalities, and responsibilities for planning have been passed from the departmental administrative tiers down to the local level. Its main impact has been on the rural population of the highlands and the indigenous peoples in the oriental lowlands. There has been a quite impressive increase in the number of mayors and councilors with a peasant or indigenous background. Until the 1995 municipal elections (the first elections following the implementation of the Law on Popular Participation), these non-urban groups had never really been represented in local democracy.

The crucial difference with the Brazilian decentralization process is the coherent system of laws which provide the legal and regulatory framework in Bolivia. This makes the implementation of the participatory planning practice at the municipal level much more a matter of commitment than it is in the Brazilian context. Failure on the part of the local authorities to formulate yearly and five-yearly development plans is sanctioned with restrictions on money transfers from central government. Even though the current (1998-2001) government of ex-dictator Bánzer is not at all sympathetic to this nationwide decentralization-cum-participation affair, it has not been able to frustrate the process because it exists within a sound, legally established framework. The process has gained its own momentum, in particular in the rural municipalities where, for the first time ever, a large share of the population feels that it is a part of society at large.

In Brazil, however, apart from the newly established constitution, no such system of specifically targeted laws has been developed. As such, it depends entirely on the political will and disposition of local authorities whether or not participatory initiatives are stimulated and supported. The case of Porto Alegre was exceptionally rewarding because of the political continuity of four consecutive PT administrations. Other municipalities have been less politically stable and this has interrupted some promising initiatives.

Although Bolivian local authorities display a more generalized commitment to participatory planning approaches, their engagement is often much less than in the Brazilian cases of participatory budgeting. In Brazil, the PT municipalities with their bottom-up approaches have a much greater ownership of their programs than Bolivian municipalities. The involvement of municipal authorities and their administrative staff is much greater in Porto Alegre and other PT-run municipalities. In Bolivia this engagement is much less, precisely because it is very much a top-down affair. This also manifests itself in the phenomenon of the outsourcing of very substantial parts of the participatory planning process. Innumerable NGOs and consultants are contracted by Bolivian municipalities to organize and supervise the planning process and to deliver the yearly operational plans. This is particularly characteristic of the rural municipalities, which lack the capacity to perform the task adequately. The Monteagudo case demonstrates a more autonomous planning process. Since this city has a larger and more qualified staff than the other municipalities in the study, the planning experience shows a slightly higher degree of ownership. However, it must be emphasized that the enormous lack of capacity among the administrative staff of Bolivian municipalities (even in the largest cities, such as La Paz and Santa Cruz) poses a real challenge to the future development of participatory planning approaches.

Another important difference is the methodology of targeting the budget at specific areas and groups. In the Bolivian system, the co-participation funds are distributed through a very simple, single-criterion methodology, i.e., the number of residents per spatial entity (municipality). In Porto Alegre the distributive policies are based on a multi-criteria methodology, which gives much weight to deficiencies in infrastructure and service provision. In other cities, such as Belo Horizonte, the administration has developed a quality of life index which determines the allocation of resources. This question of allocation of resources has been a matter of debate in Bolivia for some years now, as it is acknowledged that the instrument is too crude and does not help to attain greater social justice and equity in the municipalities. However, it is not expected that a new methodology will be agreed upon until a new, more decentralization-minded government is installed.

A very promising fact revealed by this comparative study is that participatory decision-making is an art that can be taught and learned. Having assisted at community meetings in many Bolivian municipalities, it was a highly refreshing experience to participate in assemblies and meetings in Porto Alegre. In Bolivia, these meetings are generally poorly chaired and are disturbed by many interruptions. In Porto Alegre, the inhabitants have learned how to express themselves at discussion meetings in an orderly and effective manner. Here, the fruits of more than a decade of practice in public debating and decision-making became astonishingly clear. People showed a high degree of understanding for arguments which were more convincing than their own. They were even willing to accept proposals for investments that would not directly favor their own settlement.

References

Abers, R. (1998a), 'Learning Democratic Practice: Distributing Government Resources Through Popular Participation in Porto Alegre, Brazil', in M. Douglas and J. Friedmann (eds), *Cities for Citizens*, John Wiley and Sons, Chichester, pp. 29-65.

Abers, R. (1998b), 'From Clientelism to Cooperation: Local Government, Participatory Policy, and Civic Organizing in Porto Alegre, Brazil', *Politics and Society*, Vol. 26(4), pp. 511-23.

Albo, X. (1997), 'Alcaldes y Consejales Campesinos/Indígenas: La Lógica Tras las Cifras', *Indígenas en el poder local*, Ministerio de Desarrollo Humano, Secretaria Nacional de Participación Popular, La Paz.

Alves dos Santos Junior, O. (2000), 'Gestao Urbana, Associativismo e Participacao nas Metrópoles Brasileiras', in L.C. de Queiroz Ribeiro (org.), *O Futuro das Metrópoles: Desigualdades e Governabilidade*, pp. 575-600, Editora Revan/FASE, Rio de Janeiro.

Burki, S.J., Perry, G. and Dillinger, W. (1999), *Beyond the Center: Decentralizing the State*, World Bank Latin American and Caribbean Studies, Viewpoints, World Bank, Washington.

Carvalho, M., do Carmen A.A. and Felgueiras, D. (2000), *Orcamento Participativo no ABC. Mauá, Ribeirao Pires e Santo André. Gestao 1979-2000*, Publicacoes Polis No. 34, Polis, Sao Paulo.

Correa de Oliveira, M.T. (2002), *Multi-sectoral Partnerships for Low-income Land Development in Brazil* (PhD thesis, forthcoming), Utrecht University/Institute for Housing and Urban Development Studies, Utrecht/Rotterdam.

Faguet, J.P. (2000), *Does Decentralisation Increase Responsiveness to Local Needs? Evidence from Bolivia*, World Bank, Washington.

Galindo, M. (1996), *Análisis Fiscal Financiero de la Descentralización Administrativa y Estudio de Opciones para Captación de Recursos Financieros para la Prefectura de Chuquisaca*, Prefectura del Departamento Chuquisaca, Sucre.

Gaventa, J. and Valderrama, C. (1999), *Participation, Citizenship and Local Governance*, Background note prepared for the workshop on 'Strengthening Participation in Local Governance', Institute of Development Studies, June 21-24.

Leftwich, A. (1994), 'Governance, the State and the Politics of Development', *Development and Change*, Vol. 25(2), pp. 363-86.

Lippman, H. and Pranke, P. (1998), *Democratic Local Governance in Honduras*, Impact Evaluation PN-ACA-908, United States Agency for International Development, Washington.

Litvack, J., Ahmad, J. and Bird, R. (1998), *Rethinking Decentralisation in Developing Countries*, World Bank, Washington.

Manor, J. (1999), *The Political Economy of Decentralisation. Directions in Development*, World Bank, Washington.

Martinez, J.A. (1996), *Municípios y Participación Popular en América Latina: un Modelo de Desarrollo*, CEBIAE, La Paz.

Molina Monasterios, F. (1997), *Historia de la Participación Popular*, Ministerio de Desarrollo Humano, Secretaria Nacional de Participación Popular, La Paz.

Nickson, R.A. (1995), *Local Government in Latin America*, Lynne Rienner Publishers, Boulder/London.

POA (2000), *Orcamento Participativo 2001. A Conquista do Espaco Democrático. Plano de Investimentos e Servicos 2000*, Prefeitura, Porto Alegre.

Rondinelli, D., Nellis, J. and Cheema, G. (1984), *Decentralisation in Developing Countries. A Review of Recent Experience*, World Bank Staff Working Papers, No. 581, Management and Development Series, No. 8, World Bank, Washington.

Schuurman, F.J. (1996), 'Local Government in Latin America: Some Critical Notes', in P. Gans (ed.), *Regionale Entwicklung in Lateinamerika*, Erfurter Geographische Studien, Bd. 4, pp. 4-21.

Smith, B.C. (1985), *Decentralisation: the Territorial Dimension of the State*, George Allen and Unwin, London/Boston/Sydney.

Sousa Santos, B. de (1998), 'Participatory Budgeting in Porto Alegre: Toward a Redistributive Democracy', *Politics and Society*, Vol. 26(4), pp. 461-510.

Souza, C. (2001), 'Participatory Budgeting in Brazilian Cities: Limits and Possibilities in Building Democratic Institutions', *Environment and Urbanization*, Vol. 13(1), pp. 159-84.

Verle, J. (2001), *O Orcamento Participativo em Porto Alegre*. Paper presented at the IULA/FMCU Unity Congress, 3-6 May, Rio de Janeiro.

Wilson, E., Garman, Ch. and Haggard, S. (1999), 'The Politics of Decentralisation in Latin America', *Latin American Research Review*, Vol. 34(1), pp. 7-56.

World Bank (2000), *Cities in Transition: A Strategic View of Urban and Local Government Issues*, World Bank, Washington.

11   Combining Capitals: The Assets of Community-Based Organizations and Local Government for Neighborhood Environmental Management in Lima

MICHAELA HORDIJK

Introduction

In the summer of 1998, a group of neighborhood leaders from the squatter settlements of Pampas de Juan (southern Lima) visited their mayor. The mayor was running for a third consecutive term, and his election campaign was in full swing. For the neighborhood leaders, this was an ideal opportunity to claim the political capital they had built up during their numerous visits to the municipality. They needed the support of the mayor in their demand making towards the water company. By making tremendous efforts, they had managed to get the drinking water and sewerage connections installed in their neighborhoods. For years they had been paying off their debt. Although the national government had recently announced that the debts of the poor to the public utilities would be written off, the debts of the poor in Pampas de San Juan to the water company seemed not to be considered in this debt-relief scheme. This was why the usually quarrelling neighborhood leaders had formed an ad-hoc coalition and were now visiting the mayor. They could organize the people in Pampas in order to give him more votes. The mayor in turn could use his influence, his contacts with congress members, and his friendships with the high echelons of the ruling party of President Fujimori to ensure that Pampas de San Juan would be included in the debt-reshuffling. Twenty-five neighborhood leaders from different political backgrounds joined in a meeting with the mayor to speak about this and other matters. Some reminded the mayor of his promises to construct a playground in their settlement, or to donate cooking utensils to the communal kitchen. Others complained about the activities of the provincial government in their settlement. The governor of Lima Province was also up for re-election. Since he was a member of the opposition, his interventions were as antagonistic as possible to what the district mayor was trying to achieve. Considering the many overlapping responsibilities between district and provincial government, there was little the mayor could do. But he thankfully collected the cases of mismanagement of the provincial authorities to use in his campaign, and in order to sue the governor if possible.

A few months later, the election was over and the mayor had won. The people in Pampas were still paying their debt to the water company, and the mayor – highly troubled by many corruption scandals – lost interest in them. The ad-hoc coalition of neighborhood leaders split up again, and each of them returned to the normal scheme of ritual visits to the mayor's office.

During the last two decades the realignment between the public sector, the private sector, and civil society has received a great deal of academic attention. At first, the relation between the public and the private sector came to the forefront, driven by the process of privatizing public services. Thereafter the relation between government and civil society attracted increasing attention, especially in the aftermath of the UNCED conference in Rio de Janeiro in 1992 (Mathews, 1997; Perlas, 2000).

In this chapter an attempt will be made to show whether and – if so – to what extent the currently praised approach (the partnership approach) can offer a feasible alternative for dealing with the twin problems of poverty and environmental hazards in low-income areas. This will be done by taking the current daily practice in a poor district in Lima as an example, and analyzing to what extent there is a real possibility for forming partnerships between local government and poor communities.

The Urban Poor as Purposeful Actors

Poverty is no longer seen as only a lack of income, but also as a lack of access. This includes a lack of access to income earning opportunities, as well as to basic services (education and health) and decision-making processes – even those that directly affect their living circumstances. One of the basic characteristics of poverty is 'vulnerability'; the inability to cope with and recover from long-term stresses and sudden shocks (Moser, 1998). However, people actively seek to overcome vulnerability by engaging in various kinds of action, either individually or collectively. Over the last decade the way they do so has been analyzed from the 'sustainable livelihoods' perspective. In an influential article, Chambers and Conway defined a livelihood as 'comprising the capabilities, assets (both natural and social) and activities required for a means of living; a livelihood is sustainable which can cope with and recover from stresses and shocks, maintain or enhance its capabilities and assets, both now and in the future, while not undermining the natural resource base' (Chambers and Conway, 1992).

Poor people thus possess certain assets, which they deploy in order to improve their situation. The most well-known 'asset' is their labor. But they also have their skills and capabilities. Their house, previously often classified as a basic need, can also be considered an asset. By using a room as a workshop or renting it out, it becomes a productive asset. More recently these different types of assets have been understood in terms of 'capitals'. Following de Haan (2000) we can distinguish five different kind of capitals the poor employ in their attempts to secure and improve their livelihoods. If applied to an urban context, these capitals are:

- *Human capital* (labor, skills, experience, knowledge, creativity, inventiveness);
- *Natural capital* (land, water, energy);
- *Physical capital* (housing, tools, machinery);
- *Financial capital* (money, loans/credit);
- *Social capital* (Haan, 2000, p. 15).

Households allocate the different capitals over four realms of urban life, viz. livelihood and employment; health and wellbeing; habitat and environment; and social networks and political power (Douglass and Zoghlin, 1994). The relative importance given to each of the four realms can change over time, and changes when the economic situation of the household changes, or when they reach another phase in the lifecycle. Improvements in one domain can also affect other domains. Adverse living conditions can threaten people's health and their potential to generate an income. Improving the provision of drinking water not only improves habitat conditions, but can also result in an improved health situation, and can release a considerable amount of time for women and children to perform other activities (income earning activities or education). Allocating assets or capitals to realize improvements in the realm of habitat and environment can therefore be understood as being part of the overall livelihood-cum-welfare strategies of households.

The livelihood approach – including the definition of the different assets or forms of capital – is usually limited to the level of the household (Moser, 1998; Haan, 2000). McCleod (2001) recently suggested adding a sixth category of capital, namely institutional capital. This refers to the organizational forms and relationships specifically developed by the urban poor to increase their capacity and to escape from poverty. They use various institutions for valuing, developing, applying, and leveraging their asset base. We thus should look not only at how households deploy their capitals, but also at the way they increase these capitals and create capitals through engaging in collective action and the formation of organizations. This idea of creating capital through collective action will be taken up in this chapter.

A Changing Perspective on the Role of the State in Urban Development

In the early 1950s, national governments in developing countries perceived their role as being the ruling actor in society, providing their citizens with security and development. The appropriate function of the private sector and civil society actors was to comply with the bureaucratic rules and procedures crafted by government institutions to regulate the market and the public sphere (Gonzalez et al., 2000).

During the economic crisis of the 1980s, it became increasingly clear that many states were failing to deliver these promises. In the urban context, they were not providing adequate housing, basic physical and social urban services, or employment opportunities. Gradually, the perception of the role of the state shifted from provider to enabler, i.e., the government should set the framework to enable others – the poor themselves, the private sector, or other actors such as NGOs or civil society organizations (CSOs) – to provide the services.

Enablement is now a familiar concept applied in many policy domains. The government is no longer the prime actor, and it seeks to establish cooperative relations with other actors in the urban arena, such as the private sector, NGOs, or CSOs. One of the major arguments in favor of partnerships is that the complementarity between two different kinds of actors can create a win-win situation. By combining distinct capacities and resources, coalitions can yield more efficient results than each type of organization alone. More recently, several authors have stated that coalitions between different types of organization can have an added value when the organizations merge their distinct objectives, assets, and powers. This allows them to develop innovative policies and practices (Biekart, 1999; Perlas, 2000; Baud, 2000).

Government thus comes with a certain set of characteristics that are specific to government. These specific characteristics can be expressed – in analogy with the situation at the household level – in a set of capitals. Gonzalez et al. (2000) distinguishes the following capitals of the government sector:

- *Physical capital* (financial, technological, and material resources), expressed in budget allocation and infrastructure;
- *Organizational capital* (human resources, capacity to manage, management structure, leadership, and training), expressed in the formal linking and coordination, both vertically and horizontally, of the bureaucratic structure, the creation of rules, procedures, and directives;
- *Political capital:* (power, authority, law-making, influence, and legitimacy);
- *Intellectual capital* (knowledge or know-how, mastery of relevant laws, policies, and institutional context; technical expertise on specific subjects);
- *Socio-cultural capital:* government ideals, values and ideology, civic mindedness (Gonzalez et al., 2000, p. 10).

When governments deploy their capitals to join forces with other actors, we no longer speak of government but of governance. The former refers to ruling, the latter to steering. If other actors start to take part, governance becomes a more complex process. Helmsing (2000, p. 18) pointed out that in the early stages these actors together may constitute no more than a fragmented network, but in advanced stages of development of governance structures they may have transformed themselves into a largely self-organizing network. The state can then only indirectly and imperfectly steer such networks (Helmsing, 2000, p. 18).

Partnerships

Partnerships between state and non-state actors can mobilize resources, reduce risks, and contribute to the economies of scale in production (Helmsing 2000). Various authors have indicated that it is difficult to adequately define partnerships, since partnership can occur between such different kinds of partner (government at all levels, all different kinds of private sector actors, all different kinds of civil society organizations), in different forms, in different degrees of formalization, and for different

purposes (Stoker, 1998; Pierre, 1998; Batley, 1996). General characteristics that most partnerships have in common are that:
- A partnership involves two or more actors (some authors add: at least one of which is public (Peters, 1998));
- Each partner is a principal, i.e., each is capable of bargaining on its own behalf, rather than having to consult with other forms of authority;
- A partnership is an enduring relationship between these actors (based on a written or verbal agreement, informal or formal in nature, with some continuing interaction);
- Each of the participants brings something to the partnership. Each of the partners has to transfer some resources – material or immaterial – to the partnership. The partnership is mutually beneficial (without assuming equality between the actors);
- A partnership finds it expression in concrete activities;
- A partnership implies a shared responsibility for the outcomes of the activities;
- Partnerships are meant to serve a public interest (Baud *et al.*, 2001; Peters, 1998). To distinguish them from commercial partnerships, they are now sometimes called public interest partnerships (PIPs) (Gonzalez *et al.*, 2000).

If these are the characteristics of a partnership, it is clear that certain preconditions have to be fulfilled before a partnership can be fruitfully developed. There has to be a certain degree of mutuality of interest between the actors concerning the specific goals the partnership might pursue. If each partner has to bring something to the partnership, and the partnership should be mutually beneficial, this implies that there has to be a possibility of exchange. A partnership can only function if there is a certain amount of trust between the partners, as well as mutual accountability (Baud, 2000). There has to be a certain leadership available to both sets of actors. The leaders must be willing to take some gambles and be willing to forego some of the potential credit for any success. Peters (1998) furthermore notes that partnerships more often flourish when there are no alternatives available to attain the same goals, and that partnerships tend to be more successful when the partners are sufficiently strong to bargain effectively. A seriously asymmetric relation may not create the symbiosis required for successful partnerships.

It goes without saying that if each of the participants brings something to the partnership, we must be able to understand the different contribution in terms of capitals. Partners can thus bring in financial capital, but also human, physical, organizational, political, intellectual, and socio-cultural capital. As stated; if two partners with distinct characteristics join forces, this may produce surplus value; in other words, an increase of capital. Developing partnerships is a process. Throughout the process new social capital is created, and quite often also intellectual, organizational, and even political capital. It is important to analyze the functioning of partnerships not only in terms of their material results, but also to take the capital formation into account.

Local government has become the major government actor when it comes to local governance. It is to be expected that the importance of local government will increase in face of the globalization process and the rise of inter-city competition. As local governments cannot meet the challenges of local development on their own, they therefore engage in partnership arrangements with other actors in the urban arena. But how do these two actors actually meet on common ground? How do they interact and what partnerships do they develop? These questions will be illustrated with a specific case; local goverment-CBO interaction for daily urban environmental management practices in a poor district in Lima, Peru (Hordijk, 2000).

Urban Environmental Conditions in Pampas de San Juan, Southern Lima

Presently there are over 1,000 low-income settlements (*barriadas*) in Lima, housing a third of the Limenian population. A very small percentage are situated in the city center – the inner-city slums (*tugurios*). Over 90 per cent of these barriadas are to be found in the peripheral districts of the city; the three so-called cones, where the steady growth of the city took place along the major traffic axes to the north, east, and south of the city. These peripheral districts – most of them with between 100,000 and 500,000 inhabitants – have similar socio-economic and physical characteristics. They all result from people building their own dwelling in unattractive peripheral desert areas (low-value land), with or without state support. A high proportion of the economically active population works in the informal sector.

Pampas de San Juan is one of these innumerable clusters of peripheral low-income neighborhoods. It is part of the district San Juan de Miraflores. Pampas de San Juan now has an estimated 50,000 inhabitants, a sixth of the population of San Juan de Miraflores. The area it covers is a typical Limenian desert landscape of flat areas surrounded by steep rocky hills. Invasions of the flat areas started in the early 1980s. Once these filled up, people started to invade the slopes. By the mid-1990s there was almost no space left for new invasions, but the occupation of public spaces in consolidated neighborhoods was continuous.

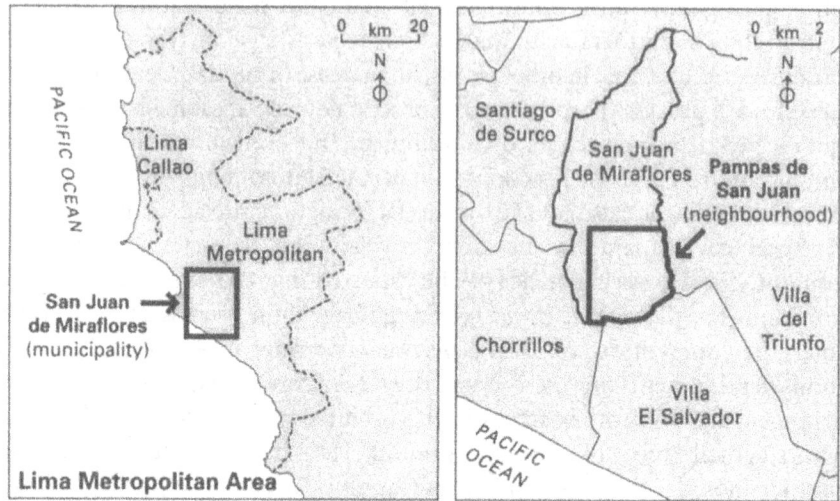

Figure 11.1   Location of research area Pampas de San Juan

This process of steady growth resulted in a heterogeneous zone in terms of income, household characteristics, neighborhood consolidation, and service provision. The older settlements are well consolidated; most houses are made of durable materials, and have a domestic electricity, water, and sewerage connection. In many of these settlements, at least some of the streets and sidewalks are paved. In the more recent settlements on the slopes, most houses are built of straw or wood on Andean-style terraces, people have to fetch water from a public tap or from water vendors, and either have built a latrine or lack any kind of sanitary service. Households on the slopes are smaller, younger, and poorer than those in the lower, flat areas. As the most important environmental problems, the inhabitants indicated water scarcity, the lack of paved roads (and the consequent dust contamination), and the deficient waste collection. There are other environmental problems – such as a lack of sanitary services, the bad quality of drinking water, and noise contamination – but these are considered of far less importance.

Household Environmental Management in Pampas de San Juan

What activities do households in Pampas de San Juan undertake to improve the living conditions in their neighborhoods, and how do they deploy their assets or capitals in this process?

Undertaking an invasion in a desert area means relying on your own resources. People undertake an invasion because they lack a very important element of natural capital; land, on which to build a house. Through an invasion they try to obtain this asset, in the Limenian case often with success in the long run. To be able to take part in an invasion, households often use their networks of kinship and friends. One hears about planned invasions or other possibilities to obtain plots only by word of mouth.

Securing household well-being in these hostile circumstances requires creativity and endurance. In the early years of invasions, most houses are built of straw or wood. Daily environmental management tasks are then fetching water from a public tap or a water tank of the water company, finding ways to deal with the waste the household produces – either by burying or burning it – and cleaning the house and the immediate environment.

Water is a scarce resource in the peripheral settlements, and for people who depend on water vendors it is expensive. The scarcity and price means that – until they have a domestic connection – households economize on the use of drinking water and reuse it whenever possible. For example, water used for washing is reused for watering the plants or for dampening the streets to keep the dust down. What households can do in the first years after an invasion depends a great deal on the security of tenure. As long as the urban development plan has not been approved, they cannot be sure about what their final plot will be, and thus they do not invest in home improvement. Only when they possess the individual land title can they get access to one of the credit schemes. But as soon as the tenure is secured, people start to concentrate on house improvement. This is a process of incremental improvement. First, the foundation and the floor are laid. If they have managed to obtain a loan, a small part of the basic walls is built, creating the skeleton of a living room, kitchen, bedroom, and toilet. Quite often the loan is not enough to also construct a concrete roof, which is the next step in the consolidation process. But many houses do have a staircase that leads to what in the future will become first a roof, and later the second floor. In these years, the improvement activities of the household are concentrated on the household and family well-being, and households are far less active in neighborhood-wide activities. Household environmental management activities are thus mainly limited to coping strategies rather than improvement activities.

There are two issues on which households can and do undertake improvement activities; home improvement and greening. Greening is mainly concentrated on the private space within the boundaries of the plot, and some communal space in front of the house. The other issues – such as water-scarcity and road improvement – are clearly issues that can only be dealt with on a collective basis.

Collective Action in Community-Based Organizations

For daily survival, people engage in many social networks of mutual support, creating and deploying their social capital. This ranges from exchanging help in daily tasks – looking after each other's children, lending money, in some cases sharing food or helping to set up a business – to fund-raising when a sudden calamity (like illness or death) befalls a family in the neighborhood. Social capital, however, is also an essential ingredient in large-scale neighborhood upgrading exercises. In the first years of settlement formation, people have to rely on collective action. Most improvements they strive for – such as obtaining security of tenure, domestic electricity, water and sewerage connections, improving the roads – can only be achieved collectively, not on an individual basis. With this in mind, they establish their own community-based organizations (CBOs).

The first organization formed after invasion is the neighborhood organization, which elects a group of leaders – the neighborhood council, headed by a *secretario general* – and holds a general assembly. All families that are future homeowners are represented in the neighborhood organization and each family has one vote. Once the neighborhood council and the leaders are registered as such at the municipality, the neighborhood leaders can act on behalf of the inhabitants, and can even sign contracts for the neighborhood as a whole.

The neighborhood organization plays a very important role in achieving habitat improvement. It is responsible for bringing about the necessary condition, viz. securing land tenure. The neighborhood organization hires a topographer to draw the settlement's perimetric plan, and then it ensures the plan's registry and recognition. Once the boundaries are set, the neighborhood council can start negotiations with the water company to get a public tap installed. In this same first phase, the neighborhood council organizes days of communal work (*faenas*) in which roads are opened up, steps are built on steep slopes, and sites are cleared for public functions, such as a community hall or day-care center. In these first years the neighborhood organizations also organize clean-up campaigns, in which all litter in the neighborhood is collected and burned. Each household is obliged to send at least one member to these faenas. Participation in the faenas is recorded by the secretary of the neighborhood council. Households that do not comply are fined. A strong sanction mechanism for non-participation is that households can be threatened that they will not be included in the register of the households entitled to get a plot.

In a next step, the neighborhood council contracts an architect to develop an urban development plan for the neighborhood; this plan also has to be legalized by a government entity. Based on this legalized plan, households can finally obtain their individual land title. With the official land title, the neighborhood organization can start negotiations with the water company to get the final water and sewerage connections installed. The most common modality for the construction of the final connections is that the neighborhood council contracts an engineer who develops a project and helps the neighborhood organization with the procedures at the water company. There are different modalities for credits for the construction of the waterworks. The construction work is often contracted out to a private company. A neighborhood organization then invites various companies to tender for the job. One of the conditions for being awarded the contract is that unskilled labor be contracted from within the neighborhood. In other neighborhoods, the population provides voluntary labor in order to keep the costs down. Some settlements in Pampas de San Juan managed to get their waterworks financed by external donors, while others constructed them with financial and technical support from NGOs.

Once the final waterworks are constructed, the neighborhood organizations can start negotiating to get the roads paved. Neighborhoods obtain their roads in many different ways. The principal roads often come under the investment programs of either the national or the local government, or as a joint effort. Here the inhabitants have little or no say in planning procedures. The internal roads are basically paved after demand making of the inhabitants, at either the national or the local government level (election campaigns are a good time for getting roads paved). In recent years, the municipality has developed a new way of dealing with the demands for paving the roads. If a neighborhood raises the necessary funds to level the roads and pave the sidewalks, and organizes the unskilled labor, the municipality provides the machinery, skilled labor, and asphalt.

Households also organize in the sphere of health and well-being. Usually, a 'Comité Vaso de Leche' (glass of milk committee) is established immediately after the settlement is formed. Since the mid-1980s, there has been a government program that provides all children under seven and lactating mothers with a glass of milk each day. To be able to participate in the program, a group of households has to nominate a committee, which registers with the program and is responsible for distributing the milk to its members. The milk is provided by a local government office. A third kind of CBO formed at the neighborhood level are the famous communal kitchens, where households jointly prepare cheap meals. Other CBOS are health committees – small groups of women that receive training to provide first aid and medication – and parents' associations, which are formed to participate in and co-manage the schools.

All these CBOs share certain characteristics. They can draw on their members and mobilize both financial and human resources. In the first years, people pay a monthly contribution to the neighborhood organizations, and the neighborhood organizations collect money for bureaucratic procedures, professional assistance (architects and engineers), or investment. Also the communal kitchens and the association of school parents have mechanisms to mobilize financial resources. Neighborhoods organizations and other CBOs are stable institutions, and the institutional conditions for their functioning are exceptionally favorable in Peru. This provides them with a solid base for establishing partnerships with the government and NGOS.

CBOS and Capitals

Similar to individuals and households, CBOs are endowed with capitals. As soon as the boundaries of a settlement are legalized, decisions on land use are taken by the neighborhood organization. The CBO therewith possesses a certain kind of physical capital; land. It is common for neighborhood organizations to negotiate with this asset. They endeavor to attract investments for the construction of schools or health posts, for which they provide the necessary space.

CBOs can deploy their human capital in many ways. They can draw on the labor force of their members for communal works. Members can be also called upon for different forms of demand making, or for pressuring and protesting. Neighborhood leaders have organizational capital, and develop linkages both inside and outside the neighborhood. Furthermore, neighborhood organizations have their own set of internal rules and procedures (such as sanctioning mechanisms for members who do not fulfil their obligations), as well as their articles of association, and their recognition at the municipality.

The political capital of the neighborhood organization is quite important. The urban poor form an important group of voters. Both national and local politicians constantly try to gain their political support. A successful way to go about this is to invest in neighborhood improvement projects coordinated by the neighborhood organizations. These linkages are then made official in covenants or by nominating the politicians as *compadre* of the school that was built, the playground that was concreted, or the roads that were paved.

Neighborhood leaders try to develop intellectual capital during the course of the process of neighborhood consolidation. It is part and parcel of the job of a neighborhood leader to constantly keep track of the changes in the legal framework, changes in the responsibilities of the other actors, and new investment or support possibilities. The more a leader is up to date, the more he can do for his neighborhood. There is a vivid exchange of this knowledge and sometimes an ad-hoc coalition building between different neighborhood organizations. It even requires specific maneuvering skills to know which information to share – in order to build up social capital with the other leaders – and which not to share, in order to prevent new competitors from accessing scarce funds.

Neighborhood organizations have their social-cultural capital. There is a shared set of values and codes on how to behave as a neighborhood organization and a neighborhood leader. This set of values and codes is shared internally – between the members – and with external actors. Neighborhood organizations are supposed to make demands towards outside actors; they have a legitimacy to do so. It is also part of the code that this should be tried first through negotiations, and only if this does not work to resort to pressuring in the form of protest marches. Neighborhood leaders are supposed to behave politely and modestly when negotiating, but it is part of the game that they should be insistent. In a similar way, government officials are supposed to grant some of the petitions and demands by performing concrete actions.

We can thus conclude that through their forms of collective action and organization, the poor create an important set of capitals. But how can the CBOs in Pampas de San Juan use these capitals to form partnerships with local government?

The Municipality of San Juan de Miraflores

Until the 1980s, the municipal governments in Peru had basically a symbolic function. Mayors were appointed by central government, and there was little they could do. In 1980, a new law (Ley Organica de Municipalidades) delegated many responsibilities to the municipal level, such as the planning and construction of roads and urban transport; planning, redesigning, and legalizing squatter settlements; planning basic social services (health and education); creating and maintaining green areas and public spaces; and performing solid waste collection. Additionally they got the mandate for a considerable series of licenses, and the obligation to set up a land registry system in order to raise local taxes. A year after the law was endorsed, it was followed by the first local government elections, in which inhabitants could choose a mayor and a council. This decentralization of responsibilities, however, was not followed by the decentralization of funds. Over the years the Peruvian municipalities have received on average around 4 per cent of the national government budget. Most of the funds they receive go to pay the salaries of the municipal workers. As a consequence of these limited financial resources, municipalities are seriously understaffed, especially in qualitative terms. A second factor that seriously inhibits the functioning of the municipalities is the fact that although responsibilities were transferred to the municipalities, they were not simultaneously curtailed at the national level, resulting in many overlapping responsibilities. In the decade under president Fujimori, there furthermore was a process of re-centralization. The issue of legalizing squatter settlements, for instance, was transferred back to a national state agency, cutting off an important planning and management tool of local governments.

In 1997 the Fujimori regime issued a new decree (Decree 776) that channeled more investment funds to the municipalities. For the municipality of San Juan de Miraflores, this meant that their budget doubled. There are, however, many restrictions on the use of these funds. They can only be used for infrastructural investments. In San Juan de Miraflores, the funds have been spent on an extensive road construction program.

Daily practice at the municipality of San Juan de Miraflores thus has very little to do with what it should be according to the municipality's mandate. It does not work with an urban development plan, nor with an environmental management plan. There are very few ways in which the municipality can respond to, for example, new invasions even if these spring up at very unfavorable locations. The municipality's record when it comes to solid waste management and the maintenance of green areas (its two major responsibilities in the management of the urban environment) is very poor. This is related to a lack of machinery and financial resources (physical capital) and of qualified staff (human capital). People are very dissatisfied, especially since the municipality levies a specific tax for solid waste collection and parks, without providing an adequate service. Yet although both issues are considered high-priority environmental problems – according to both the inhabitants and the leaders – they are not the most important topics in their negotiations with the municipality.

Most important negotiations between the neighborhood organizations and the municipality concern small-scale investments in neighborhood improvement projects, such as playgrounds, health posts, and community halls. Although the municipality has only limited funds and possibilities, it is the actor to whom the neighborhood leaders most often turn for coordination. All neighborhood leaders try to establish good relations with the mayor and/or the councilors. The general form is to present petitions for investments, and then to start the ritual of visiting the municipality over and over again. Whether or not a petition is granted has little to do with technical or management decisions, but depends on political motives. There is a surprising discrepancy between the amount of time and effort spent on coordinating with the mayor and the concrete results. Of 75 projects carried out in 47 neighborhoods – ranging from the installation of electricity and public water taps, to the construction of schools, playgrounds, and health posts – the municipality financed only three and executed only two. The majority of the projects were financed by a national credit scheme (33) or by the community itself (26), and executed by private engineers contracted by the neighborhood organizations (36) or by the inhabitants (20).

These contradictory results – a lot of effort being put into coordinating with the municipality without meaningful, concrete results – can be explained if we analyze which capitals the municipality of San Juan de Miraflores actually possesses. Financial capital is scarce at the municipality. About 80 per cent of the budget is set aside to pay salaries. The lack of financial capital also causes a lack of human capital. There are few capable professionals at the municipality. In terms of extraordinary investment budgets, the situation at the municipality has improved considerably thanks to Decree 776. Since the municipality has only very limited autonomy in decisions concerning the allocation of these investment budgets, however, it cannot directly use it in negotiations with neighborhood organizations.

Organizational capital at the municipality is also weak in several respects. Although the municipality has a clear bureaucratic structure and the ability to create rules and procedures, these are seriously hampered by the range of overlapping responsibilities that exist between different layers of government. Municipal decisions are frequently overruled by other state entities. Another problem is that the scarcity of financial and human capital inhibits proper enforcement of the rules and procedures established.

The municipality also possesses political capital. How important this capital is for both sides – the neighborhood organizations and the municipality – is shown by the fact that neighborhood leaders keep investing in contacts with the municipality, despite the fact that this leads to few concrete results. Political affiliation is furthermore a strategy for upward social mobility, both for neighborhood leaders who can become municipal officers or councilors, and for councilors and municipal officers, who apply for positions in the national government. Being mayor can even be an important stepping stone to becoming a member of parliament. This clearly available political capital might, however, be a blessing in disguise. It is one of the only capitals deployed freely at the municipality. Many decisions are inspired by political rather than technical motives. Since the other capitals are weakly present at the municipality, there are few possibilities to counterbalance the decisions taken out of political interests, which has serious implications both for the management of daily affairs and for long-term planning.

Analyzing the intellectual capital at the municipality gives a mixed result. Although there is a qualified staff with adequate legal knowledge and technical skills, these well qualified people constitute only a small minority. Due to the politicization of daily affairs, the insights and suggestions of qualified people furthermore may be overruled by political motives. Qualified people are easily fired if their proposals or behavior do not fit the political interest of the day.

Socio-cultural capital is strongly represented. Fifty years of formation and consolidation of squatter settlements have resulted in a clear set of rules and procedures on how to act, with clear roles, norms, and values for each actor in the process. It is part of the commonly shared ritual that neighborhood leaders visit the mayor to present their demands, irrespective of whether or not they have a chance of success. Both the inhabitants and the mayor expect this ritual to take place.

Even more important might be the shared ideology on how poor people are supposed to create their own shelter and habitat improvement, and what role the municipality has to play in this process. The Peruvian state was early in accepting self-help housing as a possible solution to the housing problems of the poor. Riofrío (1990) pointed out that it was also a relatively easy way to get rid of the problem. Poor people were left on low-value land, and it was considered their responsibility to solve their housing problem. The poor people in Lima thus use their own resources to build and pay for their houses and basic infrastructure. National governments have over the years developed different credit schemes to support the poor in this process; the municipality does not intervene in this issue. The mayor is expected to make small-scale investments in the neighborhoods, and assure proper solid waste collection. The performance of a mayor is frequently judged on the number and quality of the investment projects implemented during his term, more than on governance criteria. So although many capitals are scarce at the municipality of San Juan de Miraflores, many people still think that the mayor is doing a good job – as demonstrated by the fact that in 1998, they re-elected the incumbent mayor.

Conclusions

Capitals

This article illustrated how the poor households in peripheral Lima deploy their various capitals or assets in order to improve their living conditions. The analysis of neighborhood-based environmental management in Pampas de San Juan shows that it is basically through their organizations that the poor 'value, develop, apply and leverage' their assets, and that the level of the organizations of the poor thus should be included in the analysis, as proposed by McCleod (2001, p. 4).

Combining the different forms of capitals of households (Chambers, 1995; Moser, 1998; Haan, 2000; McCleod, 2001), community-based organizations (McCleod, 2001) and local government (Gonzalez et al., 2000) then gives the following result.

The deployment of capital is a dynamic process, and the 'capital stock' changes in the course of this process. Certain capitals increase or decrease in the practice of continuous interaction between the neighborhood organizations and local government. However, it is important to distinguish whether this capital formation is deployed for personal benefit, for collective benefit, or for both.

A clear collective benefit is the organizational or institutional capital that has been formed throughout the years of neighborhood-state interaction. Today, there is a clear set of roles and procedures on 'how to go about neighborhood improvement.' This includes established forms of formal and informal linking, and the formally established responsibilities and rights of the different actors. This organizational capital is accompanied by socio-cultural capital; a set of shared ideology and codes of behavior for the various players in the game. Both the inhabitants and their leaders know how to behave in their demand making. They know, for instance, when they will have better chances if they behave politely, and when pressuring by means of protest marches will have a better chance of success. Government officials know how they are expected to respond. It is part of the game that petitions

	Households	Community-based organizations	Local government
Human capital	Skills, labor, health	Mobilization of labor force of their members	Availability of staff
Financial capital	Money, loans or credits	Financial resources	Budget, autonomy in budget allocations, loans or credits
Physical capital	Housing, basic infrastructure, tools, machinery	Physical infrastructure (community hall, school, health post) Land	Machinery, autonomy in land-use planning
Organizational or institutional capital	Participation in formal and informal networks, pooling of household labor resources	Formal and informal linking and coordinating, both horizontally and vertically, internal rules and procedures (membership and rights and obligations)	Formal and informal linking and coordinating, both horizontally and vertically, bureaucratic structure, creation of rules, procedures
Political capital	Votes	Political affiliation, demand making, lobbying and representation, legitimacy	Political will and support, formal authority, access to the political system
Intellectual capital	General knowledge of survival strategies in the urban context	Mastery of relevant laws, general knowledge of survival strategies and collective action	Mastery of relevant laws, technical expertise on specific subjects
Socio-cultural capital	Ideals, social relations, and kinship ties	Government ideals, values, and ideology	Government ideals, values, and ideology

Source: Adapted from Gonzalez et al. 'Opting for Partnerships: Governance Innovations in South East Asia, Ottawa 2000, p. 10

Figure 11.2 Capital inputs

are sometimes granted and sometimes not. Together the accumulation of these two types of capital strengthens the ties that connect citizens and public officers (embeddedness).

The interaction between neighborhood leaders and the state also has repercussions for their political capital. Neighborhood leaders know that adopting a confrontational strategy towards local government often decreases their political capital. It requires coalition building between different CBOs to create sufficient political capital to pressure the government, as was described in the introduction. Leaders often opt for a more individual approach that can result in a direct benefit for just their settlement. These are then material benefits – such as the construction of a playground or leveling of the roads – without challenging the existing power structures. A local government, and especially the mayor, has to be responsive to the demand making of the inhabitants in order to maintain or increase its/his political capital.

There is a process of human and intellectual capital formation, especially in the formation of new leadership, both within community-based organizations and at the municipality. Leaders quite often engage in a process of learning by doing, and gain in different ways from their experiences as leaders. Often these capitals are later capitalized in upward social mobility, and then thus deployed for the personal benefit of the leader or municipal functionary. It highly depends on the intention of the leader and his leadership capabilities whether or not he/she manages to combine personal with collective benefits. Inhabitants accept a certain personal benefit for neighborhood leaders, as long as there is also a collective benefit. As soon as the personal benefit for the leader exceeds the unspoken codes of what is acceptable, this erodes the socio-cultural capital base in the neighborhood. People lose trust and no longer participate in collective action. Neighborhood improvement then comes to a standstill.

The apparent paradox between the efforts neighborhood leaders invest in coordinating with local government, and the limited material results of this coordination can only be understood if we also take into account the non-material capitals created in this process. By constantly visiting the municipality, the neighborhood leaders not only seek material benefits for their settlement, but also create social, political, and intellectual capital they can later deploy for both personal and collective benefit.

Partnerships

This analysis also made clear that the local government of San Juan de Miraflores cannot deploy its capitals as freely as is necessary to develop partnerships with the neighborhood organizations. It lacks the necessary autonomy. Furthermore, its financial, physical, and human capital is limited, as is its organizational capital. However, it does have significant political and socio-cultural capitals, which it uses to maintain cooperative relations with neighborhood organizations. As a consequence, the cooperative relations established with the neighborhood organizations only lead to small-scale concrete results. The vast majority of the investments in neighborhood improvement come from the inhabitants themselves. Nevertheless, the shared government ideology seems not to be contested, and both parties maintain their efforts to meet and coordinate.

It can also be concluded that the relationships between the neighborhood organizations do not meet all criteria to qualify as a partnership. There are two or more partners, including one public, and there is a mutual interest – local governments seeks visible results and electoral support, neighborhood organizations seek neighborhood improvement – and each partner can bring something to the partnership. The decisive hindrance is that the municipality cannot act as a principal. It can be (and often is) overruled by other government entities. Furthermore, it lacks the necessary resources to qualify as a principal. The collaboration results in few concrete activities. But in the process of working together, new capital is created, albeit without much direct effect on the ground.

Many of these limitations can be seen as a result of the political situation in Peru over the last decade. Ten years of Fujimori dictatorship halted the process of improving local governance that had started so promisingly in the early 1980s. The recently elected president, Alejandro Toledo, announced increased transfers to the municipal level (in his election rhetoric, he even promised raising it from the current 4 per cent to 20 per cent in the near future), and a new process of decentralization. Developing good governance is a long-term process. It is thus not to be expected that the situation at the municipality will soon improve. For the people in Pampas de San Juan, it is already of decisive importance that they can again hope for future improvements.

The analysis of the situation at the municipality of San Juan de Miraflores is thus not meant to disqualify the partnership approach in neighborhood-level urban environmental management. On the contrary, the analysis of the activities of the neighborhood organization made clear that there are many promising entry points for developing these partnerships. But neighborhood organizations need a 'principal' as partner. Hopefully Alejandro Toledo's *'Peru Posible'* will indeed make this come true.

References

Batley, Richard (1996), 'Public-Private Relationships and Performance in Service Provision', *Urban Studies*, Vol. 33(4-5), pp. 723-752.

Baud, I.S.A. (2000), *Collective Action, Enablement and Partnerships: Issues in Urban Development*, Inaugural address, Free University, Amsterdam.

Baud, I.S.A., Grafakos, S., Hordijk, M. and Post, J. (2001), 'Quality of Life and Alliances in Solid Waste Management – Contributions to Urban Sustainable Development', *Cities*, Vol. 18(1), pp. 3-12.

Biekart, Kees (1999), *The Politics of Civil Society Building: European Private Aid Agencies and Democratic Transitions in Central America*, International Books and Transnational Institute, Utrecht.

Chambers, Robert and Conway, G. (1992), 'Sustainable Rural Livelihoods; Practical Concepts for the 21st Century', IDS Discussion Paper, No. 296, Brighton.

Chambers, Robert (1995), 'Poverty and Livelihoods; Whose Reality Counts?', *Environment and Urbanization*, Vol. 7(1), April, pp. 173-204.

Douglass, Mike and Zoghlin, Maria (1994), 'Sustaining Cities at the Grassroots. Livelihood, Environment and Social Networks in Suan Phlu, Bangkok', *Third World Planning Review*, Vol. 16(2), Liverpool University Press, Liverpool, pp. 171-87.

Evans, P. (1996), 'Government Action, Social Capital and Development, Reviewing the Evidence on Synergy', *World Development*, Vol. 24(6), pp. 1119-32.

Gentry, Bradford and Fernandez, Lisa (1997), 'Evolving Public-Private Partnerships: General Themes and Urban Water Examples', in OEC, *Globalization and the Environment: Perspectives from OECD and Dynamic Non-Member Economies*, OECD, Paris, pp. 19-25.

Gonzalez J, Lauder, K. and Melles, B. (2000), *Opting for Partnerships, Governance Innovations in South East Asia*, Institute on Governance, Ottawa.

Haan, Leo de (2000), *Livelihood, Locality and Globalization*, Nijmegen University Press, Nijmegen.

Helmsing (2000), *Decentralization and Enablement; Issues in the Local Governance Debate*, Inaugural address, University of Utrecht, Utrecht.

Hordijk Michaela (2000), *Of Dreams and Deeds; The Role of Local Initiatives in Community-based Urban Environmental Management. A Case Study from Lima, Peru*, Thela Thesis, Amsterdam.

Mathews, Jessica, T.(1997), 'Power Shift', *Foreign Affairs*, Vol. 76(1), pp. 50-66.

McCleod, R. (2001), *Experiences of Linking Community-based Housing Finance to Formal Finance Mechanisms*, Paper presented at the Gavle meeting on Housing Finance, held in Sweden, March 28, 2001, http://www.theinclusivecity.org/Bridging_the_finance_gap/case_studies.htm

Moser, Caroline, O.N. (1998), 'The Asset Vulnerability Framework: Reassessing Urban Poverty Reduction Strategies', *World Development*, Vol. 26(1), pp. 1-19.

Perlas, N. (2000), *Shaping Globalization, Civil Society, Cultural Power and Threefolding*, CADI, Quezon City.

Peters, G. B. (1998). "With a Little Help from our Friends': Public- private Partnerships as Institutions and Instruments', in Pierre, J. (1998), *Partnerships in Urban Governance; European and American Experience*, Macmillan Press Ltd., London.

Pierre, J. (1998), *Partnerships in Urban Governance; European and American Experience*, Macmillan Press Ltd., London.

Riofrío, Gustavo (1990), *Producir la Ciudad (popular) de los '90: Entre el Mercado y el Estado*, DESCO, Lima.

Stoker, G. (1998), 'Theory and Urban Politics', *International Political Science Review*, Vol. 19(2), pp. 119-30.

12 New Partnerships in Urban Solid Waste Management and their Contribution to Sustainable Development: Experiences in Accra (Ghana) and Chennai (India)

ISA BAUD AND JOHAN POST

Introducing Partnerships

In the debates on making urban management and local governance more effective in the developing world, a major hallmark is the realignment between government, the private sector, and civil society. The new wisdom is that governments should concentrate on creating the institutional framework that enables private sector actors, both commercial and non-profit, to directly provide housing and urban services. Within these debates, much attention is paid to the potentials of partnership or co-management arrangements between actors in realizing such provisions (Rakodi, 1999; Baud, 2000; Helmsing, 2000; Stoker, 2000). Partnerships are said to enhance the effectiveness of actions by (a) taking on board all relevant stakeholders and avoiding problems of exclusion and fragmentation, (b) recognizing the complex social dynamics surrounding interventions, and taking these into account in the design and implementation of actions, and, most importantly, (c) saving on costs through the resource input and commitment of civil society actors and the synergy resulting from combining skills and resources of various actors. Furthermore, there is a strongly normative claim made for the participation inherent in partnerships (Johnson and Wilson, 2000, p. 1892). Obviously, the potentials of partnerships do not materialize automatically. In the real world, there are many obstacles, such as the unequal power relations between external actors and project beneficiaries, the difficulty of ensuring wider participation, and the transaction costs involved in dealing with a variety of actors (Baud, 2000).

Partnerships can be defined as more or less enduring, mutually beneficial relationships between two or more actors based on a written or verbal agreement, and having a concrete, physical manifestation (in the case of waste management, such things as garbage bins, transfer stations, disposal sites, and collection vehicles). Furthermore – and to distinguish them from exclusively commercial relationships – they contribute either directly or indirectly to a public goal (linking these relationships to governance). Partnerships include both formal and informal arrangements, e.g., those that are supported by the rule of law, and those that are embedded in established social practices. In principle, partnerships provide each of the actors involved with benefits, but this does not imply equality among them, for in most such relationships issues of power are at stake. Although partnerships suggest a degree of stability, they should nevertheless be seen as expressions of people's practices that have an inherent tendency to evolve, adapt, and dissolve in response to changing circumstances (Baud *et al.*, 2001; see also the chapter by Hordijk in this volume).

When studying partnership arrangements, a distinction can be made between the objectives, the internal dynamics, the socio-economic and political context, and the outcomes of partnerships. In the domain of urban basic services, the core objective of partnerships is to provide these in a more efficient and effective way. However, the overall goal may very well be subordinate to the particular needs and objectives of the actors. In reality, therefore, the challenge is to look for compatibility of objectives, for example between the profit motive of the private sector and the community desire of affordability and equitable coverage (UNCHS, 1993). The internal dynamics of partnerships refers to the nature of the collaboration between different social groups having different values, concerns, and resources. In this respect, the concept of social capital – reciprocity within and between individuals or groups based on trust derived from social ties – has emerged. Differences in social capital lead to different degrees of synergy[1] in the outcome of partnerships (Evans, 1996; Ostrom, 1996; Baud, 2000). Although collaboration is rarely on a truly equal footing, concrete projects and interventions through partnerships can help to manage differences in power and other social inequalities, as well as build new norms, values, and practices that contribute

---

1. Synergy refers to the win-win situation that may arise from collaboration. According to Evans (1996, pp. 1120-21) it requires complementarity of inputs by the actors involved as well as embeddedness, that is, ties of loyalty and trust that connect the actors.

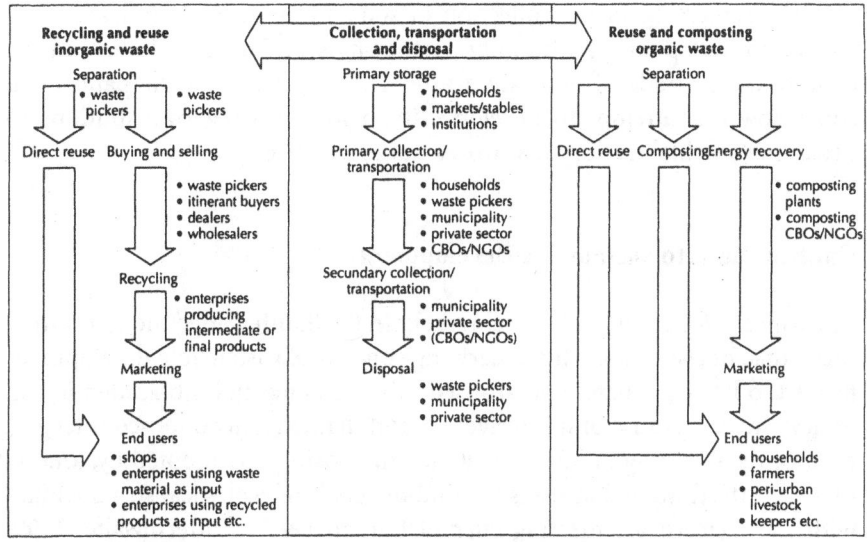

Figure 12.1 Actors and relationships in solid waste management

towards long-term development goals (Johnson and Wilson, 2000, p. 1895). As far as the context of partnerships is concerned, there are many external macro-level factors over which local partners have very little control, but that do influence the nature and outcomes of partnerships. It is generally believed that market-led macro-economic policies, decentralized systems of administration, and institutionalized forms of popular participation (democratic conditions) create a favorable environment for the rise and performance of partnerships (UNCHS, 1996; Post, 1997; Helmsing, 2000). Finally, the outcomes of partnerships are the ultimate test of their usefulness as a development tool. To what extent are they able to bring about perceptible improvements in the living and working conditions of urban citizens, notably the urban poor and simultaneously to protect the environment, i.e., promote sustainable development? This is the question taken up in this chapter.

The term partnership is used here to describe established relationships between actors in urban solid waste management (see Figure 12.1). It is important to map the various relationships that exist in a concrete setting in order to avoid a preoccupation with the most dominant ones, and to come to an appreciation of the potentials of the others. Having said that, however, we will confine ourselves to the analysis of a few selected partnerships across the spectrum of solid waste management. The examples concern a public-private partnership in the collection of solid waste in Accra (Ghana), and two important public-community partnerships in Chennai (India), in the collection and trade of domestic waste. The major aim of the paper is to show how our attempt to develop criteria for assessing contributions to urban sustainable development works out in practice.

Contributions to Sustainable Development

The concern for sustainable development in the South gained momentum in the course of the 1980s. The underlying concept of sustainable development has led to heated debates and aroused mixed feelings in both academic and policy circles, because of its elusiveness and diametrically opposed interpretations. As a starting point, we will take the position as adopted by, among others, Satterthwaite that seeks to combine goals of ecological sustainability with the concern for meeting current human needs (Satterthwaite, 1997; Hardoy, Mitlin, and Satterthwaite, 2001). Striving for ecological sustainability implies that the use of non-renewable resources should be minimized, renewable resources should be used in such a way that regeneration of the resource is ensured, and the capacity of local and global sinks should not be exceeded in either case.

With respect to the development component, the situation is less straightforward. There is tremendous controversy concerning what human needs entail, how their satisfaction relates to ecological sustainability, and what the acceptable levels of trade-offs are. This is apparent, for example, in the contrast between the advocates of the green and the brown agenda in urban environmental improvements. The former emphasize ecosystem health, the impact of cities on rural resources and surrounding regions, and the threat posed by urban consumption to the fulfillment of the needs of future generations. The latter focus on environmental hazards and social justice, and are more concerned with immediate problems at local level, notably those faced by the urban poor (McGranahan and Satterthwaite, 2000). In this paper we will work from an understanding of sustainable development that sees it largely in terms of welfare in its broadest sense. It fits in with current approaches that seek to create and conserve various forms of capital, including physical, human, social, and environmental (see Pugh, 2000).

Solid waste management (SWM) is a typical brown agenda issue and its impacts are largely, albeit not exclusively, local. This is reflected in the 'localized nature' of the criteria we selected to assess the contribution to sustainable development of various partnerships in SWM. However, in view of the multifaceted nature of sustainable development, we have tried to pay attention to various dimensions, notably ecological sustainability, socio-economic goals, and environmental health concerns. With respect to the first, SWM systems need to work towards the following goals:

- To minimize the amount of waste generated.
- To maximize reuse and recycling.
- To dispose of remaining waste in a controlled fashion in order not to exceed the capacities of local sinks.

The goal of minimizing the production of waste is primarily a national government (and private sector) responsibility, and can be pursued through policies that induce production and consumption practices that reduce the input of materials, make more efficient use of these inputs, and increase closed-loop recycling. Whether or not consumers, industries, and institutions contribute to this goal depends on their assessment of the social, economic, and environmental costs and benefits involved, as well as their levels of awareness. The maximizing of waste reuse and recycling can be carried out at primary level – within households, firms and institutions – or at secondary level, that is after materials have entered the municipal waste stream. A very important aspect is the extent to which source separation occurs and is officially endorsed and promoted (Lardinois and Furedy, 1999). The contribution to sustainable development lies in the reduction of volumes of waste to be disposed of, and the reduction in use of virgin materials. Controlled disposal is included because the amount of municipal waste that actually reaches the official dumpsites – and, consequently, how much is disposed of illegally and pollutes the urban environment – is an important indicator of the quality of an SWM system. Finally, the method of final disposal – in developing countries, largely through crude dumping or sanitary landfills – determines to what extent ecological sustainability and environmental health are impaired through contamination of surface and groundwater or soils by leakage, air pollution by waste burning, and spread of diseases by different vectors.

The socio-economic dimensions used to assess SWM systems encompass both consequences at the level of actors and impacts on the efficiency of the entire system (city level). Four criteria are used:

- Financial viability and affordability for the local authorities, consumers, and/or entrepreneurs involved (these may conflict among groups).

- Employment providing a living wage and a certain level of job security.
- Legitimacy from the perspective of the authorities (legal) and the public (social).
- Effective monitoring and enforcement of standards.[2]

The continuity of an activity ultimately depends on its financial viability, i.e., the assurance that the revenues will continue to balance the costs incurred. Considering the 'public good-nature of SWM, authorities often have to accept a considerable degree of subsidization. However, the financial sustainability of the system depends on the authorities' solvability (through own revenues or grants) and the political willingness to pay the price of adequate servicing. Contributions from residents can help to increase the financial viability of waste collection – this is expressed in the concept of allocative efficiency (Batley, 1996, p. 743), the extent to which charges cover the cost of the service – but if the charges are beyond what they can afford, it will incite them to opt out of the service or to engage in free-rider practices. Within this criterion, we also deal with the issue of productive efficiency, which refers to the operational performance of the service provider measured by such things as labor productivity and costs per ton (ibid. p. 743). The contribution SWM makes to gainful employment is a key aspect of our assessment scheme. It tries to ascertain whether jobs within the sector provide a living wage and a certain degree of job security. In addition, it seeks to compare the labor conditions of various social groups. The legitimacy criterion distinguishes between the legal situation and public attitudes. Legal recognition of a partnership may provide both advantages (access to credit and facilities; absence of harassment) and disadvantages (costs of formalization), and the same applies to non-recognition. Social legitimacy refers to acceptance in the eyes of the public. The fourth criterion aims to find out whether mechanisms are put in place to monitor performances – in all three dimensions – and sanctions are applied in case agreed norms – output criteria, health standards, labor codes, environmental rules – are violated.

---

2. In an earlier version (Baud et al., 2001) we spoke of better coordination within the SWM sector which was discussed in terms of a clear demarcation of tasks and responsibilities (avoiding overlap). To assess this aspect we looked at the existence of policies and bylaws, and capacities for monitoring and law enforcement. Good coordination was supposed to bring about superior system efficiency. In practice, this aspect turned out to be very difficult to test. Therefore, we decided to narrow it down to effective monitoring and enforcement of standards, while discussing the legal framework under the legitimacy criterion, and efficiency under the heading of financial viability.

The third criterion assesses contributions to environmental health. The goals are:

- To bring about greater effectiveness in achieving a clean urban environment.
- To minimize occupational health hazards.
- To minimize environmental health hazards to man and animals related to the use of waste in agriculture.

The contributions to a cleaner environment can once again be investigated at two levels, that of the neighborhood where the activity takes place, and that of the city as a whole. From the perspective of SWM, cleaner neighborhoods largely depend on the quality of waste collection (service effectiveness), notably the frequency and the reliability of the service. However, pollution produced by local industries dealing with waste materials (air, water, soil) or by collection vehicles (air) also has to be taken into account. At city level, the contribution partnerships make to increasing spatial coverage of collection services is of prime importance. The goal of reducing occupational health hazards is quite obvious. It depends on the level of exposure to waste, especially to dangerous fractions of waste, and can be mitigated by the use of appropriate safety equipment. Finally, when waste – either decomposed or composted organic waste or unsegregated waste – is applied in peri-urban agriculture, possible negative impacts on animal health, soil conditions, and the quality of food crops also have to be considered.

In the subsequent analysis, three important partnership arrangements in two cities are evaluated in terms of their contribution to sustainable development using the above template. The empirical material is derived from studies carried out by Obirih-Opareh (2000) in Accra, and Dhanalakshmi and Iyer (1999) in Chennai. However, as these investigations were not explicitly designed to evaluate our sustainable development model, it was not always possible to come up with appropriate information for all criteria.

Public-Private Partnership in Solid Waste Collection in Accra

Solid Waste Collection (SWC) in Accra

Accra is a fast growing and sprawling metropolis. Its estimated three million inhabitants produce about 1,500 tons of waste every day. Until 1995 the municipal Waste Management Department (WMD) was virtually the sole service provider. Collection performance was far from adequate, and only about 60 per cent of the total volume ended up at official dumpsites. The urban landscape used to be blighted by mountains of uncollected rubbish, especially in the ill-served poorer quarters. These heaps of rubbish constituted potential sources of disease. Moreover, large quantities of household waste often flowed straight into river basins and bodies of water, creating serious public health risks.

swc in Accra is based on either the house-to-house (HtH) system or the central communal container (ccc) system. Until 1999 both systems could be run by either the public sector or private operators. HtH systems are only used in rich and some middle-income areas, whilst the ccc system is applied in the remaining areas. Each area is served exclusively by one provider, which is expected to collect and transport the waste to designated dumpsites. In the ccc system, the Accra Municipal Authorities (AMA) normally provide the containers and bear all the costs. In the HtH system, residents are obliged to register with the WMD or the accredited contractor and to pay a user charge. Private franchisers operating the HtH system have to pay a fee to the AMA for dumping at the designated sites. In terms of relative importance, the ccc and HtH systems cover 70 per cent and 30 per cent, respectively, of the areas actually receiving swc services.

Recently, a major central government intervention entirely changed the situation in Accra. In July 1999, City and Country Waste (ccw), a Canadian-Ghanaian joint venture, was granted a monopoly in swc services in the capital. Under the contract, the AMA procured equipment at a total cost of US$ 10.3 million for the ccw on a five-year lease. The reason for the government to interfere in local government affairs was its growing indignation about the failure of the AMA/WMD to adequately deal with the mounting problem of swc, despite modest improvements made through its privatization policy.[3] The AMA were ordered to hand over all their collection trucks, equipment, and workshops to the ccw, effectively putting the WMD out of business. Although the ccw is under no obligation to engage the infant local waste collection industry, it has sublet several areas to local contractors who perform well.

---

3. The agreement was shrouded in so much secrecy that even members of parliament from the government party for Accra did not know what it entailed when the issue was put before the assembly for approval. Despite questions and a press conference with the opposition parties, both the (NDC controlled) parliament and the AMA were forced to swallow the government's decision on the issue.

Ecological Sustainability

The PPP in SWC does not add to the minimization of waste production as this is not part of its mandate. Furthermore, the arrangement does not encourage people to sort their rubbish in order to reduce waste flows going to the dump, and, therefore, its contribution to maximizing recycling and reuse is nil.[4] However, SWC has appreciably improved in terms of volumes of waste collected since the private sector stepped in. The overall annual collection performance went up from 639,000 cubic meters in 1998 to 753,000 cubic meters in 1999, of which by the end of 1998 about 70 per cent was collected by private service providers. Therefore, the new partnership seems to have led to an increase in the volume of waste actually arriving at official dumpsites (disposal in a controlled fashion). However, a few environmental drawbacks need to be mentioned. Most contractors use old, second-hand vehicles that are a serious source of air pollution. The trucks are usually open and the requirement to cover the waste with nets in order to prevent littering during transportation is often violated. In addition, some contractors and/or drivers active in HtH collection avoid going to the dump and paying dumping fees to the AMA. Finally, the privatization policy has not affected the method used to treat waste at the dump site (crude dumping) and therefore has not led to safer disposal.

Financial Viability and Affordability

As the CCC system does not at the moment attract user fees, all the costs have to be borne by the AMA. In 1999 they paid local contractors ¢10,000 to remove one ton of waste through the CCC system. Although the fee was enough to keep firms in business, operators considered it an absolute minimum. For the HtH system, the situation was more attractive. In 1999 the services generated revenues of between ¢8,000 (US$ 2) and ¢10,000 (US$ 2.5) per month per bin. The private operators involved used to work (until

---

4. Separation at the source is largely confined to items that people can either use themselves or give to their neighbours. It is common practice in the poorer communities of Accra to use organic waste (food leftovers) to feed domestic livestock, and some people even sell organic waste to livestock owners. However, the composting plant that was set up by the government in Teshie in the 1970s has been a big failure due to lack of demand. Contrary to many other poor cities across the developing world, there is no substantial sector of waste pickers in Accra who collect and sort household waste on behalf of merchants, recycling firms, or composting units. The recycling industry is small, perhaps with the exception of the iron scrap industry.

mid-1999, when CCW took over) on a franchise basis, and were very successful in collecting the fees due to them with levels of recovery of over 95 per cent (simultaneously attesting to the affordability of the charge). They performed substantially better than the WMD, which was faced with default rates of as high as 30-40 per cent. Whilst the private sector employs all means possible to collect their fees (as payment of their wages and salaries depend on it), public sector agencies do not. However, with the arrival of CCW the franchising system was abolished and contractors ceased to collect fees.

Although accurate data on the productive efficiency of public and private SWC are lacking, it is possible to provide a number of arguments that attest to the efficiency gains of privatization. First of all, private contractors have lower overall wage bills than the government (see below). Secondly, they often (albeit not exclusively) use old, second-hand vehicles and unsophisticated equipment (much manual labor) helping them to save considerably on investment and depreciation costs. Finally, private waste collection firms are under great pressure to perform. In the CCC system, contractors are paid for each recorded waste-carrying trip to the designated dumpsites, and in the HtH system the willingness of residents to pay their dues depends on whether they receive value for money. Such direct financial incentives are absent from WMD operations.

Since CCW stepped in, the level of productive efficiency has fallen dramatically. The company is paid an overall rate of ¢77,000 per ton (in 1999 prices) which is almost three times the average price per ton in the pre-CCW period. Furthermore, the local contractors were able to provide profitable HtH servicing at a cost of ¢8,000 – ¢10,000 per house, whereas the new rates approved in April 2000 are ¢40,000 per month in first-class areas, ¢25,000 in second-class areas, ¢10,800 in third-class areas, and a daily rate yet to be fixed by the AMA in fourth-class areas. These amounts are much higher than a correction for inflation would justify. It is very uncertain whether and, if so, to what extent the authorities will succeed in getting people to pay these excessive charges.

A final issue to be considered under this aspect is the financial sustainability of privatized servicing at city level. The AMA have seen their spending on waste management (which is more than collection) increase from ¢1.27 million in 1995 to ¢2.24 million in 1998, largely due to the privatization campaign. The net deficit in the sector went up by 40 per cent and constitutes over 10 per cent of the revenue collected by the AMA in 1998. The difficulties arising from this mounting deficit are apparent in the inability of the AMA to pay local contractors (the AMA owed ¢800 million by July 1999 for unpaid services in the CCC system for eight months). With the arrival of the CCW, the costs of SWM have skyrocketed and moved even further beyond local government affordability. Whereas the AMA collected ¢13 billion from their own sources in 1999, the contract with the CCW is for ¢22.5 billion per year (at 1999 prices).

Employment and Labor Conditions

Considering the virtual ban on recruitment in the public sector, privatization was the only available avenue to increase the labor input in SWC. Privatization has indeed created additional employment opportunities in the sector (several hundred extra jobs throughout the city), especially while most privately run schemes have adopted labor-intensive technologies.

Working conditions for those working in SWC are rather unattractive. Collection crews have to work under unhygienic conditions and at low wages. When comparing employers, it appeared that remuneration levels for various categories of workers are pretty much the same in the indigenous private sector, the WMD (until 1999), and the CCW (since 1999), and correspond to minimum wage levels set by the government. However, fringe benefits for government workers and CCW personnel (taken over from WMD), including allowances for housing, transportation, risk, and hazards, and full medical care for the worker and his/her family, are substantially better than in the local private sector – namely by about 20-30 per cent. In addition, employees in the latter are usually not reimbursed for hospital and medical expenses, do not have clear employment contracts, and are frequently troubled by irregularity of payment. Because these workers are not organized, their bargaining power is very weak. This helps explain why labor turnover in the indigenous private sector is so high.

Legitimacy

Privatization is official government policy and the new public-private arrangements are supported by law. Furthermore, public attitudes towards the privatization of SWC proved overwhelmingly positive. This is somewhat remarkable, considering that most respondents believe that privatization will lead to price increases. Apparently there is a strong public desire for better services, and a belief in the private sector's potential to deliver these. Nevertheless, residents feel the AMA should remain in charge of setting and regulating user fees in order to avoid overpricing by profit-seeking entrepreneurs. Social legitimacy of privatization, however, is likely to suffer a blow now that user fees have been increased considerably.

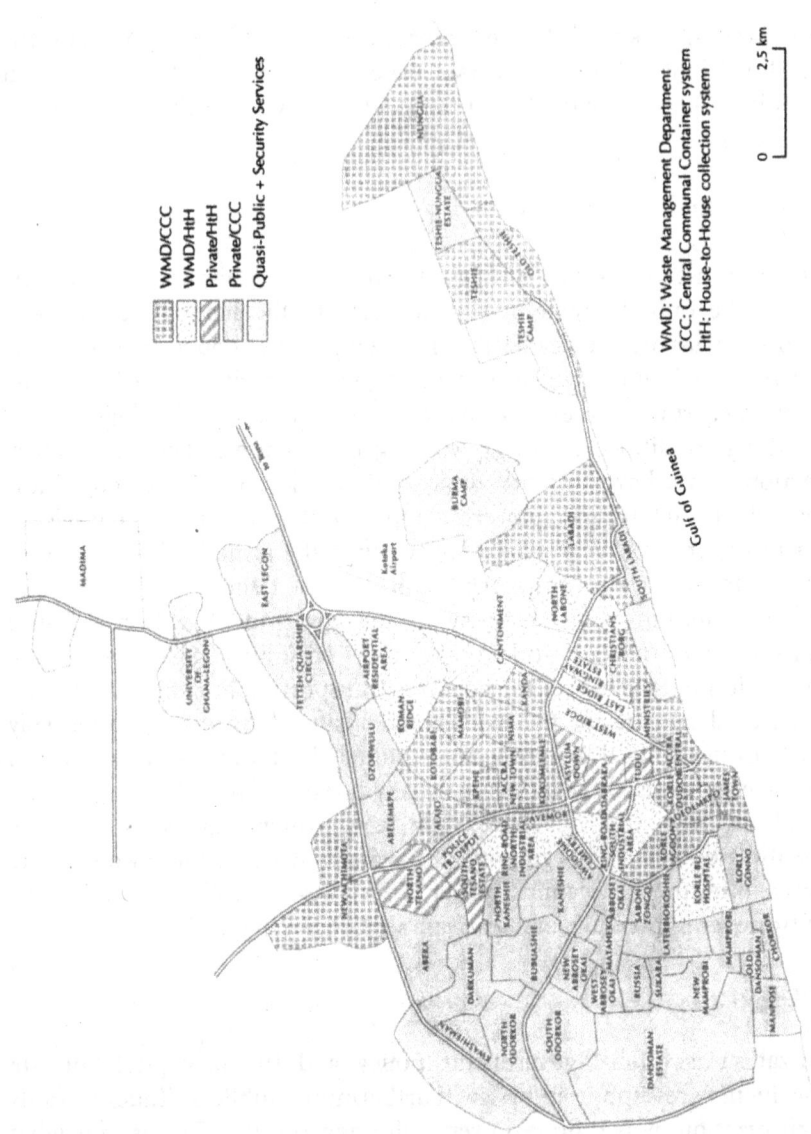

Figure 12.2 Coverage of public and private modes of SWC in Accra in 1998

Monitoring

The official actors in SWC are the WMD (sanitation officers) and the Environmental Health Department (health inspectors), who are expected to regulate and monitor the quality of service delivery and sanitary conditions, respectively, and to sanction possible offenders. In addition, consumers themselves (by filing complaints) and their representatives (assembly members) have a watchdog function. However, official monitoring is exceptionally weak due to bad logistics, under-staffing, low remuneration, and corruption. Evidence shows that the local service providers continuously flout contract specifications and/or sanitary bylaws. However, despite an extensive list of complaints – waste collectors not wearing protective clothing, using the same containers to collect solid waste and night soil, failure to cover open containers with nets during transportation, poor record-keeping of complaints, etc. – they are hardly ever sanctioned by the authorities. Although our material does not allow to differentiate in terms of complaints and the handling thereof between public and private HtH systems, the previous franchise system did offer – at least in theory – a clear advantage. By establishing a relationship of direct dependence between contractor (offering a service and collecting a fee) and consumer (receiving a service and paying a fee), adequate and reliable servicing is fostered. However, these advantages largely pertain to the quality of the service in the narrow sense of the word, for consumers are largely indifferent to the labor conditions inside the firm or its environmental practices.

Cleanliness of Neighborhoods

Dissatisfaction with the frequency of services was the single most important problem identified by the residents (62 per cent mentioned it as their major objection). In the CCC system, the major reason for this is irregularity of services leading to waste piling up at container sites. There is a significant difference between CCC performances under public provision and those under private provision. Local contractors generally provide better services, probably because they are paid according to the number of container-loads they actually transport to disposal sites. For HtH services, the appreciation of frequency is highest in the cantonments and the Airport Residential Area, which are run by the WMD. These areas receive a service twice a week, rather than the officially stipulated once a week (and this is not reflected in the rate they have to pay). The reason is that these are the wealthiest areas in Accra, housing prominent government officials, top foreign dignitaries, and high-level businessmen. They are able to ensure prompt and regular servicing, among others by tipping waste collection workers. However, levels of satisfaction in the areas with privately run HtH collection are good, as is apparent from the low incidence of free riders.

At city level, privatization has resulted in increased spatial coverage of swc in the metropolis. A number of residential areas that were previously not served or were under-served have been put under private provision, while servicing in some middle-income areas has been upgraded from ccc to HtH collection.

Since ccw took over, the situation has improved considerably in those areas where the WMD used to operate the ccc system. Areas such as Nima – a low-income quarter with a high population density and a limited number of containers and container sites – are now receiving regular, twice per day waste collection.

Public-Community Partnerships in Chennai

Solid Waste Collection in Chennai

Chennai is the capital of Tamil Nadu, and the fourth largest metropolitan city in India. In 1991, the population of the Corporation area totaled 3.8 million people, and of the larger metropolitan area 5.3 million people. An estimated 2,500-2,800 tons of garbage were generated daily in 1993-94. The Corporation is responsible for solid waste collection, which in principle is carried out throughout the city, including slum areas; in practice, only around 75 per cent of the city is served. However, difficulties in maintaining a sufficient workforce and a shortage of transportation vehicles have led to private contractors being used as and when necessary. The backlogs experienced in collecting and disposing of waste are clearly visible in the city, in the waste dropped around neighborhood bins, and areas where waste is separated and stored for recycling in slum areas by waste pickers, traders, and wholesalers. swc is based on communal storage bins, provided by the Corporation throughout neighborhoods and areas where bulk waste is generated (markets, marriage halls, etc.). The Corporation provides the means to transport the waste, first to transfer stations, and subsequently to the two dumpsites in Chennai. The Corporation bears the full costs of this system.

As a result of the difficulties experienced in effective collection at the neighborhood level, different types of NGOs have been active in developing partnerships around these problems. They have done so from two perspectives. One set of NGOs worked with street children selling waste materials; they contracted with the Corporation to provide localized house-to-house collection services with the help of waste-picking youngsters, employing them legally and providing them with alternative training and employment opportunities in the end. Another type of NGO, Civic Exnora, became active in the early 1990s in organizing largely middle-class residents, based on the voluntary services of neighborhood committees. Their activities also concern house-to-house collection at the neighborhood level, through a hired 'street beautifier'; households are expected to pay a nominal fee for this service.

The contrast between the effects of the two types of NGOs is marked. The NGOs working with street children had a one-year contract with the Corporation to cover a number of neighborhoods under the Clean and Green Madras City project. The Corporation provided the funding for clothes and equipment, and for the salaries of the youngsters recruited through the NGOs. The contract was not renewed, however, as conflicts occurred in the financial dealings between the Corporation and the NGOs (personal communications).

Civic Exnora, on the other hand, has become a major urban movement in Chennai, taking up activities other than solid waste collection and spreading to other cities in India. In Chennai, Civic Exnoras now also function as bridgeheads between elected councilors and the people who elect them in the areas where they are active (Anand, 1999, p. 162).

Limiting the discussion to SWC, a survey among a number of Exnoras in Chennai showed that they served on average 189 households, of whom almost 90 per cent paid their monthly dues. Exnoras are concentrated in the Corporation area, and they are much fewer in number in surrounding towns and rural areas. The survey also shows that they have a middle-class bias in their outreach (Anand, 1999, pp. 167-168).

Ecological Sustainability

The public-community partnerships did not add to the minimization of waste production as this was not included in their objectives.

Households carry out different degrees of source separation for economic reasons. Paper, bottles, and plastic are generally sold by housewives or servants in Chennai. Neither type of partnership encourages households to carry out further source separation of waste in order to reduce waste flows. The NGOs working with street children did encourage the collectors employed to sort wastes and resell them in order to increase the incomes derived from their work; environmental motives played a minor role in this. Vermi-composting has been encouraged by a small number of Exnoras, but the positive effects of reducing waste volumes seem more than offset by the environmental health hazards it presents at local level, especially the attraction of rodents and snakes to composting pits (Anand, 1999, p. 175). Therefore, the contribution of the partnerships to increasing reuse and recycling does exist, but is not maximized as much as it could be. This is a pity, because at this point in the process, waste is still relatively unmixed and has a higher economic value.

Although the primary collection of waste at the neighborhood level is made more effective by the public-community partnership, it does not follow that it contributes to the controlled disposal of waste. This is related to the fact that activities are limited to primary collection, and secondary collection is left to the Corporation (through transfer stations and transportation to the dumps). Ecologically, therefore, there is transfer of the problem to a higher level and geographical scale.

Financial Viability and Affordability

The municipal system of SWM in Chennai is paid for by general taxes provided previously to the Health and Conservancy Department, and currently to the Solid Waste Management Department. Recent cost estimates made by the Corporation put the costs of waste removal at 515 Rs. per ton for primary removal, 150 Rs. per ton for transportation, and 32 Rs. per ton for disposal at the dumpsite; totaling almost 700 Rs. per ton of waste.[5] The World Bank is planning to fund upgrading activities throughout the SWM cycle, particularly in transfer stations and landfill upgrading. The 2,100 million Rs. needed for such activities could not readily be funded by the Corporation from its yearly funds. In fact, although the Corporation budget for SWM was increased in the early 1990s, the number of sweepers decreased in that period.[6]

The public-community partnership is an efficient addition to the primary collection of waste carried out by the Corporation. The Corporation estimates its costs for primary collection – by using neighborhood bins – at 515 Rs. per ton. Exnora collects half a ton daily from its neighborhoods,

---

5. www.corporationofchennai.com/depart/waste.html
6. State government has allocated new funding for privatization and large-scale recycling initiatives in Chennai; however, these have not yet been realised.

for which households pay 120 Rs. per year. The Corporation, therefore, is replaced by Exnora in its primary collection activities. The costs the Corporation would incur for such service has been calculated at 496 Rs. per household per year (calculations made by the authors), which is clearly higher than the costs incurred by Exnora. This is due to the low wages paid to the 'street beautifiers', and the 'free time' put in by Exnora organizers. The arrangement has helped to enhance productive efficiency, while simultaneously producing, for the first time ever, an element of cost recovery (allocative efficiency). Furthermore, service effectiveness has gone up in Exnora neighborhoods, given the greater satisfaction with local cleanliness expressed by residents and the fact that they no longer have to bring the waste to the bins. The Corporation does not financially contribute to the system, as it feels responsible only for the basic service.

The costs incurred by the four NGOs for cleaning several neighborhoods with the help of former waste pickers is not known. However, the difficulties with financial transactions and the suspicions of corruption suggest a higher level of transaction costs for these arrangements.

The affordability for the middle-class neighborhoods served by Exnoras is very high. This may change now, because waste cannot be easily dumped nearby but needs to be brought to transfer stations, raising the costs of transportation. Anand expresses reservations about the future viability of the system, particularly for more distant and isolated neighborhoods.

Employment and Labor Conditions

There was a stop on recruiting public sector sweepers, so that community hiring is an important alternative way to increase labor input, which especially the Exnora initiative has done. Although the sweepers recruited by both community / NGO groups have less favorable contracts than municipal sweepers, compared with their own previous informal and illegal status, the formalized context of their work reduces harassment and insecurity. In addition, the NGOs offered alternative technical training and savings schemes, in an effort to get youngsters into alternative types of employment. However, street youngsters often prefer higher daily levels of income and more insecurity to working for the NGOs. In the contract period, some 250 youngsters worked in this context.

Working conditions for the people working in community initiatives are similar to those for municipal sweepers, with protective clothing being provided but often not used. In community initiatives, workers also do not have the fringe benefits of housing, bonuses, and health care that municipal workers have. However, the conditions are a vast improvement on the previous ones.

Legitimacy

The legitimacy of the community initiatives was guaranteed through the contract the NGOs had with the Municipal Corporation. The withdrawal of the contract made their activities almost impossible, as residents are very suspicious of street pickers unless they come under the umbrella of a known organization. Exnora's legitimacy is based on the official neighborhood committee guiding activities, and on the status of the parent Exnora International. The middle-class bias in the movement makes it easier for residents and the Corporation to accept the partnership. The legitimacy of the street children's NGOs with the Corporation lay only in the known status of the NGOs involved.[7] Even then, the sweepers needed personal connections with the NGO in order to be trusted by households.

Monitoring

In these public-community partnerships, monitoring was carried out by the local committees of the community organization. Combined with collecting fees, this was their primary task. The effectiveness of the service was related to the strength of the monitoring involved. The Exnoras still have the original enthusiastic leaders, who are willing to put in a great deal of unpaid time. The question is whether this enthusiasm will still be there in the future. As the Corporation is left outside the arrangement, it does not interfere with the monitoring.

Cleanliness of Neighborhoods

The cleanliness of the neighborhoods has improved, in comparison to the situation when the Corporation carried out the service. However, Anand suggests that initially environmental problems were externalized to other neighborhoods, because the Corporation continued to have a daily backlog of waste, which is not collected (estimated at 500 tons per day). The type of externalization has changed because waste now has to be brought to intermediate collection points, from where it is taken to eight transfer stations

---

7. These included a religious order, the Asian Youth Centre, Nesaharam, and Asha Nivas.

throughout the city. He suggests that this may raise the costs of the primary collection by Exnora, because the transportation costs have increased.

Conclusions

The acclaimed synergetic potential of partnership arrangements seems to be confirmed by the outcomes of our assessment in Accra and in Chennai. In both cities the partnerships have helped to raise levels of productive and allocative efficiency as well as service effectiveness in comparison to the previous situation when the public sector was the sole responsible actor. These gains, however, have to be qualified somewhat. The labor conditions of those who found employment within the new partnership framework compare unfavorably with government employees in terms of wage levels, security, and fringe benefits. At the same time, if workers are drawn in whose previous work was more insecure and irregular, this still implies an improvement. Another mitigating factor is that transaction costs – the supervision of private operators in Accra, and the facilitation by NGOs in Chennai – fall outside the equation. Although they are difficult to quantify, they are likely to be substantial.

A second major observation is that while the partnership debate is certainly a hot one, local authorities still seem to feel rather uncomfortable with the entire idea. There is little development of regulatory frameworks and human capacities within local government bodies to facilitate partnerships in SWM and to adequately perform their remaining monitoring and control functions. Furthermore, there is a strong inclination on the part of local authorities to think in terms of 'big is beautiful' and to disregard or disrespect small-scale, indigenous solutions and/or community initiatives in SWM. This was especially the case in Accra, where an overzealous central government, preoccupied with concerns of environmental health and city beautification, sought to overcome the financial problems troubling the local public-private arrangement in a technocratic manner by granting monopoly rights to a foreign company.[8] The findings in the two cities further suggest that if things are left to the local authorities, community participation remains of almost no concern to authorities (Accra), and when the community does play a leading role (despite the fact that it is through a middle-class movement), the authorities remain aloof from it (Chennai). This implies that an important actor defending the public/communal interest is either

---

8. A recent paper by Bharat Dahiya (2000) also points to this problem in Chennai.

ignored or overburdened, while this is one of the acclaimed strengths of partnerships.

Assessments of SWM activities (and partnerships) are rarely carried out from the more encompassing sustainable development perspective, and are usually based on ideas of greater service efficiency and effectiveness, and environmental health concerns, with occasional attention to equity/justice considerations. Possible contributions to ecological sustainability are usually ignored. The partnership arrangements investigated here also suffered from this neglect, as sustainability concerns were either entirely absent (Accra) or played only a minor role (Chennai). Obviously, more effective collection does help to reduce the burden on local sinks (neighborhood), but this has been a welcome externality rather than a specific goal of the partnerships concerned. The cases show that very little is done to operate across the waste management hierarchy, especially by linking collection, transportation and disposal practices to waste reuse and recycling. This means that opportunities for developing positive spin-offs are not grasped sufficiently, which could improve the functioning of the entire system in accordance with a sustainable development perspective. Finally, an important strength of the sustainable development template that we have adopted – one that does not really emerge from the analysis of the partnerships investigated here – is that it points to the necessity of looking at impacts both at the level of the partnership activity as such, as well as at the level of the entire SWM system, and at the level of the city/region. This integrative perspective is likely to lead to different conclusions than when activities are considered separately, and avoids the danger of sweeping away those activities whose contributions cannot, and should not, be judged in purely economic terms only.

References

Anand, P.B. (1999), 'Waste Management in Madras Revisited', *Environment and Urbanization*, Vol. 11(2), pp. 161-76.
Batley, R. (1996), 'Public-Private Relationships and Performance in Service Delivery', *Urban Studies*, Vol. 33(4-5), pp. 723-51.
Baud, I.S.A. (2000), *Collective Action, Enablement and Partnerships, Issues in Urban Development*, inaugural address, Free University, Amsterdam, 27 October 2000.
Baud, I.S.A, Grafakos, S., Hordijk, M. and Post, J. (2001), 'Quality of Life and Alliances in Solid Waste Management', *Cities*, Vol. 18(1), pp. 1-10.
Dahiya, B. (2000), *Managing the Urban Local Commons: Conflicts and Governance in Valasaravakkam town in South India*, Paper presented to the DSA conference on Environmental Resources and Sustainable Development Study Group, University of Bradford.

Dhanalakshmi, R. and Iyer, S. (1999), *Solid Waste Management in Madras City*, Pattipaggam Ltd., Madras.
Evans, D. (1996), 'Government Action, Social Capital and Development: Evidence on Synergy', *World Development*, Vol. 24(6), pp. 1119-32.
Hardoy, J.E., Mitlin, D. and Satterthwaite, D. (2001), *Environmental Problems in an Urbanizing World, Finding Solutions for Cities in Africa, Asia and Latin America*, Earthscan, London.
Helmsing, A.H.J. (2000), *Decentralisation and Enablement, Issues in the Local Governance Debate*, Inaugural Address, University Utrecht, 27 April 2000.
Johnson, H. and Wilson, G. (2000), 'Biting the Bullet: Civil Society, Social Learning and the Transformation of Local Governance', *World Development*, Vol. 28(11), pp. 1891-906.
Lardinois, I. and Furedy, C. (1999), 'Source Separation of Household Waste Materials – Analysis of Case Studies from Pakistan, the Philippines, India, Brazil, Argentina and the Netherlands', *Urban Waste Series* No. 7, WASTE, Gouda.
McGranahan, G. and Satterthwaite, D. (2000), 'Environmental Health or Ecological Sustainability? Reconciling the Brown and Green Agendas in Urban Development', in C. Pugh (ed.) *Sustainable Cities in Developing Countries*, Earthscan, London, pp. 73-90.
Obirih-Opareh, N. (2000), *Institutional Arrangements and Stakeholders' Perspectives of Solid Waste Management in Accra*, Report to NIRP.
Ostrom, E. (1996), 'Crossing the Great Divide: Co-production, Synergy and Development', *World Development*, Vol. 24(6), pp. 1073-87.
Post, J. (1997), 'Urban Management in an Unruly Setting, the African Case', *Third World Planning Review*, Vol. 19(4), pp. 347-366.
Pugh, C. (2000), 'Sustainable Urban Development: Some Millennial Reflections on Theory and Application', in C. Pugh (ed.), *Sustainable Cities in Developing Countries*, Earthscan, London, pp. 21-52.
Rakodi, C. (1999), *Urban Governance, Partnership and Poverty, a Preliminary Exploration of the Research Issues*, Theme Paper, No. 8, International Development Department, School of Public Policy, University of Birmingham.
Satterthwaite, D. (1997), 'Sustainable Cities or Cities that Contribute to Sustainable Development', *Urban Studies*, Vol. 34(10), pp. 1667-91.
Stoker, G. (2000), *The New Politics of British Local Governance*, MacMillan Press, Basingstoke.
UNCHS (1993), *Public-Private Partnership in Enabling Shelter Strategies*, UNCHS, Nairobi.
UNCHS (1996), *Global Report on Human Settlements*, Oxford University Press, Oxford.
www.corporationofchennai.com/depart/waste.html

PART III

Livelihoods, Rural-Urban Linkages and Regional Development

13 About Trade and Trust: The Question of Livelihood and Social Capital in Rural-Urban Interactions

LEO DE HAAN AND PAUL QUARLES VAN UFFORD

Introduction

In this paper, rural-urban interactions are considered as linkages across space reflected in the flows of people, goods, services, finance, and information between urban and rural areas. We will draw mainly upon findings of research in West Africa, although our argument has a much wider purport. We do not attempt to exactly define the 'urban' and the 'rural', since every such attempt is controversial. 'Rural' activities like agricultural and livestock breeding occur in cities, and an activity usually classified as 'urban' (such as manufacturing) may turn up in the countryside. Moreover, in Africa a settlement of 5,000 people is typically 'urban' in morphology and functions, while in India such a settlement is classified as 'rural'.

Over the last decades, rural-urban interactions in developing countries have expanded. For instance, in the Club du Sahel's famous West Africa Long-Term Perspective Study, Cour and Snrech (1998, p. 34-62) found that (1) population growth, (2) changes in the natural environment, and (3) brutal exposure to world markets occasioned a rapid increase in rural-urban interactions. Cities expand and extend their influence on the countryside, which in its turn modernizes many aspects of social and economic life. Export crops and food production for urban markets have made agriculture gradually more market-oriented. Urban markets influence rural settlement patterns and agricultural production, in the sense that rural population densities have increased along the same geographical lines as urban markets have developed. However, while rural areas now quickly respond to urban demand for food, the flow of urban goods and services to rural areas generally lags behind. This can be explained by, firstly, the increased diversification of rural production, which directly meets rural demand for particular goods and services. The non-farm share of African rural household income is estimated at 25 per cent-30 per cent, while it amounts to almost 40 per cent in the Sahel (Cour and Snrech, 1998, p. 55). Secondly, it can be explained by the failure of urban areas to produce sufficient (both in quantitative and qualitative terms) goods and services for the rural areas. This is still considered to be the weak link, which has to be improved if full complementarity between urban and rural areas is to be achieved. Thirdly, rural-urban interactions may comprise clear-cut competition. For instance, the land market in the rural-urban contact zone is troubled by speculation and conflicts between modern and traditional law over property rights.

The three above-mentioned driving forces not only altered production and the flows of goods, services and finance, but also resulted in a significant increase in people's mobility. Today, the physical distance between urban and rural areas forms less and less of a constraint on social relations. Migration from the countryside to the towns is rapidly increasing, and migration trajectories are becoming more complex. In West Africa, urban areas have absorbed two-thirds of the region's population growth. The proportion of town dwellers rose from 13 per cent in 1960 to 40 per cent in 1990 (Cour and Snrech, 1998, pp. 45-47). Soon, a clear-cut majority of the region's population will live in urban areas. The regional urban network takes the shape of a relatively normal rank/size distribution.

This being the general picture of rural-urban interactions in West-Africa, the question arises how these interactions are being shaped by the people concerned. We have already defined rural-urban interactions as linkages across space of flows of people, goods, services, finance, and information. We take these interactions to be reciprocal – i.e., to the possible benefit of both parties – rather than exploitative, i.e., to the detriment of one of them, generally the countryside.

Moreover, rural-urban interactions can only be properly understood if analyzed as a manifestation of people's livelihood strategies. Therefore, we will first elaborate on the concept of livelihood. Next, we will use this concept to improve our understanding of rural-urban interactions, grounding it with research findings in West Africa. We will show that social capital is a key concept in understanding these interactions, and will use case studies of agricultural marketing networks to underpin our argument.

Livelihood

As one of us has already pointed out (De Haan, 2000a, p. 343), people in developing countries – and poor people in particular – undertake manifold activities which yield them food, housing, and a monetary income.

> 'The most common of these are the production of crops, livestock, clothing and housing for home consumption; the production of crops and livestock for sale; trade; handicrafts such as basket weaving, pottery, carpentry; seasonal or permanent wage labor, which includes children; remittances by kin who have emigrated; loans, alms, gifts and sometimes corruption.'

Thus, a person's livelihood is not necessarily the same as that person having a job. Moreover, although obtaining a monetary income is important, it is not the only aspect that matters in livelihood. It is quite conceivable for somebody with a low monetary income to be better off than someone with a higher monetary income.

Nowadays, livelihood – even in the remotest corners of the world – is subject to a multitude of influences from a broader national and international economic, social and political context. According to De Haan (2000a, p. 344), to achieve a livelihood people make use of various assets and resources, which are called capitals. People apply various blends of these capitals, which represent various strategies that result in different livelihoods. Thus, although the actual mixture may change per livelihood, the capitals involved are: Human capital (not only labor, but also skills, experience, creativity, and inventiveness); natural capital (land, water, forests, pastures, minerals, etc.); physical capital (food stocks, livestock, jewelry, equipment, tools, machinery, etc.); financial capital (money in a savings account at the bank or in an old sock, a loan or credit, etc.); and social capital (i.e., the quality of relations between people).

The discussion on such concepts as entitlement (Sen, 1981), claims (Chambers and Conway, 1992), and access (Blaikie et al., 1994) has made it clear that the various forms of capital do not necessarily have to be held as private property. All these concepts refer to the general ability of actors to use the capital at reasonable (i.e., unimpeded) costs when needed and wanted. Land can be rented; water and forests can be communally owned; a plough can be borrowed or hired; food can be bestowed. What matters is one's access to the capital. According to Blaikie et al. (1994), every social group, every household, and every member of it has a particular access profile to capitals, which depends on rights by tradition or by law and the way these are exercised. They differ per individual, per household, and per group, and may change over time. Actors like social groups, households, and individuals decide on a choice of livelihood strategies on the basis of their access profile.

We consider livelihood as sustainable when the outcome of the processing of different types of capital is meaningful in terms of human well-being, and viable in terms of securing people against shocks and stresses. 'Shocks are violent and come unexpectedly; stress is less violent, but can last longer. Both have their impact on one or more of the vital 'capitals'. An environmental shock like a flood or an earthquake has its impact on natural, human and physical capital. Drought is an example of a high-level environmental stress; seasonality is a well-known example of low-level environmental stress' (De Haan, 2000a, p. 347). In West Africa, the droughts of 1967-1975 and 1984-1986 were a major driving force behind the change in rural-urban interactions They not only forced agriculture southward, but also induced the flight of ecological refugees to towns in search of food and employment. Many of them stayed, and switched from rural to urban livelihoods. Many of those who remained in the countryside nowadays supplement their rural livelihoods with a temporary job in town; other rural households are supported by remittances from migrants in cities.

Another source of shocks and stresses is the economy. 'After independence, the new West African states were plunged into the world markets and into a level of economic competition for which they were poorly prepared' (Cour and Snrech, 1998, p. 35). They continued to depend on the export of low-priced commodities. Investments aimed at increasing productivity and diversifying the economy failed. Loans to cover increasingly expensive import bills after the 1973 oil crisis resulted in a debt crisis in the 1980s. Price policies, aimed at keeping food prices in the cities low, chronically frustrated the income generation of food producers in rural areas. Subsequent programs of structural adjustment undercut social services and only reinforced the integration in low-priced raw material markets. All the time, these countries remained heavily dependent on international donor transfers. At the same time, increased market integration became the second driving force behind the expansion of rural-urban interactions, notably because increased market integration stimulated the flow of goods, services, and finance between rural and urban areas.

The impact of these environmental and economic shocks and stresses was aggravated by the third driving force: Rapid population growth. Although sustainable development and population growth do not exclude each other by definition (see for an extensive argumentation, De Haan, 2000b), the average 2.7 per cent annual population growth rate after 1960 made the shocks and stresses more dramatic.

Sen (1981; Drèze and Sen, 1989) has shown that livelihood depends not only on direct access to capitals, but also on how the use of capitals is embedded in a wider social, economic, political, and natural context. He observed that droughts result in famine only under certain conditions. First of all, people can run out of food, but if they find employment and thus earn money to buy food, there will be no famine. Sen noted that food is sometimes exported from famine areas, precisely because of a lack of purchasing power. Second, where food scarcity leads to increasing food prices, markets would normally attract enough food from elsewhere, unless they are malfunctioning. Thus, according to Sen, various contextual factors like market organization, the labor market, and price policy contribute to or even cause the stress in livelihood.

In short, the concept of livelihood refers not only to access to, and the subsequent processing of, capitals, but also to the particular interaction of social groups, households, and individuals with their wider context. Livelihood is dynamic because people do not process capitals automatically, but with an eye to opportunities offered by the wider context, as they are sometimes forced by the same context to resort to particular strategies. Thus, people are neither powerless objects nor free agents who can become whatever they choose (De Haan, 2000a, p. 350).

The increased exposure to world markets, continued population growth, and drastic events in the natural environment finally resulted in an adapted livelihood. It is this adapted livelihood that gave way to and shaped the intensification of rural-urban interactions.

However, we do not think that some kind of an equilibrium has been reached in West Africa, represented by a stabilized adapted livelihood. In the present epoch of globalization, equilibrium and stability are far away. 'Globalization places a premium on flexibility and adaptability, and those least able to respond to change are likely to be those adversely affected' (Ellis and Seeley, 2001, p. 1). Thus, livelihood in West Africa is continuously undergoing change. In particular, it is becoming increasingly multi-local, i.e., using capitals that are found in different locations, countryside, and city alike. Besides, livelihood is becoming multiple or multidimensional, i.e., social groups, households, and individuals are combining various livelihood strategies. Nowadays, agricultural production is generally combined with rural or urban off-farm employment and trade. The general picture of livelihood in West Africa is therefore one of continuous rearrangements of strategies using various capitals in different locations. As there is no such thing as *the* West African livelihood, today one often speaks about livelihoods in plural. A proper understanding of rural-urban interaction can only be achieved if this general picture is taken into account.

Networks: Livelihood and the Shaping of Rural-urban Interactions

As argued in the preceding section, rural-urban flows can be considered as manifestations of livelihoods, and because of the multi-locality and multi-dimensionality of livelihoods, flows of goods, services, people, finance and information, they 'are not usually limited within the regional boundaries of a town and its hinterland. Migrants can go to a variety of places, including international destinations, and goods and services can be sold and purchased in many different locations. From the perspective of a rural household, the pattern of flows is thus more likely to resemble a *network* [our italics] involving multiple linkages with a number of villages and towns, rather than revolving around a single urban centre' (Tacoli, 1998, p. 12). Thus, networks are the way in which livelihoods reveal themselves and shape rural-urban relations.

We consider networks as a set of relations, or ties, between actors. In this case, actors can be understood as organizations, social groups, households, or individuals. Social relations or ties may range from kinship, friendship, and village membership to patron-client relationships, union or political party membership, and ethnic bonds. Social relations are not confined to a local scale. Even kinship becomes increasingly multi-local, with relatives migrating to various urban and rural areas. Any social relation can be mapped as a tie having both a content and a form. It should be noted that social relations can overlap and that people may be part of various networks. Note also that we consider with Granovetter (1985) all economic actions as embedded in social relations, which means that economic behavior can only be understood as part of social behavior. Markets, for example, have to be considered as social institutions as well. This implies considering the supposed non-rational residue factor of an actor's behavior in economic analysis, as a rational choice.

The content of a tie can include anything from goods, services, friendship or love, to money, information, and advice. The form of a tie concerns the strength of the relation and may range from weak to strong. Relations between family members, friends, and close colleagues are considered to be strong ties. So too are those between people who frequently communicate with each other and with other actors in the same network, and who put a high value on their relations. Weak ties occur between members of different networks, i.e., between people who have less contact and who value their relations less. At first sight, strong ties seem eminent in sustaining a livelihood. In family and friends one has trust, and they are the first to call upon. Agricultural work and food are shared among family and friends in the village. Remittances from migrants in the city are mostly received by kin. Granovetter (1983), however, has pointed out an interesting issue that may also help to shed light on the value of different forms of ties for globalizing livelihoods. He argues that weak ties are important for people looking for a job. Even the modern meaning of 'networking' emerged in this context: People looking for a job benefit more from contacts with members of other networks than with the one(s) they are part of. Contacts with members of another network may yield new information about job opportunities or may once more lead to new contacts. This does not mean that complete strangers offer the most valuable information. Granovetter shows that employers in search of personnel prefer to recruit candidates who are vouched for by others. There is only one complication. People usually value information from strong ties as more trustworthy than information from weak ties. This may hinder the recognition of feasible opportunities offered by weak ties. At this point, it is of importance to refer to what has been argued about livelihood in globalization : If globalization places a premium on flexibility and adaptability, leading to continuously changing multi-local and multidimensional livelihoods, then this premium on adaptation is perhaps better realized through weak rather than strong ties.

Finally, Rose (1998, p. 3) usefully summarizes the relevant distinction between informal and formal networks that actors use in procuring a livelihood, at the same time revealing the overlap with strong and weak ties. Informal networks 'are face-to-face relationships between a limited number of individuals who know each other and are bound together by kinship, friendship or propinquity. Informal networks are institutions in the sociological sense of having patterned and recurring interaction. Lacking legal recognition, full-time officials, written rules, and their own funds, they are not formal organisations'. Informal networks are therefore more likely to display strong ties. Formal networks 'are rule-bound bureaucratic, have legal personality and secure revenue from the market or the state. A formal organization can have individuals as its members', such as a political party, or its members can be organizations such as an urban NGO providing support to village credit cooperatives. 'Formal organisations are a necessary part of a *modern* [italics in original] society, for it requires impersonal bureaucratic organisations of state and market that can routinely produce complex goods such as automobiles'. There are many links between informal and formal networks, and sometimes the distinction between them is vague. 'Even if a network has a formal identity, such as a rural cooperative, face-to-face networks tend to be horizontal and diffuse and an individual's reputation for helpful cooperation is more important than cash payments and bureaucratic regulations'. Formal networks do not preclude strong ties, even though weak ties are more likely to occur than in informal networks. We will return to this matter after the following section.

Rural-Urban Interactions: Food trade in Benin

The West African coastal state of Benin stretches roughly 800 km from the sub-humid coastal zone at the Bight of Benin in the south to the semi-arid Sahel zone at the Niger river in the north. Because of the presence of various agro-ecological zones, food production is highly diverse. However, when it comes to rural-urban interactions in the form of food trade, maize, yam, and cattle are prominent on a national scale. The trade in these goods is in the hands of private traders and integrated into larger international West African markets.

Maize Trade

Maize is produced in both the south and the north, but only in the south is it a vital subsistence crop for farmers. Yet, the major maize granaries are located in the north.

Maize is traded from rural areas to urban areas (and in periods of shortage, back to rural areas) through informal and formal markets. In the south, the first exchange of maize at harvest time often takes place along the road between the farm and the formal market place. Difficulties of transport, road conditions or lack of funds to pay formal market taxes are the reasons why farmers accept the risk of selling at a lower price than at the market place itself. Informal market transactions occur mainly in the north when quantities are large or roads are inaccessible to public transport. Subsequently, the maize finds it way through formal markets, starting with the village market where producers sell to consumers as well as to assemblers, retailers, and local wholesalers. Most traders, in turn, sell the maize at the urban regional market, which has strong linkages with the village market. Especially in the north, flows of maize are assembled and channelled to urban consumer markets. The latter are pure distribution markets where maize and other goods are sold by wholesalers and retailers, and bought by retailers and consumers throughout the year (Lutz, 1994, pp. 61-63).

In the period of abundance (June-January), maize is typically traded from the rural areas in the south and center of the country to urban areas in the south, and from the rural areas in the north to urban areas in Niger, and to a lesser extent in Togo (Klaasse Bos and Krogt, 1991). In the lean season (March-June), the reduced supply from the south and center is compensated for by the north.

It was argued in the previous sections that livelihood strategies explain the way rural-urban interactions, such as these maize flows, are shaped. In fact, maize farmers, mostly sell their surplus in relatively small quantities whenever some kind of household expense needs financing. Thus their maize stock represents a liquid type of physical capital. This leads to the frequent selling of small quantities and laborious collection activities at the start of the marketing channel. However, the poor accessibility and high transportation costs also orient their sales strategy towards informal markets at farm gate or roadside. A fine-meshed rural collection pattern of markets is the result. The same applies to the maize distribution in urban areas: As most urban consumers have very limited financial capital at their disposal, they buy in very small quantities.

With respect to the livelihood strategies of other actors, Lutz (1994, pp. 66-71) distinguishes wholesalers and retailers. The former buys from farmers and retailer-assemblers and sells to the latter, who in turn sells to retailers. Wholesalers completely depend on their own financial capital, and the significant dissimilarities among them are linked to this. Wholesalers with limited financial capital cannot invest in credit and storage. Despite their low turnover, these petty wholesalers perform an indispensable function at the first stage of the marketing channel. The number of wholesalers with much financial capital is limited. They buy much larger quantities and are able to invest in buying and selling networks. This means that they are also much more flexible in their choice of markets at which to buy and sell maize. This ability is crucial to understanding food marketing in Benin, because these traders are in fact the only ones capable of directly connecting rural supply and urban demand, which are hundreds of kilometers apart.

Retailers buy maize from wholesalers for sale to consumers at convenient locations and times. Moreover, by re-packing, sorting, and processing they are able to offer maize in the requested forms and quantities. To increase the volume assembled, some retailers have joined forces to set up their own assembling networks.

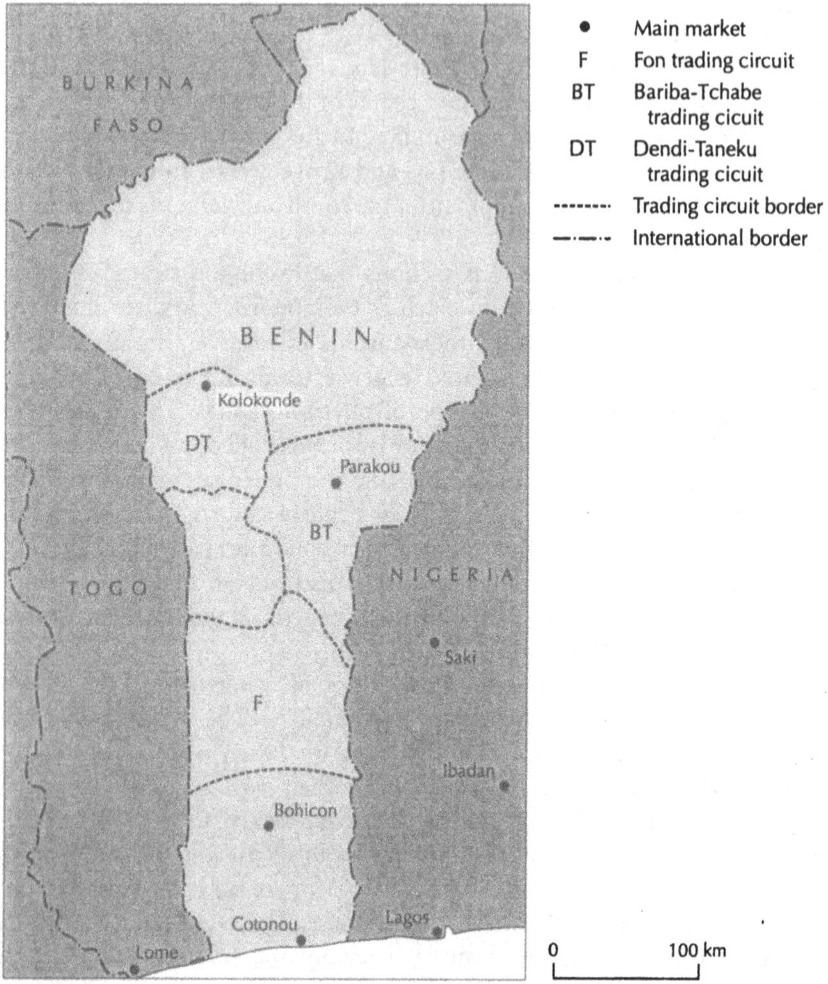

Figure 13.1 Benin: main markets and trading circuits

In addition to wholesalers and retailers, commission agents such as brokers and assemblers are key actors in the marketing channel. Non-resident wholesalers arriving at the large urban markets of Bohicon or Cotonou find it hard, especially in the period of abundance, to sell their maize without much delay to retailers, whom, moreover, they hardly know. To save time, they store their produce in a broker's warehouse. Subsequently, and on a commission basis, the broker sells the maize to retailers on behalf of the wholesaler. The broker knows the retailers well and often sells on credit, which considerably speeds up the sale of the wholesaler's stock. Some wealthy wholesalers do not even wait for their stock to be sold, but return to the production zone for more produce and collect their cash later. Others simply send a truck of maize to their broker without appearing in the city.

Assemblers buy maize on behalf of wholesalers at the farm gate, roadside, or village market. Like brokers, they do not incur a financial risk since their transactions are pre-financed by the wholesaler. Their work is advantageous to both farmers and wholesalers. Farmers save time and transportation costs; wholesalers save time and contract out an activity for which specific skills are required. '... assembly is quite a time-consuming activity: One has to attract farmers willing to sell their surpluses and negotiate a suitable price or measured quantity. Assemblers master the necessary local measuring techniques which consist of procuring the maximum of produce per unit measure, the price being more or less determined by the type of measure used' (Lutz, 1994, p. 69).

In practice, there is no clear distinction between the groups involved in trading maize from rural to urban areas. Brokers may do wholesaling at their own risk if opportunities are good. Petty wholesalers may turn into assemblers if their financial capital is insufficient to trade for their own account, and may start to wholesale again alongside assembling for a wealthy wholesaler when their financial capital has grown again.

Yam Trade

Yams are produced in central and northern Benin. As well as being locally consumed, they are mainly traded to the south, where the urban market of Cotonou constitutes the main outlet. Adanguidi (2000) distinguishes three separate, ethnically (Fon, Bariba-Tchabe, and Dendi-Taneka) dominated trading circuits through which fresh and processed yams from different production zones are traded to Cotonou.

Yams are purchased predominantly at the farm gate. Wholesalers transport the produce to the city. Various reasons are found for the ethnic specialization in trading circuits. Firstly, yams tend to have specific characteristics in taste and texture according to their production zone. Consequently, the consumers who belong to an ethnic group that originates from a particular production zone, typically prefer to buy yams that are grown there. Secondly, at the Cotonou market, the use of measures to determine weight and quantity differs according to the ethnicity of wholesalers and retailers. For example, Fon wholesalers sell by balance, a technique which has not been mastered by their Bariba or Tchabe colleagues, who prefer to sell by pile or sack. The third reason seems to be the most important, however: When his truckload of yams arrives in Cotonou, it is hard for the wholesaler to sell them all at once. Storage is needed, but storage capacity is scarce and, moreover, it is important to sell as quickly as possible if prices are favorable. Therefore, each wholesaler guarantees his access to the market by cultivating relations with a group of retailers, who typically belong to the same ethnic group. For instance, to ensure sufficient storage capacity for yams or yam flour, Fon wholesalers maintain good relations with the market officials who rent out storage rooms from time to time. In addition, wholesalers mainly sell to retailers belonging to their own ethnic group, since much of the produce is provided on credit. Otherwise, the wholesalers use the services of brokers who store the produce in their warehouse in exchange for a commission and subsequently sell to retailers, again for a commission.

Adanguidi (2000, p. 119) concludes that there is a strong personal content and a clear regional-ethnic bias in the various relations that constitute the trade organization and, consequently, the type of rural-urban interaction. Although relations are personal, he does not consider them as power-neutral. Mainly because of differences in available financial and social capital, different actors in the trade organization have different powers. Nevertheless, he considers this type of rural-urban interaction as a relation of partnership rather than patron-client.

Cattle Trade

Compared to other West African coastal countries, Benin has a large cattle population. Most cattle keeping is concentrated in the north, because the south is infested with the tsetse fly. Some three-quarters of the cattle supply originates from pastoralists; the remainder stems from farmers who mainly sell draught animals.

As in maize marketing, a distinction can be made between informal and formal markets, which are situated along the marketing channel that links rural and urban areas. The informal market is represented by farm-gate transactions between pastoralists, farmers, butchers, and traders, who sell and buy cattle in order to expand herds, to train draught animals, to slaughter, or to make a profit on a subsequent sale, respectively. Usually, three types of formal markets are distinguished. At collection markets, local traders buy from pastoralists and farmers. These markets are considerably less numerous, and consequently more dispersed, than the village maize markets, indicating the importance of informal cattle marketing. Distribution markets are typically second-level markets where local traders sell to long-distance traders, who in turn sell to butchers at the urban markets of Lome (Togo), Cotonou (Benin), Ibadan and Lagos (Nigeria). However, cattle flows between rural and urban areas may provide a more complicated picture (Quarles van Ufford, 1999, pp. 119-151). This is mainly due to the multitude of transactions between formal and informal markets in the north. The expanding cotton economy in particular explains the rise in the number of local transactions for animal traction, cattle breeding or investment purposes.

As with the maize trade, different types of traders are active in the cattle trade. Yet, due to the diverging characteristics of the produce involved, both trades have developed their own specializations and concomitant organization. The maize trade organization, as outlined above, is dominated by a relay type of transaction carried out by independent actors. In relay trade, the commodity is effectively exchanged and ownership is transferred from one actor to another (farmer-trader, trader-consumer). In network trade, no transfer of property occurs; the commodity changes hands between different representatives or employees of a chief trader (farmer-network-butcher-consumer). Both types of trade organization are not mutually exclusive. Assemblers and brokers in the maize trade, for instance, acting on behalf of wealthy traders and retailers sometimes purchase maize through assembling networks. However, maize is much easier to standardize in terms of quality and measure than cattle are. This makes the maize market more transparent and explains its organization around the most ordinary form of consecutive transactions between sellers and buyers. Cattle trade is to a much larger extent vertically integrated and leaves less room for individual maneuver.

What can be said about the archetypal composition of a trade network? Central to the network is the network chief. His position is based on a combination of material wealth, prestige, and an extensive network of personal relations. He decides upon most of the transaction details (such as time schedule, numbers, and destination) and takes care of all financial arrangements.

For the purchase of cattle, the chief may employ various collectors. In relay trade, these would be independent retailer-assemblers. In the cattle trade, however, collectors are part of the chief's network. He advances them a certain amount of money to buy cattle at informal markets or small local collection markets. Usually, the collectors are experienced cattle buyers who typically confine their activities to a specific area. Even at formal market places, the collectors, as well as the traders, use the services of brokers.

Brokers are omnipresent at cattle markets all over West Africa. For a fixed commission from both buyer and seller, they witness the transaction, assure the solvability of the buyer, the origin and state of health of the animal, and guarantee that the animal has not been stolen. Typically, a broker is well acquainted with the cattle market in question and will try to find potential buyers for his clients, who are mostly pastoralists. They entrust the broker with the cattle they have for sale. As such, he performs a crucial service in the negotiation process, alternately informing buyer and seller about the respective bids. Using their prestige and material wealth, traders attempt to win over certain brokers by providing them with the occasional, financial favor. Brokers are prone to providing seller-pastoralists with erroneous information about the maximum traders are willing to pay, or about the alleged absence of other potential buyers. Thus, establishing relations with brokers is clearly to the financial advantage of the traders (Quarles van Ufford, forthcoming).

An itinerant trader may be in charge of transporting the animals to the final destination market. Besides the cattle, a sum to cover various transaction costs is entrusted to him. Upon return, the sales revenue is returned to the chief in cash or in the form of consumer goods which he ordered before departure. Yet, most chiefs prefer to make the final sale at the destination market themselves. In the absence of price standardization, only marketing experience can determine the right price. Still, an experienced herder will take care of trekking the cattle over at least part of the itinerary. The risks involved in this, as well as the considerable value of cattle entrusted to the herder, explain the observation that the chief typically prefers to maintain a network relation with this person who is so crucial to his trading activities.

At the sales markets on the West African coast, a crucial function in the trade network is performed by the landlord-broker who accommodates the itinerant long-distance traders and assists them in selling their cattle. In fact, he can be considered a cross-cultural broker, since the butchers to whom cattle are sold typically belong to a different ethnic group. The landlord is permanently established at the destination market. A chief trader will usually deal with one landlord to whom he may be related by kinship, ethnicity, or common region of origin. To lodge the traders, a landlord operates one or more residences. He provides meals and market information, and accompanies the trader to the market. Because of his acquaintance with the butchers, he is able to identify creditworthy and reliable customers, and is even prepared to run a debt collection service. Until the departure of the trader, he keeps the money and takes care of the administration (Quarles van Ufford, 1999, pp. 47-51).

Discussion: Reassessing the Role of Social Capital and Networks in Rural-Urban Interactions

The strategies of maize, yam, and cattle traders revealed that rural-urban interactions are shaped to a large extent by people's livelihood strategies. It is also clear that although trade is an economic activity, rural-urban interactions are embedded in social relations. This prompts us to reassess the role of social capital in rural-urban interactions and consequently in livelihood and to demonstrate that networks, personal contacts, trust, and prestige are vital determinants of the patterns we observe.

There is no fixed definition of social capital, and the concept is discussed in many contexts other than in relation to livelihood. According to the Social Capital Initiative (World Bank, 1998, p. 1), social capital 'includes the institutions, the relationships, the attitudes and values that govern interactions among people and contribute to economic and social development'. It is 'not simply the sum of institutions which underpin society, but also the glue that holds them together'. Within this overall perspective, three concepts of social capital can be distinguished. The original and most narrow one is associated with Putnam's (1993) analysis of civic traditions, democracy, and regional development in Italy. He explained regional differences in development by corresponding differences in social structures and networks. To him, social capital consists of social networks and associated norms that have an effect on the productivity of the community. He pointed at the tradition of rich networks of organized reciprocity and solidarity, embodied in guilds, religious fraternities, and neighborhood organizations in Italy, that laid the foundations for successful economic development. Trust-fostering norms, coordination of actions, information about trustworthiness of members, and the potential to serve as platforms of collaboration for new types of activity make these networks so interesting to Putnam.

Secondly, Coleman (1988) defined social capital much more broadly, as a variety of different entities which have in common that they consist of some aspect of social structure and facilitate certain actions of actors within the structure. Where Putnam (1993) thinks that vertical relations based on authority have a limited capacity for collective action and economic performance, and horizontal relations based on trust and shared values are more likely to have economic success (Bebbington 1999), Coleman values both horizontal and vertical organizations by arguing that certain forms of social capital may be useful for one action but useless or harmful for another. The key elements to Coleman are trustworthiness, the capability of information provision, and the execution of effective sanctions.

Thirdly, Olsen (1982) and North (1990) include in social capital the most formalized institutional relationships and structures such as government, law, and civil liberties. Clearly, these three concepts of social capital are not mutually exclusive, but overlap and encompass each other.

Although the debate about social capital sometimes takes euphoric dimensions, it is evident that it cannot be a panacea for development. Nor will social capital have positive effects for everyone in all cases. If it has positive effects on one group, it may be to the detriment of others. Nevertheless, social capital clearly has the potential to enhance people's livelihood, and one may expect that it improves the sustainability of that livelihood in terms of coping and adaptation. The role of social capital is particularly interesting with respect to the access it may provide to other capitals and to wider institutions of state, market, and civil society. Especially Bebbington (1999) dwells upon the relationship between social capital and access from both the inside out and the outside in. With respect to 'from the inside out', he points at the mobilization of social relations for accessing capitals, so-called claim-making. Shared cultural identity and strong intra-group communication etc. facilitate group members' access to local capitals. Examples are access to financial capital through rotating saving schemes, or to arable land through a common property regime. Moving up the scale, strong networks with state or civil society actors may facilitate access to health and educational services. In the same vein, networks with other market actors may open up new markets. Finally, on a national scale, strong social capital in the form of regional or national political parties or trade associations may influence trade policies. With respect to 'from the outside in' Bebbington (1999) notes that little is known about how external institutions, such as state institutions, can reach down to enhance people's access to capitals. He mainly points at synergistic relations in service provision between state institutions and local formal organizations.

From our discussion of the maize, yam, and cattle trade it has become clear that social capital plays an important role in trade organization and in the livelihood of traders, producers, and consumers. Contacts, trust, and information about the trustworthiness of actors and the trustworthiness of market information are prominent issues in this respect.

In the organization of the yam trade, for instance, strong personal ties and a clear regional-ethnic identity were depicted. Yam wholesalers must trust retailers to pay them once the latter have sold the produce to consumers. Equally they must trust brokers for selling their stock at a reasonable price. Since written contracts hardly exist or can hardly be enforced in the absence of collateral, trust on the basis of long-standing personal contacts and endorsed by regional-ethnic bonds is the only alternative.

Also in the maize trade, wholesalers establish relations of trust with their brokers, who store and sell their produce. They also lend assemblers money to buy maize at the farm gate, roadside, or village market. Lutz (1994, p. 60) believes that retailers provide consumers with credit for social rather than economic reasons. In view of the above, we agree with Granovetter (1985) that economic and social considerations cannot be separated from each other. Providing credit to consumers is as much a socially embedded economic act as a wholesaler's providing a retailer with produce on credit. In the cases Lutz mentions, trust (i.e., social capital) substitutes financial capital, which is scarce. As such, social capital guarantees the maintenance of the clientele and the continuity of the business.

Finally, it appeared that social capital is equally indispensable in the cattle trade. For instance, a trader requires a minimum of contacts with suppliers, herders, brokers or butchers to facilitate his transactions. In the past, his file of potential suppliers – i.e. pastoralists - was even more important given the near absence of formal cattle markets. It is interesting to note in this respect that until recently the relationship with a trader constituted an important asset for a pastoralist as well, notably to get access to 'urban affairs'. A trader could, for instance, assist in contacting local authorities in order to resolve problems concerning tenure, cattle thefts, and the like. Hence, upon establishment in a particular area, pastoralists would seek to contact a local trader in order to build a sustained relationship of 'mutual services'. Nowadays, this particular manifestation of social capital bridging the rural-urban divide has lost some of its importance, since many pastoralists have integrated urban markets in one way or another, and have become acquainted with city life. For traders, however, preferential sales contacts with pastoralists remain of substantial weight in their trading practices.

In the cattle trade as well, social capital and trust are intimately related. Giving large sums of money to a collector to buy cattle demonstrates the confidence of the network chief in his collaborator. Sending thirty head of cattle on the hoof over the Nigerian border to avoid customs controls and to sell at more profitable prices at the Ibadan terminal market, means putting a lot of confidence in herders. In fact, a brief description of the management of trading networks gives us a perfect insight into how social capital can be created, maintained, and expanded, and how trust is obtained.

Generally, there are three types of relations a chief trader maintains with his collaborators. Firstly, there are kinship relations with his children or cousins. This is less obvious than it seems at first sight. Although sons do participate in his network, the working relation with their father may be less close than expected. Given the often large number of sons in view of the polygamous households of many traders, and the danger of dispersal of the inheritance and decline of the enterprise when Islamic heritage laws are applied after his death, a father-trader may select his successor at an early stage and transfer a substantial part of the business to him. Intense work relationships havealso been observed between a trader and his cousins. In general, kinship relations are crucial for starting traders, since they benefit from the experience, prestige and financial capacity of their father or uncle.

A second type of relationship is the matrimonial alliance. In this case, an individual becomes linked to the chief through marriage to one of his daughters or female kin. In fact, this often concerns the revaluation of an employer-employee relation to a kinship relation, and happens to the best performing employees. They will subsequently have many more opportunities to start their own business, while remaining close to the chief-trader.

Thirdly, there is the employer-employee relationship, which usually takes the form of a patron-client relation or an apprenticeship. Here, the apprentice is 'indebted' to the chief because the latter has rendered him one or more specific services – such as the provision of food, lodging or a trade education – or has helped him out with a particular problem. The apprentice reciprocally performs trade activities for the trader. In due time, these trade activities typically become more complicated and involve increasing responsibilities and trust, as in the case of an apprentice selling his patron's cattle at a far away market. His education completed, the apprentice will be symbolically liberated. At that time, he will have accumulated his own working capital and will thus be able to set up his own business as an independent trader, even though he will certainly maintain close economic and social ties with his former chief.

These examples reveal the substance of social capital. In turn, social capital may provide access to other capitals such as information. Through privileged contacts, a trader obtains information on prices, trekking routes, etc., in a market typically characterised by the non transparency of such parameters. Social capital may have a religious underpinning, too. In West Africa, the traditional trade sectors – such as those for food grains and cattle – are generally dominated by Moslem traders. Islam is often referred to as providing traders with a set of elementary trading regulations as well as binding them together into a supra-community. It provides a set of norms and values which have a significant impact on trade organization and the strategies of traders. 'For a long time, the function of landlord-broker has enjoyed considerable prestige. In the Islamic setting of long-distance trade, the fact of receiving multiple visitors certainly contributes to this. "Guests are presents from God" a landlord once said' (Quarles van Ufford, 1999, pp. 22 and 50). The title *El Hadj*, earned by a completing a pilgrimage to Mecca, adds to a trader's prestige and trustworthiness. For that matter, Bebbington (1999) would prefer to call this cultural capital. Note that Islam not only supported the bonds in the West African pre-colonial Haoussa trade networks and diaspora, but protected the minorities in the different trading towns from what Portes and Landolt (1996) call the downside of social capital. Successful entrepreneurs are often besieged by relatives and friends, who expect to receive assistance from the wealthy businessman. This might become such a burden to him that the continuity of the business is threatened. The different religion of the diaspora made its members less vulnerable to claim-making from the host society. We may conclude this discussion on the meaning of social capital for livelihood as follows. Social capital plays a key role in livelihood maintenance. It is defined as the institutions, relationships, attitudes, and values that govern interactions between people and contribute to economic and social development. Social capital can be a value in itself, because it contributes to people's sense of well-being through belonging and identity. What is crucial, however, is that the processing of the other vital capitals in pursuit of a livelihood is mediated through social capital, because social capital gives the actor access to other capitals. Our analysis of the cattle trade convincingly demonstrated that social capital may provide a person with access to other capitals. Both kinship relations and apprenticeships are types of social capital creation through which other vital capitals (information, skill, finance) in cattle marketing become accessible to the starting trader.

However, some traders succeed to make their way into trade relying only partly on kinship relations or apprenticeships. This shows that the role of social capital should not be glorified to the extreme, nor should its importance be neglected. The observation rather partly confirms the analysis of Granovetter (1983) concerning strong and weak ties. To become successful in cattle marketing, newcomers who do not belong to the inner circle of insiders have to create social capital, but they do so by exploring weak ties. Their entry is not facilitated by social capital based on strong ties, but primarily by the possession of other capitals, i.e., skill and finance. Notwithstanding this, comparatively more success is still gained through the kinship and the apprentice modes, which falsifies Granovetter's opinion of strong ties. With respect to the informal and formal kinds of networks identified by Rose (1998), we did not come across any significant formal network in trade organization that contributed to a trader's livelihood. This complies with our general impression that rural-urban interactions in West Africa, also when they concern flows of people, mainly comprise informal networks.

More practically, social capital consists of (1) relationships of trust, reciprocity, and exchange that facilitate cooperation, reduce transaction costs, and provide safety nets amongst actors; (2) networks, either vertical or horizontal, that increase people's trust and ability to cooperate and expand their access to wider institutions; and (3) membership of more formal groups, which often entails adherence to common rules, norms, and sanctions (DFID, 1999).

Through social capital, the quantity and quality of the other forms of capital can be improved. Mutual trust and reciprocity lower the costs of working together. Lower costs improve the efficiency of economic actions, and therefore reinforce financial capital. Rules and sanctions prevent the overexploitation of natural resources and induce its conservation. When people are linked by common norms and sanctions they may more easily form new organizations to pursue interests, including claim-making in the political domain.

Finally, at least two other vital capitals (in addition to human, natural, physical, financial, and social) have been detected in the analysis of rural-urban interaction, i.e., information capital and religious/cultural capital. We feel that there are good arguments to classify religious or cultural capital under social capital, since religion is so closely linked to norms, sanctions, trust, and formalized groups. However, in the case of trading strategies it was appropriate to discuss them separately. With regard to information capital, our analysis showed that information is provided through networks of social relations, and even that information (about the trustworthiness of the members) is one of the prerequisites for a successful network. However, in the case of marketing, information does not necessarily have to be obtained through social networks; soon in fact – if the formalization of markets continues at the present pace – it will not be obtained through such networks at all. Therefore it may be advisable to include information as a vital resource in the livelihood analysis of rural-urban interactions.

Conclusion

We have oriented our analysis of modern rural-urban interaction toward livelihood strategies that shape the flows of food items from rural to urban areas in West Africa. By paying attention to food trade, we were also able to pay additional attention to other interactions such as flows of people and information. Our approach showed that it pays off to analyze rural-urban interactions such as trade as socially embedded economic activities.

Through an analysis of networks and social relations, we have determined the prominent role of social capital in livelihood. The processing of vital capitals in the pursuit of a livelihood is mediated through social capital, precisely because social capital facilitates access to these other forms of capital. We therefore consider social capital as a historical requirement in linking the rural and the urban.

One question that remains to be answered concerns the endurance of our conclusions in the light of increasing globalization. Market structures in West Africa are increasingly formalized. This formalization appears with the emergence of more formal markets, new modes of market organization, and the subsequent decline of such traditional institutions as brokerage. This results in highly personalized informal exchange configurations between buyer and seller, becoming impersonal formal market relations. Informal markets become outshone by formal markets. Brokers on formal markets give way to marketing committees, which officially register transactions. Price information is increasingly distributed through public channels and more rapidly available, reducing the benefits of network information. Yet, this tendency is unevenly developing in different markets. We have already pointed at differences between the maize and the cattle market. Standardization is easier in the maize trade than in the cattle trade, which explains the prevalence of relay relations in maize trade as compared to network relations in cattle trade. Moreover, formalization in market relations is more ahead in more densely populated areas with a certain volume of market production than in sparsely populated, remote areas. We expect that increasing formalization will result in a decline in the significance of social capital in market relations. On the other hand, because globalization places a premium on flexibility and adaptability, we postulate that the premium on adaptation is easier to cash in by maintaining social capital.

References

Adanguidi, J. (2000), 'La Personnalisation de l'Impersonnel. Reflexion Autour du Commerce de l'Igname a Cotonou', APAD *Bulletin*, No. 19, pp. 105-20.

Bebbington, A. (1999), 'Capitals and Capabilities: A Framework for Analyzing Peasant Viability, Rural Livelihood and Poverty', *World Development*, Vol. 27(12), pp. 2021-44.

Blaikie, P., Cannon, T., Davis, I., and Wisner, B. (1994), *At Risk. Natural Hazards, People's Vulnerability and Disasters*, Routledge, London.

Chambers, R. and Conway, G. (1992), *Sustainable Rural Livelihoods: Practical Concepts for the 21st Century*, University of Sussex, Institute of Development Studies, Discussion Paper, No. 296, IDS, Brighton.

Coleman, J. (1988), 'Social Capital in the Creation of Human Capital', *American Journal of Sociology, (Supplement)* S195-S120.
Cour J. and Snrech, S. (1998), *Preparing for the Future. A Vision of West Africa in the Year 2020. West African Long-Term Perspective Study*, OECD/Club du Sahel, Paris.
De Haan, L. (2000a), 'Globalization, Localization and Sustainable Livelihood', *Sociologia Ruralis*, Vol. 40(3), pp. 339-65.
De Haan, L. (2000b), 'The Question of Development and Environment in Geography in the Era of Globalization', *GeoJournal*, Vol. 50, pp. 359-67.
DFID (1999), *Sustainable Livelihoods Guidance Sheets*, DFID, London.
Drèze, J. and Sen, A. (1989), *Hunger and Public Action*, Clarendon Press, Oxford.
Ellis, F. and Seeley, J. (2001), *Globalization and Sustainable Livelihood: An Initial Note*, DFID, London.
Granovetter, M. (1983), 'The Strength of Weak Ties: A Network Theory Revisited', in P. Marsden and N. Lin (eds), *Social Structure and Network Analysis*, Sage, Beverly Hills, pp. 105-30.
Granovetter, M (1985), 'Economic Action and Social Structure. The Problem of Embeddedness', *American Journal of Sociology*, Vol. 91(3), pp. 481-510.
Klaasse Bos, A. and Krogt, S. van der (1991), *Les Echanges Frontaliers de Quelques Produits Vivriers entre le Bénin et le Niger*, Réseau Néerlandais de Recherche, Working Paper, Maastricht.
Lutz, C. (1994), *The Functioning of the Maize Market in Benin: Spatial and Temporal Arbitrage on the Market of a Staple Food Crop*, Department of Regional Economics University of Amsterdam, Amsterdam.
North D. (1990), *Institutions, Institutional Change and Economic Performance*, Cambridge University Press, New York.
Olsen, M. (1982), *The Rise and Decline of Nations: Economic Growth, Stagflation and Social Rigidities*, Yale University Press, New Haven.
Portes, A. and Landolt, P. (1996), 'The Downside of Social Capital', *The American Prospect*, No. 26, pp. 18-21.
Putnam, R. (1993), 'The Prosperous Community. Social Capital and Public Life', *The American Prospect*, pp. 35-42.
Quarles van Ufford, P. (1999), *Trade and Traders. The Making of the Cattle Market in Benin*, Thela Thesis, Amsterdam.
Quarles van Ufford, P. (forthcoming), *The Wealth of Relations. Networks of Cattle Traders in the Republic of Benin*.
Quarles van Ufford, P. and Zaal, F. (forthcoming), *The Transfer of Trust: Ethnicities as Economic Institutions in the Livestock Trade in West and East Africa*.
Rose (1998), *Getting Things Done in an Anti-Modern Society; Social Capital Networks in Russia*, Social Capital Initiative Working Paper No. 6, World Bank, Washington.
Sen, A. (1981), *Poverty and Famines. An Essay on Entitlement and Deprivation*, Oxford University Press, Oxford.
Tacoli, C. (1998), *Bridging the Divide: Rural-urban Interactions and Livelihood Strategies*, Gatekeeper Series 77, IIED, London.
World Bank (1998), *The Initiative on Defining, Monitoring and Measuring Social Capital. Overview and Program Description*, Social Capital Initiative Working Paper 1, World Bank, Washington.

14 The Provisioning of African Cities, with Ouagadougou as a Case Study

TON DIETZ AND FRED ZAAL

Population Growth and Urbanization in Africa

Africa is still one of the world's least urbanized regions. In 1960 – when most of Europe's colonial possessions in Africa had, or were about to, become independent states – only 10-13 per cent of Africa's total population lived in cities, that is, 33 million people as opposed to the 220 million inhabitants of the vast rural areas (Broek and Webb, 1967, p. 426; World Bank, 1983, pp. 190-91). Only along the Mediterranean coast and in South Africa and Congo-Brazzaville did more than a quarter of the population live in cities. South Africa was the most urbanized country on the continent (47 per cent, using a very broad definition) and the only African country with more than 40 per cent of its population living in urban areas. Only three cities in tropical Africa had more than half a million inhabitants, Ibadan and Lagos in Nigeria, and Kinshasa in Congo/ Zaire.

Between 1960 and 1980, Africa's population growth rate was explosive, with an average annual rate of 3.2 per cent. The rural population increased from 220 million to 370 million, and the urban population more than tripled, from 33 million to 110 million. Almost a quarter of the African population lived in cities in 1980. Tunisia had become the most urbanized country on the continent (52 per cent of its people living in cities), but South Africa, Algeria, Egypt, Morocco, Congo-Brazzaville, and Zambia each had an urban population of at least 40 per cent (World Bank, 1983, pp. 148-49; World Bank, 2000, pp. 274-77).

Between 1980 and 2000, population growth slowed to 2.5 per cent per annum, but the urban explosion continued, with annual increases of close to 5 per cent. Africa's urban population almost tripled (to 300 million), and the rural population further increased, to 500 million. Table 14.1 shows the

Table 14.1 Africa's urbanization process: urbanization rates in percentages in 1960 and 2000 compared

in 1960	Urbanization percentage in 2000					
	<10	10-19	20-29	30-39	40-49	50+
<10	Burundi Rwanda	Burkina Faso Ethiopia Eritrea Uganda	Chad Lesotho Malawi Niger Gabon	Kenya Mozambique Tanzania		Botswana Mauritania
10-19			Madagascar Mali Sudan	Angola Sierra Leone DR Congo Togo Guinea Zimbabwe Namibia	Benin Cameroon Ivory Coast Nigeria	
20-29				Ghana	CAR Senegal Zambia	Morocco Libya
30-39					Egypt	Algeria Rep. Congo Tunisia Mauritius
40-49						South Africa
urban in 2000	1m	17m	23m	66m	113m	72m
total in 2000	15m	102m	89m	196m	252m	127m

Note: There are no data for Somalia or Liberia (together approx. 12 million people in 2000)

geographical differences in this urbanization process, comparing 1960 with 2000 (World Bank, 1983, pp. 190-91; World Bank, 2000, pp. 274-77).

In Africa in 2000, 379 million people (almost half of the continent's population of 800 million) lived in a predominantly urban country (>50 per cent), or one which will soon become predominantly urban (40-50 per cent). In northern Africa, these urban countries form a contiguous zone from Mauritania, through Morocco, Algeria, and Tunisia to Libya and Egypt. In southern Africa, South Africa, Botswana, Zambia, and Mauritius belong to this category. In West and West-Central Africa, Senegal, Ivory Coast, Benin, Nigeria, Cameroon, Congo-Brazzaville, and the Central African Republic have also become urban countries. Other African countries still have a more rural character, although almost all of them have experienced rapid urban growth (the only exceptions are Burundi and Rwanda). All African countries, with the exception of these two, made a jump from one ten-per cent category to at least the next one. Table 14.1 shows that ten African countries made a jump of 10-20 per cent, although in absolute numbers the increase is even more impressive. A rural country like Burkina Faso had an urban population of barely 5 per cent in 1960 (less than 200,000 people); in 2000, this percentage had quadrupled to almost 20 per cent, or close to 2 million urban people, representing a tenfold increase. Nineteen African countries had made an urbanization jump of 20-30 per cent, and eleven a jump of more than 30 per cent. Of this group of countries undergoing relatively very fast urbanization, two – Botswana and Mauritania – went from a very low urbanization level (less than 5 per cent in 1960) to more than 50 per cent in 2000.

Of Africa's 300 million urban people in the year 2000, 100 million live in 39 urban agglomerations of more than 1 million people. Table 14.2 gives an overview of all urban regions in Africa with more than 1 million inhabitants.

Table 14.2　All urban regions in Africa with more than 1 million inhabitants in 2000

Pop. (mill.)	Urban regions
>10	Cairo, Egypt (14.5)
3-6	Lagos, Nigeria (6.0), Kinshasa, DR Congo (4.6), Addis Ababa, Ethiopia (4.0), Alexandria, Egypt (3.8), Casablanca, Morocco; Antananarivo, Madagascar (both 3.6), Abidjan, Ivory Coast (3.4), Cape Town/ Khayelitsha/Cape Flats, South Africa; Arusha, Tanzania (both 3.1), Greater Khartoum, Sudan (3.0)
2-3	Algiers, Algeria (2.8), Soweto, South Africa (2.7), Kano, Nigeria (2.6), Johannesburg, South Africa (2.5), Dakar, Senegal; Dar es Salaam, Tanzania (both 2.3), Ibadan, Nigeria (2.0)
1-2	Tunis, Tunisia (1.8), Accra, Ghana and Lusaka, Zambia (1.7), Rabat, Morocco and Nairobi, Kenya (both 1.6). Harare, Zimbabwe, Mogadishu, Somalia and Durban, South Africa (all 1.5), Luanda, Angola and Bamako, Mali (both 1.4), Conakry, Guinea, Oujda, Morocco and Pretoria, South Africa (all 1.3), Ouagadougou, Burkina Faso, Maputo, Mozambique and Douala, Cameroon (all 1.1), Lubumbashi, DR Congo; Yaounde, Cameroon; Ogbomosho, Nigeria; Port Elisabeth, South Africa; Kumasi, Ghana (all 1.0)

Sources: Own estimates based on http://www.urbanobservatory.org/indicators/database/pdf/ population.pdf, April 2001 (UNCHS); http://www.weltalmanach.de/staaten (Der Fischer Weltalmanach); Grote Winkler Prins Encyclopedie; 'Landenreeks' series of KIT/NOVIB/11.11.11; Grote Bos Atlas (52nd edition, 2001). The population data are an estimate of urban and peri-urban populations living in an urban region. Often such data include the administrative regions immediately bordering the urban or metropolitan administrative region.

Figure 14.1 Major urban regions in Africa

Figure 14.1 gives an overview of these urban regions in Africa. Contrary to popular belief, half of all major African urban regions are located in the continent's interior, while the other half are located on or near the coast, directly connected to international harbors.

Figure 14.2 shows the changes that occurred in population density between 1960 and the mid-1990s (Dietz et al., 2001, p. 43). The figure shows a dramatic redistribution of Africa's population in the last four decades, with some areas being depopulated (e.g. dryland areas hit by climate change, as well as areas hit by violence and insecurity), and the population of other areas more than quadrupling. Almost all coastal areas belong to these zones with very fast population increases; however, also some inland areas around

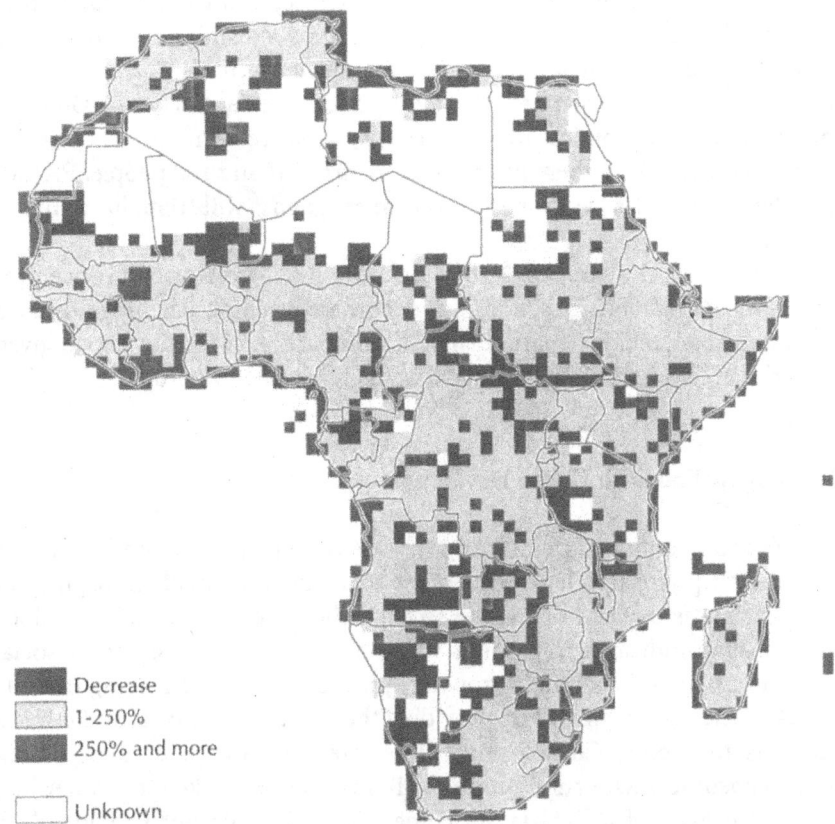

Figure 14.2 Changes in population densities in Africa, 1960 to mid-1990s

capital cities and in expanding mining areas have undergone considerable population growth. Much of this growth in population densities goes together with urban expansion.

It is difficult to rely on forecasts about African population growth and urbanization. The demographic impact of Aids and TB, widespread violence, the deterioration of state-provided health care, and emigration can become considerable. It is not likely that the African net population growth rate will be higher than 2 per cent per annum in the period 2000-2030 (cf. Reitsma, 1997, p. 163). We may assume that rural population growth will not be much more than 1 per cent per annum, resulting in a rural population of 650-700 million people. For the urban population, a combination of natural growth at 1-2 per cent per annum and continuing rural-urban migration may result in a net urban growth of 2-3 per cent per annum. In 2030 there might be 650-700 million urban Africans, or twice as many as there are today; in other words, there might be more urban than rural people. Providing these urbanites with basic consumer goods will remain a major challenge.

Note that as Aids happens to be a disease with a strong urban concentration in most areas in Africa, and Aids deaths are reaching alarming numbers in some urban regions (particularly in Southern Africa), the above-given scenarios are even more speculative than they normally would be.

A Changing Focus on Urban Development

Africa's urban boom started during the late colonial period and in the first decade after political independence. The social-psychological atmosphere in most areas was one of hope and a strong belief in planned, rapid development. Urban-industrial expansion was thought to be the engine of social modernization and economic growth, with the countryside feeding the coffers of the new governments by providing them with agricultural and mining products to export. Consequently, little attention was paid to providing urban consumers with rural products (Binns, 1994). Unlike most other historical processes of urbanization in the world, the continued rapid urban growth in Africa since 1970 has taken place in a situation of slackening growth, increasing climatic, economic, and political insecurity, and – since 1980 – economic and political collapse and social-psychological despair in many countries in the region. For large numbers of rural people, urbanization became an escape from rural misery and catastrophes, and the 'migratory basis of urban growth' as it was called by Little (1974, quoted in Verkoren and van Westen, 2000, p. 173) was one of the main driving forces of urban growth at that time. Droughts in the Sahel, the Horn, and southern Africa created a massive rural-urban (and rural-rural) migration process. For example, Nouakchott in Mauritania swelled from 20,000 inhabitants in 1960 to over 200,000 in just a few years, and to over 600,000 today (Mauritania's urban population increased from less than 5 per cent in 1960 to over 50 per cent in 2000). Bamako and Ouagadougou, the capital of Mali and of Burkina Faso, respectively, had annual population growth rates of more than 10 per cent during the drought years between 1976 and 1983; in just those few years,

Bamako was confronted with a quarter of a million new inhabitants, all of them poor and many rather desperate (Broekhuis and De Jong, 2001, p. 86). In other areas, violence created rural no-go areas with hundreds of thousands of refugees living in refugee camps (e.g. the refugee city of Goma after the Rwanda massacres) and urban refuge areas (e.g. Kuhlman, 1994, about the city of Kassala, catering for the refugees from Ethiopia/Eritrea).

Next to these calamity-driven driving forces of urbanization, rural-urban migration is also very much caused by expanding education. In sub-Saharan Africa in 1970, 50 per cent of the relevant age group was enrolled in primary education, 7 per cent in secondary education, and only 1 per cent in tertiary education. In 1992, these figures had increased to 67 per cent, 18 per cent, and 4 per cent, respectively, and the education enrollment of girls had increased from 41 to 60 per cent in the primary school age group and from 5 to 16 per cent in the secondary school age group (World Bank, 1995, p. 217). This had a double impact on urbanization. First, there was an urban concentration of better schools, which resulted in rural-urban school migration, and some of these children remained in the urban environment afterwards. Second, education – also in the countryside – often resulted in alienation from the rural background, as children were trained for white-collar jobs, and it created expectations of much better prospects in urban compared to rural environments. The expanding government-related job market in African cities in the 1960s and 1970s, filled by the early generation of educated Africans, who often had a rural background and maintained many rural ties, had also created urban footholds for children longing for an urban education and for urban jobs. In the 1990s, however, this picture changed. In a number of countries, the enrollment percentages stopped rising. In war-ravaged countries this is understandable. In a country like Angola, the primary enrollment plunged from 83 per cent in 1980 to 35 per cent in 1997. But also in countries without a civil war, enrollment figures showed dramatic decreases. Tanzania's primary enrollment was 34 per cent in 1970, 68 per cent in 1980 and 1992, but only 48 per cent in 1997. In many other countries, enrollment figures stagnated. Burkina Faso's primary enrollment went from 13 per cent in 1970 and 15 per cent in 1980 to 31 per cent in 1992, and only 32 per cent in 1997 (data from World Bank, 1995, p. 216 and 2000, p. 284). As some of the countries also made their school curriculum more rural, the education-driven urbanization of the 1990s became less pronounced. The rapid urbanization together with stagnating or deteriorating economic and social conditions led to a situation Armstrong and McGee called 'urban involution' in an Asian context (Armstrong and McGee, 1976), and de Bruijne, following Geertz and Wertheim, called 'shared poverty' in a 'dualistic urban economy' (Bruijne, 1976, p. 135). It created a large number of urban inhabitants who did not work in the formal sector, but in the mushrooming, chaotic, and mostly (but not always) low-rewarding informal sector, even if they had a rather high level of education. For many urban households, the key to survival changed from specialization to diversification, along with an astonishing mobility and mobile attitude, called 'circular migration' by some scholars (Mortimore, 1998). Many people who were counted as urban by censuses and in surveys in fact combined urban and rural residences and livelihoods, a situation called 'multi-spatial livelihoods' by Foeken and Owuor (2001). Many rural people had strong and fluctuating urban linkages, and many rural families had one or more part-time members who were part of a mobile labor force, moving from place to place, often combining geographical pathways which contained more than one city and more than one rural area. Urban-rural networks enabled support from rural parts of the livelihood of people to urban parts and the other way around, depending on seasons, and on 'relative stress' (Foeken, 1997; Foeken and Mwangi, 1998; Foeken and Owuor, 2000). Not only were urban people supported with food provided by their rural family members, but many of them still cultivated their own fields in their rural area of origin and/or in newly acquired fields in the rural areas around the urban region, where they also reside during part of the year. Many urban parts of multi-locational extended households' livelihoods also consisted of forms of urban agriculture, and many rural parts had urban elements in them. Both from a demographic and from a livelihood perspective, the differences between urban and rural became blurred. From a social-psychological perspective, it is better to regard people as mobile and multi-locational (and multi-occupational) than to use such rigid categories as urban and rural, or agricultural and non-agricultural.

However, despite the importance of direct provisioning of food, water, and energy in and around the cities by households themselves, and provisioning based on rural-urban family networks for urban inhabitants, the large majority of consumer basics for urbanites comes to cities through a commercialized network. The urban fraction of the population can no longer be regarded as a demographically marginal group. Its increase from 30 million in the late 1950s to over 300 million people now (and from 13 per cent to over 35 per cent for the continent as a whole) has forced a complete reorganization of the supply-demand networks. One of the first scholars to write about the challenges of provisioning the urban masses, Vennetier (1976, based on research in the late 1960s), could still write that most of the rural people in Africa lived in an almost closed economy. If they were partly integrated into a commercial market, it was for export products, in a continuation of colonial patterns. Writing about the rapidly expanding cities in central Africa (e.g. Brazzaville and Bangui), he observed that suddenly a very large urban consumer market had emerged for products which had hardly ever been traded before. Supplying a fast-growing and generally poor urban clientele with cassava, grains, milk, meat, water, firewood, and charcoal became a major challenge to traders and their providers. In most colonial and early post-colonial countries, very little attention had been given to improving the production and marketing of food and energy products. Newly established governments suddenly saw their capital cities (and other towns) undergoing explosive growth, and that the urban demand for basic necessities was not always adequately supplied. Hoarding, fluctuating prices, and large-scale market uncertainty sometimes resulted in riots and political tension, which could easily undermine the positions of the newly established political elites. Many of the new political leaders chose to step in with political means, by controlling markets and price formation and sometimes by taking over markets through pseudo- or para-governmental agencies which got monopoly positions. The corruptness of these agencies, their lack of quality, and their inadequate means often resulted in the breakdown of provisioning systems, and in the growth of all types of illegal and informal trading initiatives. The lack of efficiency was further aggravated by the grossly inadequate transport system which, having been improved in the 1960s and 1970s in many countries, deteriorated after 1980. Urban life became expensive and the urban poor had to spend so much money on basics that they had to 'ruralize' their urban lives (see above), and in some countries quite a number of urban people had to return to rural areas (at least for part of the year) to eke out a living there, especially in those cases where structural adjustment measures resulted in the retrenchment of large numbers of government personnel, or where civil servants were no longer paid regular salaries. In many capital cities, a rather large, government-related middle class had been formed, which functioned as a sponge for related migrants from their home areas. After 1985/1990 many members of the middle class were hit by the economic crisis, while at the same time the number of rural-urban migrants who would like to benefit from their rich relatives' presence in the cities in many cases continued to increase. A considerable number of these rural-urban migrants had attained quite high educational standards and their outlook was obviously urban. The urban crisis of the 1990s forced people to reduce their standard of living and to lower their expectations to levels many regarded as being far below what they deserved. The despair this created made many urban centers turn into violent pools of criminal behavior, further threatening the orderly provisioning of basics.

In some countries there developed a strong reliance for many urban basics on imports from foreign (often far-away) sources, some of it connected to subsidized provisions (e.g. food aid). Some urban coastal centers became very dependent on imported food and energy sources. Dakar is a well-known example of this. In the early 1990s, 29 per cent of Senegal's import package consisted of food and 16 per cent consisted of fuel (World Bank, 1994, p. 188) and a lot of it was meant to appease the urban population of Dakar. But also Burkina Faso had a very high food and fuel element in its import package; 25 per cent of its imports consisted of food and 16 per cent consisted of fuel, and also here a lot of it (although less compared to Dakar) was meant to provide its urban citizens (particularly those in the capital, Ouagadougou) with basics from abroad.

Gradually, however, most African urban centers created their local rural hinterlands. It is an interesting hypothesis to state that these will resemble a von Thünen-type pattern, with water, firewood, milk, eggs, poultry, and horticultural products near (or in) the city and its outskirts, and grains/starch, charcoal, and meat coming from farther away, with the commercial fingers of the functioning transport lines stretching out hundreds of kilometers into the countryside (Dijkstra, 1997). In many cases, providing the urban poor with energy meant widening the circle of environmental destruction around the metropolis to perhaps hundreds of kilometers, as was the case with Dakar, Ouagadougou, and Nairobi, until prices for charcoal and firewood became so high that alternative sources (paraffin, electricity, gas) took over, part of it imported or produced with imported resources. In some places, this pattern is continuing.

The provisioning of the rapidly growing urban regions in Africa with such basics as food, water, and energy by providers in rural areas surrounding the urban centers, very much depends on the agricultural possibilities of those rural environs of the big cities, on the organizational skills of entrepreneurs bringing demand and supply together, on the competition from overseas, and on the positive (enabling) or negative roles played by the government and agencies in civil society. The agricultural possibilities of the rural environment depend on the agro-ecological and the hydrological situation, on population densities, on the existence and quality of investments in skills, built environment (waterworks, agro-landesque capital, roads), means of transport, and communication. The existence of a trading community, its financial strength (and the quality and reliability of formal and informal credit and insurance systems), and its ability to work in often adverse circumstances comprise a crucial element. The public and semi-public sector may partly undertake these entrepreneurial roles, but since the mid-1980s this has been strongly discouraged by the Bretton Woods institutions and many donor governments. The impact of abolishing these institutions and letting the market actors take over depended very much on the earlier effectiveness and efficiency of the non-formal traders' networks. For livestock and meat, usually little changed as they were based on well-developed networks (Quarles van Ufford, 1999; Quarles van Ufford and Zaal, forthcoming), but with regard to grains, the impact was sometimes considerable (Meijling, 1999). With a growing impact of what is popularly called the urban crisis in Africa, and the withdrawal or breakdown of state agencies which used to deal with food, fuel, and water provisioning, many civil society agencies took initiatives to improve urban life. Tostensen *et al.* (2001) put a lot of emphasis on the growing importance of what they call 'associational life in African cities', as the popular response to the urban crisis. 'The onset of the urban crisis in the mid-1980s ... seems to have had a dramatic impact on the number and nature of associations in urban areas. Their role increasingly became centered on providing urban services that the state could not deliver (such as housing, water and sanitation)' (ibid. p. 22). Conceptual boundaries between state, civil society associations, formal traders, and informal traders also become ever more blurred.

However, it is not wise to regard the current state's function as completely marginalized. Even if governments are not at all directly active as traders, government does matter in maintaining law and order, in providing a legal and monetary framework for entrepreneurial activities, in improving and maintaining infrastructure, in taxing, and in cushioning or aggravating the impact of natural calamities (droughts/floods) on supply and demand. Contrary to the attitude in the 1960s to the mid-1980s, with a government attitude preferring to import basic needs from abroad (paid for by aid money or commercial loans), this is now seen as undermining the production and trade activities of entrepreneurs in the urban hinterland. Urban elite groups and governments in coastal areas may be tempted to consume foreign produce, and not to invest in productive activities in their own rural hinterlands. Urban elite groups and governments in inland areas, far from coastal harbors with relatively cheap foreign imports of food and energy, can be expected to rely more on their own direct hinterland, even if that hinterland is not well endowed with productive opportunities.

The Example of Ouagadougou

As an example of such an inland urban situation in a problematic agricultural environment, we will briefly look at the situation in and around Ouagadougou (capital of Burkina Faso), which is located 900-1,100 long, difficult, expensive, and time-consuming kilometers from the coastal harbor cities of Lomé (Togo), Accra (Ghana), and Abidjan (Ivory Coast). We are mainly interested in the research question how the fast growing need for food, fuel, and water in this city has been accommodated. The geographical question to be answered is where these basic goods come from and what geographical trends can be discerned. But a related sociological question also interests us; which agents played a role in bringing together supply and demand, and what alliances (if any) developed between state agencies and market agents?

Ouagadougou is one of the examples of fast demographic growth of both a city and its immediate surroundings in an inland and stressful part of Africa. At the time of independence in 1960, the city of Ouagadougou hardly existed. The Mossi area, of which it was an important traditional center, was still largely a rural zone, although rather densely populated by Sahelian standards. The sub-colony of Haute Volta was part of French West Africa. The overall colonial capital was Dakar in present-day Senegal, and Ouagadougou only had a minor function in the French administrative set-up. At independence, the city had a meager 59,000 inhabitants. In 1975 this had increased to 180,000, although with a doubling of the city's administrative area (Verkoren and Westen, 2000). Then Burkina Faso was hit by a period of drought and drought-related disasters, resulting in a rapid rural-urban refugee migration. In 1985, Ouagadougou had 460,000 inhabitants. In the 1980s Burkina Faso experienced a major primary education boom, increasing the primary school enrolment from 15 per cent to 30 per cent, followed in the late 1980s and early 1990s by a secondary education boom (from 5 per cent to 13 per cent) (data: World Bank, 1995 and 2000). Ouagadougou was one of the core areas of educational expansion, and many rural-urban migrants were attracted by better educational and employment opportunities. The 1996 census counted 752,000 people in Ouagadougou proper; currently, the urban population is estimated to be close to 900,000, and will probably exceed one million in 2004. Grand Ouaga (Kadiogo Province and some urban fringe areas nearby) had a population of over 1.1 million in 2000 (Ministère des Infrastructures, 1997, p. 27). In the first 15 years after independence, the annual growth rate of Ouagadougou proper was a considerable 7.7 per cent, increasing to 9.8 per cent per annum in the period

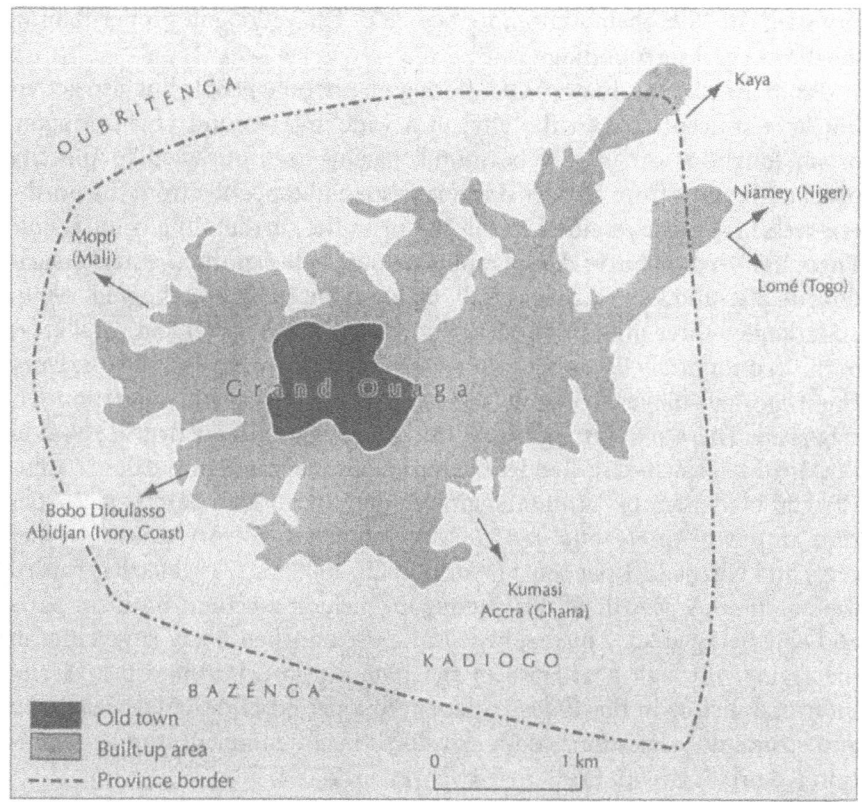

Figure 14.3 Ouagadougou and its immediate hinterland

of the droughts (1975-1985) and slowing down to 4.6 per cent per annum between 1985 and 1996 (Ministère des Infrastructures, 1997, p. 19). Also the direct surroundings of the city itself (i.e., up to 30 km) experienced an increase in population and a rapid change in landscape and economic activities (De Jong et al., 2001). The three provinces Bazega, Kadiogo, and Oubritenga/Koureweogo together – which includes Greater Ouagadougou (see Figure 14.3) – experienced a population growth of 4 per cent per annum between 1975 and 1996 (i.e., from 655,000 to 1,479,000). This means that the population of the non-Ouagadougou parts of these provinces increased from 475,000 to 727,000, an annual increase of 2 per cent, which is below the annual population growth for Burkina Faso as a whole (which was 2.6 per cent for this period). In relative terms, this means that in 1975 the direct rural surroundings of Ouagadougou still had 2.6 times more people than the city itself. In 1996 there were more people in Ouagadougou proper than in the direct rural surroundings.

From the surroundings of Ouagadougou, not only people but also activities have concentrated in the city; in a wide area around Ouagadougou, urban functions can hardly be found, having been attracted to the city proper. Migrants from all over Burkina Faso (and especially from the northern areas) have settled either in the city or in the surrounding countryside. There has been intensive demographic contact between the Greater Ouagadougou area and Ivory Coast as well. Between the 1960s and the mid-1990s, an estimated three million Burkinabé migrated to the urban and rural areas of this economically booming country. However, since the early 1990s, Ivory Coast has had major economic and security problems, and migration has stagnated. There are even signs that Burkinabé migrants are drifting back to Burkina Faso (including Greater Ouagadougou), because of the better security and higher annual economic growth rates in Burkina Faso (e.g. 2.7 per cent growth of GNP/capita in 1998/99), compared to Ivory Coast (1.1 per cent) and Ghana (2.1 per cent) (World Bank, 2000, p. 274). This has caused the continuous growth of Ouagadougou, including certain business parts and elite living areas. This happened in a period when many large cities in the region, through a collapse of the state-supported administrative and industrial sectors in the 1990s, experienced a period of de-industrialization and economic stagnation, and a slowdown if not complete stop of migration-led urban growth (Verkoren and Westen, 2000).

Generally, many of the first-generation migrants to Greater Ouagadougou were actively involved in the production of food, wood, or charcoal for the urban population. They did this partly in the rural parts of Greater Ouagadougou, and partly in the urban wastelands and the direct peri-urban fringe areas. This was not a random process. Analysis of SPOT remote imagery shows the results in terms of land use and land-use change (De Jong et al., 2001). From the center of the old colonial town to the fringes of the present city, typical land use patterns – characterized as intensive urban agriculture, commercial livestock production, and fruit production – spread outwards. Then comes a degraded fringe area where intensive agriculture and spontaneous settlement compete for space, followed by old peripheral areas slowly becoming densely populated, thereby attaching themselves to the earlier high-density central parts of the city (see also Beeker and Guièbo, 1994 and Tindano, 1989).

Beyond the peri-urban environment, agricultural and sylvicultural products come from areas all over Burkina Faso, with some areas specializing in cereals (millets and sorghum; the central and south-eastern areas of Burkina

Faso), tubers (the south-western parts), meat (the north), and milk and vegetables (center-north), and irrigated areas in the south and south-west (Rouers and Bos, 1999). For most products, the marketing chains are short. Produce is bought in the producing areas, transported to the cities, and traded by wholesalers to retailers. Some wholesalers in the cereal business are also involved in import-export trade, and their investment capital can be considerable. Urban traders also invest in upgrading rural production processes by introducing new varieties and crops and new livestock breeds, and providing capital for capital-intensive forms of production (poultry, irrigation, sheds).

Food

The result in terms of production increases in agriculture geared to the catering to the urban market has been relatively good. The agricultural expansion in the hinterland of Ouagadougou was hindered between 1976 and 1985 by 20-30 per cent less rainfall than usual. In those years, food aid from abroad became an absolute necessity for survival, and as a cushion against extreme price fluctuations. Since 1986, the rainfall situation has followed an upward general trend (although with drought years in 1990 and 1996/97), enabling better production results (Put, 1999). In addition, a lot of investments were made environmental improvements (soil and water management, irrigation in valley bottom areas) (see Reij et al.,1996; Mazzucato and Niemeyer, 2000), and in better agricultural tools (oxen traction) and skills (higher overall education levels, higher agricultural knowledge, and more and better knowledge and extension institutions). Burkina Faso as a whole doubled its food production volumes between 1980 and 1997, resulting in 34 per cent more food per capita (own calculations, using World Bank, 2000, p. 288). The overall improvement of agricultural production enabled a rather successful commercialization of food products to cater to the rapidly expanding urban demand, even if this demand was different from the typical rural consumption patterns. This growing demand created price increases for such products as vegetables, wheat, rice, milk, meat, and eggs, which also spurred investments by urbanites in agricultural expansion in and around the city. The rich became involved by investing in capital-intensive forms of agriculture (e.g., poultry farms), and the poor by using wasteland and the areas around their houses for production for sale (alongside production for home consumption, which they had always done whenever there were opportunities to do so). Spurred by high cereal prices in the 1980s, some of the urban agricultural investors also supported considerable production improvements in the staple food production (rice, sorghum, millet), resulting in higher yields (Yonli, 1988), quite near areas of more traditional rural self-supporting production of millet and sorghum. Careful urban management in some parts of the expanding city enabled the production of garden agriculture, which was partly commercial as well. On the eastern side of the city, however, this poses a health hazard, because of considerable pollution in the area (personal comment, Coen Beeker). Still, a steady urban growth, together with variable, but basically rather stable, basic grains production levels in the wider area around Ouagadougou, has meant a steady increase of the cereal deficit, and thus an increasing need for cereals from further away (Rouers and Bos, 1999). Depending on the rainfall situation and the geographic spread of infrastructure, prices for cereals in Ouagadougou reflect production circumstances in the N'Gourma region or regions further south, and may not be lower than those in the structurally deficit areas of the far north of the country, even though they are more stable due to better market integration of the Ouagadougou market in the national market (Zaal, 1998). An early liberalization of the cereals trade (1978) has helped the early development of a trade network linking producers more directly to wholesalers from Ouagadougou, partly from the N'Gourma region, partly from the west (Dano, Nouna, Boromo, and Bobo-Dioulasso), and from areas around Ouagadougou (Ziniaré, Kombissiri, and – further away – Manga).

Biomass Fuel

The production and trade of biomass for fuel can be regarded as more problematic than the production and trade of food for the expanding urban population. Biomass fuels are still the most important type of household fuel (for cooking and boiling water), and are also important as raw material for small-scale industrial production (e.g. brewing beer). Urban households in Ouagadougou have changed their biomass consumption from the use of wood to the use of charcoal, with the exception of the urban elites who combined this with the use of gas. A few remaining areas of urban wood (a forest and a park in the northern parts of the city) had effectively been illegally logged between 1986 and 1996, forcing almost all urban inhabitants to look for another type of fuel. There are still forest patches in the north-east, officially well protected but increasingly used for agriculture and no longer a source of firewood (De Jong *et al.*, 2001, p. 3 and 6). Instead, massive government and donor supported reforestation projects (14,000 ha and 10,410 ha, respectively) added to the policy measures of green belt, village forestry, and agro-forestry initiatives to provide fuel wood for the future. Since 1985, the government's influence in providing wood has become more pronounced, both by more strict implementation of rules and by becoming involved as traders; some sections of the army have become deeply involved (personal communication, Ouindinda Nikièma).

The costs of charcoal are still lower than alternative sources of energy, because the raw materials are regarded as a free good, and wages and profits in the charcoal production branch are relatively low. The biomass production sector provides a lot of employment for people with a 200-kilometer radius of the city (in the 1950s, the radius was only 20 kilometers). They also provide an opportunity for informal sector entrepreneurs to make a living, and for some rich merchants to invest in the more lucrative parts of the market and to make large profits. Gradually increasing prices (by a factor of 22 between 1970 and 1992) and increased fuel efficiency (by using improved stoves) resulted in a strong reduction in the daily consumption of charcoal between 1974 and 1992 (from 2.8 kg to 0.5 kg). In the mid-1990s, the population of Ouagadougou consumed 300,000 tons of biomass fuels (wood-equivalents) per annum, or 400 kg/capita (Rouers and Bos, 1999). In a large area around the city, the cutting of wood for firewood and especially charcoal production has resulted in large-scale landscape changes ('an expanding ring of desolation', according to Dankelman and Davidson (1988, p. 67), even though this strong wording should be placed perhaps against the more generally felt despair of the time) and in biomass fuels being collected from an ever-expanding area and sold for an ever-increasing price. Urban use clearly competes with rural use, as the larger part of biomass consumption within 200 kilometers of Ouagadougou is still consumed in rural areas (partly collected for household consumption, partly commercialized). However, wherever there are through-roads to the capital city, the trade in charcoal becomes urban-bound. According to some researchers, there the collected quantities of wood exceed the natural production substantially, resulting in net deforestation (Broekhuis and De Jong, 2001, p. 91). The situation became so alarming that the Burkinabé government, despite pressure from abroad to withdraw from direct intervention in matters of production and trade, decided to take action by means of price policies, trade regulation, and forestry plantations.

Water

The production of water for the growing urban population in a dryland region that has a structural deficit of rainfall as compared to potential evaporation, is the most pressing task. Here there is potential major urban-rural strife, as the urban water demand competes with increasing demands for water for people, animals, crops, and wood production in the rapidly changing watershed area feeding Ouagadougou. In 1996 it was estimated that 70 per cent of all urban households were in one way or another connected to a clean water source, mainly through the dams and wells north of the city center, which provide the city with 15 million m3 in a normal year, and 10 million m3 in a dry year. However, the current demand is 16 million m3 per year. Water consumption per capita has strongly decreased in Ouagadougou, reflecting increasing scarcity; from 57 liters daily in 1978 to 39 liters in 1986 and 26 liters in 1993 (Rouers and Bos 1999). The waterworks could not supply the growing number of clients sufficiently, partly because of technical problems (breakdowns, leaks), but mainly because of a supply-demand problem. In the dry season in particular Ouagadougou suffers from water shortages. In a relatively dry year, the available amount of water is as much as one-third less than in a normal year. Since 1994, the urban consumption of water at a low estimate of 40 l/cap/day has exceeded the availability of water in an average dry year; by 2003, it is expected that this phenomenon will occur in average normal rainfall years (Rouers and Bos 1999). A new dam across the Nakambé River at Ziga, 50 km north-east of Ouagadougou, should help ease the problem until 2010, when demand will be 52 million m3.

As ever more peri-urban land is used for irrigated agriculture and semi-industrial agriculture (e.g. poultry), and water needs are most pressing in the dry seasons in the dry years there as well, there is major competition between agro-industrial pressure groups and domestic water users, and between the urban core areas and the peri-urban fringes. The liberalization of water provisioning in the stressful situation Ouagadougou finds itself in, may result in a major struggle for water, and in the rapid commercialization of water and sharp price rises. The urban poor, particularly those in unauthorized settlements, are already faced with high and increasing water prices, and in some periods with loss of access to what may be regarded as the most basic of all basic needs. They may end up paying a high price for water from wells and boreholes within the city, instead of using public taps. However, water from wells is often polluted and public health may be at risk. Also, most wells are dry in the period between March and June, when needs are highest. As with wood-fuel provisioning, the government of Burkina Faso is now caught between a rock and a hard place, i.e., between the internal political need to step in again by providing cheap and reliable water for the urban population, and the externally induced wish to maintain a distance from market parties and to provide only a legal and incentive structure.

Conclusion

The experiences in Ouagadougou show that the challenges of organizing a major expansion of the provisioning of food, water, and energy to fulfill the needs of a rapidly growing urban population have been taken up with surprising success. Although government legislation and agencies are still important (in water provision in particular), liberalization and deregulation meant that most of the organizational challenge was taken up by private entrepreneurs, in the formal and informal sectors. Tensions between supply and demand materialize during dry seasons in relatively dry years. In the water and charcoal sectors there are potential major structural problems. Access to water in particular, and competition for water between various uses, and between relatively rich and relatively poor sections of the urban population, may result in so much social stress that public interventions may become more important again. In fact, in the food sector this has happened whenever a drought threatened the supply of food to the urban poor. Foreign aid provisions then cushioned the poor from the adverse impacts of these droughts. One may expect that also in the other basic provisions, government and pseudo/non-governmental agencies will in a flexible way step in, whenever the fluctuating context demands such, and then step out again when the situation normalizes. The recent role of sections of the army in wood provisioning is an interesting example. This demands a good ability to intervene in a flexible manner, and then to withdraw in a flexible manner. In the case of Burkina Faso and Ouagadougou, many actors seem to have mastered this art of fluctuating care, leaving most of the organizational work under normal circumstances to private initiatives. In water provisioning, however, privatization in a situation of high competition may result in a dramatic deterioration of the quality of life of the urban poor.

Acknowledgments

Thanks to Liesbeth van den Bos and Frank Rouers for a lot of fact-finding; to Coen Beeker, Leo de Haan, and Ouindinda Nikièma for advice; and to Els Veldhuizen for compiling

Figure 14.2. The map was one of the results of the research project Impact of Climate Change in Drylands, funded by NOP.

References

Armstrong, W.R. and McGee, T.G. (1976), 'Revolutionaire Verandering en de Stad in de Derde Wereld: een Stedelijke Involutietheorie', in G.A. de Bruijne, J. Hardeman and J.J.F. Heins, *Perspectief op Ontwikkeling?*, Romen, Bussum, pp. 115-33. (Orig. Revolutionary Change and the Third World City, *Civilisations*, 1968, Vol. 18, pp. 353-378).

Beeker, C. and J. Guièbo (1994), *Plotting the Urban Field of Ouagadougou*. Third World Planning Review, Vol. 16, no. 3.

Binns, T. (1994), Urban Africa, in: T. Binns, *Tropical Africa*, pp. 115-151. London and New York: Routledge.

Broek J.O.M. and J.W. Webb (1967), *A Geography of Mankind*. New York, McGraw-Hill Book Company.

Broekhuis, A. and A. de Jong (2001), Urban-rural linkages and climatic variability, in: T. Dietz, J. Verhagen and R. Ruben (eds.) (2001), *Impact of Climate Change in Drylands, with a Focus on West Africa*. Final Report to NOP. Amsterdam etc./CERES etc., pp. 85-93.

Bruijne, G.A. de (1976), 'Over de Urbane Problematiek van de Ontwikkelingslanden', in G.A.de Bruijne, J. Hardeman and J.J.F. Heins, *Perspectief op Ontwikkeling?*, Romen, Bussum, pp. 134-43.

Dankelman, I. and Davidson, J. (1988), *Women and Environment in the Third World*, Earthscan, London.

De Jong, S., Teeffelen, P. van, Bagré, A. and Deursen, W. van (2001), *Monitoring Trends in Urban Growth using SPOT imagery. The Case of Ouagadougou, Burkina Faso*, BCRS, Utrecht (http://www.geog.uu.nl/fg/UrbanGrowth).

Dietz, T., J. Verhagen and R. Ruben (eds) (2001), *Impact of Climate Change in Drylands, with a Focus on West Africa*, Final Report to NOP, CERES etc./ Amsterdam etc.

Dijkstra, T. (1997), *Trading the Fruits of the land: Horticultural marketing channels in Kenya*, Ashgate, Aldershot.

Fischer, Weltalmanach (2001), http://www.weltalmanach.de/staaten (consulted April 2001).

Foeken, D. (1997), 'Urban Trajectories in Rural Livelihood Strategies: Household Employment Patterns in Kenya's Coast Province', in D.B. Bryceson and V. Jamal (eds), *Farewell to Farms. De-agrarianisation and employment in Africa*, Ashgate, Aldershot, Research Series of the African Studies Center, Vol. 10, pp. 119-36.

Foeken, D. and Mwangi, A.M. (1998), 'Does Access to Land have a Positive Impact on the Food Situation of the Urban Poor? A Case-Study in Nairobi, *East African Social Science Research Review*, Vol. 14(1), pp. 19-32.

Foeken, D.W.J. and Owuor, S.O. (2000), *Urban farmers in Nakuru, Kenya*, ASC Working Papers No. 45, Leiden/ Center for Urban Research University of Nairobi, Kenya.

Foeken, D. and Owuor, S.O. (2001), 'Multi-Spatial Livelihoods in Sub-Saharan Africa: Rural Farming by Urban Households. The Case of Nakuru Town, Kenya', in M. de Bruijn, R. van Dijk and D. Foeken, *Mobile Africa*, Brill, Leiden.

Grote Bos Atlas (2001), 52nd edn., Wolters Noordhof, Groningen.

Grote Winkler Prins Encyclopedie (1990) 9th edn. (and subsequent Year Books), Elsevier, Amsterdam and Antwerpen.
Koninklijk Instituut voor de Tropen, NOVIB and 11.11.11 (various years; various authors), Landenreeks, Amsterdam.
Kuhlman, T. (1994), *Asylum or Aid? The Economic Integration of Ethiopian and Eritrean refugees in the Sudan*, African Studies Center Research Series 2 (Avebury), Leiden.
Little, K. (1974), *Urbanisation as a Social Process. An Essay on Movement and Change in Contemporary Africa*, London.
Mazzucato, V. and Niemeijer, D. (2000), *Rethinking Soil and Water Conservation in a Changing Society. A case study in eastern Burkina Faso*, Wageningen University Tropical Resource Management Papers, No. 32, Wageningen.
Meijling, H. (1999), 'Maize Marketing in Kenya, 1976-1996. Liberalization and Food Security, in L. van der Laan, T. Dijkstra and A. van Tilburg (eds), *Agricultural Marketing in Tropical Africa, Contributions from the Netherlands*, ASC research series 15/1999.
Ministère des Infrastructures, de l'Habitat et de l'Urbanisme (1997), Sécrétariat Général, Direction Général de l'Urbanisme et des Travaux Fonciers, Projet Villages-Centers Banlieu de Ouagadougou, 1997, *Schéma directeur d'Aménagement du <Grand Ouaga> (Horizon 2010)*, Ouagadougou (Document Provisoire).
Mortimore, M. (1998), *Roots in the African Dust. Sustaining the Drylands*, Cambridge University Press, Cambridge.
Quarles van Ufford, P. (1999), Trade and Traders. The Making of the Cattle Market in Benin, Thela Thesis Amsterdam.
Quarles van Ufford, P. and Zaal, F. (forthcoming), *The Transfer of Trust. Ethnicities as Economic Institutions in the Livestock Trade in West and East Africa*, Draft.
Put, M. (1999), *Climate Change and Climate Variability in Dryland West Africa*, AGIDS, Amsterdam (internal report for ICCD project).
Reitsma, H. (1997), 'No More Regions of Explosive Population Growth', in T. van Naerssen, M. Rutten and A. Zoomers, *The Diversity of Development. Essays in Honour of Jan Kleinpenning*, van Gorcum, Assen, pp. 157-65.
Reij, C., Scoones, I. and Toulmin, C. (eds) (1996), *Sustaining the Soil. Indigenous Soil and Water Conservation in Africa*, Earthscan Publications, London.
Rouers, F. and Bos, L. van den (1999), *Etude de Cas de la Cellule de Ouagadougou*, AGIDS/ Amsterdam, internal report for NOP-ICCD research.
Tindano, M. (1989), *Ecologie Urbain de Ouagadougou: Etude de Cas*, Mémoire de maîtrise, Université de Ouagadougou, Département de Géographie, Ouagadougou.
Tostensen, A., Tvedten I. and Vaa, M. (2001), *Associational Life in African Cities. Popular Responses to the Urban Crisis*, Nordiska Afrikainstitutet, Uppsala.
UNCHS (2001), http://www.urbanobservatory.org/indicators/database/pdf/population.pdf (consulted April 2001).
Vennetier, P. (1976), 'Stedelijke Voedselvoorziening in Zwart Afrika', in G.A. de Bruijne, J. Hardeman and J.J.F. Heins, *Perspectief op Ontwikkeling?*, Romen, Bussum, pp. 177-86. (Orig. 'Reflexions sur l'approvisionnement des villes en Afrique noire', in La croissance urbaine dans les pays tropicaux. Travaux et documents de géographie tropicale, Bordeaux, 1972, pp. 1-14).
Verkoren, O. and A.C.M. van Westen (2000), 'Gedaanteveranderingen van de Afrikaanse Stad', in O. Verkoren and E.J.A. Harts-Broekhuis (eds), *Tropisch Afrika*, van Gorcum, Assen, pp. 165-96.

World Bank (1983), *World Development Report* 1983, World Bank/Oxford U.P., Washington.
World Bank (1994), *World Development Report* 1994, World Bank/Oxford U.P., Washington.
World Bank (1995), *World Development Report* 1995, World Bank/Oxford U.P., Washington.
World Bank (2000), *World Development Report* 2000/2001. Washington: World Bank/Oxford U.P.
Yonli, P.E. (1988), *Marchés et Prix dans l'Approvisionnement du Plateau Mossi en Sorgho et Mil*, AGRISK/CEDRES, Groningen/Ouagadougou.
Zaal, A.F.M. (1998), *Pastoralism in a Global Age. Livestock Marketing and Pastoral Commercial Activities in Kenya and Burkina Faso*, Thela Thesis, Amsterdam.

15 Economic Networks and the Importance of Rural-Urban Linkages, with the Focus on Sub-Saharan Africa

SJOUKJE VOLBEDA

Introduction

This chapter discusses the vital importance of economic networks for development. Economic development can only occur through the specialization and subdivision of labor. Such specialization will generate a higher standard of living through a mechanism of exchange, which can in turn only be productive through interactions in a network of functional economic relations. Such relations have an important institutional dimension, as pointed out by the New Institutional Economics paradigm, which indicates that the neoclassical model of an efficient market only obtains when transactions are costless. This leaves little cognizance of peculiarities of time and place (cf. Harriss *et al.*, 1995). In fact, these transactions are constrained by all kinds of institutions and also by the spatial dimension. When all the transactions are mapped out, it will be seen that the nodal points in these networks coincide with the urban settlements.

This chapter looks at a framework of understanding to improve pro-poor economic development. To do so, a balance must be sought between the dominant economic discourse and the geographical discourse. Only then can we account for the spatial impact of economic phenomena. In other words, we need to understand the spatial implications of issues such as market integration. Both globalization and decentralization can only be fully understood if attention is paid to the spatial implications of economic market integration. As areas become more and more integrated locally, regionally, and globally, we need not only to address the urban-hinterland relationships, but also to focus on the wider context of economic networks and regional differentiation within larger areas. This requires the analysis of quite extensive areas (often beyond national borders) in order to show the comparative advantages of the different regions within a larger area, while at the same time keeping a clear eye on macroeconomic developments (cf. Snrech, 1995).

To stimulate pro-poor economic development, we need to understand how the various networks arise, how they function, and in what direction they may develop. Which networks are the most efficient? How can an existing network be optimized? How can an existing network be extended to include more poor? How are certain network subdivisions or components localized? How do we interpret the potential of a place or region? As pointed out, we want to look at these markets as real places, unevenly distributed over the earth's surface, between which there are real flows of goods and services that are both visible and measurable. Important in this respect is the notion of the virtuous cycle, a process through which a regional economy grows by maximizing its comparative advantages (Evans, 1993). This will only happen if transaction costs are lower than the profit generated. This means that we need to look at catalysts that stimulate the economic interactions and the flow of people, capital, goods, and services.

We will first explain why economic networks are important, why the rural-urban symbiosis should be the starting point in development thinking, and how rural urban linkages are the lifeblood of economic networks. Using the model devised by Evans (1993), the economic links between urban and rural areas are to be seen as transactions or, more generally, interactions between urban and rural areas, while catalysts ensure that the transaction effectively take place. The interactions consist of labor, capital, goods, and services; these are discussed subsequently in a second section. Infrastructure, transport, information, and education are examples of catalysts; these are reviewed in the third section. In the last section, conclusions and recommendations are presented. In general, the focus is on sub-Saharan Africa.

Why are Economic Networks Important?

The Habitat Agenda (section 10) acknowledges that cities, towns, and rural settlements are linked through the movement of goods, resources, and people, and that rural-urban linkages are of crucial importance to the sustainability of human settlements. The World Development Report 1999-2000 (World Bank, 1999a) cites two key trends that will have a major influence on international cooperation during the 21st century; globalization and localization. Globalization, or increasing involvement with the global economy, is leading to progressive global integration. Globalization has economic as well as social and cultural aspects. In economic terms it means not only that more and more international links arise (Dicken, 1998), but also that qualitative changes appear such as the emergence of global commodity chains or GCCs (Gereffi and Korzeniewicz, 1994). The outcome of this process is at best a patchy pattern of insertion of local producers. Some producers will hook up to centrally administered international production systems or to decentralized network production systems, while others are excluded. At the local level, this patchy pattern results in the formation of clusters of globally connected, locally disconnected producers (like Gereffi's global commodity chains; also see Porter 1990 and Helmsing 1997 (pp. 56-73) and 2000), next to locally connected, globally disconnected producers. One may imagine that a few highly competitive producers manage to be connected both ways. Pederson and McCormick (1999, p. 110) speak in this respect of the fragmentation of African business systems, because on this continent the lack of coherence appears to be the dominant feature.

Culturally and socially, globalization means that developments in one hemisphere are having a growing impact on populations in the other, and within ever shorter timeframes. It is therefore crucial that we respond rapidly and effectively to new developments. At the same time, more and more population groups are demanding a greater influence over their own lives, and this is reflected in the ongoing democratization of governance and decentralization of tasks and responsibilities to lower levels of government. These developments also tie in with the decentralization programs that many countries are implementing in the context of administrative reform. As a result, local and regional authorities are confronted with a number of new tasks.

One of the biggest challenges facing local and regional governments is regional economic development. Economic growth helps to combat unemployment, widen the economic base, and boost revenue from taxation. The last-mentioned factor is especially important for local and regional authorities, given that central governments generally provide them with little or no financial assistance when devolving responsibilities (Bergen, 1998).

When all transactions are mapped out, it will be seen that nodal points in these networks coincide with the urban centers. This could even be used as a definition for urban centers. Similarly, the integration of rural areas into a market economy can also be seen. This means that rural-urban relations are of vital importance for sustaining an economic network. The process of integration can be depicted in a time series of such transaction maps. This yields a dynamic concept and a better understanding of the development of such networks and relations. Due to the improved use of satellite images and the geographical information systems used to analyze them, we no longer need to define regions in advance; instead, the area demarcation could result from the analysis.

Since economic transactions are vital to the development of a region, it is important to consider how access to the national and global economy can be improved. Access of course has everything to do with institutions and their formal and informal rules and regulations, norms of behavior, conventions or codes of conduct, as in general these have been established over long periods of time. To cope with this notion, a paradigm of New Institutional Economics (NIE) has been spelled out, which brings 'history' back into the explanation of the neo-classical theory (Harriss et al., 1995, chapters 2 and 11). NIE incorporates a theory of institutions into economics. The reasoning is the following. Institutions are formed to reduce uncertainty in human exchange, and together with the technology employed they determine the costs of transaction (and of producing). Baldly stated, the neo-classical efficiency of markets only obtains when it is costless to transact. And when it is costly to transact, institutions matter. Institutions, however, are generally created to serve the interests of those who have the bargaining power to create new rules. (North, 1995, pp. 17-26). This means that institutions have a differentiating effect economically, politically, socially, and culturally. This is in line with Pedersen and McCormick's (1999, p. 130) finding of the fragmentation of the African business systems and with their findings that Structural Adjustment Policies (SAPs) and their inconsistent implementation have favored some and worsened the business climate for others. Apart from bringing 'history' back into economic explanation, we also need to bring back a cognizance of the peculiarities of 'place' (Harriss *et al.*, 1995, p. 5; World Bank, 2000). Access is constrained not only by institutions, but also by proximity, connectivity, or accessibility in real space. Global integration at the local level may be possible by satellite communication and make producers 'footloose', but whenever real goods need to be transported over distances it requires considerable costs and time. So good interregional and intraregional links are essential. These institutional and spatial links are generally established between urban centers (rural-urban linkages), with cities serving as the hubs between them. Stronger links enhance the effectiveness and efficiency of regional markets, and thus contribute directly to the growth of economic networks. This understanding has led to a revival of international interest in economic networks (UNDP, 1997; UNHCS, 1999; see also Haan, 2000, pp. 29-41 and World Bank, 2000).

Networks and Economic Growth

Economic value is generated through land, capital, labor, and knowledge. In theory, anyone can use these inputs unilaterally to try to satisfy their own individual needs. In practice, the division of labor (in which all individuals are responsible for and depend on a specific output) leads, or can lead, to a higher level of prosperity per capita. It is better to do a few things extremely well than to do many things inadequately. This applies not only to individuals but also to larger groups such as communities, regions, and even countries. One necessary precondition for generating a higher standard of living through specialization is the existence of an exchange mechanism. For example, a barber must be able to exchange his services for basic necessities, such as bread, otherwise he will go hungry in spite of his professional skills. First of all, he needs to know that there is a baker nearby (information network). Then he must be able to physically go to the baker to offer a haircut in exchange for bread (infrastructure network). Alternatively, it would be more practical for the barber to cut his clients' hair for money, so that he can pay the baker in cash (financial network).

In short, then, specialization requires transaction networks that have important spatial and institutional dimensions. The interplay of both dimensions results in real space as flows of people, goods, or services. These flows can be represented on a map by lines joining their source and destination. If all the transactions in a network are plotted, some locations will be seen to have a large number of interactions, while others will have very few. The pattern results in a spatial hierarchy of central places; the urban settlements (Christaller, 1933). Lambooy (1980, p. 20) defined these as the nodes of regional networks. Depending on their institutional and spatial function, the character of these nodes may vary. The size of such a nodal region or network may change dramatically and suddenly, for instance through the opening up of new transport lines. In other words, urban settlements are the hubs of these transactions in the networks. If it is true that transactions lead to greater prosperity, then the locations with few transactions will be economically weak. To stimulate economic growth, then, we need to know how the various networks come into being, how they operate, and how they develop. Which networks are the most efficient? How can an existing network be optimized? How can an existing network be extended? Where are the various network components located? How should the potential of a location be evaluated? What institutional and spatial environment is instrumental in fostering a pro-poor economic growth, generally seen as economic growth that favors the poor more than others?

As a result of global economic integration, national networks are gradually merging with international networks. Some observers argue that this is leading to the 'death of distance', in the sense that modern communication methods are negating distance. Yet distance is still a factor, especially when goods or people are being moved, and more so in developing countries with poor infrastructure and limited capital. But even in an economically well-integrated area, a regional production environment seems to be highly important for the formation and localization of certain clusters, including the so-called footloose activities. Footloose is therefore no longer an accurate term. In the light of the NIE paradigm, economic markets are imperfect due to spatial as well as institutional factors, meaning that proximity still obtains as a localization factor, resulting in the formation of clusters of production systems or of global commodity chains. As stated above, the process in Africa at least shows a patchy pattern, indicating that the process does not evolve gradually, but rather by fits and starts, which explains the fragmentation of African business systems composed of more and less connected producers (and consumers).

The Rural-Urban Symbiosis

Economic networks rely on economic links or connections. The hubs between these interactions are the cities. Urban and rural areas are therefore interdependent. Urban centers depend on rural areas for food production, and rural areas obtain many of their amenities from cities. In frontier regions, this symbiosis between rural and urban areas is visible from the moment the region is first opened up. Research shows that urban development actually precedes the development of the frontier of agricultural and mining activities, because it is not possible to develop the latter without the support of urban institutions in the vicinity (Volbeda, 1984 and 1997). Thus, by viewing the development of urban and rural areas simultaneously and approaching them as such, we can encourage regions to develop as a balanced whole. Only through the creation of hubs of transaction can we channel flows of goods and people, and deliver services effectively.

There are many different types of links between rural and urban areas, known as 'rural-urban linkages' (cf. Douglass, 1998; Tacoli, 1998a). Some of these links are primarily social, others are economic, and yet others are environmental. These various links are closely interconnected. If an individual moves from a village to a city to look for work, this can be seen as an economic link, since a member of the labor force is leaving a rural area for an urban center. Seen from another angle, the same event can be described as a social link, in that the worker is leaving his family and friends behind in the village, but will doubtless stay in touch with them. It is also quite likely that he has found his new job through a social network (cf. Fall, 1998; Manona, 1999; Titus, 2000). The individual's departure will also affect the environmental link, since it will reduce the burden on the rural environment while increasing the claim on the ecological space (ecological footprint) in the city (see also the chapter by Baud and Hordijk in this book).

Economic Rural-Urban Linkages

What exactly is the significance of economic links between rural and urban areas? A regional economy grows when a region is able to use its comparative advantages. In less developed regions, these advantages will usually consist of the ability to grow agricultural produce cheaply. The sale of these products on the external market boosts growers' income. This in turn creates more demand for other food and consumer goods. The increase in demand creates jobs outside the primary sector, especially in nearby cities, and growing employment in the secondary and tertiary sectors generates yet more demand for agricultural produce, and so on. This process is often referred to as the virtuous cycle in literature on the subject (cf. Evans, 1993; Tacoli, 1998b). As will be shown in the following sections, the process can work both ways; urban growth through investments financed by agriculture, as well as agricultural growth through investments financed by urban activities. This two-way process is at the heart of the rural-urban symbiosis.

A virtuous cycle is only established when the transaction costs are lower than the profit generated by the region's comparative advantages. If a producer of goods or services has to pay a relatively high price for e.g. market information, legal levies and bribes, storage and/or transport, little or no interaction will take place. To keep transaction costs low, therefore, either the regional economy must be closely knit or it must have highly developed rural-urban linkages. These are the lifeblood of a regional economic network. They include not just the links within the region itself but also the links between regions. A regional market is usually internally not large enough to generate economic growth by itself, which is why the region must have good connections to the outside world. After all, only through interregional trade can a region's comparative advantages be exploited. Without adequately developed internal and external links, the virtuous cycle will not function effectively.

Production Factor Flows

This section discusses the economic production factors of land, capital, and labor, which are used to produce goods and services. All of these factors (except land) can be geographically displaced. Land can change hands but cannot be physically relocated. However, it can change its function, which is relevant since this involves a shift in spatial designation. Such shifts can also alter the relative distance between places, and can promote (or discourage) their integration into a network. Examples include the transition from rural agricultural land to urban construction land. Land policy may be regarded as a catalyst that facilitates (or hampers) economic growth, through a pricing system, land as a taxation base, zoning, etc. However, this chapter does not include a separate section on land (nor on land policy), since land cannot be physically moved and therefore only has an indirect effect on those factors which can be moved, such as labor, capital, goods, and services.

Labor

Over the past two decades, labor markets in most developing countries have declined sharply or failed to keep pace with supply. Moreover, in many countries the number of formal jobs has been severely reduced in the wake of SAPs, especially in the public sector. Also employment in the agricultural sector has shrunk in recent years. This is due less to the mechanization of farming, as in Asia and Latin America, than to the monetary crises, the liberalization of the agricultural sector, and the structural reduction in prices on the world market due to intense competition from food producers outside Africa. As a result, many African smallholders have more or less been forced to fall back on subsistence farming (Pedersen and McCormick, 1999; Bryceson, 1999). The decline in jobs in the primary sector has been accompanied by a sharp rise in the population in practically all developing countries, thereby creating a large labor surplus. Most of this extra workforce has migrated to the informal urban economy (ILO, 1998), leading to the rapid expansion of some urban centers and generally reducing living standards there (see cf. UNDP, 1997). Despite this, cities appear to offer many people a more attractive existence – either a temporary or a long-term one – than rural areas. This is primarily because there are more job opportunities in and around cities than in the countryside, in terms of both numbers and the level of income they provide. Mulat Demeke (1997) found that in North Shoa, Ethiopia, there was a 200 per cent wage gap between the area around the regional capital of Debre Berhan and the city of Ankober just 45 kilometers away.

The pull exerted by urban centers is intensifying competition for jobs in many cities, in both the formal and the informal sector. According to El Hadi El Nagar (1998), jobs in the formal sector are becoming so scarce in relation to the intensifying demand, that university graduates are competing for informal jobs as waiters, builders, street traders, and housekeepers, thus putting unskilled workers in an even worse position than before. Labor migration flows do not move solely from rural to urban areas, but also from urban centers to rural areas, from city to city and from rural area to rural area (NAR, 1991). Urban workers, for example, return to the country as day-laborers to help with the harvest (Kamete, 1998). The rural Lozi from Barotseland, Zambia, work in the South African mines, which are also located in a rural area (Staaij and Wiel, 1999).

The degree to and the distance over which labor migration occurs depends largely on the historical context of a region. Non-agrarian regions with a long tradition of labor migration tend to have highly mobile populations. People travel enormous distances to look for work. Most of these migrants stay away for some considerable time. This type of migration occurs in Zimbabwe and South Africa, among other places. In the Sahel countries, traditional dramatic fluctuations in crop yields (due to a very short growing season) have led to a tradition of labor migration over long distances (cf. Bryceson, 1999; Hendrix and Slob, 1999). In rural regions combining an agricultural tradition with historic links to an urban center, much of the population is engaged in trade. The proportion of such traders has increased sharply over recent years (cf. Jambiya, 1998; Chukwuezi, 1999). SAPs have made a major contribution to this process. Many countries have liberalized their trade, while foreign goods have now become so expensive as a result of the SAPs that cheap, rurally produced goods are proving an attractive alternative for urban dwellers, despite their often inferior quality. Although these traders travel huge distances, they tend to use their local village as their operating base. The remoter regions frequently have little interaction with the cities (Mulat Demeke, 1997; Bryceson, 1999). Apart from historic ties and the impact of the SAPs, population pressure is another key factor. Madulu (1998) and others see the scarcity of land as a driving force behind labor migration.

Labor migration to urban centers tends to assume a more permanent form than other types of migration. In Africa, there are comparatively few commuters travelling between their urban place of work and their rural home (cf. Mwamfupe, 1998; Manona, 1999). Yet migration to the city does not automatically mean that the village is permanently left behind. Many households try to minimize their income risks by having some members of the family working in the town and some in the village. In most cases, it is the young men who go to the city to look for work while the women remain in the village. However, in recent years an increasing number of young women have been joining the migration process (Jambiya, 1998; Bol, 1999). For many older farmers, the emigration of young people is a source of concern, since it is creating a shortage of labor to work the land (Madulu, 1998). Yet at the same time, remittances from family members working in the city are often badly needed to supplement rural household incomes (Jambiya, 1998)

The village is a home base and a fall-back for many migrants. If for some reason they cannot survive in the fiercely competitive environment of the city, they may return, temporarily, to their village (Potts and Mutambirwa, 1998; Jambiya, 1998). Many city dwellers maintain links with their village through visits to their families, ownership of rural property, and sending back money (cf. Potts and Mutambirwa, 1998; Smit, 1998). In Gaborone, the capital of Botswana, many migrants still own land and livestock in their home village. The land is usually farmed by family members who have remained behind, and the livestock is looked after by paid herdsmen (Krüger, 1998).

Meagher (1999) found evidence of another form of fall-back in Nigeria. Returning migrants used the knowledge they had acquired in the city to set up their own micro-business in their home village. This assists the transfer of knowledge and helps to widen the economic base of the village. Yunusa (1999) has identified a reverse trend among successful rural entrepreneurs who, once they have acquired enough capital, move on to the more competitive, but more profitable, urban centers. Nevertheless, many migrants continue to regard their village as their real home (cf. Smit, 1998; Krüger, 1998) and therefore cherish hopes of moving back permanently once they stop working (Chukwuezi 1999).

Finally, it should be noted that labor migration in some countries is also accelerating the spread of Aids and other sexually transmitted diseases (cf. Mung'ong'o, 1998). Although this is primarily a social rural-urban link, Aids will clearly have major economic repercussions, especially in the long term. The first signs of this are already visible (cf. Wilkins, 1999).

Capital

The financial sector in sub-Saharan Africa is poorly developed. There is often no adequate provision of services, especially in rural areas. For this reason, the movement of capital between urban and rural centers tends to veer towards informal channels. One of the main channels for capital movement is through migrants who send part of their wages home to their relatives. This flow generally moves from the urban centers to the rural areas. Cultural variations also create different patterns of capital movement within regions. In Dakar, Senegal, almost 70 per cent of migrants provide their family members at home with substantial financial support (Fall, 1998). In Melani in South Africa's Eastern Cape Province, Manona (1999) found that the vast majority of households obtained a substantial part of their income from relatives who had emigrated. By contrast, Zanen (1999) found that the remittances from Burkinese labor migrants were highly erratic and selective.

The importance of remittances (or financial contributions) could lessen in the future. Growing mobility over ever increasing distances is boosting the individualization of African society. In some cases, this is undermining group solidarity, which is in turn reducing the frequency and size of the remittances. Nevertheless, the practice remains strikingly persistent, even if it only involves small amounts sent back by a few people. Mung'ong'o (1998), for example, found that the results of a 1988 survey conducted by Howe and Bryceson on the number and level of remittances in Njombe District in Tanzania still applied a decade later; namely, that only 10-20 per cent of households were sent money by emigrant family members, and the amounts involved were often minimal, in some cases less than US$ 1. Jambiya (1998) points out that the SAPs cost many city dwellers their job and hence their income, while also leading to the abolition of numerous subsidies. This has made life in urban centers far more expensive (Potts and Mutambirwa, 1998). As a result, some city dwellers have become dependent on their rural family members and/or on the income from their rural property (cf. Krüger, 1998). This ties in with the strategy described above, in which migrants tend to fall back on their home village in times of need. On the other hand, the Tanzanian case may be rather special, as higher levels of remittances play an important role in the financing of agricultural innovations in Eastern Africa, for instance in Kenya (Collier and Lal, 1986; Bevan et al., 1989).

Cross-investments are another form of informal capital movement. In much of sub-Saharan Africa, households combine agrarian and non-farm activities (NFAS), whereby the often very modest profits from one sector are invested in the other (cf. Madulu, 1998; Jambiya, 1998; Bryceson, 1999). Various authors (cf. Madulu, 1998; Jambiya, 1998) have noticed a clear shift in this practice, with older people tending to want to invest as much as possible in their smallholdings, while younger people prefer to invest in NFAS. Although many of these cross-investments are made in a single region, capital also moves between regions. The previous section described how successful rural entrepreneurs go on to try their luck in the cities, whereas older urban entrepreneurs prefer to retire to the country with their earnings (Chukwuezi, 1999). Fall (1998) found that in Senegal, some migrants reinvested the capital they had earned elsewhere in their home village, for example, by building schools or purchasing agricultural machinery.

Clearly, although informal capital flows boost economic growth, a formal banking system is also essential. The establishment of a commercially viable formal banking sector that is accessible to both the urban and the rural population is one of the biggest challenges in this field. Once this has been achieved, capital will be able to flow much more freely between urban and rural areas, and can therefore be deployed more effectively. Aryeetey et al. (1997) and Buckley (1997) have shown that the links between the formal and informal sectors in Ghana, Kenya, Malawi, Nigeria, and Tanzania are minimal. Lack of formally registered collateral is one of the hiccups (Collier and Gunning, 1999). Yet despite this, Aryeetey et al. and Buckley see opportunities for building a bridge between the sectors through informal intermediaries. Because providers of informal financial services have knowledge of the local market, this demonstrably minimizes the risks involved. Because many of these providers are travelling salesmen, they can cover quite extensive distances at low costs. However, they lack access to the formal money market. Although formal banks do not have local information and their coverage is usually limited, they do have access to formal capital (Evans, 1993; Aryeete et al., 1997). This should make informal and formal providers ideal partners.

One or two projects in Asia (Grameen Bank, Bank Rakyat Indonesia, Yaron and Piprek., 1997) and in Latin America (BankoSol, Gonzalez-Vega, 1996) have shown that it is possible to set up micro-finance institutions (MFIS), which create a bridge between the formal and the informal sector. Sancton (2000) gives a simple yet striking example of the potential impact of the availability of credit facilities. A woman in Bangladesh used a loan from the Grameen Bank to purchase what became the only mobile phone in her village. She now earns twice the average income by using it to provide telephone services. Her fellow villagers use the telephone primarily to gather information about the surrounding markets, and this has enabled them to charge higher prices for their products. Research by Duggleby (1993) and Dia (1996) on the formal and informal financial sector in Mali clearly shows that there are good opportunities in Africa for bridge-building between the two sectors.

However, alongside the handful of successful MFIS that have been established, there are many more unprofitable and/or small-scale initiatives with low success rates (Buckley, 1997). The low population density and the often extremely low incomes in large parts of sub-Saharan Africa will present major obstacles to the development of a banking network with sufficient coverage (Gulli and Berger, 1999). On the other hand, recent developments in ICT may offer new cost-effective options. In Latin America, for instance, Acción already uses hand-held PCs to evaluate and process loan applications within a mere 15 minutes (Acción International, 1999). A similar system using informal intermediaries is being tried out in Ghana under the name Computerized Mobile Bank (World Bank, 1999b). Other examples include the initiatives being launched by the ILO, which is trying – with some success – to transfer the Grameen Bank formula to West Africa (Gbézo, 1999). However, a large-scale breakthrough is still needed so that the initiative can benefit several million rather than merely several thousand households. In addition to individual loans, the issuing of credits to regional and/or local authorities following the decentralization of tasks and responsibilities is becoming increasingly important (Bergen, 1998), especially now that central governments are reducing the funding they set aside for implementation. A strong regional government, a stable source of income, and a reliable banking system are key criteria for qualifying for a loan from national and international capital providers. These criteria stress the importance of economic growth and the existence of a formal, regulated banking sector.

Goods and Services

Rural regions are traditional producers of unprocessed goods such as food and raw materials for urban centers. In return, they consume the goods and services produced in cities, such as groceries, clothing, education, and health care. The rise of urban farming and of a wide range of non-farm activities in rural areas is now blurring this clear-cut distinction and promoting greater diversity. Moreover, urban and rural areas are also increasingly exchanging goods and services as they become more regionally and globally integrated.

The West Africa Long-Term Perspective Study (WALTPS) shows that the volume and diversity of the movement of goods is closely linked to the accessibility of urban centers (Snrech, 1995). The study also found that the more closely a region is integrated with an urban center, and the more highly developed its urban network, the higher the productivity per hectare and the population density of the rural area. This overrides other characteristics such as soil fertility and the availability of water. Obviously, these factors are also crucial, but they are of secondary importance. The key prerequisite is the integration of a region into the urban network, since this is the main criterion for investments and for the purchase of inputs to improve soil quality. The proximity of an urban center provides a consumer market, thereby making these investments worthwhile. An example from another region, the Kerio Valley in Kenya, shows that good agricultural potential is not enough to foster development. The regional population there is impoverished due to its inability to find an adequate market for its goods. In Kijado, in another part of Kenya, smallholders are paid relatively high prices for their produce thanks to good links between the region and the capital city of Nairobi (Dietz and Leeuw, 1999). Even the infertile land surrounding Debre Berhan, the regional capital of North Shoa in Ethiopia, where crop yields are quite low, was found to have the highest inputs per hectare (in terms of irrigation, manure, and artificial fertilizer) (Mulat Demeke, 1997). Nevertheless, production does not always automatically increase near good consumer markets. In Botswana, for example, the supply of food to the cities is low, despite the demand. Krüger (1998) attributes this to a lack of enterprise and to years of restrictive trade policy imposed by the government.

In his case study on Zimbabwe, Kamete (1998) notes that most of the goods and services supplied by urban centers to the rural market are regarded as inferior by urban consumers. This observation has a parallel with the dynamics on the labor market, in that workers who are unable to hold their own in the highly competitive urban environment have tended to return, temporarily, to their rural village. Similarly, traditional products often cannot compete in terms of quality with their modern, foreign-produced counterparts (Mulat Demeke, 1997). Innovation and the modernization of rural production are therefore crucial. On the other hand, the impact of the SAPs is creating scope once more for local products, since imported products have become prohibitively expensive for many people.

Urban centers are not simply units of production and consumption, but also serve as important links in a trade network in which rural goods produced in one region are transported via a city to another region (cf. Kamete, 1998; Mwamfupe, 1998). The substantial increase in the number of traders in many countries suggests that this role has increased in importance and will continue to do so.

Examples of Catalysts

There will be no attempt to be exhaustive in this section, as the subject would lead us way beyond the scope of this paper. In particular if one wants to do justice to the institutional dimension of transaction costs, it would encompass such issues as legal matters, cultural matters, civil service reform, integrity systems, land policy, business environment, financing institutions, etc. Within the scope of this paper, we have chosen an exemplary approach touching briefly on infrastructure and transport, information, and education, while recommending Harriss et al. (1998) for further reading on institutional issues.

Infrastructure and Transport

Labor, capital, goods, and/or services cannot be moved from one place to another without some form of infrastructure or transport. It is therefore not surprising that in their respective studies in Malawi and Tanzania, Tellegen (1997) and Madulu (1998), among others, have observed a strong correlation between the proximity of roads and the viability and diversity of non-farm activities. One advantage of isolation for a region is that there are no competing external activities. Certainly in places where the local non-farm production consists of traditional crafts, this can benefit employment in that sector, given that modern alternatives will probably be highly competitive both in terms of quality and price (Mulat Demeke, 1997). The disadvantage is that there are no commercial opportunities, and this will restrict the growth of the region (cf. Staaij and Wiel, 1999).

The influence of infrastructure can also be seen in the Dutch regional development projects in sub-Saharan Africa. For example, livestock prices in Zambia are inversely proportional to their distance from the rail infrastructure (cf. Staaij and Wiel, 1999). Dietz and Leeuw (1999) state that the road network in the Kerio Valley in Kenya must be substantially improved before the agricultural potential of the region can be fully exploited. The fact that investments in infrastructure can assist growth is also seen in various districts in Tanzania. The construction of roads has made urban markets easier to reach, thereby giving farmers access to a much bigger market for their goods. In some cases, average income rose by as much as 50 per cent following the improvements in infrastructure (Bol, 1999). Although many of the infrastructure projects were beset by numerous problems, according to the author they were the only project components that had demonstrably positive effects for large groups of people. Another study by Jambiya (1998) found that the horticulture sector in Lushoto District, also in Tanzania, did not fully develop until the road to Dar es Salaam (a city with approximately three million inhabitants) had been made passable.

The proximity of infrastructure not only assists the spread of goods and services, but also encourages the distribution of labor and information. Both

Mung'ong'o (1998) and Jambiya (1998) noted a higher mobility among the working population in the villages with the best transport links. According to Bryceson (1999), the proximity of roads has become more important in recent years following the liberalization and privatization initiatives launched by the SAPs. Although the semi-publicly owned transport companies offered a reasonable service to rural regions, the privatized companies that replaced them did not serve farms and villages that were located too far from the main roads (cf. Jambiya, 1998; Mung'ong'o, 1998). This has made it more difficult for rural inhabitants to obtain the necessary inputs and to market their products. Consequently, it is not surprising that in the more remote areas, parents urge their children to look for work in the cities (Jambiya, 1998), which they do in large numbers (cf. Sterkenburg and Wiel, 1999). Many young people in fact need little encouragement to do so. The SAPs have also had a positive effect on the transport sector. It has now become easier to import motorized vehicles and spare parts, many arterial roads have been upgraded, and there are now many more private transport companies. This is reducing transport costs between the urban and rural regions served by these companies, and is also making products on both urban and rural markets cheaper, thereby stimulating reciprocal demand (Bol, 1999). Conversely, regions that are excluded from the network are becoming further marginalized (cf. Bryceson, 1999).

The improvement of road networks must take into account local demand. In the past, many infrastructure projects failed because they did not devote enough attention to actual demand. In practice, this means that it may sometimes be better for investments in infrastructure not to go ahead or for preference to be given to lower quality solutions. Evans (1993) and others have stressed the need to construct simple footpaths. Although they may be less suitable for motorized traffic, they cost far less to build and can therefore be used to create a denser network between villages and cities and between individual villages. Douglass (1998) maintains that a dense network of this kind is vital for the development of a region; he argues against concentrating all the regional amenities in a single urban center with a large rural catchment area, but instead advocates the creation of a network of villages with specialized, complementary amenities. According to Douglass, this will make a huge contribution to the diversification of the local economy. Douglass' ideas are very similar to the concept of the network city as described in the introductory memorandum to the Fifth Spatial Planning Policy Document (Ministry of Housing, 1999). Like Douglass' model, the network city in the Netherlands also consists of several hubs, all of which have their own specialization and are linked by a high-grade public transport network.

Hardoy and Satterthwaite (1988) also conclude that each urban center already has one or more historically evolved specializations, but that few authorities are making the most of them through the formation of networks.

Madulu (1998) describes an initial phase in the development of such a network. Although the villages in his study area (the central village of Mabuki and its outlying settlements in Sakumaland, Tanzania) do not yet have a highly evolved specialization, he nevertheless describes an active and dynamic trade between the various villages in the study area and between the study area and the urban centers. Young people acquire chickens in exchange for products such as salt, soap, pans, and second-hand clothes. They sell their chickens at the market in Mabuki to traders who cycle with them to the regional capital 50 kilometers away, or else take them by bus to more distant cities. In return, these traders offer products from the city in exchange for the chickens. In addition to the chicken market, which is held three times a week, there is also a weekly general market where rural and urban produced goods can be traded.

In addition to passable roads, vehicles are also needed to move goods and/or services. The infrastructure projects carried out in the context of the district programs in Tanzania have already been mentioned in this regard. One of the consequences of the improved road network has been the rise in the number of transport services (cf. Bryceson, 1999; Bol, 1999). This ties in closely with the findings of Jambiya (1998), who attributes the sluggish economic growth of Kweminyasa (Lushoto District, Tanzania) to inadequate transport facilities; in nearby Lukozi, which has good communications with the capital city and other urban centers, economic growth is healthy.

Even simple means of transport such as bicycles can have a major impact on trade networks in places where handcarts and 'head loading' are the norm (Mulate Demeke, 1997; Bryceson, 1999). The trade network in Tanzania described above, for example, is heavily reliant on bicycles. Moreover, the productivity of smallholders in the same region also increased following the introduction of ox carts, which enable them to transport larger quantities of goods to market (Madulu, 1998). Another example is found in Mbeya, Tanzania, where canoes and bicycles are used to operate a cross-border trade network (Mwamfupe, 1998). Investments in relatively cheap, low-tech forms of transport can substantially boost the reach of producers, allowing them to target markets that were previously inaccessible to them. More carrying capacity can also greatly improve efficiency.

Information

In addition to roads and means of transport, information is another vital factor assisting the movement of labor, capital, and goods. Rural job-seekers are more likely to migrate to the city if they know that their prospects will be better there. Similarly, loans are only made if the credit provider has some knowledge of the investment opportunity. Before offering goods and services, producers need to know precisely what customers want. A shortage or complete lack of information will greatly slow down economic growth. Both the quality and the quantity of information supply is at a low ebb in many African countries (Alemna, 1998). Setting up and maintaining local information systems concerning, say, market developments, local directories, and so on, will need to be addressed very actively if a market is to operate efficiently. According to Helmsing (2000, pp. 19-38), the exchange of knowledge and information between individual businesses and between businesses and public and semi-public agencies will become increasingly important. Reliable information is also vital for properly substantiated and verifiable planning.

Information therefore acts as a catalyst for the movement of labor, capital, and goods. At the same time, information itself moves from place to place. As such, it is part of the overall supply of services. The use of ICT will become progressively widespread in the 21st century. However, sub-Saharan Africa is struggling with a serious lack of modern telecommunications infrastructure, especially in rural areas. Telephone density is often extremely low (International Telecommunications Union, 1998), partly due to the high costs of laying a fixed network. This could be overcome through the development of cable-free technology (cf. RAWOO, 1998; Sancton, 2000). The application of such technology in Africa is gaining more and more ground, even when the relative costs involved are high. 'Market mammies' in West Africa use mobile phones to exchange information on cross-border prices, while the Grand Coast Fishing Operators' Union in Senegal uses the Internet to advertise its products, to consult information on export markets, and to conduct price negotiations (Sancton, 2000). The World Bank and other institutions are also funding experimental solutions under the InfoDev program (World Bank, 1999b) and the recently launched idea of setting up a Global Development Gateway. Traditional media such as radio, TV, and newspapers will continue to be important, while knowledge and information will also be disseminated through labor migration. Even so, developments in ICT will have an impact on urban rural links over the course of time, and probably sooner than many people expect. The most likely scenario is that existing information will eventually be more or less directly available throughout the whole of the African continent, even in the more remote regions, thereby reducing the existing disparity in information density between urban and rural areas.

Education

Education probably does not immediately come to mind as a catalyst for rural-urban linkages. Nevertheless, education does have an influence on links between individual urban centers and between rural areas and cities. Educated youngsters, for example, are more likely than their unskilled contemporaries to look for work in an urban environment. Also, the type of schooling provided in sub-Saharan Africa often does not properly tie in with market demand (cf. Evans, 1993; El Hadi El Nagar, 1998). The quality of rural education in particular is frequently so poor that when young people migrate to an urban environment, they find themselves at a serious disadvantage (cf. Mung'ong'o, 1998). As a result, rural immigrants often cannot compete with their better-educated urban peers (cf. El Hadi El Nagar, 1998). Moreover, urban youngsters also generally have a better social urban network, which can be important in securing an apprenticeship (cf. Fall, 1998). Because knowledge is likely to become increasingly crucial in the future, the importance of education will continue to grow.

Keyzer (1998) points out that education also influences international migration patterns. The majority of international migrants are well-educated city dwellers. Because many education and training projects focus special attention on improving schooling for girls, the proportion of women in the migration flows is also growing (cf. Jambiya, 1998; Titus, 2000). Despite this, however, most women end up in a less-well paid job because their level of education still tends to be lower (cf. Jambiya, 1998; Mung'ong'o, 1998). Finally, the availability of knowledge will play an increasingly important role in the regional economy. Regions with a poor knowledge infrastructure will be further marginalized, as will urban centers with an inadequate road network (cf. Helmsing, 2000).

Conclusions

1. *The operation of rural-urban linkages in the framework of economic networks in sub-Saharan Africa must be studied more closely*
This initial inventory of rural urban linkages in the framework of economic networks in Africa highlights the need to tackle the lack of interest in this

topic. It contains many indications that these networks and their linkages are crucial to the development of a region. By devoting specific attention to rural-urban linkages, we can increase the success rate of programs geared towards economic development.

There are very few examples of studies that focus on both economic networks and regional development. Such studies have a longer time span and a wider geographical coverage than is usual in economic research. However, this is necessary because we can only obtain sufficient insight into developments if we look at both the macro-economic and the macro-geographic context. A broad, multidisciplinary approach is also required, given that multiple links are involved. The OECD's West Africa Long-Term Perspective Study (Snrech, 1995) is one of the first detailed studies in this field that manages to go beyond a limited survey of urban centers and their immediate hinterlands. It looks at far more extensive regions, many of which reach beyond national borders. The regional development programs that have been launched by countless donors from the 1960s to the present day have largely neglected the cities. So although they have covered extensive areas, they have not been a fruitful source of quantitative or qualitative data (cf. Bol, 1999). While there have been some publications on related sub-themes, these have generally approached the issue from an entirely different perspective. They are therefore used in this paper merely as examples. Also, most of the studies are short on firm figures, so that it is not yet possible to assess the relative importance of specific rural-urban linkages. We therefore cannot enter any validated weightings of the various parameters in econometric models. Nor can we gain adequate insight into the consequences of world-wide trends such as global integration and computerization. Rapid developments in technologies designed to monitor changes in land-use via satellites and to analyze these changes using geographical information systems provide a source of hope, however. They will make it possible to avoid defining regions in advance, but instead to delineate their various roles on the basis of the spatial dynamics identified by the analysis. If we continue this line of research, we can gain a better understanding of the spatial dynamics of economic networks.

2. *The spatial interaction patterns of labor, capital, goods, and services are the lifeblood of the linkages between economic networks*

In contrast to what we know of other continents, the urbanization of sub-Saharan Africa has in most cases not gone hand in hand with economic growth (World Bank, 1999a). In this part of the world, urbanization has been less a consequence of mechanized farming than of increased joblessness due to rapid population growth coupled with low levels of production and revenue. The virtuous cycle – in which profits from agrarian activities are invested in non-farm activities and vice versa – has generally not happened on a substantial scale in Africa. One possible reason for this is the malfunctioning or even absence of linkages between economic networks. If there is too little economic interaction within and between regions, economic growth appears to stagnate. These interactions create an exchange mechanism in which land, capital, labor, and knowledge can be used to generate economic value. An exchange mechanism is a necessary precondition for raising living standards through specialization. Investment in rural urban linkages in terms of infrastructure and transport possibilities as well as in terms of institutional assets (such as good governance and business environment) will be very vital for generating economic growth. To make this a pro-poor growth strategy detailed analysis is needed to accommodate the needs of the poor.

3. *The rural-urban symbiosis needs to be the starting point for development interventions*

Economic networks have a spatial dimension; they can, for example, be represented on maps. The hubs of the interaction patterns in these networks are the urban settlements. Most interactions tend to take place along rural-urban linkages, although rural-rural and urban-urban linkages are also possible. These rural-urban linkages operate, naturally enough, in two directions. In view of this fact, the failure of the larger regional development programs to include the urban centers in their focus is a serious omission, since it neglects the essence of development.

4. *Economic growth accelerates as rural-urban linkages improve*

The WALTPS (Snrech, 1995) shows that regions that are more fully integrated into the urban network – measured in terms of accessibility (rather than proximity) to urban centers – undergo more rapid economic growth than regions without these links. It also clearly shows that a higher level of integration results in a higher yield per hectare, and also a higher (and increasing) population density in rural areas. More remote areas appear to be characterized by low yields, low population density, and the out-migration of indigenous populations in absolute terms. Between these two extremes, many other regions are also experiencing out-migration, but are nevertheless growing in relative terms.

5. *Regions without good rural-urban linkages will become more marginalized*
There are indications that as a result of SAPs, regions that lack good links with urban centers could become even more marginalized. For remote regions in particular, it is relevant to ask what can be done to reduce transaction costs or to improve links with consumer markets. If these opportunities are limited, as is the case with the majority of remote areas, we may have to conclude that substantial investments in such regions – which in any case have extremely low and declining population densities – are less worthwhile (Sterkenburg and Wiel, 1999).

6. *Development interventions should focus primarily on the catalysts for economic interactions, addressing spatial as well as institutional issues*
In view of the importance of rural-urban linkages for economic interactions (as the lifeblood of economic networks), policy measures should focus primarily on the catalysts which influence these links favorably. The organization of the links (i.e., the movement of labor, capital, goods, and services) is generally regarded not as a government task but as one that is left to the market. To enhance easy movement should be seen as investing in an enabling environment.

We should also ask ourselves the fundamental question whether the various policy interventions we launch in the context of development cooperation are spatially neutral. It is after all likely that without fully considering their impact, we are implementing measures which may inadvertently be affecting the existing spatial economic structure and existing spatial economic links. The SAPs are an example of this. Clearly, when we have a better idea of the economic processes we are dealing with, we will be able to tailor our policies accordingly.

This paper discussed the movement of labor, capital, goods, and services, and the catalysts that influence them, namely, infrastructure, transport, information, and education. The list of catalysts is by no means exhaustive. Examples were chosen to give some idea of possible implications. In practice, each region will need to be treated individually on the basis of a spatial and institutional economic analysis. The insights gained should then be translated into a policy geared towards the maximum pro-poor growth of the regional economy within the constraints imposed by the need for sustainability.

Acknowledgements

I would like to thank Dirk van Barneveld for his extensive literature survey. Together we prepared a position paper for the standpoint of the Council of the European Union in the prepcom for the Istanbul5+ conference held in Nairobi in May 2000. This chapter draws heavily on this work. Also I wish to thank Jan Willem Gunning, Bert Helmsing, Jan Lambooij, Guus van Westen, Isa Baud, Tom Segaar, Jan Sterkenburg, Hans Slot and participants of the seminars at the Institute of Social Studies and the Ministry for Development Cooperation, and the Utrecht University of the CERES research school for their valuable comments and discussions. However, I am totally responsible for the content of this chapter.

References

Accion International (1999), 'Palm Pilots: Lending Efficiency to Micro-credit', *Ventures*, Autumn, pp. 1-3.

Alemna, A. (1998), 'Information in African Society', *Information Development*, Vol. 14(2), pp. 69-72.

Aryeetey, E., Hettige, H., Nissanke, M. and Steel, W.F. (1997), 'Financial Market Fragmentation and Reforms in Ghana, Malawi, Nigeria, and Tanzania', *The World Bank Economic Review*, Vol. 11(2), pp. 195-218.

Bergen, M. (1998), 'Credit Ratings: What the Experts Look For. *Urban Age*, Vol. 5(4), pp. 24-5.

Bevan, D., Collier, P. and Gunning, J.W. (1989), *Peasants and Governments: an Economic Analysis*, Oxford Univ. Press, Clarendon.

Bol, D. (1999), 'District Rural Development Projects in Tanzania', in J. Sterkenburg and A. van der Wiel (eds), *Integrated Area Development. Experiences with Netherlands Aid in Africa*, Ministry of Foreign Affairs, The Hague, pp. 59-77.

Bryceson, D.F. (1999), *Sub-Saharan Africa Betwixt and Between: Rural Livelihood Practices and Policies*, ASC Working Paper, No. 43, African Studies Center, Leiden.

Buckley, G. (1997), 'Microfinance in Africa: is it the Problem or the Solution?', *World Development*, No. 7, pp. 1081-93.

Chukwuezi, B. (1999), *De-agrarianisation and Rural Employment in Rural Igboland, Southeastern Nigeria*, ASC Working Paper, No. 37, African Studies Center, Leiden.

Christaller, W. (1968), *Die Zentralen Orte in Süddeutschland*, Wissenschaftliche Buchgesellschaft, Darmstadt.

Collier, P. and Lal, D. (1986), *Labor and Poverty in Kenya, 1900-1980*, Oxford University Press, Clarendon.

Collier, P. and Gunning, J.W. (1999), 'Explaining African Economic Performance', *Journal of Economic Literature*, Vol. 37, March, pp. 64-111.

Dia, M. (1996), *Africa's Management in the 1990s and Beyond, Reconciling Indigenous and Transplanted Institutions*, World Bank, pp. 194-219.

Dicken, P. (1998), *The Global Shift: Transforming the World Economy*, Chapman, London.

Dietz, A.J. and Leeuw, W. de (1999), 'The Arid and Semi-arid Lands Programme in Kenya', in J. Sterkenburg and A. van der Wiel (eds), *Integrated Area Development. Experiences with Netherlands aid in Africa*, Ministry of Foreign Affairs, The Hague, pp. 37-57.

Douglass, M. (1998), *Rural-Urban Linkages and Poverty Alleviation. Toward a Policy Framework*, Paper presented at the International Workshop on Rural-Urban Linkages, Curitiba, 10-13 March.
Duggleby, T. (1993), *Comparative Study of Informal and Formal Finance in Mali*, unpublished paper for Dia, M., World Bank 1996.
El Hadi El Nagar, S. (1998), *Pastoralists' Adaptations to Market Opportunities*, Paper presented to the workshop on Pastoral Resource Competition in Eastern Africa, August, ISS, The Hague.
Evans, H.E. (1993), *Rural-Urban Linkages: Operational Implications for Self-sustained Development. Draft*, Pasadena.
Fall, A. (1998), 'Migrants' Long-Distance Relationships and Social Networks', *Environment and Urbanization*, Vol. 10(1), pp. 135-45.
Gbézo, B. (1999), 'Microcredit in West Africa: how Small Loans Make a Big Impact on Poverty', *World of Work*, No. 31, pp. 13-5.
Gereffi, G. and M. Korzeniewicz (eds) (1994), *Commodity Chains and Global Capitalism*, Preager Westport, Connecticut.
Gonzalez-Vega, C. (1996), *BancoSol. The Challenge of Growth for Micro-finance Organization.*, Ohio.
Gulli, H. and Berger, M. (1999), 'Microfinance and Poverty Reduction – Evidence from Latin America', *Small Enterprise Development*, Vol. 10(3), pp. 16-28.
Haan, L.J. de (2000), *Livelihood, Locality and Globalization*, Inaugural address, Nijmegen University Press, Nijmegen, pp. 29-41.
Hardoy, J. and Satterthwaite, D. (1988), 'Small and Intermediate Urban Centers in the Third World', *TWPR*, Vol. 10(1), pp. 5-26.
Harriss, J., Hunter, J. and Lewis, C.M. (1995), *The New Institutional Economics and Third World Development*, Routledge, London.
Helmsing, B. (2000), *Externalities, Learning and Governance Perspectives on Local Economic Development*, Institute of Social Studies, The Hague.
Hendrix, H. and Slob, A. (1999), 'Irrigated Rice Cultivation in the Office du Niger, Mali', in J. Sterkenburg and A. van der Wiel (eds), *Integrated Area Development. Experiences with Netherlands Aid in Africa*, Ministry of Foreign Affairs, The Hague, pp. 123-38.
Howe, J and Bryceson, D. (1988), *Baseline Study of the Songea-Makambako Road, Tanzania. Interim Report, Vol. II*, Ministry of Overseas Development, London.
ILO (1998). *The Future of Urban Employment*, ILO, Geneva.
International Telecommunications Union (1998), *World Telecommunication Development Report: Universal Access*, ITU, Geneva.
Jambiya, G. (1998), *The Dynamics of Population, Land Scarcity, Agriculture and Non- agricultural Activities: West Usambara Mountains, Lushoto District, Tanzania*, ASC Working Paper, No. 28, African Studies Center, Leiden.
Kamete, A. (1998), 'Interlocking Livelihoods: Farm and Small Town in Zimbabwe, *Environment and Urbanization*, Vol. 10(1).
Keyzer, M. (1998), *Economische Gevolgen van Internationale Migratie*, Paper for course on development issues, Amsterdam.
Krüger, F. (1998), 'Taking Advantage of Rural Assets as a Coping Strategy for the Urban Poor: The Case of Rural-Urban Interrelations in Botswana', *Environment and Urbanization*, Vol. 10(1), pp. 119-34.

Lambooy, J.G. (1980), 'Het Begrip 'Regio' in de Geografische Theorie en Methode', KNAW 1980, pp. 15-23.
Madulu, N. (1998), *Changing Lifestyles in Farming Societies of Sukumaland: Kwimba District, Tanzania*, ASC Working Paper, No. 27, African Studies Center, Leiden.
Manona, C. (1999), *De-agrarianisation and the Urbanization of a Rural Economy: Agrarian Patterns in Melani Village in the Eastern Cape, South Africa*, ASC Working Paper, No. 32, African Studies Center, Leiden.
Meagher, K. (1999), *If the Drumming Changes, the Dance also Changes: De-agrarianisation and Rural Non-Farm Employment in the Nigerian Savannah*, ASC Working Paper, No. 40, African Studies Center, Leiden.
Ministry of Housing, Spatial Planning and the Environment, (1999), *De Ruimte van Nederland. Startnota ruimtelijke ordening* 1999, Staatsuitgeverij, The Hague.
Mulat Demeke (1997), *Rural Non-Farm Activities in Impoverished Agricultural Communities: the Case of North Shoa, Ethiopia*, African Studies Center, Leiden.
Mung'ong'o, C. (1998), *Coming Full Circle: Agriculture, Non-Farm Activities and the Resurgence of Out-migration in Njombe District, Tanzania*, African Studies Center, Leiden.
Mwamfupe, D. (1998), *Changing Village Land, Labor and Livelihoods: Rungwe and Kyela Districts, Tanzania*, ASC Working Paper, No. 29, African Studies Center, Leiden.
NAR (July 1999), National Advisory Council for Development Cooperation No. 97: *Advies Migratie en Bilaterale Ontwikkelingssamenwerking*, DOP, The Hague.
North, D.C. (1995), 'The New Institutional Economics and Third World Development', in J. Harriss, J. Hunter and C.M. Lewis (1995, reprint 2000), *The New Institutional Economics and Third World Development*, Routledge, London, pp. 17-26.
Pedersen, P.O. and McCormick, D. (1999), 'African Business Systems in a Globalising World', *The Journal of Modern African Studies*, Vol. 37, pp. 109-35.
Porter, M.E. (1990), *Competitive Advantage of Nations*, Free Press, New York.
Potts, D. and Mutambirwa, C. (1998), 'Basics are Now a Luxury: Perceptions of Structural Adjustment's Impact on Rural and Urban Areas in Zimbabwe', *Environment and Urbanization*, Vol. 10(1), pp. 55-75.
RAWOO (1998), *Information and Communication Technology and Development. RAWOO Lectures and Seminar*, RAWOO, The Hague.
Sancton, T. (2000), 'A Great Leap. Developing Countries are Finding Ways to Leverage Advances in Information Technology and Help Narrow the North-South Divide', *Time*, Jan 31, Europe edition, pp. 42-6.
Smit, W. (1998), 'The Rural Linkages of Urban Households in Durban, South Africa', *Environment and Urbanization*, Vol. 10(1), pp. 77-87.
Snrech, S. (1995), *Preparing for the Future: a Vision of West Africa in the Year* 2020, Summary Report. OECD, Paris.
Staaij, F. van der, and Wiel, A. van der (1999), 'Rural Development Support in Western Province, Zambia', in J. Sterkenburg and A. van der Wiel (eds), *Integrated Area Development. Experiences with Netherlands Aid in Africa*, Ministry of Foreign Affairs, The Hague, pp. 79-105.
Sterkenburg, J. and Wiel, A. van der (1999), *Integrated Area Development. Experiences with Netherlands Aid in Africa*, Ministry of Foreign Affairs, The Hague.
Tacoli, C. (1998a). Rural-Urban Interactions: a guide to the literature, in *Environment and Urbanization*, vol. 10, no. 1, pp. 147-166.

Tacoli, C. (1998b), 'Rural-Urban Linkages and Sustainable Rural Livelihoods', in D. Carney (ed.), *Sustainable Rural Livelihoods. What Contribution Can We Make?*, Department for International Development, London.

Tellegen, J. (1997), *Rural Enterprises in Malawi: Necessity or Opportunity?*, Ashgate, Aldershot.

Titus, M. (2000), *Determinant and Trends of Urban Development in Ujung Pandang, Indonesia*, Draft, University of Utrecht.

UNDP (1997), *Rural-Urban Linkages: Operational Implications for Self-sustained Development*, Draft, New York (Interim draft, September 2000).

UNHCS (1999), *Habitat Debate*, Vol. 5(1), UNCHS, Nairobi.

Volbeda, S. (1984), *Pionierssteden in het Oerwoud, Stedelijke Ontwikkelingen aan een Agrarisch Kolonisatiefront in het Braziliaanse Amazonegebied*, Nijmeegse Geografische Cahiers No. 26, dissertation, Nijmegen.

Volbeda, S. (1997), 'A Comparison between Pioneer Towns and Rural Service Centers in the Amazon region of Brazil', in P. van Lindert and O. Verkoren (eds), *Small Towns and Beyond. Rural Transformation and Small Urban Centers in Latin America*, Thela Publishers, Amsterdam, pp. 15-30.

Wilkins, N. (1999), 'HIV/AIDS and the Informal Sector', *Aids analysis Africa*, No. 1, pp. 7-10.

World Bank (1999a), *Entering the 21st Century. World Development Report 1999-2000*, World Bank, Washington DC.

World Bank (1999b), *Quarterly Report from InfoDev. Third quarter 1999*, World Bank, Washington DC.

World Bank (2000), *Rural-Urban Linkages and Interactions: Synthesis of Issues, Conclusions and Priority Opportunities Emerging from the 9 March Workshop and Related Discussions*. Draft, World Bank, Washington DC.

Yaron, J. and Piprek, B. (1997), *Rural Finance. Issues, Design and Best Practices*, Environmentally and Socially Sustainable Development Studies and Monograph Series, No. 14, World Bank, New York.

Yunusa (1999), *Not Farms Alone: A Study of Rural Livelihoods in the Middle Belt of Nigeria*, ASC Working paper, No. 39, African Studies Center, Leiden.

Zanen, J. (1999), 'Natural and Human Resource Management in Kaya Burkina Faso', in J. Sterkenburg and A. van der Wiel (eds), *Integrated Area Development. Experiences with Netherlands Aid in Africa*, Ministry of Foreign Affairs, The Hague, pp. 105-122.

16 Resource Flows and Urban Governance: Approaching Environmental Transitions in Cities and their Hinterland

ISA BAUD AND MICHAELA HORDIJK

Introduction

Several major changes that occurred in the global economy in the 1980s and 1990s have affected the pattern of growth of cities in developing countries. Such changes include (1) the rapid growth in international trade, and a shift away from trade in goods to trade in business and financial services, (2) the transformation of production processes, leading to localized production systems coupled to centralized control, (3) advances in telecommunications, and (4) the global mobility of capital flows and increased foreign direct investment in certain developing countries. At the same time, structural adjustment programs in the 1980s reduced levels of investment by governments in urban infrastructure, housing, and services despite the rapid growth of urban areas (UNCHS, 1996). Developments in the world economy have been accompanied by major shifts of populations from rural to urbanized areas. This is related to demographic, economic, and political changes, which have led to changing roles for urban areas (UNCHS, 1996).

Both demographic and economic trends lead to a concentration of resource flows into cities to provide their populations with food, shelter, energy, and material goods. A city draws heavily on natural resource flows (water, air, energy, soil, raw materials) from outside its boundaries. It uses the capacity of the local and global sinks for the flows it discharges (polluted air, water, waste materials, noise). Although the majority of resource flows are used for production and consumption in the city itself, there are also flows of products and information that leave the city to 'feed' the hinterland.

The increase in these flows threatens the ecological sustainability of the natural environment in both the city and its hinterland. This is the result of impacts deriving from the extraction of resources from outside the city, both in the area of extraction ('the ecological rucksack'; Sachs et al., 1998), as well as through the wastes and the pollution they generate in and around the city. It also threatens the natural environment through the degradation of natural ecosystems, threatening the regenerative capacity of such ecosystems.

These flows can also threaten the health of urban inhabitants to various degrees. Environmental impacts within cities are very uneven. The urban poor suffer more than the urban rich from lack of access to basic urban services with which they can organize shelter, food, water, and basic sanitation. They are also more exposed to the threats to their health resulting from the wastes and pollution generated by the production of goods (cf. Hardoy and Sattherwaite, 1993; *Environment and Urbanization*, 1999).

Relations between cities and their hinterland have generally concentrated on socioeconomic flows. In this chapter, we will examine the ecological dimension of activities related to basic urban services and the built environment, by addressing the question how resource flows into and out of cities can be made ecologically more sustainable. Although we recognize the importance of the ecological dimension of urban economic production, we will not deal with it here. We will use examples related to the provision of basic urban services, such as water and solid waste management. As the city is an open system in terms of flows of resources into and flows of wastes and emissions from it, it is all the more necessary to consider such relations at the city-hinterland level. It is hoped that by looking at issues of ecological sustainability at the level of cities and their hinterlands, a contribution can be made to discussions on how cities can more effectively tackle environmental problems in a larger eco-regional context, defined as the area of resource extraction and the area of environmental impact of urban activities.

Sustainability and Sustainable Development

A great deal has been written about concepts of sustainability and sustainable development, ranging from conceptions of social, economic, and political sustainability to more specific concepts of ecological sustainability. An excellent summary of such discussions in the context of development studies is provided by an article written by Mitlin and Satterthwaite (1996). They distinguish ecological sustainability on the basis of the following criteria; minimizing the use or waste of non-renewable resources, sustainable use of renewable resources, and keeping wastes from cities within the absorptive capacity of local and global sinks. The element of 'development' includes social, economic, and political needs for current and future generations. Together these elements form the potential for 'sustainable development' (cf. Mitlin and Satterthwaite, 1996, pp. 31-32). Their definitions are used as starting points in this chapter. Sustainability and sustainable development are seen as policy goals that form the backdrop against which to assess current resource flows and the natural systems from which they emanate, competing demands for resource flows, the organization of their transformation and distribution, and the issues of governance regulating them. Given the current state of affairs – societal, political, scientific, and with respect to technological innovations – it is more realistic to talk about striving for a transition towards a more sustainable way of urban life, or 'the transition to sustainability' (O'Riordian, 1998). Realizing completely ecologically sustainable development is still a Utopian goal.

Sustainability – as the word is used in this chapter – has a number of key features. Firstly, there are absolute physical limits to growth, imposed by the 'limited carrying capacity of ecosystems, the recuperative efficiency of natural resources, and the availability of raw materials' (Sachs et al., 1998, p. 12). Together these form the 'environmental space' – defined by Opschoor and Constanza (1995) as the area human beings can use in the natural environment without doing lasting harm to its essential characteristics – humans can use to satisfy their basic needs. The flows into cities and the environmental impacts they generate must remain within that 'environmental space'. This means we should pay attention to the natural environment in its own right, and acknowledge the strength of environmental impacts and natural regeneration processes independent of human agency.

According to the report by the EU Expert Group on the Urban Environment in the context of the European Sustainable Cities Project of the EU (ESC Report, 1994), determining where these limits lie is not an easy process, and very precise limits may not always be determinable. In such cases, avoiding essential risks to the natural ecosystem must have priority over other considerations (the precautionary principle). This requires the development of preventive reduction of resource extraction as a complementary strategy in any discussion of strategies aimed at achieving sustainability (Sachs et al., 1998, p. 20). The goal must be to maintain the existing capital of natural resources, as well as the self-regulatory capacity of ecosystems (Sachs et al., 1998).

Secondly, the precautionary principle implies that human activities must remain within the limits set by the natural environment. This requires policies and strategies aimed at managing human demands – i.e., at reducing or redirecting them – rather than meeting them *in toto* (ESC Report, 1994). Also required in this process of management are greater 'environmental efficiency' and 'social efficiency'. 'Environmental efficiency means achieving maximum economic benefit for each unit of natural resources used and waste produced' (ESC Report, 1994). The reduction in natural resources extraction and use mentioned above is a major part of such strategies. 'Social efficiency means obtaining the greatest human benefit from each unit of economic activity' (ESC Report, 1994, p. 43).

The final, political point is that strategies aimed at achieving sustainability should promote equity in various forms. Types of equity identified include that between different geographical areas of the world (geographical equity) – such as between industrialized and developing countries – between groups with different income levels (intra-generational equity), and between current and future generations (inter-generational) (Haughton, 1999).

Limitations

When trying to apply the concept of ecological sustainability to city-hinterland relations, one faces several limitations. First of all, a comprehensive analytical model combining the different levels of analysis needed for the urban context has not yet been developed. Researchers have focused either on natural ecosystems – analyzing the impacts of human activity, and providing us with a wealth of information on changes in biodiversity in different ecosystems – or on the management of natural resources and the resource requirements for maintaining certain standards of resource delivery for the urban population (applying health standards and ignoring the limits set by the regenerative capacity of ecosystems). One well-known approach is the 'ecological footprint' concept (Rees, 1992). This footprint measures the total land area required to maintain the food, water, energy, and waste-disposal demands per person, per product, or per city. It is a summary indicator of environmental impacts of human activity, but it does not – nor is it meant to – capture the social or political dimensions of such activities (Bossel, 1999, p. 13).

A second limitation is that we are dealing with complex and dynamic relations whose internal feedback loops are not well known. Many natural processes fluctuate over varying periods and spatial scales in an unpredictable manner, and interact with other variables in an unknown manner (Jensen, 1998). This applies to ecosystems within a city and, presumably, even more so to flows which link urban areas and their hinterland. And we have to take into account that even if a causal relation – expressed in measurable factors – has not been scientifically proven, this does not necessarily mean that no such relation exists (O'Riordian and Voisy, 1998, p. 11).

A third limitation is that – as is expressed in the ecological footprint – city-hinterland relations nowadays include relations that affect the entire globe (Jensen, 1998). For instance, emissions from industries in China have been detected throughout the Pacific region, including the continental USA. However, in this chapter the focus on the impact of resource flows between city and hinterland is limited to a more local 'eco-region'.

The question how city-hinterland resource flows can be made more ecologically sustainable while promoting equity both temporally and spatially, therefore raises more questions than answers in this chapter. However, the question is raised in order to develop parts of a preliminary model, to be used to promote further discussion on these themes and lead to a research agenda for the coming years. This chapter focuses on some specific processes which form part of such a model. These processes are:

- The main flows of resources into a city, and the competing demands for their use made by groups within that city and in the surrounding rural areas (resource availability, demand, and changes over time);
- The environmental stresses resulting from pollution and waste generation as resources are consumed, and changes in the pattern of stresses as cities develop, including spatial and temporal transfer mechanisms (impact of pollution and waste and changes over time);
- Management and governance of resource flows, i.e., public-private partnerships and institutional arrangements through which a more equitable distribution of resources can be achieved (co- management of resources and governance); and
- What processes can improve sustainability at relevant city-hinterland levels, moving from pollution reduction only to reducing resource inputs as part of such a process (strongly sustainable resources policy and management).

The City and its Hinterland: Natural Environment, Built Environment, and Society

The OECD defines the urban context as interweaving a mixture of natural, built form, organized through political, economic, social, and cultural relationships (OECD, 1990). The physical urban environment consists of the natural environment and the city's built form. The elements of the city's

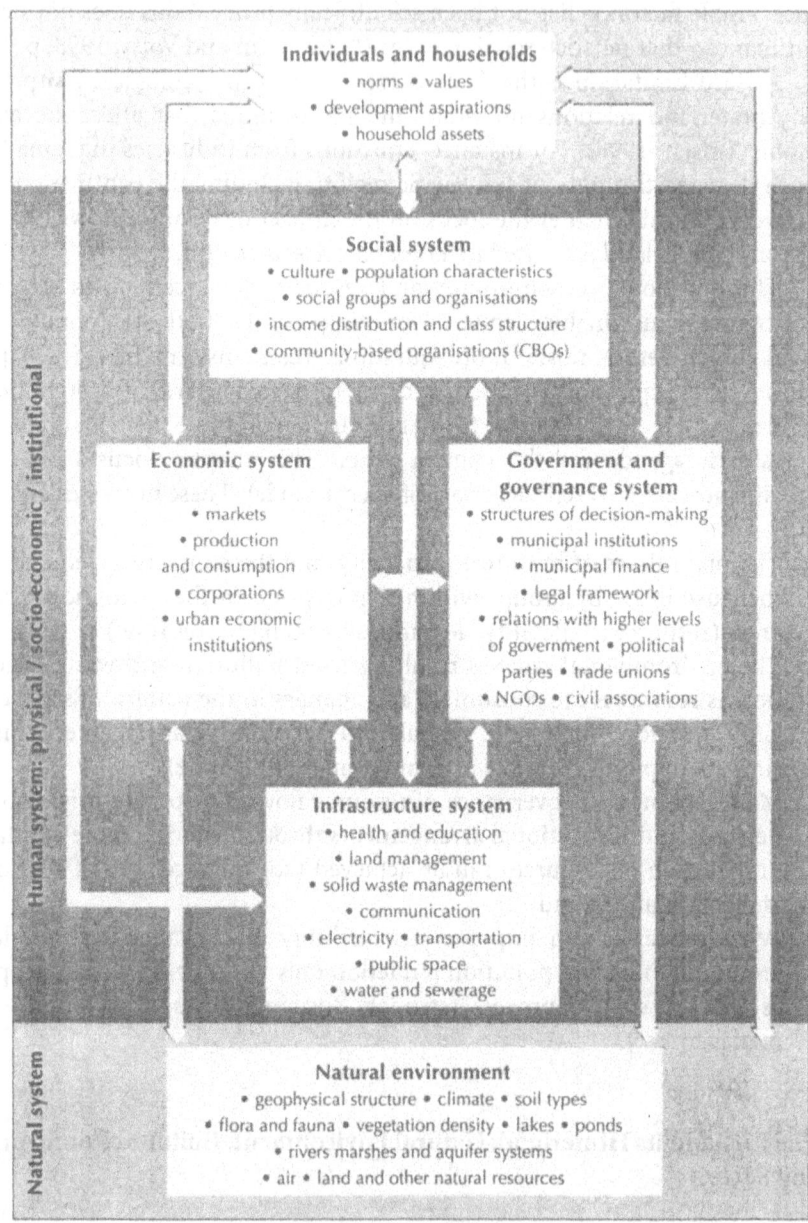

Figure 16.1 The system of the city and its subsystems

natural environment are geophysical structure, soil, air, water, flora, fauna, and climate; the built form consists of housing, infrastructure, and urban services; society consists of the inhabitants and their cultural, economic, political, and social institutions. The model on the following page groups these dimensions together. The question examined here is what kind of rural-urban interactions can be discerned within this model. The perspective used is that of the urban point of view, the bias of which we acknowledge.

Three levels of analysis are brought together in the model. The natural resource system surrounding urban areas provides the basis for all human activities, although it follows its own laws independent of human agency. The built environment is the result of public or private companies transforming natural resources into goods, basic services, and infrastructure, which are demanded by urban inhabitants for consumption purposes. Finally, the human environment is the system of governance comprised of government bodies, civil society organizations, and the private sector, which together determine what patterns of production and consumption take place, and whose demands are met most fully.

There are competing models concerning the relationship between human activities and the natural environment. A basic difference in assumptions is between, on the one hand, models in which economic activities are the primary concern, and environmental issues are defined primarily in terms of negative spin-off (pollution) which needs to be mitigated, and, on the other hand, models which start from the primacy of the natural environment in which humans can undertake activities within the limitations set by nature (cf. Sachs *et al.*, 1998). There is a second set of related differences between the 'green' agenda (concerning long-term ecological sustainability) and the 'brown' agenda (concerning the immediate negative environmental health impacts of economic activities). In this model, an attempt is made to see to what extent a further unraveling of the processes within the model can help define areas of consensus and tension in integrating the 'green' and the 'brown' agendas (cf. McGranahan and Satterthwaite, 2000)

Resource Extraction Processes and Rural-Urban Interaction

Urban inhabitants draw on natural resources from the surrounding region in order to fulfil their demands for shelter, food, water, and material goods. These resources include water; timber and stone (building materials); fuel for transport, cooking, heating, and industrial production; and raw materials for the production of goods. The main type of rural-urban linkage in this area then is resource extraction. Resource extraction is often represented as a flow into a city, without indicating how organizational structures channel and distribute such flows. Natural water systems are channeled by the infrastructure provided by public or private water companies into sources of drinking water for the urban population. Forests are transformed by logging companies into timber for housing.

It is important to determine the extent to which firms and public utility companies recognize linkages between urban and rural areas other than resource extraction. This influences how much care they take to reduce pollution resulting from their activities and to stay within the ecological boundaries of the systems from which they extract resources, and how much effort they are willing to put into regenerating such systems. The example of logging companies extracting trees will do as an example. Do they raze whole areas to the ground for the type of trees they want, and then leave the area to recover without any inputs? Or do they replant the areas they have denuded, or perhaps extract carefully only the type of tree they want and leave the rest of the area relatively undisturbed?

Therefore a second rural-urban linkage to take into account is the way firms and utility companies organize their extraction activities. A major question is whether companies are willing to reduce the ecological impact of their production methods by introducing methods of cleaner production. These aspects include reduction of raw material use per unit of production, changing to the use of renewable resources, reducing waste and emissions, and providing help in regenerating the natural systems from which they draw resources.

The processes of extraction of resources and the interactions between urban and rural areas change when a city becomes larger and wealthier. When comparing cities at different levels of economic development, McGranahan found that the urban consumption of water, energy, fuel, and raw materials increased as inhabitants of cities became wealthier generally, although obviously differences remain as wealth is spread unevenly within the urban population (McGranahan *et al.*, 1996). The implications for resource flows are that cities will draw on increasingly wider geographical areas in order to satisfy the demand for resources. It may also imply a shift in the sources from which inputs are drawn. For example, small cities may draw on rivers for drinking water and water for industrial production. When such sources become polluted, groundwater sources may be used increasingly for such purposes, drawing on aquifers from increasingly larger distances from the urban area itself.

Similarly, the types of resources utilized can shift as cities grow wealthier; rather than using wood as a source of fuel, urban inhabitants may increasingly make use of fossil fuels for stoves. Rather than walking or using bicycles for transportation, urban inhabitants may make increasing use of motorized transportation, either public transport or private cars.

Environmental Impacts of Resource Use in the Urban–Rural Context

When we look at the environmental impact of resource use in urban areas, and its linkages to rural areas, we can again distinguish the three levels of analysis. The first concerns the type of environmental impact resource extraction has on the natural environment in the rural area of extraction itself. Sachs terms this impact the 'ecological rucksack', by which he means the damage done to the natural environment in the areas where resources are extracted – 'the mountainous slag heaps, kilometers of tunnels, and tons of churned-up earth' (Sachs *et al.*, 1998, p. 12). The natural environment is also impacted by the wastes generated as energy and materials are transformed into products, and the wastes produced by city inhabitants (solid wastes, wastewater, polluted air) as a result of their consumption patterns.

A second question concerns the way firms producing goods and utility organizations providing basic services allow the impact of their activities on both urban and rural environment to occur. This will vary according to the level of technology they utilize for production itself, and the extent to which it is used to reduce the use of inputs per unit of production, and limit the wastes generated. The extent to which ISO 14000 guidelines – which aim at reducing the pollution impact of production processes, and at working towards cleaner production processes on a continual basis – are used by companies (both those producing goods and those providing basic services) is an important method of determining levels of impact. In India, interestingly, urban planners working in the areas of solid waste management and water provision focus on reducing pollution effects, whereas researchers working on energy and transportation systems are already discussing the reduction of inputs as a necessary complementary process.

A third question concerns the governance surrounding the impact of pollution processes. The emphasis governments are currently putting on the privatization of services is changing the ways in which government can influence the provision of services. Although the debate on the extent to which governments should keep control of provision through setting standards and stipulations in contracts with private providers, the monitoring and control of proper provision is a fairly new role for many local governments. A second element in governance is the question what alliances or partnerships are developed with local populations. Local participatory planning processes (such as envisaged in Local Agenda 21 planning) offer the opportunity to draw in local residents and their concerns, as well as organizations for monitoring and control with their new agendas.

Preventing the negative ecological impacts of activities in cities is an area which requires more attention in terms of integration within local government policies. It also requires partnerships with regional and national actors, as the jurisdiction of local government may not extend far enough to develop effective prevention policies.

Changes over Time and Level of Development

As wealth increases, the environmental impacts created by a city's functioning tend to shift from direct health-threatening impacts (including water, air, and soil contamination in the direct living environment, caused by a lack of adequate drinking water provision, a lack of sanitation, and a lack of adequate waste management) within the city to long-term impacts generated over a wider geographical region. In general, it can be said that:

- The urban environmental impacts generated in poor cities are the direct health-threatening problems that are local in nature. Poor households in poor cities contribute very little to either the processes of resource extraction or discharges of wastes, effluents, or emissions.
- The most extreme examples of city and regional-level environmental stresses are found in and around middle-income mega-cities, and in the industrial cities of the formerly planned economies. This is the result of intensive industrial processes, coupled with few environmental controls, which creates a situation in which high levels of polluting wastes and emissions are directly discharged into the city and surrounding region.
- In high-income cities in the North, the impacts are characterized by being regional or global in nature, and health risks are indirect and a result of long-term cumulative exposure. The lifestyles of urban inhabitants demand high levels of resource extraction (including from long distances), and the emissions and effluents created cause the majority of the global environmental problems (McGranahan *et al.*, 1996).

The main reason for the changes in the ways the impact of pollution is experienced is the fact that, with increased wealth, cities can more easily transfer such impacts both temporally and spatially.

There are three basic ways in which environmental impacts can be transferred. They can be transferred: (1) to a higher geographical level of scale, (2) through time, drawing on the resources of future generations, and (3) from the individual to the collective level (NAR, 1993). Most visible and well known is the transfer of consequences to other spatial levels of scale. Transferring the consequences can almost become a policy, as is the case in developed countries where chimney heights are increased to ensure that the air pollution created will have its effects further away. In a similar way, hazardous waste from developed countries is shipped and transported to developing countries.

Transfer through time occurs when consequences are transferred to future generations, the often cited effect of 'compromising the needs of future generations'. Transfer over time is most often related to the over-exploitation of natural resources and supersession of the absorption capacity of the sinks.

Examples of the transfer from the individual to the collective level, where the sum of all individual rational actions leads to collective unacceptable consequences, are more difficult to identify. The discharge of a limited amount of wastewater into a river by one private enterprise might be environmentally sound; however, the sum of all discharges by all industries into the same river exceeds the self-cleaning capacity of the stream and leads to a decrease in water quality. These transfer effects are illustrated in Figure 16.2.

Governance and Impact of Resource Use in Urban-Rural Linkages

A third important linkage is the system of governance under which resource extraction takes place. Currently, three basic trends characterize changes in urban governance; decentralization, privatization, and an increased sharing of the planning process with other actors. This development is a result of the national and local Agenda 21 processes that are taking place in many countries.

The first two trends reduce the power of local authorities to regulate the extraction activities of private sector companies, and even of utilities when they are privatized. This makes it more difficult to encourage companies to adopt strategies for more ecologically sustainable production, particularly when extraction takes place in the rural areas outside urban jurisdiction.

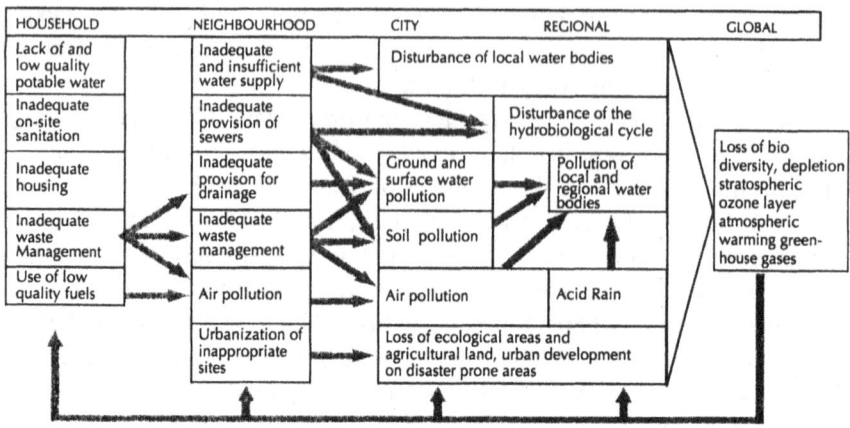

Source: Hordijk M.A. (1999)

Figure 16.2   Transfer mechanisms over different geographical scales

Cities may also be in more direct competition with each other when it comes to attracting new investments, and therefore may be reluctant to set high environmental standards for companies moving to their area (cf. Luz Velasquez, 1999).

With the process of decentralization, planning efforts are being increasingly concentrated at the level of the city. There are few mechanisms that challenge urban authorities to view the functioning of their city within its region as being outside their jurisdiction.[1] Generally, municipal boundaries are quite close to the built-up urban area. Since authorities have to serve their voters and do a good job within their jurisdiction, they tend to bother less about what is happening outside it. They are less concerned with the effects of extraction of water for urban use on the rural area from which it is drawn (upstream). They are also less concerned about what happens downstream, in terms of pollution from wastewater flowing out of the city. The fact that they can transfer the consequences over space and time, and that what happens in distant regions and for future generations is outside their legal responsibility, enables them to do a good job in the city in the short term.

---

1. This is why some countries – for example, Bolivia – define the boundaries of municipalities such that they include the municipality's hinterland. Bolivian municipal authorities therefore govern a region made up of urban and rural areas. But examples such as Bolivia are rare.

An increasing involvement of many different actors in the urban planning process – the third recent trend – can counterbalance the tendencies of local authorities and companies to limit their views on maintaining ecological sustainability in the extraction of resources, driven as they are by electoral and economic interests. The increasing strength of civil organizations in themselves (especially ecological movements, consumer organizations, and others), as well as the increasing importance given to processes of consultation, can broaden views over space and time. It does, however, depend on the kind of actors involved, and the kind of interests they represent. The involvement of different actors at least ensures more comprehensive planning. But residents' organizations may well focus on the short term and on immediate environmental impacts, rather than on the longer term. Representatives of community-based organizations are more likely to fight for pollution reduction than for a reduction of inputs. If environmental organizations are included in the consultative process, there is more chance that long-term and 'long-distance' interests will also be represented.

Good governance of natural resources in an eco-region as a whole may well require cooperation between municipal authorities, and greater cooperation with national government in setting new standards with which companies have to comply. In Peru, for example, more and more consultative bodies are being set up, comprising the mayors of various municipalities in a river basin who are trying to coordinate their activities. In India, the World Bank is encouraging municipal authorities to set up dumpsites for several towns jointly. But these kinds of initiatives are still in an infant stage, and have not yet led to concrete results. This suggests that although the outcomes of decentralization processes can be favorable for many other aspects of urban governance, they can have undesirable side effects for the transition to sustainability.

A similar argument can be made for the process of privatization. There is increasingly a tendency to hold companies accountable for the pollution their production generates. However, emphasizing the importance of reducing resource input is a far more recent phenomenon. The process of improved business performance in this wider understanding of the transition towards sustainability has just started. And for utility companies, so far few demands have been put on their environmental performance. For the time being, such companies are concentrating more on the quality of their service and on their financial viability, than on the environmental impacts over space and time.

Conclusion: Implications for Research

The points mentioned in this chapter lead to a few basic conclusions for future research. The first is that the different levels of analysis discussed above need to be further integrated into a common framework, which should include:

- An analysis of ecosystems and the extent to which they limit the environmental space humans can use to satisfy their basic needs. This means that in any analysis we must recognize the role of the natural environment in its own right within and around urban areas.
- Secondly, such an analysis should include the way in which natural resources are transformed into products used in human activities. For example, the way natural water sources are channeled through a public utility company into drinking water for urban inhabitants, or into water used in industrial production.
- Thirdly, it should include an analysis of the competing demands made on resources by different groups of urban and rural inhabitants, the conflicts concerning resource use, and the possibilities to reduce such conflicts.
- Finally, it should include an analysis of how more participatory styles of governance influence the direction of demand on resource use, the equitability of the resource use socially, spatially, and over time, and how partnerships can contribute to solving existing conflicts.

Such an analysis should be carried out through empirical studies on a number of basic urban services, such as water supply, energy use and transportation, sanitation, solid waste management, and building materials and housing. Such sectoral studies would provide the evidence for a further expansion of the framework proposed, which is at present an empty shell.

Which methodologies can assist in such an integrated framework of analysis? The most promising is that of lifecycle assessment. So far, this methodology has been most widely used for analyzing the environmental impact of the way companies produce their services and goods. In private companies, this way of thinking is already becoming more common in the form of ISO 14000 guidelines (see the website of the World Resource Institute – 1999 Conference). Lifecycle assessment (LCA) as applied in the framework of ISO 14000 is an environmental management tool that examines every stage of the lifecycle of a certain product, service, or activity 'from cradle to grave'. For each stage of the lifecycle – from the winning of raw materials, through manufacture, distribution, and use, to possible reuse/recycling and final disposal – the inputs (in terms of raw materials and energy) and the outputs (in terms of emissions to air, water, and as solid waste) are calculated. These are then converted into their environmental impacts. An LCA conducted within a framework of ISO 14000 also includes the identification of possible responses. It does not – and is not intended to – cover the social and political dynamics.

The objectives mentioned above imply that models of analysis should be based on a combination of analyses of natural resource flows (such as is used in LCA analysis) in combination with social, economic, and political analyses which are more inclusive of a number of dilemmas (the conflicts of the model presented), and recognize different levels of interaction. Such analyses should be carried out for the various resource flows going into cities, at the level of the specific sectors involved. These include water supply, energy and transport, production, and solid waste management, although this list is not exhaustive.

What we need is interdisciplinary research that – although starting from a sectoral point of view – manages to oversee the consequences from each factor in the system in the eco-region (city and hinterland) as a whole. For a sector such as that of water, this would mean a lifecycle assessment of extraction, use, and discharge of water from the ecological perspective combined with an analysis of economic, social, and management structures that induce this extraction-use-discharge process. Can we envisage a system of resource management that covers the three systems introduced in this chapter, i.e., natural environment, built environment, and human environment? Can we develop a framework of analysis that will enable us to identify the hidden dynamics in these systems, related to each of the 'sectoral issues' that shape the flows going into and leaving cities? Such a program of research will develop a better understanding of the various relationships posited in the model above, and how targets and strategies can be developed in order to achieve greater sustainability combined with equity of different types.

References

Bossel, H. (1999), *Indicators for Sustainable Development, Theory, Method and Applications*, IISD, Winnipeg.

Bhutani, S. and Mazumdar, M. (1998), 'Urban Environmental Legislation in India: A Macro Study', *Urban India: Special Issue on Urban Environment*, Vol. 18(2), pp. 19-48.

Environment and Urbanization (1999), Special Issue – Healthy Cities, Neighbourhoods and Homes, Vol. 11(1).

ESC Report (1994), *European Sustainable Cities, First Report* 1994, Sustainable Cities Project, EU Expert Group on the Urban Environment, Brussels.

Hardoy, J. and Satterthwaite, D. (1993), *Environmental Problems in Third World Cities*, Earthscan Publications, London.

Haughton, G. (1999), 'Environmental Justice and the Sustainable City', in D. Satterthwaite (ed.), *The Earthscan Reader in Sustainable Cities*, Earthscan Publications, London, pp. 62-80.

Jensen, M. (1998), 'Ecologists go to Town, Investigations in Baltimore and Phoenix Forge a New Ecology of Cities', *Science News*, Vol. 153, pp. 219-21.

McGranahan, G., and Satterthwaite, D. (2000), 'Environmental Health or Ecological Sustainability? Reconciling the Brown and Green Agendas in Urban Development', in C. Pugh, *Sustainable Cities in Developing Countries*, Earthscan Publications, London, pp. 73-90.

McGranahan, G., Songsore J., and Kjellen, M. (1996), 'Sustainability, Poverty and the Urban Environmental Transitions', in C. Pugh (ed.), *Sustainability, the Environment and Urbanization*, Earthscan Publications, London, pp. 103-34.

Mitlin, D. and Satterthwaite, D. (1996), 'Sustainable Development and Cities', in C. Pugh (ed.), *Sustainability, the Environment and Urbanization*, Earthscan Publications, London, pp. 23-61.

NAR (1993), *Milieu, een Mondiale Zorg. Naar een Politiek van Duurzame Ontwikkeling*, NAR, Den Haag.

OECD (1990), *Urban Environmental Policies for the 1990s*, Inception Report Sustainable Cities Project, OECD, Paris.

Opschoor, H. and Constanza, R. (1995), 'Environmental Performance Indicators, Environmental Space and the Preservation of Ecosystem Health', in J. Jaeger, A. Liberatore and K. Grundlach, *Global Environmental Change and Sustainable Development in Europe*, European Commission DG XII, Office for Publications of the EC, Luxembourg 1995, pp. 157-91.

O'Riordian, T. (1998), 'Civic Science and the Sustainability Transition', in D. Warburton (ed.), *Community and Sustainable Development; Participation in the Future*, Earthscan Publications, London, pp. 96-116.

O'Riordian, T. and Voisey, H. (1998), *The Transition to Sustainability: the Politics of Agenda 21 in Europe*, Earthscan Publications, London.

Rees, W. (1992), 'Ecological Footprints and Appropriated Carrying Capacities, What Environmental Economics Leaves Out', *Environment and Urbanization*, Vol. 4(2), pp. 121-130.

Sachs, W., Loske, R., Linz, M. (1998), *Greening the North, A Post-Industrial Blueprint for Ecology and Equity*, Zed Books. London.

UNCHS (1996), *An Urbanizing World: Global Report on Human Settlements 1996*, Oxford University Press, Oxford and New York.

Velasquez L. (1999), 'The Local Environmental Action Plan for Olivares Commune in Manizales', *Environment and Urbanization*, Vol. 11(2), pp. 41-50.

Website World Resource Institute: http://www.wri.org

17 Regional Development Planning in Latin America: Towards a More Sustainable Use of Space

ANNELIES ZOOMERS

Introduction

In Latin America, the need for regional development planning was widely accepted during the 1950s and the 1960s. Regional disparities had increased due to rapid urbanization and governments developed different kinds of regional policy in order to tackle the consequent problems – i.e., the rapid growth of primate cities and the congestion in metropolitan areas such as unemployment, housing problems and criminality – while simultaneously stimulating the economic growth of poor regions and increasing the level of territorial integration.

Common elements of regional policy – usually implemented by regional development agencies – were programs for industrial deconcentration, the improvement of infrastructure provision, and schemes for marginal or isolated areas (e.g., the agricultural colonization of the Amazon). Occasionally, governments even constructed new capital cities (e.g., Brasilia) and industrial growth centers (e.g., Ciudad Guyana in Venezuela). Reshaping the settlement system and creating a physically integrated hierarchy of places was expected to play a crucial role in the process of regional development. According to Rondinelli (1983, p. 197) 'Secondary cities can play important roles in balancing the distribution of the urban population and economic activities, in stimulating rural development and in generating a more socially and geographically equitable distribution of the benefits of urbanization, when secondary urban centers are economically strong and linked to each other and to larger and smaller settlements in their region' (see also DHV, 1985; Dusseldorp, 1971; Johnson, 1970; Mosher, 1969; Rondinelli and Ruddle, 1976). Reducing urban primacy and contributing to more equitable forms of regional development were considered important goals of regional planning.

However, regional planning programs were not very successful in this. Many of the programs were more rhetorical than real, and/or did not contribute to slowing the growth of major cities; nor were they successful in reducing regional disparities and/or encouraging growth in the poorest regions. In general, there was considerable disappointment regarding their performance (Gilbert 1997, p. 181).

From the 1980s onwards, structural adjustment programs encouraged most Latin American governments to cut back on state expenditure and reduce most forms of public intervention and national planning. The neo-liberal model recommended that governments should facilitate the private sector rather than perform activities themselves. Regional development agencies were closed and the budget for planning was reduced in favor of privatization policies and attempts to liberalize the market. The role of governments was to ensure that markets worked and that prices were not distorted. This was expected to contribute to sustainable or – at least to some extent – equitable economic development (Zoomers and Haar, 2000, p. 21). In this policy context, there was little room for ambitious regional schemes. 'Regional development planning was effectively dead' (Gilbert, 1993; Richardson, 1989 in Gilbert 1997, p. 181).

Ironically, the moment governments stopped planning, there was a dramatic shift in regional trends. Neo-liberal development programs went hand in hand with declining levels of metropolitan growth, urban primacy decreased and spatial development became more equitable. A number of intermediate cities began to expand rapidly, the economies of some poorer regions grew swiftly, foreign investors began to develop new resources (especially minerals), and internal migration slowed down. After years of ineffectual regional planning, some of the goals of regional development were achieved in the 1980s without any public intervention at all (Gilbert 1997, pp. 181-182; see also Valladares and Prats Coelho, 1993).

During the 1990s, the interest in regional planning further declined due to the introduction of new information and communication technology such as the Internet. In many respects, the meaning of distance in social and economic interaction has changed ('the death of distance'), and the old logic of space is no longer the same. According to Castells (1996, p. 380): 'Space and time, the material foundations of human experience, have been transformed, as the *space of flows* dominates the *space of places*. Actors in different localities are nowadays linked with different levels of scale, which may be globally connected but locally disconnected.' The relative importance of the city-region relationship has decreased with respect to the importance of the relationships which interlink various cities in different regions and countries. 'New activities concentrate in particular poles and that implies an increase of disparities between urban poles and their respective hinterlands. Regions and localities do not disappear, but become integrated into international networks that link up their most dynamic sectors' (Castells, 1996, p. 380). Established spatial metaphors – such as nation, region, and even global and local – are no longer sufficient (Bebbington, 2000).

The aim of this article is to make a conceptual update of the regional planning debate. Now that the logics of space have changed, it is necessary to shed some light on current spatial trends and to reassess the need for spatial intervention.

Given the goal of sustainable development – that is, 'Development that meets the needs of present generations without compromising the ability of future generations to meet their own needs' (WCED, 1987, pp.8 and 43) – it is striking that so little attention is given to the spatial dimension. The sustainable use of space – or spatial sustainability – is hardly on the policy agenda. In so far as attention is paid to current spatial trends, there is a tendency to emphasis that the old problems have been solved. The negative process of constantly increasing congestion and population concentration has stopped, regional disparities have declined, and people have become increasingly free in their locational behavior. The free operation of market forces and processes of institutional change, such as decentralization and participatory planning, are expected to help produce efficient space and more equitable patterns of development. The 'modern' pattern of dispersed urbanization and increased mobility, i.e., the death of distance, is usually described in positive terms. It is suggested that there is no need for further interventions.

In this article it will be argued, without going into empirical details, that current trends are not always in line with the goal of sustainable development, nor do they automatically contribute to efficient, equitable, or sustainable space. Whereas regional planning in the 1950s and 1960s was aimed at reducing urban primacy and regional disparities, i.e., at creating a physically integrated system of urban and rural centers, we are now faced with a new set of spatial problems, and these are often neglected in the development debate. Even though spatial disparities have declined, it is an oversimplification to assume that spatial matters are no longer relevant, or that the organization of space must be left to the operation of market forces. It will be shown that, now the logics of space have changed, there is a new need to put spatial matters on the policy agenda.

Assessing Current Spatial Trends

Regional development planning has rapidly lost ground since the beginning of the 1980s. Nowadays, it is usually seen as an unnecessary and superfluous activity. Rather than planning, free market operation is considered a more efficient way of producing a spatially desirable situation. The old hierarchy of places as the ideal distribution pattern for the provision of services etc. might still be applicable, but along with improved transport and communication, distance (or overcoming space) is less and less seen, in comparison to former times, as a bottleneck. From the moment urbanization became dispersed and mobility increased, regional planning agencies closed down and the goal of reducing regional disparities disappeared from the policy agenda.

However, an assessment of the spatial processes that have taken place since the 1980s shows that dispersed urbanization and increased mobility produce all kinds of spatial transformations which cannot be described only in old terms. An analysis of the current situation reveals that the following spatial trends are taking place.

The Blurring of the Rural-Urban Gap

Whereas in the 1950s and 1960s much attention was paid to reducing the urban-rural gap (expressed in terms of population density, income, service level, etc.), we now have to deal with the blurring of the rural-urban interface. During the final decades of the 20th century, rural-urban relationships underwent profound changes, whereby it became increasingly difficult to make a physical distinction on the basis of population or area characteristics. After a period of rapid rural-urban migration, during which rural populations settled permanently in cities, urban growth became increasingly locally-based, i.e., driven by natural growth. Since then, along with the current process of dispersed urbanization, there has been a growing tendency for people living in the hinterland of a city to become a commuter, that is, to visit the urban area on a regular basis. Increasing numbers of rural populations are now working in cities without changing their area of residence. In addition, within the rural area, the population is increasingly involved in urban-based activities (farming is no longer the principal source of income), and many urban dwellers are involved in urban agriculture, for example food production, often as a strategy for reducing risk and coping with a crisis situation. The rural population can no longer be characterized as a counter-group for urban groups, and vice versa. The blurring of the rural-urban sphere has important consequences for the reality of households' livelihoods, which often include both rural and urban elements (see also Bryceson, 2000; Reardon et al., 2001; Tacoli, 1998; Zoomers and Kleinpenning, 1996). Instead of having an interest in closing the rural-urban gap, people are inclined to live in the two worlds, using the rural-urban interface as a continuum.

The distinction between rural and urban is often difficult to make, especially in the peri-urban areas. The landscape usually is extremely diversified; land-use patterns are fragmented, chaotic, and constantly changing. In these areas, land markets are developing in a chaotic fashion (see also Iaquinta and Drescher, 2001), and land fragmentation and landlessness are increasing. A considerable proportion of all farmland belongs to non-farmers, some of whom are affluent urbanites who obtained the land by foreclosing on loans. Increasing land values have led them to look upon land as an attractive commodity for investment purposes (Zoomers and Haar, 2000, pp. 69-70).

More active land markets tend to accelerate processes of land fragmentation. Most sellers try to retain some of their land as a safety valve, rather than selling it all. Many vendors of land – who usually own several parcels located in different places – are inclined to sell their property piece by piece, because they get a better price than they would if they sold everything at once. As land fragmentation increases, a process which often goes hand in hand with individualization and privatization, the usual result is an increase in land prices. This is often followed by the gradual squeezing out of rural land use.

Arable farming and cattle ranching are increasingly replaced by urban plots and *quintas* (plots used for recreation). Within a wide radius of cities and in the immediate vicinity of important arterial roads, rural land is disappearing. Due to increasing land prices, rural dwellers are stimulated to sell their land. Given the price level, most farmers cannot buy back their land after they have sold it, forcing them to become urban or to re-establish themselves farther from the cities, in the more marginal areas. Due to the higher transport costs, this will finally have an adverse effect on their profitability, restricting the opportunities for agricultural development.

New Patterns of Mobility

During the 1950s and 1960s, population mobility was mainly seen as a reflection of spatial inequality (i.e., push pull-migration), but nowadays it is explained in terms of the newly acquired freedom of locational behavior. Improved transportation and communication, combined with the processes of economic restructuring, are held responsible for increased mobility; this is usually perceived as a positive rather than a negative development. Now that the mobility of the population has increased, and transport and communication have improved, the old hierarchy of places based on 'distance decay' is no longer considered the basic principle in the planning of services or infrastructure, or for the dissemination of innovations. Improved mobility is supposed to have 'killed' distances, and people have become mobile and flexible.

If one analyses the current situation in Latin America, however, it appears that in many situations distance has not 'died'. Processes of economic restructuring are making new spatial demands which are not fulfilled by the free operation of land markets; new mobility problems have appeared, requiring new types of interventions. Mobility patterns and the spatial distribution of roads do not coincide.

In many urban and peri-urban areas, the capacity of roads – many of which were planned in the 1950s and 1960s within the framework of regional plans – is no longer sufficient, given the new mobility patterns and traffic increase. In cities and their direct hinterland, roads are often congested, there are a large number of traffic accidents, and people are confronted with high costs, in terms of both money and travelling time. In practice, travelling and 'bridging space' is not as easy as is often suggested by those who speak of the death of distance.

Many areas in Latin America still lack all-weather roads. Even in those areas connected to more permanent roads, mobility is often hindered by floods and other extreme weather conditions. In many cases, the road network is constantly under repair. Little attention is paid in the current debate to the need to reconsider whether roads (or populations) need to be relocated as a means of preventing future disasters (for example in response to climate change) and avoiding the need to pay high repair costs.

The lack of coincidence between space and mobility is especially clear in border areas. International connections are usually difficult to make, even between countries within regional blocks, such as Mercosur (Brazil, Uruguay, Paraguay, and Argentina). The lack of connecting roads has direct implications for the comparative advantages and the competitiveness of countries, as well as for migration facility and the possibilities for migrants to maintain contact with their place of origin. Despite the rhetoric of 'spaces of flows', practice shows that mobility is not as smooth as one may expect.

Resettlement and Multilocational Space

Whereas the 1950s and 1960s were dominated by the problem of settlement (agricultural colonization, frontiers), today resettlement – or relocation – is an important aspect of spatial transformations. The old question of 'how to attach people to the land', has become 'how to deal with migrants and refugees'. Focusing on the current processes of relocation, we see that large groups of Latin Americans have been forced to move – or flee – in response to economic crisis, natural disasters, or conflict situations, leaving a vacuum in their area of origin.

While most of these groups resettled in nearby areas, others decided to cross international borders. Some did so with the intention to stay, while others did so on a temporary basis. Large numbers of Paraguayans and Bolivians decided to leave 'home' and now live in the *barrios* of Buenos Aires, and Peruvians, Mexicans, and Central Americans have now become residents of the United States. In many cases, neighborhoods are named after their villages of origin, as an attempt to maintain the old place-identity. Rural groups originating from the Andes now live and work – usually on a temporary basis – in Europe, Israel, and Japan (Cortes in Zoomers, 2001), and growing numbers of Koreans and Japanese have decided to come to Latin America.

Instead of being attached to one place, family networks are now based on a wide range of different localities. Their lives are highly interconnected via a global network. Places can no longer be seen as a portion of geographical space, and the romantic notion of place (stable, homogeneous place-based communities) is out of date. Along with increased mobility, the individual's attachment to particular places, and the degree of places linking events attitudes and places (homogeneous place-based communities, or organized sites on the basis of social relations, meanings, and collective memory) is becoming less and less common. It is important to recognize 'the open and porous boundaries of places as well as the myriad interlinkages and interdependencies among places' (Massey, 1997; Perose, 1993; Young 1990 in Johnston *et al.*, 2000, p. 583). According to Castells (1996, pp. 380-381) 'The dominant tendency is towards a horizon of networked, a-historical space of flows, aiming at imposing its logic over scattered, segmented places, increasingly unrelated to each other, less and less able to share cultural codes.' While some assume that globalization has homogenizing effects, reducing the particularity of places and increasing placelessness, others point to its uneven effects across the globe and the defensive reaction which seeks to maintain or recover place differences. According to Massey (in Johnston *et al.*, 2000, p. 586) 'the persistent identification of place with community is a mistaken romanticism. Any single location can be very different places to different types of people'. Due to globalization, the old notion of a sense of place can no longer be maintained.

The Need for Conceptual Change

Taking a fresh look at some of the concepts, we see that space can no longer be described in the old terms. Old disparities are no longer there, and concepts used in the 1950s and 1960s are no longer in line with the spatial problems of our time. There is a need to redefine the problem and to reformulate the concepts and instruments to deal with the new situation.

Starting with the rural-urban divide, it is no longer realistic to make a distinction between rural and urban as complementary categories. The two populations can no longer be characterized as separate, co-existing groups, because often they overlap. From the perspective of the population, the rural-urban gap is a continuum. By crossing the border, it is possible to get the better of two worlds. Rather than focusing on the differences (population density, income level, etc.), more attention should be paid to the flows of goods, capital, and people constantly crossing the border. Official statistics shed insufficient light on the significance of this mobile rural-urban population. In practice, large parts of the rural population registered in villages spend most of their time in the city. The population should therefore be expressed not only in number per location, but also in 'people months' (Zoomers, 1999, p. 84).

In addition, the concept of urbanization needs to be more precisely defined. Dispersed urbanization often occurs in the rural sphere – which is very different from previous processes of metropolitan growth. Rather than defining urbanization as 'the process of becoming urban' (i.e., the relative concentration of a territory's population in towns and cities (Johnston et al., 2000, p. 883), more attention should be paid to the context in which this is taking place (is it rural, peri-urban, or urban?), which will have important implications for changes in livelihood and/or landscape. There is no general category of 'urban dwellers', and a distinction should be made between the various subcategories.

In the literature, the peri-urban landscape is usually regarded as an intermediary stage between the rural and the urban. It is necessary, however, to perceive the peri-urban sphere as an autonomous space, and not as post-rural or pre-urban. It should not be perceived as an evolutionary or transitory stage that will develop into a urban landscape. Given the negative developments linked to peri-urbanization (fragmentation, social exclusion) efforts should be made to restrict further expansion and focus on consolidating the area as it is (and preventing further urbanization). Rather than continuing down the road of dispersed urbanization, more attention should be paid to consolidating the situation ('compact' cities), facilitating rural-urban livelihoods, but keeping mobility within acceptable limits. Controlled growth seems to provide better opportunities for the sustainable use of space than dispersed urbanization.

It is essential to acknowledge that space often performs different functions at the same time. For some groups, it is used as a territory (exclusive rights to land and/or resources); for others it is a place of residence, a historical site (cultural heritage, *fiestas*), or a possible location for tourism or relaxation. Because of this multifunctionality of space, it is not realistic to expect the price mechanism (or free land markets) to lead to optimal allocation.

It is striking that in the current debate so little attention is paid to the human side of ongoing spatial transformations. Dispersed urbanization and increased mobility – two important dimensions of spatial change – are usually described in neutral terms, as no attention is paid to the social implications. Rural people living in the hinterland of a growing city are often forced to cope with a rapidly changing situation (de-agrarianization, disappearing landscapes, etc.). Also improved mobility often has important – and sometimes dramatic – consequences for social life. Having more freedom in locational behavior means in practice the dispersion of family life (there are always people left behind); migrants, who often comprise the poorest segments of the population, see themselves forced to spend scarce resources (time and money) on travelling (distances are not dead for those who have to move); migrants run the risk of becoming ill, especially if they are not familiar with the new climate; and many migrants lead a rather risky life and lack the old security mechanisms of the home community.

Many migrants never manage to become a full member of their host society, even after spending a large part of their life in their new country. In times of economic crisis, many are forced to return 'home'; however, reintegration is often difficult because after so many years the place of origin is no longer the same.

Given the importance of multilocational livelihood, regions can no longer be defined as a closed or bounded space. People base their livelihood on a chain of places, involving various regions at the same time. The old-fashioned vertical man-place relationship (people's attachment to one place) is increasingly being replaced by horizontal relations (people's attachment to a combination of locations in transnational space).

Changes in the Institutional Landscape: the Need for Planning

Whereas regional planning in the 1950s and 1960s was aimed at reducing urban primacy and regional disparities, i.e., creating a physically integrated system of urban and rural centers, we are now faced with a new set of spatial problems: Decentralized urbanization – through the rapid expansion of the peri-urban zones – poses a threat to the landscape, and results in land fragmentation and the gradual squeezing out of rural land use. Insofar as population mobility has increased, there is often a mismatch with the infrastructure, and the implications are often not in line with the objectives of sustainable development. Finally, due to globalization (and the threat of cultural destruction and the homogenization of transnational space) the uniqueness of particular places and place-based identities are increasingly at risk.

Even though spatial disparities have declined, it is an oversimplification to assume that spatial matters are no longer relevant, or that the organization of space must be left to the operation of market forces. Now the logics of space have changed, there is a new need to put spatial matters on the policy agenda.

Since the end of regional planning in the 1980s, important changes have taken place in the institutional landscape. Whereas in previous times spatial development was mainly performed by the state (through planning agencies), it is now the domain of a broad range of actors, including the local population, municipal governments, the private sector, NGOs, the state, and international organizations.

Making an assessment of developments from the early 1980s (the withdrawal of the state, the end of regional planning), we see that in the course of time, old-fashioned top-down planning has been replaced by a modern version of participatory planning, often carried out in the framework of decentralization policy (local governments collaborating with NGOs and the private sector). Also the planning goals have changed. The old focus on regional growth or reducing regional disparities (i.e., spatial goals) has been replaced by the goal of 'sustainable development'; instead of aspiring to 'territorial integration', planners nowadays aim at environmental conservation and/or protecting indigenous groups or cultural sites; finally, along with the introduction of remote sensing and satellites, much more attention is currently given to monitoring global trends (climate change etc.) than in previous times. Analyzing these types of 'modern' planning in more detail, we see, however, that this is not always in line with the current needs.

Decentralized, Participatory Planning

Compared to top-down planning, decentralized, participatory planning is usually described as a positive development. Indeed, a decentralized participatory approach is desirable from the local point of view (giving priority to the projects supported by the local population), but will not always be able to solve the current set of spatial problems. Many of the current spatial trends need a solution at the supra-local level, requiring the intensive collaboration of various actors, and not only between local government, NGOs, and/or the population.

A decentralized, participatory approach will not necessarily be in line with regional – or spatial – needs (how to stop peri-urbanization; how to improve the match between infrastructure and mobility patterns), and may even worsen the situation by accelerating the process of spatial fragmentation. In a country like Bolivia, decentralization and popular participation have resulted in the implementation of local plans (improvement of the *plaza*, or construction of a school and local roads), reflecting little consideration for relationships between communities, especially if relationships transcend municipal boundaries. Resources are assigned according to the number of inhabitants in a community, with little attention paid to the fact that nowadays a substantial portion of the rural population resides in other places (usually cities, but also abroad) for a few months each year.

Decentralized, participatory planning often results in the fragmentation of space, also because of the role of NGOs, who often have their own projects which are not always carried out in close coordination with local government. Coordination with other NGOs is usually rather weak. NGOs usually have their 'own' areas of intervention, and will often be inclined to concentrate their efforts in villages that can be reached easily, have good market access, a relatively good infrastructure (electricity, water), and a concentrated population. In more isolated areas, where the infrastructure is poor and the population dispersed, considerably fewer development interventions are in progress. For development organizations, concentrated activity areas are advantageous. They reduce operational costs (e.g., for transport) and provide opportunities to take such local aspects as culture into account. In a strictly defined area, results can be achieved more quickly and efficiently, especially in the relatively large and easily accessible villages where the infrastructure is good. This suggests that development organizations are inclined to choose their areas of intervention on the basis of the likelihood of success rather than on the need for intervention.

Protective Planning

Since the 1980s, along with the end of regional planning, new forms of territorial planning have come into existence. One example is the creation of *reservas indígenas* (indigenous reserves) which provide indigenous groups with land rights in their own territories (ILO Convention 169, 1989). The ILO Convention, which has been given the status of national law in many Latin American countries, facilitated the protection of 'the total environment of the areas which the peoples occupy or otherwise use' (Art. 13-2); this included 'safeguarding the rights of peoples concerned to use lands not exclusively occupied by them but to which they have traditionally had access for their subsistence and traditional activities' (Art. 14-1). In the framework of this mode of territorial planning, some 100 million hectares were set aside for indigenous peoples of the Amazon region between 1960 and 1996 (Roldan, 1996 in Assies, 2000, p. 98), often supported by international NGOs.

A second example of such reserve-model planning consists of the creation and management of national parks and biosphere reserves, as a response to increasing international concern over environmental issues (Agenda 21 etc.) and the greening of the development agenda. These reserves are aimed at the sustainable exploitation of forest areas, providing a solution to the problem of deforestation and conservation of biodiversity. In Costa Rica, where efforts to create parks began as early as 1969, protected areas, national parks, and biological reserves now constitute more than 12 per cent of the country and over 27 per cent of the land is protected. Other examples of regions where much attention has been paid to the goal of environmental protection and the conservation of the biological diversity are the Amazon (mainly Brazil, but also Ecuador, Bolivia and Peru), Central America, and Mexico (see Herrera and Garcia, 1995; Kyle and Cunha, 1992; Richards, 1996; Schabel, 1997 in Zoomers and Haar, 2000, p. 312).

Finally, a third example of protective planning is related to UNESCO's World Heritage Sites. Ninety-six sites in Latin America and the Caribbean are on the list and thus receive special protection. Most of these sites (45) are in Mexico, Brazil, or Peru; others (28) are located in Argentina, Bolivia, Cuba, Colombia, and Ecuador. The other 23 sites are dispersed over 12 countries, i.e., Chile, Paraguay, Uruguay, Venezuela, and other countries in Central America. Of the protected sites, 42 per cent are protected due to their quality as a historical and/or archaeological site (cave art, fossils, sculptured rocks), 32 per cent are historical cities (or cities with historical centers or architectural value, including Jesuit ruins), and 26 per cent are protected for their natural beauty, biodiversity, and/or wildlife (forest reserves, glacial lakes, mountains, wetlands, etc.). Sixty percent of the sites were put on the list in the period 1980-1994, and 40 per cent in the period 1995-2001 (World Heritage Centre, 2001).

Terrestrial Monitoring and Mapping

Thanks to new technology (geographical information systems, remote sensing/satellite images, agrometerological technologies, etc.) there is increased interest in analyzing spatial trends, focusing in particular on urbanization, land cover change, desertification, climate change, etc.

Since the 1990s, many organizations (FAO, UNEP, etc.) have invested increasing amounts of funds in long-term terrestrial monitoring and research activities. Many of these projects aim at collecting information on land cover/land use, while mapping/classifying and monitoring global trends; in addition, efforts are being made to provide a standardized approach to describing and classifying trends, and to homogenize definitions, statistics, and data material. According to the FAO, 'There is an increasing need to be able to precisely describe and classify land cover and uses in order to define sustainable land use systems that are best suited for each place. Land needs to be better matched to its uses to increase production, while at the same time attempting to protect the environment, biodiversity, and global climate systems. It is therefore essential to have detailed and in-depth knowledge of potentials and limitations of the present uses. This information is considered necessary for many aspects of land use planning and policy development; it is also a prerequisite for monitoring, modeling and environmental change, and as a basis for land use statistics at all levels' (FAO, 1999).

The lack of a global agreement on the definition and classification of both land use and land cover is increasingly regarded as a bottleneck: There are many classification systems and innumerable map legends, and maps and statistics from different countries (and in many cases, even from the same country) are incompatible. 'Technological advances, such as the vast amount of remote sensing data having become available from earth observation satellites, make it increasingly possible to map, evaluate and monitor land cover and land use over wide areas' (FAO, 1999).

According to a recent evaluation of space-related activities (FAO, 1999), implementation has been rather slow: 'Whereas progress of land cover mapping is well underway, little progress has been made so far on land use data collection. A serious consolidated effort is needed to collect this type of information in parallel with ongoing efforts on land cover. (...) Creation of such a system would enable national and local planning of sustainable land use. Awareness should be created internationally and nationally that one cannot attempt to effectively protect the environment, biodiversity and global climate systems if one of the key elements of information to do so is unavailable.'

In conclusion, the current spatial problems (fragmentation, mobility problems and social exclusion, disappearing landscapes) will not be solved by present planning efforts. Decentralization and the elaboration of participatory plans will not result in improved levels of territorial integration, but rather stimulate the further fragmentation of space. The territorial mode of planning (*reservas* etc.) might benefit those directly affected, but have negative consequences for those groups not included. Examples of excluded groups are poor farmers who are no longer entitled to make use of resources (now part of the reserve) and – in the case of World Heritage Sites – Peruvian traders who were evicted from the historical center of Lima (see Seppänen, 2001). This 'planning for protection' often develops into new conflict situations, which cannot be solved by local and/or participatory planning.

The tendency to monitor and visualize spatial trends might in the long run facilitate the planning process by providing a basis for the implementation of early-warning systems (prevention of natural disasters) and the reassessment of space (establishing the best location for roads or houses, given the risk of floods, hurricanes). There is a danger, however, that spatial planning will increasingly be seen as a technical matter and the world as a globally uniform space. However, to achieve a more sustainable use of space, it is not sufficient to focus on the technical aspects. It is important to focus more closely on the human face of space, i.e., people's attachments to place and territories should be taken as an important starting point for future planning.

Conclusion

The aim of this article is not to continue the old discussion about the usefulness, or uselessness, of regional planning as a strategy for sustainable development, but to make an update of the debate on the basis of current (i.e., post-1980s) spatial trends, and to reflect on the desirability of giving more priority to the spatial aspects of sustainable development.

Dispersed urbanization and increased mobility are too easily mentioned as positive spatial trends, and as a motive for nullifying the need for regional planning. However, practice shows that dispersed urbanization and the rapid expansion of the peri-urban sphere also have a problematic side, which often is not mentioned in the current debate and will not be solved by the free operation of market forces. Current trends will increasingly result in land fragmentation, the squeezing out of rural land use, and social exclusion (especially in peri-urban areas); increased mobility is not only a 'spatial matter', but might have negative implications for family life; increased traveling and/or migration means additional costs (time, money), extra risks (accidents, illness), and often results in the disruption of social life. Current spatial trends are not in line with sustainable development, and current planning efforts – which emphasize participatory planning, protection, monitoring – will not steer spatial trends in the right direction; they might even worsen the situation, by accelerating processes of spatial fragmentation.

Future planning efforts should aim at a more sustainable use of space; rather than accepting 'dispersed urbanization', planners should analyze to what extent preference should be given to the development of *compact* cities, giving priority to controlling urban growth, streamlining rural-urban linkages, and removing the spatial bottlenecks with respect to transport and communications. In addition, instead of accepting 'increased mobility' as a common element of modern life, it is necessary assess to what extent people give preference to a 'locally-based life' (lower costs, less risks).

Whereas regional planning in the 1950s and 1960s was aimed at reducing urban primacy and regional disparities, we are now faced with a new set of spatial problems which are often neglected in the development debate. Even though spatial disparities have declined, it is an oversimplification to assume that spatial matters are no longer relevant, or that the organization of space must be left to the operation of market forces. Current trends are not always in line with the goal of sustainable development, nor do they automatically contribute to efficient, equitable, or sustainable space. The logics of space have changed, and thus there is a new need to put spatial matters on the policy agenda.

References

Assies, W. (2000), 'Land, Territories, and Indigenous Peoples' Rights', in Annelies Zoomers and Gemma van der Haar (eds), *Current land policy in Latin America, Regulating land tenure under neoliberalism*, KIT publishers and Iberoamericana/Vervuert Verlag, Amsterdam/Frankfurt, pp. 93-110.

Bebbington, A. (2000), 'Re-encountering Development: Livelihood Transition and Place Transformation in the Andes', *Annals of the Association of American Geographers*, Vol. 90(3), pp. 495-520.

Bryceson, D. (2000), 'Peasant Theories and Peasant Policies: Past and Present', in Bryceson, D. Kay, C. and Mooij, J. (eds), *Disappearing Peasantries? Rural Labour in Africa, Asia and Latin America*, Intermediate Technology Publications, London, pp. 1-36.

Castells, M. (1996), 'The Rise of the Network Society', *The Information Age: Economy, Society and Culture*, Vol. 1, Blackwell Publishers, Massachusetts/Oxford.

DHV (1985), 'Theoretical Considerations', *Aspects of Rural Centre Planning*, Vol. 1, DHV studies 11, Amersfoort.

Dusseldorp, D. van (1971), *Planning Service Centers in Rural Areas of Developing Countries*, International Institute for Land Reclamation and Improvement, Wageningen.

Gilbert, A. (1997), 'Poverty, Regional Convergence and Development: What Kind of Relationship?', in G.M. Hilhorst. Bert Helmsing and João Guimaraes (eds), *Locality, State and Development. Essays in honour of Jos*, Institute of Social Studies, The Hague, pp. 181-204.

Herrera, A. and Garcia, G. (1995), *La Reserva de la Biosfera Sierra del Rosario*, Cuba, Working papers South-South Cooperation Programme on Environmentally Sound Development in the Humid Tropics (UNESCO), No. 10.

Iaquinta, D. and Drescher, A. (2001), *Defining the Peri-Urban: Rural-Urban Linkages and Institutional Connections* (www.fao.org/DOCREP).

Johnson, E.A.J. (1970), *The Organization of Space in Developing Countries*, MA: Harvard University Press, Cambridge.

Johnston, R.J., D. Gregory, G. Pratt and M. Watts (eds) (2000), *The Dictionary of Human Geography*, 4th edition, Blackwell Publishers, Massachusetts/Oxford.

Kyle, S. and Cunha, A. (1992) 'National Factor Markets and the Macroeconomic Context for Environmental Destruction in the Brazilian Amazon', *Development and Change*, Vol. 23(1), pp. 7-33.

Mosher, C. (1969), *Creating a Progressive Rural Structure*, MA: Harvard University Press, Cambridge.

Reardon, T., Berdegué, J. and Escobar, G. (2001), 'Rural Nonfarm Employment and Incomes in Latin America: Overview and Policy Implications', *World Development*, Vol. 29(3), pp. 395-409.

Richards, M. (1996), 'Protected Areas, People and Incentives in the Search for Sustainable Forest Conservation in Honduras', *Environmental Conservation*, Vol. 23(3), pp. 207-17.

Rondinelli, D. and Ruddle, K. (1976), *Urban Functions in Rural Development: an Analysis of Integrated Spatial Development Policy*, Washington, USAID.

Rondinelli, D. (1983), *Secondary Cities in Developing Countries: Policies for Diffusing Urbanization*, Sage, London/Beverly Hills.

Schabel, H. (1997), 'Integrating a Research Station into Community Development and Area Protection in Nicaragua', *Journal of Sustainable Forestry*, Vol. 4(3-4), pp. 127-38.

Tacoli, C (1998), 'Rural-Urban Linkages and Sustainable Rural Livelihoods', in Diana Carney (ed.), *Sustainable Rural Livelihoods: What Contribution Can We Make?*, Department for International Development, Overseas Development Institute, London, pp. 67-82.

Seppänen, M. (2001), *Rescaling a World Heritage Site: Lettered City and Colonial Arcadia in the Historic Centre of Lima*. A paper to be presented at 'space and place in development geography, August 30-31, University of Utrecht, the Netherlands.

FAO (1999), *Space Related Activities of FAO* (www.fao.org/sd/eidirect/eire0076.htm).

Valladares, L. and Prats Coelho, M. (1993), 'Urban Research in Latin America. Towards a Research Agenda', *Urban Research in Latin America* – Discussion paper series, No. 4, UNESCO (www.unesco.org/most/valleng.htm).

WCED (1987), *Our Common Future*, World Commission on Environment and Development, Oxford University Press, Oxford.

World Heritage Centre (2001), *Brief Descriptions of the Sites on the World Heritage List* (www.unesco.or/whc/brief.htm).

Zoomers, A. and Kleinpenning, J. (1996), 'Livelihood and Urban-rural Relations in Central Paraguay', *TESG*, Vol. 87(2), pp. 161-74.

Zoomers, A. (1999), *Linking Livelihood to Development. Experiences from the Bolivian Andes*, KIT publishers, Amsterdam.

Zoomers, A. and G. van der Haar (eds) (2000), *Current Land Policy in Latin America. Regulating Land Tenure under Neoliberalism*, KIT publishers and Iberoamericana/Vervuert Verlag, Amsterdam/Frankfurt.

Zoomers, A. (ed.) (2001), *Land and Sustainable Livelihood in Latin America*, KIT publishers and Iberoamericana/Vervuert Verlag, Amsterdam/Frankfurt.

PART IV

Urban Poverty Reduction: Mapping the Policy Arena

18 Urban Poverty Reduction Options at Local Level in a Globalizing World[1]

EMIEL WEGELIN

Urbanisation, Poverty and Environmental Degradation

At the start of the new millennium, the world saw the dawn of the urban age. For the first time, the majority of the population of the world will be urban. Although this shift has been taking place over many thousands of years, the last century saw a dramatic increase in the rate and pace of urbanization. This is not only through the growth of mega-cities, but increasingly through the growth in size and number of smaller settlements past the urban threshold. Global urbanization is expected to continue; by 2025, two-thirds of the world's population will live in urban areas, implying average urban population growth rates of about 5 per cent per annum. The bulk of this urban growth will be in developing countries – the developed part of the world is already highly urbanized. Most of urbanization in absolute terms will be in Asia, which today already holds over 40 per cent of the world's urban population. This is expected to reach some 60 per cent by 2025.

The situation, of course, varies a lot from place to place, but clearly, along with the global trends of an urbanising population, poverty is being urbanised, as well. Within a few decades, the number of households living in poverty in urban centres will far exceed those in rural areas: currently 50 per cent percent of the world's poor live in cities. With urban growth as noted above, this will only get worse. The World Bank estimates that the number of urban poor will almost treble from 650 million today (1999) to 1,500 million by the year 2025 (World Bank 2000a).

Infrastructure and services deficiencies, and environmental degradation have also urbanized. The speed of the changes has stretched the capacity of governments, local governments in particular, to keep up as far as urban

---

1. This paper draws heavily on Mumtaz and Wegelin, 2001, and Vanderschueren et al., 1996.

infrastructure and municipal services provision is concerned. At least 600 million people, most of them poor, already live in health- and life-threatening situations in decaying urban environments. A third of city dwellers live in substandard housing. At least 250 million urban residents have no ready access to safe, piped water, and 400 million do not have adequate sanitation, according to the World Bank. Without an appropriate response, rapid urban population growth is likely to exacerbate the often mutually reinforcing effects of poverty and environmental damage.

Globalization and Localization

Since the late 1980s, several important factors – the end of the Cold War, global technological change related to information and communication technology, and trends towards economic liberalization – have heightened concerns about global and regional interdependence. Many governments have correctly perceived the opportunities for growth in a globalizing economic environment. They have taken measures to liberalize their economies, while being fully aware of the uncertainties and risks of operating in a global competitive environment. At the same time, national governments allow, or are forced to accept, greater decentralization in a situation of growing urbanization: globalization is combined with localization.[2]

As a result, large cities today increasingly compete at global and regional levels for direct international investment. This requires national governments to take a second look at their urban development strategies to find ways to support their cities as economic hubs and to exploit their comparative advantages. Often, this occurs in conjunction with cities or regions in neighboring countries.

These trends are beginning to redefine national urban strategies with regard to the traditional concerns of growth and equity. As globalization continues, the space for national policies diminishes. Increasingly, national governments are moving towards providing an enabling and supportive environment for cities to compete on local policies.

This implies a larger role for local/municipal government, and new roles and responsibilities at that level. City governments find themselves suddenly having to deal with the economic development of their local jurisdiction vis-

---

2. These twin trends as labelled in the World Bank's 1999/2000 World Development Report comprise the progressive integration of the world's economies on the one hand, and decentralisation and urbanisation on the other.

à-vis the international community, while at the same time having to shoulder additional responsibilities for social policies, which before were the exclusive responsibility of national governments. Regulatory and financial arrangements were not geared towards this. Given the serious capacity constraints generally prevailing at local levels, local authorities are shouldering them in partnership with other actors – the private sector, NGO groups, community representatives, and other agencies of government.

Options for Urban Poverty Reduction at Local Level

Though the reduction and elimination of poverty is of major concern for national governments as well as international and bilateral assistance agencies, it has only recently been seen as having an urgent urban management dimension. The increasing demographic shift to an urbanized population will also mean an increase in the number of urban poor, and that urban rather than rural poverty will become of greater overall significance. The nature of urban poverty is less well understood and actions for its reduction less well tested. Studies of social exclusion, coping mechanisms, vulnerability, and notions of urban sustainability are only now beginning to be converted into policy (see e.g Chambers, 1995; Kabeer, 2000; Moser, 1998). This section focuses on how action at the local level, as part of urban management, can have an effective impact on poverty reduction both through direct action and by tackling the impact and consequences of poverty.

A large, and often major, part of the earnings of urban households goes, after food, towards accessing municipal services, land, and shelter. Any reduction in the costs of accessing these has a direct bearing on the amount of disposable income available to an urban household, and therefore has an obvious impact on poverty.

Definitions of poverty vary (see e.g., Wratten, 1995; UNDP, 1999; World Bank, 2000b), but the various measures of absolute and relative poverty indicate the extent of the problem faced worldwide. Obviously, poverty is more than a lack of income or employment. Poverty includes perceptions of deprivation, at different levels, both personally and as group. New definitions of poverty also include access to and exclusion from a variety of social and physical services, and the extent to which social capital is available.

Poverty reduction programs have tended to be carried out at two levels. At the macro level, such programs concern policy and program interventions defined and implemented by central government, and include investment, subsidy, pricing, and credit. At the local level, they concern activities, which involve working directly with community groups in supporting a variety of activities (e.g., credit, basic infrastructure and slum upgrading, micro-enterprise development, and strengthening community participation). Traditionally the first has been more targeted by the international agencies and development banks working with national governments, while the second has been promoted and supported more by NGOs and CBOs working with donor agencies.

Given globalization and localization trends, there is an urgent need to address poverty issues at a third, intermediate level, that of the municipalities. These can translate national policies and programs into local action, and lend support to the activities of local and community-level actions and activities, as well as support to the informal sector. Local government has the opportunity to act in specific areas, which can systematically reduce poverty, in the short and long-term. Measures could include improving access to housing and basic urban services through land tenure, housing, housing finance, and area upgrading schemes. For local governments to undertake poverty reduction does not necessarily require a change in mandate or power, nor necessarily additional funding, as the examples of possible action given below illustrate. Particularly if a participatory approach is used in partnership with local communities and NGOs, existing resources can be efficiently deployed to undertake poverty reduction measures.[3]

However, local government action may be made difficult or constrained by financial and/or political dependence on central government, a lack of clarity of functions and responsibilities, or lack of a coherent policy in this area. Possible changes in the responsibilities of local government and the authority to act as a financial intermediary would require intensive dialogues with central government.

International agencies such UNDP, UNCHS (Habitat), the World Bank, regional development banks, and bilateral support agencies increasingly share the above perspective and have begun supporting poverty reduction activities at the local level (see e.g., Asian Development Bank, 1999, and World Bank, 2000a).

The reduction, alleviation, and elimination of poverty must also be of concern to urban management, because the extent and level of poverty directly affects its operational viability. On the one hand, the existence of large numbers of poor or widespread poverty reduces the number and

---

3. For a range of city-specific experiences along these lines see: *Environment and Urbanisation*, vol. 7 no. 2 1995: Urban poverty II: from Understanding to Action, and *Environment & Urbanisation*, vol. 11 no. 2: Poverty Reduction and Urban Governance, 2000.

proportion of households that are able and willing to pay for urban goods and services, thereby reducing the city's income and income-generating possibilities. On the other, since municipalities and local governments are increasingly obliged to meet the essential and basic shelter and service needs of the poorer households, and if these have to be provided for free or at low or subsidized rates, there is a strain on the budgetary capabilities of local governments, reducing their ability to be active and effective in other areas.

Employment, Credit and the Informal Sector

The extent and impact of poverty on urban populations, as well as on urban and national economies, would be much greater were it not for the informal sector. Variously described as unregulated, largely self-employed and small-scale activities, this previously 'hidden' or 'unrecognized' part of the economy often provides a source of employment for as much as 60 per cent of the urban population, and may well serve the needs of an equally high proportion of citizens through the provision of goods and services. Numerous studies in a variety of contexts have established that the informal sector is better integrated with and recognized by the formal sector than its dichotomous title would suggest. It has been shown that it is far more buoyant and elastic in absorbing an increasing urban labor force and providing employment than the formal sector. It has a number of other advantages over the formal sector. Due to its small-scale of operations and low levels of capitalization, it not only provides employment at a far lower cost per job, but also requires fewer skills and/or less training. Coupled with a lack of regulation and controls, the relative ease of entry enables it to absorb newcomers to the labor force and rural-urban migrants. In particular, when local economies are affected by the impact of structural adjustment or that of the global economy, the informal sector provides the main 'safety net' for those made redundant or unemployed. The relative growth of the informal sector during the recent Asian crisis is a case in point.

However, the informal sector has its limitations. The low productivity found within the sector means that the income and earning levels are often lower than in the formal sector. The very nature of the sector makes earnings both more erratic and intermittent. The irregular and often illegal nature of many of its activities make them subject to official harassment or persecution, as well as prone to Mafia-style protection rackets. The unregulated nature of the sector makes it difficult, and perhaps impossible, to obtain access to credit or other facilities necessary for increasing earnings or moving up or out of the sector. And the informal nature of many of the activities makes it difficult to protect those who are engaged in them, whether as paid workers or as unpaid family members. One much-publicized example is that of child labor, where the 'rights of the child' may be in direct conflict with the survival strategies of the family.

Within the informal sector, there are also a range of opportunities and earning possibilities. For many, entering the informal sector during periods of general economic decline or crisis is likely to be a coping mechanism, part of a survival strategy, or as a last resort. For women this is most likely to focus on domestic and other service employment, while for men this means self-employment. Households are also likely to aim at increasing the number of those engaged in income-earning activities rather than being engaged in non-waged activities or at school. The influx of greater numbers into the informal sector reduces their earnings capacity, and many may find themselves severely underemployed.

What can urban managers do to work towards lessening the negative impact while creating opportunities for poverty reduction and elimination? The key to poverty reduction and eradication lies in productive employment and income generation. While little headway can be made without sustained, broad-based economic growth at the national level, and a flexible and well-trained labor force, the process can be aided by supply-side inputs such as access to credit, information, and markets.

Options for Action
Once a local government or municipality is ready, willing, and able to develop and implement poverty eradication programs, the following options should be considered:
Opportunities for employment generation through municipal works
In a number of countries (e.g., Pakistan, Egypt, Colombia, Jamaica, and Sri Lanka), programs of community-based small-scale public works and contracts have been successfully implemented. Some cities have made the relative employment generated an explicit criteria for assessing and evaluating all bids for municipal tenders and contracts. The participation of women (especially as managers, supervisors, store-keepers, etc.) should not be overlooked and their general participation and involvement should be encouraged.
Regulatory support to informal sector activities
Local government must recognize the contribution the informal sector makes to employment and income generation, and should remove regulatory impediments limiting the opportunities for informal sector operators (e.g., hawkers, traders, waste recyclers) to enhance the economics of their activities. Municipalities may monitor the operation of land-use and zoning regulations and infrastructure provision to support and facilitate marketing, manufacturing, and employment generation activities.

Establishment of credit for small-scale and micro-enterprises
Credit for small-scale and micro-enterprises should be established, preferably through providing funds for on-lending to NGOs or CBOs, or by providing guarantees for them to financial institutions, rather than embarking upon a municipal banking operation. Biases against women either as borrowers or as entrepreneurs should be actively removed.
Mitigating the impact of economic shocks
Emergency credit facilities (small, very short-term loans available on a fast-track basis, triggered) should be made available to reduce the vulnerability of low-income households and businesses to economic shocks and fluctuations in market conditions.
Provision of marketing advice and information support
Credit schemes and facilities should be linked to marketing, market intelligence, information, and advice centers. Assistance and advice should be made available on business networking and exchange of information amongst micro-enterprises, as well as vertically with other up- and down-stream enterprises. This would facilitate in-business support, as well as encourage enterprises to move up the value-adding ladder, perhaps through joint, collaborative, or cooperative actions and initiatives. Local government may also assist in the formation of 'chambers of micro-commerce', through which it can have a direct channel of communications and feedback for its activities and support to employment generation and poverty eradication programs.
Provision of training and capacity building support
Vocational and other practical training and skills development and capacity building courses and opportunities should be provided. These should particularly focus on and encourage the participation of women, incorporating child-care, crèche facilities, and other such provisions without which their participation is severely constrained.
Provision of security of land tenure
Providing security of tenure for 'owner-occupiers' in illegal settlements greatly increases the value of their assets and their ability to access credit. It also reduces the risks of eviction, thereby encouraging investment in plant and equipment, particularly that associated with manufacturing or assembly. Provision of titles or security of tenure to women, rather than men, often has a greater multiplier impact on improvements and income generation.

Access to Urban Services and Land

The poor, like other urban dwellers, need access to municipal services, as such services directly influence their living conditions and health status. As housing has a vital role to play in the survival strategies of the poor, the provision of well-serviced housing with secure land tenure fulfils that role much more effectively than inadequate housing lacking a clear land title and devoid of water supply and reasonable sanitary conditions (Vanderschueren et al., 1996).

The poor essentially face the problem of limited access to all municipal services: Even if poor (informal) neighborhoods are not excluded from municipal services delivery on account of their perceived illegality, they are usually not the first to receive road upgrading, water supply, sewerage, drainage, or municipal solid waste collection. Women (or girls) bear the brunt of such inadequacies in water supply, sanitation, drainage, and garbage collection, and often fail to get their needs and priorities recognized in community dialogue.

Such exclusion is exacerbated by the near-universal tendency to set design and service standards (and capital costs) at levels unaffordable by the city (limiting expansion of service networks) and by the poor. A related factor further limiting access by the poor is the fact that municipal infrastructure and services are often not designed to allow for incremental upgrading as poor communities improve their habitat and their incomes and affordability to pay for services increase. As a consequence, subsidies for municipal infrastructure and services, often do not reach the urban poor, but are preempted by middle and higher income groups served by the system. Often, effective community level organizations have been established for neighborhood services provision and management in poor areas in many cities. However, these community initiatives are often not recognized and effectively linked into municipal delivery networks, thus reducing the provision effectiveness of the entire system, and adversely affecting cost-recovery potential.

Some specific issues germane to various elements of municipal services delivery are discussed below on a sector by sector basis.

Water Supply Issues: Disparity in Access

Invariably there is a disparity in access to public sector supply facilities between different income groups in urban areas. The poor tend to have less access and poorer quality of water. In many cities, the per capita water supply to the poorer sections of the population is much below the recommended minimum. Thus, formal water supply is generally subsidized in a non-discriminating or insufficiently discriminating manner, effectively resulting in not only a disparity in water supply coverage, but also in the accrual of the benefits of the subsidy.

For services which can be individualized and for which a price can be charged (water supply, solid waste collection, public transport), inadequate and subsidized municipal/public supply to poor neighborhoods is usually substituted for by informal sector supply – in the case of water supply mostly through brokers and vendors, often drawing on the same bulk water supply sources as the public supply system. Private sector drinking water is usually provided at prices the low-income market can bear. In having to rely on such mechanisms, the poor usually end up paying more per unit for comparable services, or for services of lower quality than the better-off, who have access to the subsidized public system.[4]

Water supply: Options for action
Market approach to water supply provision
In designing municipal water supply systems, it is important that the starting point is a well-designed market survey of demand for water by all segments of the population to be served, including the urban poor, who, as indicated above, have often much higher ability and willingness to pay than is assumed by water agencies (viz. amounts actually paid per unit consumed).
Low-income households sometimes share a water meter if they live in an apartment building or compound they share with others. Households without connections often obtain their water from public systems indirectly, purchasing it either from neighbors who do have connections or from water vendors.
The practice of reselling publicly supplied water, rather than being prohibited, should be legalized and encouraged, as it will not only enhance the water supply agency's net revenues (both through higher sales, as well as reductions in administrative and technically unaccounted for water), but also will tend to drive down water vendors' prices (reducing the extent of rent-seeking).
Incorporate community participation in system design
A high level of community participation in the planning, implementation, and subsequent management (operation and maintenance as well as collection of charges) of small water supply systems, or the tertiary distribution end of large systems, will ensure that supply will be better targeted at community demands and also safeguard operation and maintenance of the network. Such participation should involve training at the community level as well as of the local water agency's staff.
Introduction of community and shared standpipes
Provision of specific central and/or local government subsidies for the installation of water supply networks incorporating publicly accessible taps (community or shared standpipes), without such subsidies adversely affecting the financial results of the water agency (which would provide a disincentive to the agency to provide them). It is important to promote community management of such standpipes, including the encouragement of water sale at remunerative levels for the operators, which would reduce vendors' rent-seeking.

Sanitation and solid waste management issues

The disparity between lower and upper income groups in terms of sanitation facilities is significantly higher than in the case of water. Latrine facilities are more common in the higher income brackets, as are flush latrines connected to the sewerage system. Where sewerage systems exist, these are often managed and maintained by the municipality and a nominal user charge is levied on households. Again, subsidized sanitation facilities are often available to relatively well-off sections of the population. These not only have the privilege of latrine facilities but also their exclusive use. The pattern for poor households is just the opposite, with shared facilities being common.

The urban poor can more easily develop their own neighborhood solutions to sanitation deficiencies than to water deficiencies.[5] This may be through individual household arrangements (such as the conventional hiring of sweepers for both solid and human waste disposal, as is common throughout the south Asian subcontinent, and through the implementation of on-plot low-cost sanitation solutions such as soak-pits) or on a neighborhood or community basis (communal toilets, shallow lane sewers and collective community solid waste collection arrangements, often on a lane basis).

Often there is little public recognition of existing community activities in waste collection and recycling, and of the economic functions these activities have for the poor. In consequence, desirable support for and the linking of

---

4. Differentials in the cost of water in selected cities (ratio of price charged by water vendors to prices charged by the public utility):

City	Price ratio
Abidjan	5:1
Dhaka	12:1 to 25:1
Istanbul	10:1
Kampala	4:1 to 9:1
Karachi	28:1 to 83:1
Lagos	4:1 to 10:1
Lima	17:1
Lome	7:1 to 10:1
Nairobi	7:1 to 11:1
Port-au-Price	17:1 to 100:1
Surabaya	20:1 to 60:1
Tegucigalpa	16:1 to 34:1

Source: World Bank, World Development report 1988

5. Unless there are abundant shallow well resources available, centrally provided bulk water supply is unavoidable.

such 'informal' activities with the formal municipal waste collection and disposal system are rather rare.

Waste management: Options for action
Separate focus of municipal and community responsibilities
The local government must recognize the distinction between public provision and community provision. In doing so it must devote its scarce resources to focusing direct public provision only on sewage treatment, the trunk sewer system, and main collector lines, and on disposal sites and main routes in the solid waste collection system. The neighborhood level of sewage and solid waste disposal can be dealt with by community-based solutions such as those mentioned above; municipal regulations and practices should stimulate such solutions rather than prohibit them or consider them second rate.
Promote municipal-community cooperation
The local government must actively promote municipal-NGO/CBO cooperation at the interface of public and community based disposal and recycling elements. This is critical considering that the majority of the poor live in informal and unserviced areas, and that a significant number of the urban poor derive their income from such community based disposal and recycling activities.

Public Health and Primary Health Care Issues

Primary health care, comprising both preventive measures (health education, environmental health awareness and immunization campaigns) and curative facilities at neighborhood level, though often a statutory municipal function, has not generally been well integrated with other municipal services. Primary health care also has generally not adequately been targeted at or adapted to urban poor neighborhoods.

As a result, the urban poor lack access. This is partly because in some countries primary health care is seen as an extension of the rural-oriented national health care system, rather than as an element of municipal services. Although local governments almost universally are responsible for the maintenance of public health within their jurisdictions, this is usually narrowly interpreted as a responsibility for cleanliness of streets, abattoirs and public markets. Hence, where this applies, primary health care often is dispensed under the auspices of the ministry of health, rather than by the municipalities.

As in the case of other municipal services, provision of primary health care has also been hampered by the conflict between provision standards and financial constraints, effectively further limiting access by the poor.

Primary health care: Options for action
Provision of primary health care to low-income neighborhoods
Municipalities need to stimulate the provision of appropriate primary health care, particularly targeted at low-income (slum) neighborhoods. This may take the form of direct provision of such services (clinics, doctors, nurses, primary health care workers and training them, medicines, and information materials) by the municipality or supporting and directing/redirecting the efforts of others, including provision of services by the health department, private commercial entities, and NGOS/CBOS. Training of local health volunteers may also be particularly beneficial.
Set more modest, appropriate standards
Provision standards should be modest, with a strong emphasis on training community residents to provide preventive measures, including environmental health awareness/information campaigns in conjunction with the provision of sanitation services (such campaigns have proven particularly effective in conjunction with solid waste collection services).
Integrate primary health care with other neighborhood infrastructure provision
As much as possible, primary health care should be integrated with the provision of neighborhood infrastructure affecting public health (water supply, sanitation, including solid waste disposal, roads and footpaths, drainage, and flood prevention) in slum areas. Effectively this would mean that primary health care would become a regular element of slum upgrading.

Primary Education and Vocational Training Issues

Literacy and vocational training are two basic factors enabling poor children to be well prepared to enter the primary labor market. Primary education plays a crucial role in the social and economic integration of children into a city or a nation. In addition, the level of education of girls not only contributes to their employment potential, but also constitutes an important variable in better preparation for bringing up children and for spacing births. The experience of the last decade indicates that the percentage of drop-out or illiterate youngsters originating from low income families is increasing in some countries. Where this is the case, this is largely caused by affordability problems, sometimes exacerbated by a decrease in the quality of primary education.

In many countries, the responsibility for primary education and vocational training is split between central/provincial governments, municipal government, the private sector, and voluntary agencies. This is often a result of history rather than a conscious policy decision. As a result, low-income areas are usually under-endowed with primary education facilities, teachers, and training materials.

The lack of public investment in the development or maintenance of schools in poor areas limits the coverage and quality of primary education. Where this is compensated for by private/NGO activities, such schools often suffer from similar quality deficiencies and from lack of government recognition. The lack of qualified teachers – aggravated by the shift from teaching to other more profitable activities or private sector schools for well-off families – further reduces the quality of primary education. This further contributes to enlarging the gap between social classes.

Vocational schools have limited outreach due to lack of resources to buy appropriate equipment, and many children from poor urban families have no option but to get their technical background from the poor technical environment of the micro-enterprises.

Education: Options for action
Target primary school provision and supply
Municipal investment in education should target primary schools and the quality of teachers, equipment, and environment, as these areas of concern generally fall at least in part within the orbit of statutory municipal responsibilities. As much as possible, primary education should be integrated with the provision of other services such as health services or neighborhood infrastructure in slums.
Offset indirect costs of school attendance
Local government could provide additional incentives to encourage children in poor neighborhoods to attend school, such as the provision of breakfast at school (many children go to school without having eaten) and subsidies for school uniforms and basic school materials (pens, pencils, notebooks, books; some materials from better-endowed schools could be recycled).
Encourage parents' participation in education management
The municipality could encourage participation of parents in the support of or management of primary schools. Some primary schools built by residents with the support of the municipality or the private sector have become cultural centers or meeting places for the families. The municipality could also encourage more effective control of school attendance (basically an important social control) as a way of reinforcing parental responsibilities.
Support adult and youth literacy campaigns and programs

The municipality could promote short courses for illiterate children and/or adults, to be organized by NGOs, CBOs, and religious structures and organizations. Home-based schools for girls should be developed by NGOs and CBOs with municipal support and encouragement in those socio-cultural environments in which the formal education system does not reach girls from poor families.
Support private and community ventures
Local government could promote and encourage the private (formal and informal) sector to provide vocational training. Impediments to recognition of private/CBO/home (primary) schools should be removed, so that such schools will have access to regular government support for curriculum development and teaching materials and that their pupils can transfer credits to formal government schools.

Urban Transportation Issues

Availability of public (formal and informal) transport is of significant importance in the survival strategies of the urban poor. Availability of transport has an important bearing on the question of access to employment and markets. In many cities in the developing world, public transport systems are poorly developed and therefore need to be complemented by private operators, some of whom are not officially registered. Municipalities have the power to issue (sometimes in conjunction with central government) operating permits and road/routing licenses, and to impose operating conditions.

Access to employment and markets are often a problem for the urban poor, because they typically live in informal, unplanned areas relatively far away from job opportunities, which are often poorly serviced by roads. The costs of both formal and informal public transport are often prohibitive to the urban poor (particularly in African cities), confining their transport options to walking long distances in search of income opportunities. This has become particularly acute in countries facing economic recession. It has also led to restrictions on mobility and a premium on proximity: Social and economic activities tend to be restricted to those parts of the neighborhood within walking distance.

Municipalities (and central governments) usually lack resources to develop mass transport systems to adequately service urban areas. Prevalent public transport systems are often highly inefficient. Where such systems are subsidized, the subsidies more often than not accrue to the middle class rather than to the poor, who often do not have easy access to the transport routes.

In some cities municipalities impose severe restrictions on the operations of private operators of minibuses and non-motorized informal means of public transport (becaks, rickshaws), which the poor can afford, and which are able to service poor neighborhoods effectively.

Urban transport: Options for action
Make better use of existing instruments
The authorities in charge of transport, including municipalities, have a number of instruments at their disposal to direct public transport supply and to manage the coexistence of various forms of public transport. Such instruments could be used in developing a coherent urban public transport strategy, as e.g., demonstrated in the well-known example of Curitiba in Brazil:
Physical organization and design of street furniture, including roads design, layout of bus stops, location of transfer stations;
Technical control of roadworthiness of vehicles;
Terms and conditions of operating licenses, including mandatory routings and rates to be charged;
Terms and conditions for financing the purchase of vehicles;
Acknowledgement of professional organizations of owners, drivers, and driver assistants;
Dissemination of information on user demand, supply, and transport safety.
Incorporate and support the informal sector
In most cities in the developing world, it has been recognized that the role of private informal transport operators is crucial in the provision of public transport services to the cities. In Africa, most municipalities now facilitate the operation of such informal transport systems, although there are often problems regulating such operators. Municipalities could facilitate the development of effective formal and informal public transport systems in order to maximize access by urban residents including the poor.
Encourage competition between public and private sectors
Local government may influence the effective functioning of public transport systems, by encouraging healthy competition between the public and private sectors, while still retaining a measure of control over route coverage and fees charged through the judicious application of terms and conditions of operating licenses. Municipalities should encourage the private sector to be efficient and remove unnecessary harassment and penalties for operators. The local authority may also negotiate inter-modal or interline arrangements to reduce the rates of a specific trip.
Support non-formal modes

Local government should support non-formal modes of transport wherever possible, and create appropriate infrastructure for bicycling and other non-motorized forms of transport. Non-motorized transport, such as bicycles, should be considered as forming part and parcel of a long-term urban transport solution, and therefore investments should be oriented towards this way of transport. Walking is the main way of transport for the urban poor, suggesting significant investments in walkways and rearrangements of public space in favor of pedestrians. Specific types of short-distance popular transport (e.g., rickshaws, becak, motoconchos) could be encouraged and regulated after negotiations between users, operators (drivers and owners), and the municipality, both in the interest of providing safe, cheap, and convenient public transport for short distances, and in the interest of creating low-income employment. Safety should be ensured by enforcing traffic rules, as well as by checking the level of maintenance and source of pollution of public transport vehicles.
Introduce and use traffic management measures more effectively
Local government can take a host of traffic management measures to eliminate traffic jams and encourage the utilization of bus transport instead of private cars, such as the designation of reserved routes for buses or public transport, regulation of parking places, implementing toll roads in some areas, operation of traffic lights control from public buses, and the modification of labor timetables. The benefits of these measures should be transferred to the users and particularly to poor users.

Other Major Infrastructure Provision Issues

For other municipal services and infrastructure, such as roads, drainage, and flood protection, a similar lack of access by the poor and problems of standards apply. These are often more serious than for water and sanitation, public health care, and urban transport, because the absence of the direct cost-recovery option in principle precludes the possibility that such services can be provided in a free-standing, financially sustainable way. Instead, provision levels depend on the limited financial and institutional capability of local governments or specialized delivery agencies, such as development authorities, public works departments of higher levels of government, and on the priority such provision enjoys among these agencies' other development spending options.

Particularly for drainage and flood control, the urban poor in a sense face a 'double whammy':
- these non-revenue yielding types of urban infrastructure are generally relatively underprovided in the overall priority-setting for urban infrastructure, as compared to water and sanitation, public health care, and urban transport (i.e. all segments of the urban population have generally lower access to adequate drainage and flood protection than to the provision of drinking water and sanitation services);

- as the poor (particularly in coastal cities) are typically housed in relatively flood-prone areas, the lack of adequate protection makes them much more vulnerable to floods than the middle class population of the city.

Neighborhood Infrastructure and Land Tenure in Slum Areas

The upgrading of slum areas is one of the prongs of the enabling approach to improving the environmental conditions of the urban poor. In many countries, municipalities have been the lead agencies in implementing such schemes. Slum upgrading programs have generally comprised neighborhood infrastructure upgrading (generally including the provision and/or upgrading of walkways, micro-drainage, neighborhood water supply distribution, solid waste collection, and sometimes communal sanitation), often complemented by legalization of land tenure, and sometimes dovetailed with a home improvement loan and/or small business development loan scheme.

However, upgrading slum/squatter areas is a highly politicized activity and requires active mobilization of communities and sensitization regarding the long-term sustainability issues. Often, upgrading is carried out as an ad-hoc and short-term project activity, and therefore does not address the real problems of supply of and demand for shelter and services.

The upgrading of slum areas tends to concentrate purely on physical upgrading and often fails to address social and economic issues. In many slum areas, the poor suffer a multiplicity of problems that cannot be addressed simply through providing infrastructure. So there is a need for a more comprehensive approach to upgrading, including social (particularly primary health care and education) and economic services. Yet where this has been attempted, additional complications have often arisen. For instance, where small business development loans provision is included in the upgrading program, there is often a coordination problem between the agencies involved (usually the municipality and one or more financial institutions). Similarly, where programs have included explicit measures to legalize land tenure, the complexity of managing this alongside services and infrastructure tends to multiply (particularly where such land titling is intended to directly contribute to cost recovery of infrastructure investments).

There is an apparent incongruence between the need for cost-recovery and the need to keep solutions affordable for the urban poor. Programs which do not have a land tenure regularization component have generally relied on indirect cost-recovery through local (mainly land/property) taxation, or have accepted that neighborhood infrastructure is a part of the wider urban infrastructure network and their associated financing problems, and that therefore cost-recovery in the narrow context of slum upgrading is not appropriate.

Slum improvement: Options for action
Municipalities must take the lead in slum upgrading schemes
The overwhelming evidence is that slum upgrading schemes have led to a moderate acceleration of the normal, organic process of low-income settlement formation and consolidation, including the provision of neighborhood infrastructure. It is important to view upgrading as an ongoing process facilitating employment and income generating opportunities. In doing so, increased cooperation with neighborhood associations and other CBOs and NGOs will be necessary in making such schemes more demand-oriented and cost-effective. Infrastructure investment priority setting and financing of investments and O&M would be done through shared responsibility with the community, rather than for the community.
Municipalities must ensure adequate security of land tenure
Security of tenure is essential in order to avoid the eviction / displacement of low-income residents and to safeguard the sustainability of the physical investment both in households' shelter and in infrastructure. Without such security, residents are unlikely to participate in or make their own investments in upgrading. Municipalities need to enhance the intrinsic cost-effectiveness of such schemes by ensuring that such neighborhood schemes are adequately linked to major trunk infrastructure.

New Insights and Challenges: Assets/Vulnerability and Social Exclusion/Integration

Over the last few years, a large proportion of the global development effort has gone into the eradication of poverty. As part of this effort, a number of studies have been carried out to define poverty (see above for some references). These studies helped move the debate very quickly away from notions of poverty that were based on a particular level of income, suggesting that income could not be held to be such a rigid indicator. The use of income as an indicator of poverty was replaced by relating poverty to a basket of goods and services that could be purchased at a particular location, and those who could not afford the minimum required for an acceptable level of existence were identified as the poor. Other studies tried to develop indicators and to measure poverty amongst different groups of households. In particular the prevalence of poverty amongst disadvantaged groups and the impact of poverty on particular groups was studied. Amongst these groups were women and women-headed households, who were shown to be doubly affected, by restrictions based on their gender roles and position, and by their low levels of income.

Increasingly, scholars are concluding that poverty is both more extensive and more difficult to define and eradicate. This is not just because of notions of relative poverty that would still leave the current poor less able to afford the acceptable levels of goods and services since the acceptable level itself was subjective and subject to change. Yet without an acceptable, working definition of poverty, it is not possible to assess who needs assisting, nor can suitable responses be designed that would reach the poor. Being able to identify the poor would also help to identify and study the strategies that the poor themselves use to overcome or minimize the impact of poverty. These could then be built upon to develop viable anti-poverty and poverty-eradication policy measures.

Studies carried out for the Urban Management Program (Moser, et al.,1996), and those based on them (Moser, 1996), are suggesting that instead of defining and measuring poverty, a better understanding can be gained through the concept of vulnerability. Unlike poverty, vulnerability is a dynamic concept recognizing that people move in and out of poverty. According to Moser (1998, p. 3) 'vulnerability refers to the insecurity and sensitivity in well-being of individuals, households and communities in the face of a changing environment, and implicit in this, their responsiveness and resilience to external shocks and stress.' Vulnerability better captures the sense of threat and the pressures felt and experienced by particular groups. Without access to an adequate store of assets, households find it difficult to survive. These assets are more than just financial assets and include individual (labor and human capital), household (housing and housing relations) as well as community (networks, infrastructure) assets that can be built up and accumulated and that are needed to fend off vulnerability.

The vulnerability of particular households within society is often greater if they belong to a particular disadvantaged caste, ethnic group, or occupation, or if they do not conform to the 'norms' of that society, as in the case of women-headed households, pavement dwellers, or street children. Community assets available to other households are often denied to these groups, leading to their isolation and exclusion. Such social exclusion, or the pressures of vulnerability, may in turn lead to the disintegration of the household, the group and even of society.

Many of those socially excluded are not amongst the poorest, but because of the way these groups are viewed by society, they are unable to avail themselves of the facilities and measures that may be in place for poverty alleviation. Similarly, it is not that all those who are poor are vulnerable, nor are all those who are vulnerable also poor. Vulnerability is as much a matter of perception as of reality.

Ironically, municipalities often embark on campaigns to 'clean up' the city, removing pavement dwellings and street children from the streets. Such actions also destroy many of the very networks and social structures that support and sustain these groups. While such action increases vulnerability, pushing these groups out of sight does nothing to solve the problem, but makes it even more difficult to locate and target. It is therefore necessary that local policies are embarked on that:

- increase awareness of the assets and vulnerability of the urban poor,
- recognise their coping mechanisms as legitimate responses and support these,
- recognise the adverse impact of social exclusion on *all* segments of urban society and promote social inclusion of excluded groups by ensuring non-discriminatory access to municipal infrastructure and services.

Social integration: Options for action
Develop information and awareness, and initiate dialogue
The municipality needs to be engaged in a constant process of information and intelligence gathering in order to improve its understanding of vulnerability and social exclusion so that it can take appropriate action. The municipality should act in concert with social and religious organizations and activists to overcome prejudices and behavior that isolates and discriminates against particular groups and initiate and endorse policies and programs of reintegration. The municipality should engage in dialogue with the vulnerable and the socially excluded to develop participatory programs of support and action. It should assist the formation of groups and associations of the poor and the vulnerable. Such groups should be encouraged and assisted to form associations in order to strengthen their ability to act collectively, thereby reducing their vulnerability and lessening their exclusion.
Improve access to markets, shelter, and urban services
As noted in the sections above, the impact of poverty can be considerably lessened through the actions of the municipality in the provision of access to land, shelter, and urban services. Additionally, the municipality should work towards eliminating legal and social conventions and constraints which hamper women and other socially disadvantaged groups in their attempts to enter the labor market, or to gain access to land, shelter, and urban services. For example, regulations preventing home-based enterprises on the ground of environmental pollution should be modified and/or flexibly interpreted, so as to enhance families' (and particularly women's) assets and income opportunities. Wherever possible, policies and measures should support and strengthen peoples' efforts, complementing rather than replacing them. Priority should be given to long-term sustainable strategies in preference to short-term handouts and compensatory measures.

Participation
Inclusion of all stakeholders, particularly disadvantaged groups, in decision-making processes regarding public investments at local level will enhance the quality of the outcome of such processes, and as such increase assets, reduce vulnerability and exclusion. The municipality needs to make special efforts to include representatives of vulnerable groups in these processes explicitly as a matter of policy.

Conclusion: the Local Government's Path to Urban Poverty Reduction

Continuing global urbanization in the 21st century will take place in a radically different environment from urbanization in the 20th century. The end of the Cold War, combined with major advances in information and communication technology, has opened up unprecedented opportunities for economic growth and development. The other side of the coin is localization: The combined forces of continuing urbanization and decentralization.

While these trends provide enormous opportunities, they also contain some risks, both globally and locally. Without new forms of global governance, the global economy will be subject to potential high volatility, as was vividly demonstrated by the Asian crisis in the late 1990s.

Additionally, and perhaps more pertinent to the poor – who in the 21st century will be predominantly *urban* poor – the burden of poverty reduction will have to be carried largely by local governments, which are often ill-prepared to deal with this challenge.

Yet, even within the conventional remit of local government, there are a large number of actions that can be undertaken by local government to reduce urban poverty, as demonstrated above under the following main headings:
- Employment, credit and the informal sector;
- Access to urban services and land, and;
- Assets/vulnerability and social exclusion/integration.

While all these are possible actions, they are not foregone conclusions. Often local government officials do not perceive that they should and can take positive action along the lines suggested, and in any event, local governments cannot handle them on their own. To implement such actions, local governments need to forge partnerships with community and private sector stakeholders, as well as work in dialogue with other agencies of government.

Additionally, the above-suggested action should be seen as a generic menu: What will be the highest priority actions on that menu obviously differs greatly from city to city and over time. To set such priorities in a sensible manner is not easy, but various participatory approaches to do so have been developed during the last decade (see e.g., Mumtaz and Wegelin, 2001, Chapter 5).

Clearly there is a need for a major effort in building the capacity of local governments and of the other above-mentioned stakeholders in living up to the task. This implies training of local government staff and their partners, as well as institutional support to strengthen the local government units concerned. This particularly applies to the consideration of assets of vulnerable groups and to the need to take compensatory inclusive action vis-a-vis excluded groups, as this often requires a radical change in mindset of the staff concerned.

Local government capacity building support by the international community is perhaps a more important type of investment than financing physical infrastructure. It is gratifying to see that governments and international development institutions are increasingly redirecting their efforts along those lines.

References

Asian Development Bank (1999), *Urban Sector Strategy*, July, Manila.

Chambers, R (1995), Poverty and Livelihoods: whose reality counts? *Environment and Urbanization*, Vol. 7 (1), pp. 173-204.

Kabeer, N. (2000), Social Exclusion, Poverty and Discrimination, towards an analytical framework, *IDS Bulletin*, Vol. 31 (4), pp. 83-97.

Moser, C. (1996), *Confronting Crisis: A Comparative Study of Household Responses to Poverty and Vulnerability in Four Urban Poor Communities*, ESD Studies and Monographs, International Bank for Reconstruction and Development, Washington.

Moser, C. et al. (1996), *Household Responses to Poverty and Vulnerability*, Vol. 1-4, UMP Policy Papers 21-24.

Moser, C. (1998), 'The Asset Vulnerability Framework: Reassessing Urban Poverty Reduction Strategies', *World Development*, Vol. 26(1), pp. 1-19.

Mumtaz, B. and Wegelin, E. (2001), *Guiding Cities – The Urban Management Program*, UNDP, June, New York.

UNCHS (1996), *An Urbanizing World. Global Report on Human Settlements*, UNCHS, Nairobi.

UNDP (1999), *Human Development Report 1999*, UNDP, New York.

Vanderschueren, F., Wegelin, E. and Wekwete, K. (1996), *Policy Program Options for Urban Poverty Reduction: a framework for action at the municipal level*, UNDP/UNCHS/World Bank – Urban Management Program policy framework paper No. 20, 1996.

World Bank (1988), *World Development Report*, International Bank for Reconstruction and Development, Washington.

World Bank (1999), *Entering the 21st Century, World Development Report* 1999/2000, International Bank for Reconstruction and Development, Washington.

World Bank (2000a), *Cities in Transition – a Strategic View of Urban and Local Government Issues*, March, International Bank for Reconstruction and Development, Washington.

World Bank (2000b), *Attacking Poverty, World Development Report* 2000/2001, International Bank for Reconstruction and Development, Washington.

Wratten, E. (1995), 'Conceptualizing Urban Poverty', *Environment and Urbanization*, Vol. 7(1), pp. 11-36.

19 Reducing Urban Poverty: Constraints on the Effectiveness of Aid Agencies and Development Banks and some Suggestions for Change[1]

DAVID SATTERTHWAITE

The Gap Between What is Needed and What is Done

There is a large gap between what is needed within low- and middle-income countries to reduce urban poverty and what the aid agencies and development banks who are meant to support this can do. At the core of this gap is the limited capacity of most international agencies to support local initiatives and institutions that respond to the needs and priorities of the urban poor to support the organizations they have formed, and to have some measure of accountability to them

Official aid agencies and development banks do not implement projects; they fund others to do so.[2] Their publications give the impression that they are implementing projects. Many list all the projects they fund in their

---

1. This paper is reprinted from *Environment and Urbanization*, Vol. 13 (1), pp. 137-157. It draws primarily on the research undertaken by IIEDs Human Settlements Programme on aid and human settlements (which Jorge E Hardoy initiated in 1978) in which the author has been involved and on the research he undertook for his PhD thesis *The Constraints on Aid and Development Assistance Agencies Giving A High Priority to Basic Needs* (London School of Economics, 1998).
2. This paper's primary focus is on 'official' development assistance agencies and not on the international non-government aid agencies, many of whom do implement projects and have a higher proportion of their staff based in low- and middle-income nations. The official development assistance agencies include the bilateral agencies of governments (most of them from high-income nations) and the multilateral development banks (for instance the World Bank, the Inter-American Development Bank and the African and Asian Development Banks).

annual reports. But very few actually implement projects, since it is not the staff of these agencies who dig ditches to allow water pipes and sewers to be installed or who build and staff health care clinics. Their staff do not work with urban poor groups and their organizations to discuss what support they need. They provide funds to other institutions to do this. They are only as effective as the institutions they fund – i.e., as effective as their local partners. The scope and potential success of any international agency's urban projects are thus dependent on the quality and capacity of their local implementors.

For official aid agencies and development banks, their 'local implementor' is generally government ministries or agencies. The whole international aid/development assistance structure was set up on the assumption that capital made available to the national governments of low- or middle-income nations, accompanied by the 'best' technical advice, would deliver 'development'. Official development assistance agencies were never set up to respond to the needs and priorities of poor communities. They were set up to provide 'recipient' governments with large capital sums (as grants or loans) and professional advice. The limitations of this concept of the role of development assistance quickly became apparent as most recipient governments were unable to be effective implementors or had other priorities.[3]

The limitations in this conventional international agency-national government relationship have long been recognized: the debates about the failure of aid to reach poorer groups and to support social development go back at least to the late 1960s. The promotion by many international agencies of a higher priority to 'basic needs' in the 1970s or the promotion of more attention to 'human development' in the 1990s were both attempts to persuade recipient governments and international agencies to give a higher priority to reducing poverty. But it has proved very difficult to change the institutional structure of development assistance agencies in response to this. It is also difficult politically for the official aid agency of a government from a high-income nation to steer aid to other local 'implementors' without the approval of the recipient government. This is even more so for the multilateral agencies; after all, the large multilateral agencies are partly owned by recipient governments (even if they do not have much voting power within the boards of the development banks).[4]

---

3. There are also many other factors which have inhibited the effectiveness of most international development assistance agencies, including political and economic objectives which they have been obliged to pursue by those who fund or control them which have little to do with the needs and priorities of low-income groups.

For the development banks and bilateral agencies that provide loans, it is the national government that has to guarantee loan repayments. This conditions virtually all the funding provided by the large multilateral funding agencies such as the World Bank and the regional banks, the Inter-American, African, Asian and Caribbean Development Banks. The same is true for the large loan-providing bilateral agencies such as the Japan Bank for International Cooperation (into which the former Overseas Economic Cooperation Fund was incorporated in 1999) or the German government's KfW (Kreditanstalt für Wiederaufbau).

Most official bilateral agencies have long steered part of their funding through non-governmental or extra-governmental channels, for instance, through international NGOs (who, in turn, often work with local NGOs) or, to a much lesser extent, direct to local NGOs. But most recipient governments seek to limit the extent of such funding. No national government in Africa, Asia or Latin America will sanction increasing funding flows to institutions over which they have little control, or approve of external agencies steering funding to citizen groups or NGOs that do not support them, or even oppose them. Even where external funding is intended for other government bodies – especially city and municipal governments – national governments are inevitably loath to lose control over which cities and which sectors receive funding, or to have international donors fund municipal authorities governed by opposition parties – for nations with democratically elected national and city governments. There are also obvious questions of sovereignty. However much one would like to see official development assistance agencies fund urban poor groups directly, for nations with democratically elected governments, there are difficult issues around whether this undermines representative government structures. This issue can be particularly problematic within city governments as local politicians who have been elected can justifiably claim to have the mandate to determine local priorities (Melo et al, 2001).[5] Yet many elected politicians do not support urban poverty reduction programmes, or they only support them in top-down clientelist ways that undermine effective, representative community-based organizations.

---

4. Example, in 1999, for the International Development Association, the arm of the World Bank Group that gives concessional loans (i.e., loans with a sufficient grant element for them to qualify as aid), 62 per cent of the votes were held by 'Part 1' members who are, in effect, governments of the high-income nations. The US had 15 per cent of the votes, Japan 10.7 per cent, Germany 7 per cent, the UK 5 per cent, France 4.3 per cent, Canada 3.1 per cent and Italy 3.0 per cent (World Bank (1999), *Annual Report* 1999, Washington DC).
5. See also chapter 10.

Most development assistance agencies cannot choose to work only with the national or local governments that are democratic and relatively effective. The success rate for international development assistance to urban areas over the last 40 years would have been greatly enhanced if this had only been provided to nations with competent, representative urban authorities. But there are not many nations where such conditions exist (although there are certainly many more such cities now in the nations where decentralization and democratization have supported the development of more effective and accountable city authorities). In addition, funding only such governments would have meant denying funding to many of the nations with the weakest economies and highest levels of poverty. Many bilateral agencies choose to focus most of their aid in nations with the lowest per capita incomes but these include many nations with weak, ineffective and often unrepresentative urban governments.

At their core, the World Bank and the regional development banks are banks. They make capital available to member governments, whether or not the member governments are representative or effective with regard to poverty reduction. These banks also need to lend large sums of money to keep their own institution going, since this is how they cover most of their own costs. This need to lend money often conflicts with the best developmental course, which is for recipient governments to keep down capital expenditures. A government should seek to minimize the amount of loan capital required to finance needed investments, in order to keep down interest payments and debt burdens. For needed urban infrastructure (for instance, to improve provision for water, sanitation and drainage), any government should be seeking locally developed solutions that minimize the need for external capital. The conflict between the priorities of development banks and local development needs is well illustrated in Arif Hasan's (1999) recent book, Understanding Karachi, which describes how a US$ 70 million loan from the Asian Development Bank for part of the Greater Karachi Sewerage Plan was not actually needed. The Research and Training Institute of the Orangi Pilot Project (1998) showed that there was a much cheaper and more effective way of improving the sewer system which could be entirely funded by the money that the local agencies were going to provide as local counterpart funds for the Asian Development Bank loan. The governor of Sindh province (within which Karachi is located) agreed to change the project so it would be built with local resources and draw on local expertise. This meant that the loan was no longer needed (and thus a large debt obligation was avoided), even though considerable pressure was exerted by the federal and provincial bureaucracy to ensure that the loan was taken up. It is rare for large projects, for which governments negotiate loans from multilateral banks, to be subject to the scrutiny of civil society. It is also rare for cities to have local NGOs, such as Orangi Pilot Project, which have the technical capacity to be able to question the design and proposed budgets for large, complex infrastructure projects (for more details see: Orangi Pilot Project; Hasan, 1997; 1995; Zaidi, 2000).

Virtually all aid agencies and development banks have turned to 'capacity-building' to increase the capacity of their local counterpart institutions to implement the projects that they fund. Funding for urban projects in low-income nations can have important 'capacity-building' components so support is included for increasing the capacity of urban governments. The World Bank's urban programme recognized the need to do this more than 20 years ago and changed its approach so that not only did loans to urban projects include capacity-building but also many loans focused entirely on strengthening urban governments (Cohen, 2001). But it is difficult for any external agency to know how to build local capacity. The structure of most external agencies and the forms in which their funding are made available (including their project cycles) are not well suited to the slow and difficult task of building or strengthening local capacity. Strengthening the capacity of urban governments is often complex, not only institutionally but also politically, since it implies less power for government agencies at state or national level (Benjamin, 2000; Cohen, 2001) It often requires a lengthy process to increase the number of well-trained, motivated and adequately paid local staff. In addition, increasing the effectiveness of local governments cuts into the power and profits of many powerful vested interests and generally requires an intimate knowledge of local context and constant local support. But most donor agencies have most of their staff in their head offices in Europe or North America and most decisions are made there. They find it easier to use consultants from their own countries, not local consultants. While many of the staff of most development assistance agencies recognize the need to enhance local government capacity and accountability, these institutions = structures, financial management systems and systems for contracting out implementation are not well suited to this task.

The Distance Between the Urban Poor and the Donors

Since the partners of official aid agencies and development banks are national governments, the effectiveness of their grants or loans is largely determined by the quality of the government agencies to whom national governments allocate the external funding. Not surprisingly, much of what is funded brings little or no benefit to urban poor groups. The less accountable and representative the recipient government, the less likelihood there is that it will allow the allocation of resources to benefit poor groups. Any look into the social history high-income nations is a reminder of the long and conflictive process that, over many decades, produced more accountable, democratic, effective local governments. Even in recipient countries with democratic governments, support to urban poor groups is limited by the power of non-poor vested interests, the dominant belief in down-sizing governments (which some donors demand as a precondition for support) and the limits that all bureaucratic structures face in being able to provide real benefits to the urban poor (Schaffer, 1986) among other factors.

As discussions of 'good governance' became a central part of the development discourse over the last decade, many international agencies began to include a commitment to accountability and transparency in their official publications. But the whole structure of international development assistance creates a great distance between the development assistance agencies and the poor. Figure 1 illustrates this for the urban poor. At the bottom of the figure are those who are meant to benefit from development. Decisions about what is funded and who receives the funding are made so far from them. The funding passes through many intermediaries and is influenced by many interests before it reaches them. Furthermore, the poor groups at the bottom of the figure have no formal means of influencing the donors. They do not vote for the politicians who oversee the bilateral agencies. Their only influence within multilateral agencies is through the 'voting power' of their government–which is very small. *This means that the people whose needs justify the whole development industry are the people with the least power to influence development and to whom there is least accountability in terms of what is funded and who gets funded.*

This is a point that requires some emphasis since the reduction of poverty in what are today the high-income nations was much influenced by the capacity of lower-income men and women to organize and eventually to get the right to vote. For instance, in Europe, this helped produce political and administrative systems that extended provision for water, sanitation and drainage to virtually all dwellings, expanded education and health care systems to all citizens and produced social security systems that provided minimum incomes and access to housing and basic services for those who were unemployed or unable to work. In other words, it greatly reduced poverty. It is difficult to see how these changes could have taken place without the voting power and political pressures mobilized by those with limited incomes and without access to basic infrastructure and services. When some new social legislation proved ineffective or some project failed, citizens could hold their government to account. But when some project funded by a development bank or a bilateral aid agency fails, the intended beneficiaries cannot hold the bank or the agency to account. They cannot make formal representation to the politicians to whom the international agency is accountable. Even worse, when some development project threatens their homes or livelihoods, it is very difficult for them to make representation to the politicians who oversee the international agencies that are supporting this project. The basic mechanisms of accountability to the poor do not exist for aid agencies and development banks.

The development banks and official bilateral aid agencies are thus seeking to reduce poverty without the formal or informal mechanisms by which those who are suffering poverty can influence their priorities and the means by which they are realized. The international agencies may seek to draw on 'the voices of the poor' (as in the 2001 World Development Report) but they do not put in place the mechanisms by which the poor's own organizations and institutions have any power or influence within their decision-making processes.

The gap between the urban poor at the bottom of Fig. 19.1 and the donor agencies at the top is also a huge physical distance, bridged by a range of intermediaries. Most development assistance agencies have most of their staff at their head offices in Europe or North America. There are some exceptions—in particular unicef, which has most of its staff based in offices within recipient nations (including a considerable proportion of non ex-patriate staff). Some European bilateral agencies have also strengthened their offices within recipient nations and increased the proportion of their funding that these offices can spend. But for agencies like the World Bank, power, decision-making and senior staff are heavily concentrated in Washington dc, even if there have been moves to strengthen the role of its local offices.

The Pressure to Keep Down Staff Costs

a. Are Low Staff Costs a Measure of Effectiveness?
All development banks and official bilateral agencies are under great pressure from the politicians and bureaucrats that supervise them to keep down their staff costs. The conventional wisdom is that the lower the proportion of development funding spent on staff costs, the better. The ratio of staff costs to total funds spent is often seen as the single most important indicator of a

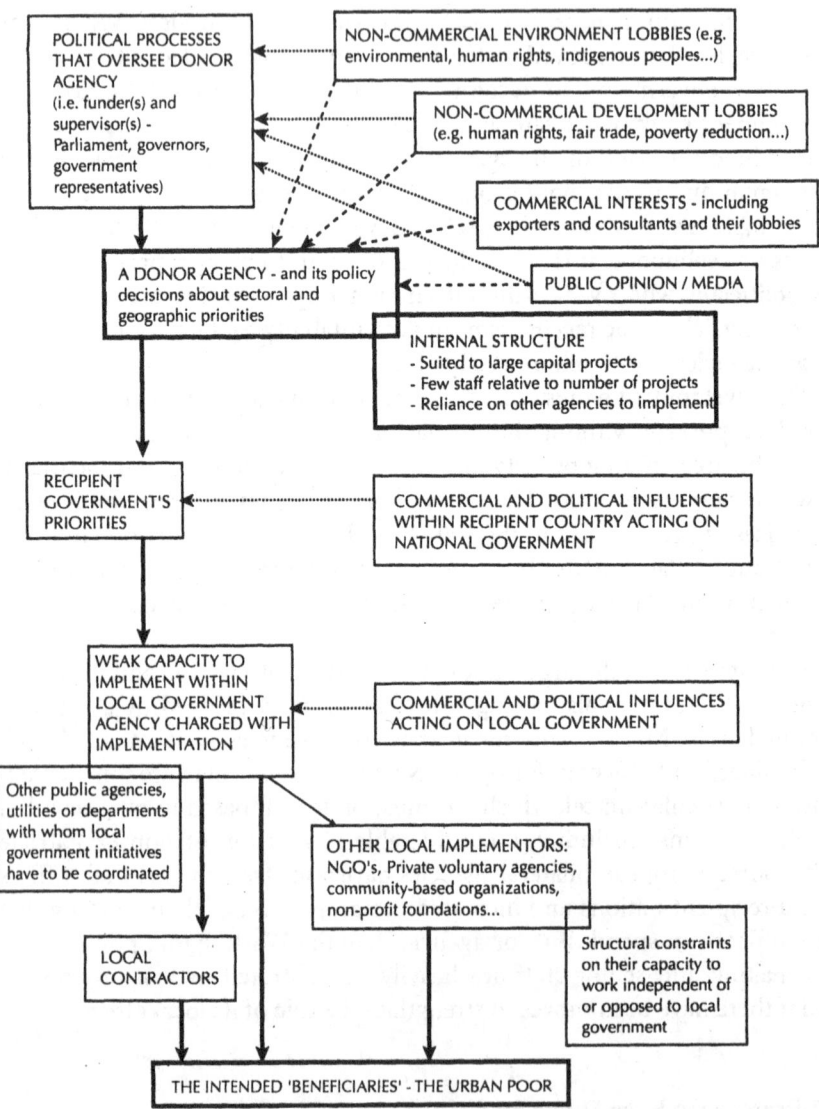

Figure 19.1 The different potential influences on a donor agency's sectoral priorities

development agency's 'efficiency'. Yet any agency that actually engages with urban poor groups knows that this takes time, and this means staff time that must be paid for. The same is true for engagement with local governments.

Agencies also know that too much money provided too quickly often damages or distorts local organizations and their capacity to build accountability and transparency into their work. Many agencies also recognize the need to keep down the costs of projects. In fact, all efforts should be made to keep down such costs since the lower the unit cost for any intervention to reduce urban poverty, the more likely it is that the intervention can be sustained and expanded. One therefore encounters the paradox of international agencies with large amounts of money that they have to spend quickly (as grants or as loans) within a 'project cycle' and very limited staff who are now trying to support local processes that often need relatively little external funding, relatively slowly and within a long local engagement. Staff from international agencies have been highlighting this paradox for many years. But, collectively, these agencies have never publicly sought to address this by demonstrating why the most effective aid is not necessarily the aid provided with the lowest staff costs. Some of the most effective aid agencies (and international NGOs) have average ratios of staff costs to total funding that are far above the average because they seek to support local processes and keep to a minimum the dependence of such local processes on external funds. Instead of defending the reasons why this is so, they seek to hide their relatively high ratio of staff costs to total funding in their accounts by inventing ambiguous categories within which some of their staff costs can be hidden.

One obvious way around this is to increase the proportion of donor agency staff based within low- and middle-income nations. But if these are ex-patriate staff, it becomes very expensive because the agency has to support not only staff salaries but also provisions for moving them there, housing them and moving them back. This conflicts with the pressure to keep down staff costs. In addition, it is difficult to build local capacity with ex-patriate staff who rarely stay in a country long enough to learn how best to support local processes; most donor agencies do not like their ex-patriate staff to stay too long in any country. The other possibility is for donor agencies to hire local staff; this has the advantage of hiring-in far greater local knowledge, people who can speak local languages and people who stay in the country. Most international NGOs and many bilateral agencies recognized the need to do this many years ago and now have a considerable proportion of their staff based in offices within recipient countries who are drawn from those countries; or else they work with local partner organizations. But for official bilateral agencies, there are obvious political complexities in having local staff in offices in 'recipient' countries responsible for spending funds provided by tax-payers in donor countries. There are also the inevitable conflicts between 'international' staff paid at international rates and local staff paid at local rates.

b. Out-sourcing Tasks; the Use of External Consultants

The other 'solution' widely used by official donor agencies to keep down the proportion of funding spent on staff costs is to use consultants. Consultants can be used for many tasks that would normally be done by agency staff – from helping to develop projects, to overseeing their implementation, to evaluating them. Although funding consultants is, in effect, funding more staff, the payments to consultants do not appear in the agency's accounts as 'staff' – as they are generally paid from country programmes or from project budgets. Large and diverse consultancy industries have developed around the headquarters of most large multilateral and bilateral agencies. As a staff member from one of the most effective European bilateral agencies pointed out, this is a ridiculous situation; his aid agency is not allowed to hire the staff it needs to effectively manage its projects and programmes but it is allowed to hire outside consultants to do so, which costs more than expanding internal staff. It may also mean that there is no 'learning' within the agency, as projects are developed, overseen and evaluated by people who are not within the agency.[6]

The multilateral banks also make heavy use of consultants. But they can pay for the costs of the consultants by including their fees in the loans they provide. In effect, it is the recipient government (and the tax payers from within the recipient country) that pays for the consultants. Most funding for consultants also goes to consultants based in Europe and North America. It is more convenient for agencies and banks to hire consultants where their headquarters are located rather than use consultants within the cities where the projects are located (who are generally much cheaper and have a greater knowledge of local context). It is common for loans from multilateral agencies to come with large consultancy fees within them, to cover the US\$ 1,000 or more per person per day charged by most international consultants. One senior official from a sub-Saharan African country told me how a loan for an urban project in his country had to include the costs of some very expensive US consultants. This official had a doctorate in urban planning

---

6. One possible counter-argument to this is that consultants may provide more continuity over time as particular consultants work over many years with the same international agency while the staff of that agency change constantly. But it is still difficult for donor agencies to internalize learning from developing, implementing and evaluating projects if much of this is done by external consultants.

from one of the most prestigious US universities. Not only did he have a much greater knowledge of the urban area in which the project was to be implemented than the consultants his government was obliged to use but he was also better qualified professionally and academically. If we accept that many aspects of reducing urban poverty requires a good knowledge of local context and local institutional structures, then expensive international consultants with little knowledge and experience of the countries in which they operate are hardly an appropriate solution. Many international consultants reproduce similar analyses and proposals regardless of the country they are in, precisely because their knowledge of each location is so limited.

By-Passing Rather Than Building Local Capacity

The work of IIED's Human Settlements Programme over the last 25 years has continuously highlighted the importance for urban poverty reduction of effective local institutions that are more accountable to the citizens in their locality and that can help address the different dimensions of deprivation (for instance, those listed in Table 19.1). Many aspects of urban poverty are rooted in local contexts, local power structures and local institutional performance (including what different government agencies do or do not do). This means that effective donor agencies need an intimate knowledge of local context and local possibilities or must support local institutions that have this knowledge. If external agencies have a constant local presence, this implies a greater capacity to adapt to changing local circumstances B for instance, to adapt an existing programme in response to a particular crisis (e.g., a flood or a sudden rise in food prices) or a particular opportunity (a local election which brings a new mayor into office who is more committed to addressing urban poverty). The form of the local institutions that have demonstrated a capacity to meet the needs of low-income or otherwise disadvantaged groups varies considerably with context; they can be community organizations or federations of community organizations, local NGOs, local foundations, municipal authorities or even, on occasion, national government agencies or local offices of international agencies. What these institutions provide, the form in which it is provided (and paid for) and the role of low-income groups in planning and delivery also varies considerably with local context but it always includes a more detailed and context-specific understanding of the needs and priorities of different low-income groups. It often includes a deliberate reshaping of the local institutions so they become more accountable to low-income groups and more transparent in the use of

Table 19.1 The different aspects of urban poverty

1. *Inadequate income* (and thus inadequate consumption of necessities including food and, often, safe and sufficient water; often problems of indebtedness with debt repayments significantly reducing income available for necessities).

2. *Inadequate, unstable or risky asset base* (non-material and material including educational attainment and housing) for individuals, households or communities.

3. *Inadequate shelter* (typically poor quality, overcrowded and insecure).

4. *Inadequate provision of 'public' infrastructure* (piped water, sanitation, drainage, roads, footpaths, etc.) which increases health burden and often work burden.

5. *Inadequate provision for basic services* such as day care/schools/vocational training, health-care, emergency services, public transport, communications, law enforcement.

6. *Limited or no safety net* to ensure basic consumption can be maintained when income falls; also to ensure access to shelter and health care when these can no longer be paid for.

7. *Inadequate protection of poorer groups= rights through the operation of the law:* including laws and regulations regarding civil and political rights, occupational health and safety, pollution control, environmental health, protection from violence and other crimes, protection from discrimination and exploitation.

8. *Poorer groups = voicelessness and powerlessness* within political systems and bureaucratic structures, leading to little or no possibility of: receiving entitlements; organizing; making demands; and getting a fair response. No means of ensuring accountability from aid agencies, NGOs, public agencies and private utilities.

NB: The table draws on Baulch, (1996), Amis, (1995), Chambers (1995), Moser (1996), Moser et al, (1993), and Wratten (1995).

funds (Souza, 2001). Some international agencies have long recognized this. For instance, when the Swedish International Development Cooperation Agency (Sida) developed programmes to address different aspects of urban poverty reduction in Central America, it set up local institutions to run them B fuprovi in Costa Rica (Sevilla, 1993; Sida, 1997) and the Programme for Local Development (prodel) in Nicaragua (Stein, 2001).

Very little official development assistance goes to these kinds of institutions. In part, this is because of the reasons noted earlier – the fact that most official development assistance is channelled through national governments who, in turn, do not direct such funds to these kinds of institutions. In part, it is because many international agencies (and most national governments) still identify and measure poverty through income-based poverty lines and fail to recognize the need for poverty reduction programmes to act on the other aspects of deprivation listed in Table 19.1. They fail to see the large potential role of local institutions to address the many aspects of deprivation other than inadequate income. They also fail to recognize that addressing these other aspects of deprivation can often contribute to increased income, for instance:

- better quality, more secure housing with better water supplies and electricity enhances income-earning opportunities for home enterprises;
- a new water supply not only improves the quality and quantity of water available to the household but also reduces the daily or weekly bill for water previously purchased from vendors and perhaps frees up time for income generation;
- better infrastructure and services greatly reduces the loss of income which results from sickness, injury or the costs of medicines and treatment (Mitlin and Satterthwaite, 2001).

An institutional structure for official development assistance that is dominated by the agency-national government relationship also means that it is difficult for the international agencies to engage in what are perhaps the two most important long-term processes for reducing urban poverty, namely, supporting the development of accountable, effective city and municipal local governments, and supporting the organizations formed by lower-income groups. New means must be found to engage with and support local government staff, where they have potential to become more effective. iied – in its work in different urban centres around the world – often finds local government officials who are struggling to fulfil their roles and responsibilities within local government structures that have made considerable improvements in terms of accountability and representation but who are ignored by development agencies and by foreign consultants. It is also common to find cities in which different international agencies (both official agencies and international NGOs) are busy funding 'their' projects with no coordination between them and with little attempt to work together to help strengthen the capacity of local institutions. For the official bilateral agencies and development banks, it may be that this is not so much a choice but, rather, is more related to the lack of local staff who knows how and when to support local processes.

Ironically, the kinds of development intervention that official donor agencies so admire in terms of cost-effectiveness and the likelihood that the initiatives will be sustained after donor assistance ceases are the ones they have the greatest difficulty in supporting. The literature published by official donor agencies may emphasize the importance of supporting community initiatives, empowerment and project 'sustainability' but they often cannot support these. If a well-organized, representative community organization wanted a loan for US$ 1,000 – for instance, to allow it to construct a central water tank from which it can develop standpipes which it will manage – it could not send this proposal to the head offices of most official development assistance agencies. Staff at these agencies cannot manage a large number and variety of small projects and cannot accept projects generated by 'the urban poor'; they were never set up to do so. It would be even more problematic for the donor agencies if they funded this US$ 1,000 project and the community organization then raised the funds to pay them back, because of the institutional difficulties the donor agency would face in managing the repayments and not spending their budgets. Donor agencies that provide loans do not want to manage cost recovery for the project loan funds since this would require a considerable expansion in their staff; they want governments to guarantee loan repayments independent of whether the project actually works or generates sufficient revenue to allow the capital costs to be repaid. If recipient governments only had to repay loans for the loan-funded donor projects that actually worked, their debt repayments would be considerably reduced.

Most official development assistance agencies have long recognized the structural limits to their capacity to support poverty reduction if funding proposals have to be approved by national government. Many have sought to steer funding direct to local governments and local NGOs (and very occasionally direct to community-based organizations). But the proportion of their funding that does not go through national governments or gets national government approval is limited. The funding that goes to local partners often fails to reach the organizations formed by low-income groups. The urban poor themselves – as individuals, households and communities – are the groups least likely to get the resources. Even if they do, these have usually been provided through projects and programmes over whose design and implementation they had little influence.

Channelling Funds to Community Initiatives

One possible way for donors to increase the proportion of funding that directly reaches urban poor groups and that supports a multiplicity of local initiatives to reduce poverty is through channelling support to a local fund. This would allow local decisions in the allocation of funding (and the terms under which it was given), to be influenced by the priorities of urban poor groups. It would allow such decision-making processes to be more transparent and accountable to urban poor groups. It would also allow a more coherent, coordinated programme of support. This fund could support requests such as the community organization requesting US$ 1,000 for a water tank noted above; it could also accept (or encourage) repayments.

The critical point is that local funds for community initiatives are needed in each city and, for larger cities, within sub-city areas (for instance, in each municipality with a high concentration of low-income groups, for cities that are organized within different municipalities). Aid agencies wishing to support community-level initiatives could channel their support through these local funds. Many bilateral agencies have recognized the need for such funds and have increased the amount of funding available for local projects through their own embassies. But having many different small grant funds located in different embassies (and presumably with support concentrated in the capital city), and with most decisions about what is to be funded being taken by a constantly changing group of ex-patriate staff, is not the same as locally staffed funds located in each area where there is a high concentration of low-income groups, that seek to set new standards of accountability and transparency to the groups that they are meant to serve.

There are some precedents on which these local funds can draw. For instance, the Thai government's Urban Community Development Office has a long-established programme to provide loans to community organizations and this has supported a great range of community initiatives. (UDCO, 2000). It also manages a small grants programme with support from danced (Danish Cooperation for Environment and Development; Boonyabancha, 1999). Some of the social funds supported by international donors have funded a large and diverse mix of projects that have brought benefits to low-income groups although these rarely have the level of accountability and transparency that local funds for community initiatives can provide and they also do not have offices easily reached and close to each concentration of low-income settlements. (Many social funds have also concentrated their support in rural areas).

The UK government's Department for International Development (DFID) is experimenting with supporting local funds for community initiatives in cities in Zambia (managed by care) and Uganda (managed by the Local Government Bureau International) and hopes to extend similar funds to other cities (Kiyaga et al., 2001) Locally based funds for community initiatives would work most easily in cities or city-districts where there are already effective, representative community organizations B or even better, as in places such as India, South Africa, Thailand and Zimbabwe, where there are also representative federations of community organizations and local NGOs that support these community organizations without imposing their professional agendas (Shack Dwellers International, 2001).

Local funds for community initiatives could:

- Provide funds under different terms, depending on who was being funded and the purposes for which the funding was intended, including loans (with varying interest rates, depending on what is to be funded and with whom) and grants. These funds could also provide technical support and, where needed, organizational support to assist the less organized and more disadvantaged groups to develop proposals for the fund, otherwise the funding would tend to go primarily to the better-organized and more articulate groups. A substantial part of the funding could be made available as loans, with further loans available, in part dependent on performance in loan repayment schedules and with loan repayments recycled into funding further local initiatives.
- Provide financial support to cover measures to address the complete range of deprivations faced by disadvantaged groups, for instance, supporting income generation, improved infrastructure and services, shelter upgrading, safety nets and improved environmental health.
- Serve as a point of coordination for the different international and local NGOs that work in that city or area of the city.

- Help support a local resource centre that provides community organizations and NGOs with information about the city and the different policies and programmes of government agencies and international agencies – such as the Urban Resource Centre developed in Karachi (Environment and Urbanization, 1994 and 2001).
- Develop the capacity to frame their support for different local initiatives in ways which, wherever possible, strengthen local government capacity. These funds would draw most of their staff from that locality since, to be effective, they need a good knowledge of the local context.
- Allow decisions about what is funded to be made locally with a minimum gap between the request and its consideration. When community-based groups or local NGOs apply for funding to donors in Europe or North America, it often takes six months before a decision is reached; it can take up to two years. With a locally based fund for community initiatives, this gap should be cut to a small fraction of this, i.e., a question of one or two weeks.
- Keep application procedures and decision-making processes completely transparent so that all groups in a city or municipality know who applies for funds, who receives funds and why. For once, the funding institution would have complete accountability downwards (to low-income citizens and their community organizations) as well as upwards (to the agencies that fund it).
- Allow local knowledge and a constant engagement with the local population to serve as an alternative to long lists of criteria that each project must meet (which so often exclude the less articulate groups). For instance, applications for support should be allowed in local languages rather than 'the language of the donor'. Very small funding requests could be managed, including requests as small as (say) US$ 50. In many instances, it is small amounts that are needed – to cover the cost that locally generated funds cannot, or to complement the support being received from the local authority.
- Allow a shared learning process between all the different community initiatives that a fund supports in any city and between funds in different cities.

These funds would also allow community-based organizations to have a direct engagement with the funding agency (and would not necessarily need intermediaries). They would also allow the priorities to be determined, or strongly influenced by, the needs and priorities of low-income groups and their organizations. This includes being able to respond to all members' needs, including the needs and priorities of children and youth. One wonders how many youth groups among the inhabitants of informal settlements have been able to develop their own proposals with some chance of these being supported by external agencies. A local fund for community initiatives should make special provision to encourage youth groups to develop proposals and should be flexible with regard to what is supported -for instance, support for youth centres that are developed, organized and managed by youth themselves or the US$ 60 that a youth group may need to buy materials to develop a hard-surface for ball games.

One final point regarding application procedures and local counterpart funding: for agencies that are considering supporting local funds, there is often discussion about how to encourage local groups to provide counterpart resources, and this often leads to a suggestion that there be a competitive process, with local groups able to offer the most counterpart resources receiving priority. Encouraging the organizations formed by urban poor groups to compete against each other for funding may be the wrong approach. Local funds could do the opposite, encouraging local groups to collaborate with each other and to learn from each other through a constant support for community-to-community exchanges (Asian Coalition for Housing Rights, 2000; Boonyabancha, 2001).

Any local fund must also include provision for helping the less organized groups, the poorer groups, the groups who face discrimination to also develop their proposals. Then, both the process of developing projects and the projects themselves will contribute to reducing poverty as, perhaps for the first time, those among the urban poor find a funding agency that responds to their needs, listens to their priorities, supports an inclusive, participatory process in developing proposals and supports the realization of the proposals. Just as the funding agency requires complete transparency from the groups they support, including rigorous checks on how money is spent, so the groups can demand the same of the funding agency that supports them. Box 19.1 gives an outline of how such a fund might operate.

What may be as important as a locally based fund for community initiatives is a fund for municipal initiatives to which urban governments can apply, although the possibilities for the success of such funds will depend much on the nature of local governments (for instance, whether they are representative and accountable to citizens) and on the relationships between local governments and national agencies and political structures. In many nations, there have been major changes towards more accountable, democratic local authorities which increase the possibilities for successful municipal funds. Like the funds for community initiatives, these would seek to set new standards in terms of transparency and accountability downwards, to local citizens. They would seek to support the processes by which local governments became more effective institutions for the low-income groups and their community organizations. Hopefully, such funds would encourage also the large bilateral and multilateral agencies to coordinate their urban investments. However, it is worth noting the political difficulties that the World Bank faced as it sought to support stronger, more reliable fiscal bases for urban local governments (Cohen, 2001).

Other Urban Agendas

Locally based funds for community initiatives are obviously only part of the solution. They fill a large gap by supporting the diverse needs and priorities of 'civil society' in ways that set new standards in terms of participation, accountability and transparency. This kind of support needs to be combined with long-term support to increase the capacity, effectiveness and accountability of city and municipal authorities, where political circumstances allow this. But there is still a need for international donors, to help ensure funding and the capacity to develop the 'big infrastructure' that most cities and smaller urban centres need to ensure good provision for water, sanitation and drainage to all city inhabitants (and ensure provision for its management and maintenance). Most community-led schemes to improve provision for water, sanitation, drainage and garbage collection need larger systems into which they can integrate.

For instance:

- most community-level water supply systems need supplies from water mains (unless there are cheap locally available ground water alternatives);
- community-level sewer systems generally need trunk sewers into which they can feed; alternatively, if on-site sanitation is more appropriate through pit latrines or latrines linked to septic tanks, there is a need for city-wide provision for cheap, efficient latrine/septic tank emptying services (Muller, 1997);

Box 19.1   A city-based fund for community initiatives

If the scale of funding to support community-level initiatives is to increase substantially, new institutional channels are needed. One possibility would be a 'Fund for Community Initiatives' set up within each city, accepting funds from external donors but managed by a small board made up of people based in that city or municipality. These board members would have to be acceptable to community groups and would usually include some staff from local NGOs who were already working with low-income groups and community organizations. It could include some locally based staff from external donors.

Functioning of the fund: Low-income groups could apply for funding for projects and also for support for developing projects. The procedures for applying for funds and the decision-making process have to be kept simple, with a capacity to respond rapidly. They would also have to be completely transparent, with information publicly available about who applied for funds, for what, who got funded and why. For funding provided as loans, the loan conditions and their repayment implications would have to be made clear and explicit – including repayment period, grace period (if any), interest rate and subsidy element.

Kinds of projects that could be supported: From the outset, the fund would seek to support a wide range of projects including health (for example, support for the construction of sanitary latrines or improved water supplies; preventive health measures including mother and child immunization; the setting up or expansion of community-based health centres); education (for example, special programmes for children or adolescents who left school early; literacy programmes); housing (building material banks, loans to community-based savings and credit schemes through which members could access loans to upgrade their homes or purchase land and build their own homes); environment (site drainage, improved water supplies) or employment (support for micro-enterprises, local employment exchanges; skill training, etc.)

Links to local government: Wherever possible, local funds should seek to work with, and strengthen the capacity of, local government. In the long term, it is difficult to reduce urban poverty without more effective, accountable local governments. But they could also work independent of local governments, in cities or districts where local governments have no capacity or interest to work with urban poor groups.

Funding: Most funding to be made available to groups or community organizations formed by low-income individuals. Funds of between US$ 500-50,000 would be made available mainly as loans. The first loan provided would generally be small, with further loans available if the project (and any planned cost recovery) proceeds to plan. Some level of counterpart funding would generally be expected (although this could be in the form of labour contribution).

Terms: Total or close to total cost recovery would be sought where feasible – with allowances made for inflation and for the cost of borrowing funds – with funding recovered shown publicly to be recycled back into supporting other community initiatives. For most projects, a short grace period would be permitted before the loan repayment had to begin (typically three months to a year) so that income generated or expenditure savings are partially realized before repayments begin. The Fund for Community Initiatives would also provide a range of support services – for instance, assistance to community organizations in developing proposals, and technical and managerial support in project implementation. Grants or soft loans could be made available for certain specific interventions where cost recovery is difficult to achieve (either because funding cannot easily be collected or because incomes are too low). Local funds should also include a capacity to give small grants to groups with very modest needs but less capacity to repay, such as youth groups.

Source   This box is drawn from Hardoy, Jorge E, Diana Mitlin and David Satterthwaite (1992), *Environmental Problems in Third Cities*, Earthscan, London. The idea of setting up internationally funded, locally based funds for community initiatives in urban areas was first elaborated by Jorge E Hardoy in a memo sent to various international agencies in 1989.

Table 19.2 Proportion of total funding going to urban poverty reduction and urban infrastructure, services and management; selected agencies, 1981-98

Proportion of total funding going to poverty reduction in urban areas

	1981-83	1984-86	1987-89	1990-92	1993-95	1996-98	1981-98
World Bank	7.0	8.6	8.4	12.2	15.9	15.4	11.3
Asian Dev. Bank	7.7	10.9	6.7	3.6	6.1	11.8	7.8
OECF (Japan)*			3.7	3.6	6.7	6.5	5.3

This analysis is based on a review of the descriptions of all project or other loan or credit commitments made by these agencies for the years shown. From this, it was possible to identify all funding commitments that went to urban projects. Six broad project categories were identified which can be said to have the explicit intention of directly reducing one or more of the aspects of urban poverty identified in Table 19.1: improving housing conditions aimed at lower-income groups (including 'slum and squatter upgrading, serviced sites, core housing and housing finance that is meant to reach lower-income households); improving or extending provision for water, sanitation, drainage and garbage collection; other components of primary health care including health care services and measures to control or prevent diseases; support for primary and basic education, including literacy programmes; integrated community development projects in urban areas which combine two or more of the above; and other projects or programmes specifically aimed at reducing urban poverty, including social funds and socially oriented public works programmes. If a project has both rural and urban components, it is included in this.

Proportion of total funding going to improving housing conditions in urban areas aimed at lower-income groups

	1981-83	1984-86	1987-89	1990-92	1993-95	1996-98	1981-98
World Bank	1.9	2.6	3.2	1.9	1.9	2.2	2.3
Asian Dev. Bank	1.9	3.6	0.4	0.1	0.8	3.4	1.7
OECF (Japan)*			0.3	0.1	0.4	0.2	0.3

NB: This includes 'slum' and squatter upgrading, serviced sites, core housing, support for housing finance that is meant to reach lower-income households and integrated community development projects whose focus is improving housing conditions and related infrastructure and service provision in urban areas.

Proportion of total funding going to improving or extending provision for water supply, sanitation and drainage in urban areas

	1981-83	1984-86	1987-89	1990-92	1993-95	1996-98	1981-98
World Bank	4.1	3.9	3.1	3.0	3.8	2.8	3.4
Asian Dev. Bank	5.1	5.5	3.5	2.0	4.4	1.7	3.3
OECF (Japan)*			3.4	2.8	6.2	4.1	4.2

Table 19.2 (continued)

In this table, only projects for water supply, sanitation and drainage that seek to extend provision to those inadequately served or unserved or which seek to improve the quality of provision are included; water and sanitation projects whose main focus is not improving or extending provision but, rather, other aspects such as sewage treatment or water reservoir construction (where the increased water supply may be used principally to serve higher-income groups or industrial and commercial concerns) are not included.

Proportion of total funding going to urban development, including all the above plus urban infrastructure, urban services and urban management

	1981–83	1984–86	1987–89	1990–92	1993–95	1996–98	1981–98
World Bank	14.8	17.5	18.7	22.5	27.7	22.1	20.7
Asian Development Bank	21.4	20.3	20.8	22.5	22.6	25.5	22.7
OECF (Japan)*			20.3	24.3	34.5	39.0	30.1

This includes not only all funding to the poverty reduction categories noted above but also funding to urban infrastructure (including ports, airports, markets, industrial estates, sewage treatment, intra-urban roads and bridges), urban services not included in poverty reduction (including higher education institutions, large hospitals, public transport and air and water pollution control), urban tourism projects and projects to support urban management.

* In 1999, OECF (the Overseas Economic Cooperation Fund) became part of the Japan Bank for International Cooperation.

Source These figures are derived from databases prepared by IIED which include details of all the urban projects that these agencies have funded for the periods shown in the table, and all other lending. These databases drew their information from the official publications of the three agencies, especially their annual reports.

- community-developed drainage networks generally need neighbourhood, district and city-level storm and surface water drain systems into which they can feed;
- community-level garbage collection services need district or city-level depots, collection points, collection services and waste dumps into which they can feed (Anand, 1999).

Similarly, systems of support for other community-led services such as primary health centres need the support of district hospitals and health centres to which the illnesses and injuries that they cannot cope with can be referred. Ensuring the efficient functioning of these broader systems within which community-based solutions can operate is also one of the greatest challenges for governments and international agencies that see privatization as the solution. Supporting community initiatives and community organizations may be one of the keys to supporting a civil society that is able to get the best out of privatized utilities.

Most international agencies allocate only a very small proportion of their funding to these kinds of interventions. Table 19.2 gives examples of this for three of the largest official agencies.

Most multilateral agencies allocate only a small proportion of their funding to interventions that directly address urban poverty or that enhance the capacity of urban governments to do so. For instance, only 5 per cent of the total project commitments by the Overseas Economic Cooperation Fund (Japan) between 1987 and 1998 went to projects to directly reduce urban poverty (see Table 19.2). For the Asian Development Bank, less than 8 per cent of funding commitments between 1981 and 1998 went to such projects. Of the three agencies, the World Bank has an unusually high proportion of funding commitments to urban poverty reduction – over 11 per cent for the period 1981 to 1998 and over 15 per cent for the period 1993 to 1998. It also gave the highest priority among the agencies to funding projects or programmes to increase the capacity of city or municipal governments.

The limited information available on the priorities of other official development assistance agencies suggests that most give a much lower priority to projects that seek to reduce urban poverty than does the World Bank (Satterthwaite, 1997; Milbert and Peat, 1999; Hardoy et al, 2001) except for the Inter-American Development Bank.[7] However, it is more difficult to analyze the priority given by most bilateral agencies to different kinds of projects because they do not publish details of all the projects they support or other funding commitments they make (which then permits an analysis of the proportion that goes to different kinds of urban projects, such as those shown in Table 19.2).

Perhaps the most telling evidence of the low priority given by most official development assistance agencies to reducing urban poverty is the lack of support for projects which improve housing conditions for low-income groups (including 'slum' and squatter upgrading, serviced site schemes, support for housing loans and integrated community development). Table 19.2 shows the very low priority they received from the World Bank, the Asian Development Bank and the OECF. For the OECF, this formed just 0.3 per cent of its funding commitments between 1987 and 1998. The World

---

7. The analysis for the Inter-American Development Bank was not completed in time to include figures here. Preliminary figures up to 1996 show an unusually high proportion of total funding going to projects to reduce urban poverty although this would be expected for an agency working in a region with around three-quarters of its population living in urban areas.

Bank supported many innovative projects in this area during the late 1970s and through the 1980s and early 1990s. They helped to establish 'upgrading' rather than bulldozing as an officially recognized approach to illegal settlements. They were among the few agencies that gave substantial support to housing finance systems, in the hope that these would increase the possibilities for lower-income groups to buy or build their own homes. However, their support for these kinds of projects dropped off during the 1990s.

The priority given to improving or extending provision for water supply, sanitation and drainage to urban populations who are unserved or inadequately served was not much higher among these three agencies – little more than 3 per cent of the funding commitments for the World Bank and the Asian Development Bank between 1981 and 1998 and 4.2 per cent for the oecf between 1987 and 1998. This is surprising given the very large inadequacies in provision for water, sanitation and drainage among the urban populations of most of Africa and Asia and much of Latin America (Hardoy et al, 2001) This low priority to water and sanitation may reflect the agencies' belief that privatization will help address this issue, so funding to governments is not needed.

The (limited) information available on the sectoral priorities of official bilateral agencies or on their urban programmes suggests that most give a very low priority to projects which help improve housing conditions for low-income groups in urban areas or which improve their access to water and sanitation (Satterthwaite, 1997; Milbert and Peat, 1999).

Part of the reason for a low priority to reducing urban poverty relates to the difficulties they have faced in the past in supporting urban infrastructure and services (or in ensuring their continued functioning after construction). Many development assistance agencies moved away from funding large urban infrastructure projects because the infrastructure they funded quickly deteriorated without the local capacity to maintain it. But this does not remove the need for large infrastructure projects. As noted above, community, neighbourhood or district-based projects to improve water, sanitation, drainage and garbage collection usually need larger systems into which they can integrate. But this means that funding for large infrastructure must be provided in ways which also enhance local capacity to build, extend and maintain it, to generate the necessary funds, and to ensure that it addresses the needs and priorities of low-income groups. Funding for large urban infrastructure is still needed but within a 'good governance' framework.

Among some agencies, a low priority to urban poverty reduction is not a result of a low priority to urban development. For instance, the oecf has a large urban programme but chooses to give a low priority to urban poverty reduction within this. Between 1987 and 1998, 30 per cent of its funding went to urban projects. But most went to support the construction of ports, airports, water infrastructure,[8] public transport, pollution control, intra-city roads and bridges, and improved electricity supplies for cities. The need for such projects is not in doubt but the priority given to these over and above those that directly address the most serious deprivations facing urban poor groups can be questioned. The heavy concentration of support for urban infrastructure projects in the countries which are or potentially will be Japan's main trading partners suggests an orientation that does not have poverty reduction as a high priority. For the Asian Development Bank, little more than one-third of its urban lending went to projects which directly address urban poverty, with most urban funding going to higher education institutions, ports, improving provision for electricity within cities, integrated urban development and, in recent years, pollution control. The World Bank gives a significantly higher priority within its urban lending to projects or programmes which bring direct benefits to low-income groups; more than half its urban lending between 1981 and 1998 went to these. The World Bank is often criticized for its over-emphasis on 'big infrastructure' but the proportion of its funding going to 'big infrastructure' has fallen considerably over the past 30 years; funding for ports, airports, intra-city roads, sewage treatment and improving provision for electricity for urban areas, for instance, has dropped from over 20 per cent of all urban funding in the 1980s to less than 10 per cent between 1990-1998. Part of the reason for this is the considerable increase in the proportion of its funding commitments going to primary and basic education and primary health care (Satterthwaite, 1998). There is debate on whether World Bank loans are the most appropriate way of funding these areas, and on the Bank's orientation with regard to how these are provided and funded (and who pays), which is beyond the scope of this paper. But in terms only of the allocation of funding, the World Bank has responded more than most official development assistance agencies to the need to give a higher priority to projects or

---

8. The analysis in Table 19.2 divides urban water projects into two categories. The first category, which is included in Aurban poverty reduction, is for projects which make provision to extend provision for water and sanitation to those inadequately served or unserved or which seek to improve the quality of provision. The second category includes water projects whose main focus is not improving or extending provision for city populations but other aspects – such as sewage treatment or water reservoir construction (where the increased water supply may be used principally to serve higher-income groups or industrial and commercial concerns).

Box 19.2 **Speculation on possible milestones of how international agencies' approaches to urban poverty reduction might change between 2002 and 2015**

2002-2003: The World Bank begins a research programme in which staff in each of its country offices assess the extent to which its US$ 1 per person per day poverty line is valid in the city in each country office is located. Initial findings highlight how large sections of the population in these cities need more than US$ 1 per person per day to avoid poverty. In some nations, the study expands to review how the minimum income needed to avoid poverty varies in different urban centres; this finds that the income needed to avoid poverty is particularly high for certain low-income groups in major cities, largely because of the high cost of non-food items (including rent, keeping children at school, payments to water vendors and pay-as-you-use toilets, fuel, transport, health care and medicines).

2002: A consortium of bilateral and multilateral agencies and UN agencies agree to set up a consultative group through which they can share knowledge and experience about programmes to reduce urban poverty.

2003: The International Union of Local Authorities sets up an expert committee of current and former mayors who have demonstrated their commitment to good governance, accountability and democratic practices. The brief to the expert committee of mayors is to consider the adequacy and limitations of current mechanisms by which city authorities can access international development funds and recommend improvements.

2003: In response to a suggestion from Shack Dwellers International (an NGO that represents federations of urban poor groups), a consortium of international NGO funding agencies agree to develop ways to allow more influence on their urban programmes by representatives from federations of urban poor groups and local NGOs.

2003: The UK Government's Department for International Development publishes the evaluation of the pilot funds for community initiatives that it supported in Kampala and Jinja in Uganda, and Lusaka and Ndola in Zambia. This acknowledges how local funds located within cities can support a more diverse, effective, community-based programme than conventional funding mechanisms, while documenting the difficulties that these funds encountered and recommending how best to expand these funds. Comparable funds are set up in many cities. The Cities Alliance agrees to start funding a programme for city-based local funds for community initiatives.

2003: World Bank replaces its US$ 1 per person per day poverty line with national income-based poverty lines based on more realistic estimates of the real income needed to avoid poverty in each nation and a more realistic allowance made for the cost of non-food essentials. The Bank also acknowledges that the 'income needed to avoid poverty' varies considerably between different areas within most nations, so its national poverty reduction strategies begin to set different income-based poverty lines for different cities and regions.

2004: A consortium of international NGOs with experience in urban development, including CORDAID, MISEREOR, Homeless International, CARE-UK, WaterAid and Oxfam, agree to work more closely together in addressing urban poverty and to recognize the need to shift from a project focus with an 'exit strategy' to a long-term engagement within each city or smaller urban centre, working with and through local NGOs and community-based groups. A code of practice is prepared with regard to the responsibilities of local NGOs to urban poor groups and their organizations.

Notes   This box borrows the idea of describing future events as if we knew that they would happen from Jorge Wilheim, as developed in his book *Faxes from the Future* (Earthscan, 1996) and in his paper in *Environment and Urbanization* Vol. 6, No. 1.

Box 19.2 (continued)

2005: The consortium of international NGOs publish a report describing their new code of practice and explaining how this will change their spending patterns. This defends the fact that staff costs may rise, within total expenditures, because many of the best local interventions keep down capital costs (so the gap between what is funded and what can be afforded is minimized) and that these and the long-term development processes that the NGOs support in each city generally imply more staff-intensive support. The tendency for staff costs to rise is partially offset by greater use of local staff.

2005: In response to the report of the IULA Expert Committee of Mayors, the official development assistance agencies' consultative group on urban development issues guidelines to which all its members agree with regard to ensuring coordination and cooperation between all the agencies working in any city and to setting new standards of transparency and accountability to the inhabitants of each city.

2005: The World Bank recognizes that using only income-based criteria for estimating the scale of urban poverty greatly underestimates the extent of deprivation, as a large proportion of the urban population with 'above poverty line incomes' still live in poor quality, overcrowded homes with insecure tenure and inadequate provision for infrastructure and services. An expert meeting is convened with staff from national statistical offices from many low- and middle-income nations to begin a work programme to develop more detailed indicators of deprivation that can be useful for local governments. One of its key tasks is to put in place the capacity of national statistical offices to rapidly provide local governments with census data disaggregated to local area units, for the new round of censuses being planned for 2009 to 2011.

2005: In recognition of the inaccuracies and inadequacies in available data on the quality and extent of provision for water, sanitation, drainage, garbage collection and health care in urban areas, the World Health Organization and UNICEF launch a new programme to support city and municipal authorities to develop better information systems and act on them. This includes support for community-driven assessments, drawing on the experience of the members of Shack Dwellers International in community-driven censuses.

2005: An assessment of the privatization of water, sanitation and garbage collection in African cities shows that the expected improvements for urban poor groups has rarely been realized. The assessment recommends that more donor support be given to publicly owned, but independently managed, utilities and to allowing non-profit institutions to compete on equal terms with private sector companies in the provision for water and sanitation.

2006: The Istanbul plus-10 conference, reviewing the extent to which governments have implemented the recommendations they agreed to at Habitat II, the second UN Conference on Human Settlements in 1996, documents a great range of innovation by city governments, NGOs and community-based organizations in implementing the Habitat Agenda but also highlights how these remain the exceptions.

2006: A consortium of international NGOs agrees to set new standards of accountability and transparency in their urban development programmes. This includes full disclosure of the funds available and how these are spent within the cities in which they are located, and describes the scope for more locally made decisions.

Box 19.2 (continued)

2007: A new WHO/UNICEF-sponsored assessment of provision for water, sanitation and drainage in urban areas shows that the inadequacies in provision had been underestimated. For instance, tens of millions of households previously categorized as having 'access to safe water' are found to receive poor quality, intermittent supplies at standpipes to which access is difficult. Tens of millions of urban dwellers previously categorized as having 'access to sanitation' are found to have only access to public toilets that are poorly managed, dirty and difficult to access. The assessment also highlights how donor support for water, sanitation and drainage has diminished and how many donors are still only supporting improvements in water supply with no provision for sanitation and drainage. The assessment recommends that donors give a higher priority to the large investments needed in city-wide water, sanitation and drainage systems but with this targeted at cities with local authorities that are accountable, and capable of supporting the investments and community-based actions that integrate into these wider systems.

2009: The various official bilateral and multilateral agencies involved in the Cities Alliance also agree to a new code of practice, similar to the one developed by the consortium of international NGOs, agree to set new standards of accountability and transparency in their urban development programmes. This includes full disclosure of the funds available and how these are spent within the cities in which they are located.

2011: A new edition of the UN Centre for Human Settlements' Global Report on Human Settlements (following on from the editions published in 1987, 1996 and 2001) documents in some detail the large and rapidly growing contribution of local non-profit institutions and non-profit city authority trusts that have greatly improved provision for water, sanitation, drainage and health care to low-income areas in many urban areas. It notes in particular how many of these have greatly reduced the unit costs of good quality provision, thus reducing the gap between what can be provided and what low-income households are prepared to pay for.

2013: The Cities Alliance, with support from a wide range of bilateral agencies, agrees to support a wide-ranging assessment of whether urban poverty has decreased, which is based both on poverty lines that are adjusted to represent the real income needed to avoid deprivation within each city and on non-income aspects of deprivation. This assessment is to inform the international donors as to whether the international targets they had set in the late 1990s for reducing poverty by 2015 have been fulfilled for urban areas.

2015: Publication of the Cities Alliance 'global assessment of the state of the world's urban poor'. Hopefully, this shows that the international donors' targets for poverty reduction have been met or exceeded.

Notes: This box borrows the idea of describing future events as if we knew that they would happen from Jorge Wilheim, as developed in his book *Faxes from the Future* (Earthscan, 1996) and in his paper in *Environment and Urbanization* Vol. 6, No. 1.

programmes that directly address the deprivations associated with urban poverty.

Rather than end this paper with a section on conclusions, Box 19.2 presents some speculations on future 'milestones' which might be achieved by international agencies as they seek to become more effective in reducing urban poverty. The milestones are given up to 2015, since this is the year by which many international development targets relating to poverty reduction are meant to be realized.

References

Anand, P.B.(1999), 'Waste Management in Madras Revisited', *Environment and Urbanization*, Vol. 11 (2), pp. 161-176.

Asian Coalition for Housing Rights (2000) *'Face to Face: Notes from the Network on Community Exchange'*, ACHR, Bangkok.

Benjamin, Solomon (2000), 'Governance, Economic Settings and Poverty in Bangalore', *Environment and Urbanization*, Vol. 12 (1), pp. 35-56.

Boonyabancha, S. (1999), 'The Urban Community Environmental Activities Project, Thailand', *Environment and Urbanization*, Vol. 11 (1), pp. 101-115.

Boonyabancha, S. (2001) 'Savings and Loans: Drawing Lessons from Some Experiences in Asia', *Environment and Urbanization*, Vol. 13 (2), pp. 9-22.

Celina Souza (2001) 'Participatory Budgeting in Brazilian Cities: Limits and Possibilities in Building Democratic Institution, *Environment and Urbanization*, Vol. 13 (1), pp. 159-184.

Cohen, M. (2001), 'Urban Assistance and the Material World; Learning by Doing at the World Bank', *Environment and Urbanization*, Vol. 13 (1), pp. 37-60.

Hasan, A. (1997), *Working with Government: The Story of the Orangi Pilot Project's Collaboration with State Agencies for Replicating its Low-cost Sanitation Programme*, City Press, Karachi.

Hardoy, J.E., Mitlin, D. and Satterthwaite, D. (2001), *Environmental Problems in an Urbanizing World: Finding Solutions for Cities in Africa, Asia and Latin America*, Earthscan Publications, London.

Hasan, A. (1999), *'Understanding Karachi: Planning and Reform for the Future',* City Press, Karachi.

Kiyaga-Nsubuga, J., Magyezi, R., O'Brien, S. and Sheldrake, M. (2001) 'Hope for the Urban Poor: DFID City Community Challenge (C3) Fund Pilot in Kampala and Jinja, Uganda', *Environment and Urbanization*, Vol. 13 (1), pp. 115-124.

Melo, M., Rezende, F. Lubambo, C. (2001), *'Urban Governance, Accountability and Poverty: The Politics of Participatory Budgeting in Recife, Brazil'* Working Paper 27, Project on Urban Governance, Partnerships and Poverty, University of Birmingham.

Milbert, I. and Peat, V. (1999), *'What Future for Urban Cooperation? Assessment of Post Habitat II Strategies',* Swiss Agency for Development and Cooperation, Berne.

Mitlin, D. and Satterthwaite, D. (2001), 'Urban Poverty: Some Thoughts About its Scale and Nature and About Responses to it', in Yusuf, S, W Wu and S Evenett (eds.), *The Challenge of Globalization: International and Local Dimensions of Development*, World Bank, Washington DC.

Muller, M.S. (ed.) (1997), *'The Collection of Household Excreta: The Operation of Services in Urban Low-income Neighbourhoods',* WASTE and ENSIC, Gouda.

Orangi Pilot Project (1995), 'NGO Profile', *Environment and Urbanization*, Vol. 7 (2), pp. 227-236.

Orangi Pilot Project-Research and Training Institute (1998), *Proposal for a Sewage Disposal System for Karachi*, City Press, Karachi.

Patel, S, Bura, S. and D'Cruz, C. (2001) 'Shack Dwellers International (SDI): Foundations to Treetops', *Environment and Urbanization*, Vol. 13 (2), pp. 45-60.

Satterthwaite, D. (1997), *The Scale and Nature of International Donor Assistance to Housing, Basic Services and Other Human Settlements Related Projects*, WIDER, Helsinki.

Satterthwaite, D. (1998), *The Constraints on Aid and Development Assistance Agencies Giving A High Priority to Basic Needs*, PhD thesis, London School of Economics.

Schaffer, B.B. (1986), 'Access: a Theory of Corruption and Bureaucracy', *Public Administration and Development*, Vol. 6 (4), pp. 357- 376.

Sevilla, Manuel (1993), 'New Approaches for Aid Agencies; FUPROVI's Community-based Shelter Programme', *Environment and Urbanization*, Vol. 5 (1), pp. 111-121.

Sida (1997), 'Seeking More Effective and Sustainable Support to Improving Housing and Living Conditions for Low-income Households in Urban Areas: Sida's Initiatives in Costa Rica, Chile and Nicaragua', *Environment and Urbanization*, Vol. 9 (2), pp. 213-231.

Stein, A. (2001) 'Participation and Sustainability in Social Projects: the Experience of the Local Development Programme (PRODEL) in Nicaragua' *Environment and Urbanization*, Vol. 13 (1), pp. 11-36.

UCDO (2000), 'UCDO *(Urban Community Development Office) Update No. 2*', Urban Community Development Office, Bangkok.

Urban Resource Centre, Karachi (1994) 'NGO Profile', *Environment and Urbanization*, Vol. 6 (1), pp. 158-163.

Urban Resource Centre, Karachi (2001) 'Urban Poverty and Transport, a Case Study from Karachi', *Environment and Urbanization*, Vol. 13 (1), pp. 223-234.

World Bank (1999), *'Annual Report 1999',* Washington DC.

World Bank (2001), *World Development Report 2000/2001: Attacking Poverty*, Oxford University Press, Oxford and New York.

Zaidi, S. Akbar (2000), '*Transforming Urban Settlements: The Orangi Pilot Project's Low-cost Sanitation Model*', City Press, Karachi.

20 The Rise and Decline of an Urban Poverty Unit in the Dutch Ministry of Development Cooperation

JOOP DE WIT

Introduction

In November 1989 a special departmental section in charge of urban poverty alleviation was created within the Netherlands Ministry for Development Cooperation. This was quite an important break with the past, as Dutch aid policy had almost exclusively been aimed at rural development, to the neglect of urban issues – until then. The new urban unit was named Spearhead Program for Urban Poverty Alleviation, thus emphasizing the focus on poverty – rather than on urban development in general – in developing countries. The name implied an expectation that the unit would somewhat forcefully draw attention to issues of urban poverty, and develop and mainstream effective policy to that effect.

The Spearhead Program (SP) got off to a good start, and managed to initiate and support different types of bilateral and multilateral urban interventions. However, in terms of budget, capacity, and operational independence within the ministry, the SP faced increasing problems. Over the years, specific Dutch urban poverty alleviation policy has tended to become less visible and more limited in scope, partly related to new policy views and foci brought to the Ministry by a new Minister for Development Cooperation who took office in 1998. In fact, there is no longer a separate urban unit; existing urban expertise has been transferred to other ministerial departments. These developments are in contrast to the presence in the Netherlands since 1987 of various groups, organizations, and individuals involved in issues related to urbanization and urban poverty in developing countries. They first lobbied for more official recognition of urban issues, and later partly supported and partly critically followed SP functioning. Today they are back again on the lobbying track.

This article describes the ups and downs of the Dutch development cooperation policy aimed at urban problems. It asks how a deliberately established urban poverty unit in the Ministry could wither away over time, while urbanization and urban poverty are increasingly serious global problems, and in spite of an active and concerned civil society. Starting in 1987, it looks at the reasons why there was a – belated – policy shift towards urban issues, including a review of the activities of various Dutch urban-focused think-tanks. Also, the objectives of the SP and its activities over time are considered. This article also assesses the achievements of the SP, and the question is asked whether these achievements warranted the termination of the special urban-poverty focused department. Finally, the implications of recent far-reaching policy shifts at the Ministry concerning the scope for a Dutch urban aid policy are explored, i.e., the increasing prominence of the 'sector approach', and the limitation of Dutch aid to a small number of countries, especially those characterized by, or moving towards, 'good governance'.[1]

1987: The International Year of Shelter for the Homeless

Dutch development cooperation has traditionally been characterized by a focus on rural development and rural issues. This has historical reasons, for example, Dutch colonialism with its emphasis on tropical agriculture, and the fact that Dutch development aid efforts started at a time when the majority of the world's population lived in rural areas. There was an awareness that rural poverty was widespread and that rural conditions left much to be desired. A related factor was that the Netherlands – with its important and sophisticated agricultural sector and abundant rural and agricultural expertise – felt itself most suited to address rural issues in developing countries. One could perhaps speak of a lobby of the Dutch agricultural sector, which not only had a large impact on overall Dutch policy, but also influenced development cooperation, where one could refer to Wageningen Agricultural University as one center of influence. But there was also a policy argument to channel aid to villages rather than cities, as it was believed that

---

1. This article has benefited much from thoughtful comments provided by Isa Baud, Joep Bijlmer, Theo Kolstee, Ed Maan, Fon van Oosterhout, and Monique Peltenburg, whose support is much appreciated. However, the views expressed here are those of the author, who is responsible for any mistakes that remain.

rural development could contribute to reducing the considerable rural-to-urban migration in developing countries.[2] Most of all, it was argued that, on average, rural poverty was much more widespread than urban poverty, and that access to and the quality of infrastructure and basic services were mostly better in cities (De Goede, 1994, p. 6).

Things started to change from about 1987 onwards, when the International Year of Shelter for the Homeless (IYSH) was organized by the UN to draw worldwide attention to problems of urbanization and urban poverty. The IYSH led to the adoption or preparation of new shelter strategies in 145 countries (UNCHS/HABITAT, 1994, p. 342). It resulted in increased attention being paid to urban issues, and, concretely, in the establishment of the Netherlands Habitat Commission (NHC) in 1986, which aimed to prepare a program of activities for IYHS. The Ministry of VROM (Housing and Planning) took charge of coordinating habitat-related activities on behalf of the Dutch government. This led to considerable attention being paid to habitat issues in the Netherlands. The NHC played a key part in mobilizing and networking efforts to keep up interest in urban issues, and to lobby parliamentarians and officials with a view to changing official Dutch development policy. It united many organizations, institutions, and individuals involved in the field of urban issues, but it may be noted that on the whole, more importance was attached to housing than to social or poverty issues. The NHC also initiated fund raising activities amongst a gradually growing group of supporters, which were eventually channelled to NGOs in the Indian city of Bangalore for small slum projects, following the concept of the 'Concentration City'. This was based on the expectation that more consolidated impacts, more comprehensive coverage, and enhanced sustainability would be achieved by concentrating aid efforts in one city (Dijkgraaf and de Wit, 1995, Habitat Platform/Harp, 1998).

In November 1989, a center-left government came into power in the Netherlands, and Minister Jan Pronk took charge of the Ministry for Development Cooperation. He ordered, oversaw, and partly wrote the most ambitious policy document to date on development cooperation, entitled 'A World of Difference', (MBZ, 1990). While the document has a strong bias towards rural poverty and rural development, it does contain the first official recognition of the significant urban problems of developing countries. It

---

2. It was later argued that aid for rural development often enhanced rural to urban migration: education led to higher expectations and a wider horizon of those educated; rural areas were opened up to markets and cities through communication and transport, leading to an increased desire to be part of money-based economies.

refers to processes of rapid urbanization in developing countries, to the many people living in urban slums, and to problems of land supply, which restrict shelter options for low-income groups. The document finally announces the establishment of the SP for Urban Poverty Alleviation (ibid., p. 342). This SP was one of four new programs. The others had a thematic focus on, respectively, the environment, women/gender and development, and research.

The Spearhead Program for Urban Poverty Alleviation

The new SP for urban poverty alleviation initially had a staff of three, and a budget of NLG 10 million in 1991. According to a 1990 Ministry document, the program budget was expected to increase rapidly, to NLG 30 million in 1995 (MBZ, 1990, p. 374). Four SP objectives are mentioned:

- To carry out research into processes of social marginalization, increasing poverty and criminality, and into the impacts of large-scale programs on urban populations;
- To support innovative activities in the field of employment and income generation;
- To make expertise available with a view to strengthening the organizations of the urban poor and marginalized groups;
- To support the development and enforcement of labor, social, and pension legislation.

It is important to stress that, in addition, the SP was to play a catalyzing role, supporting and encouraging innovative initiatives and approaches, and that it was to focus on the Ministry and multilateral donor agencies in order to mainstream urban policy in overall policy.

One of the outcomes of research and various seminars was the 1994 White Paper on urban poverty alleviation (MBZ, 1994, also Oosterhout, 1996). This is a very comprehensive text, dealing with a variety of state-of-the-art issues as diverse as urbanization, employment, habitat, and international donor agencies. One chapter deals with the SP itself. Emphasis is given to sustainable development, enabling strategies and employment, and the creation of institutional frameworks for local development, including local government and NGOs. In this context an approach is advocated 'from within' and 'from below', taking into account the position and perceptions of the urban poor (ibid., p. 131ff). It may be noted that the SP took a broad view of urban poverty, one not limited to what may be termed 'habitat', the living environment, and the provision of tangible services. In a way it set a trend which would become more important in the Ministry – and in development debates – only later: A focus on institutional development, good governance, and capacity building. It is finally important to note the elaborate research agenda of the SP under three broad areas: enhancing the employment and incomes of the urban poor; upgrading the physical habitat; and enhancing control and decision-making powers at the grassroots level (ibid., p. 142ff).

The SP White Paper was published in the same year (1994) as the Advisory Report on Urban Poverty, written by the National Advisory Council for Development Cooperation (NAR, 1994). There are many similarities in the analysis of the urban problems in the two documents. However, there was much less agreement on the policy recommendations derived from the analysis. De Goede (1994, p. 9) expresses a concern that the two documents on the same problem area diverge so widely in terms of policy recommendations. He argues that the Ministry Policy Note offers a clear framework for an operational program, but that it is too broad, and that no priority is given to activities addressing the deeper causes of urban poverty. Perhaps these divergent views are illustrative of deeper differences of opinion between the SP on the one hand and some urban experts, consultants, and scientists in the Netherlands on the other. A rift rather than a convergence eventually developed between the SP and some parts of the Dutch urban expert community, to some extent undermining and constraining the SP as the conflicts of opinion gradually came to influence and reduce support from the Minister and Dutch politicians. It seems certain that the Dutch public's support for the themes of new SPs on Women & Development, and the Environment was larger, and that its constituent groups were more united.

Multilateral and Bilateral Urban Activities

The SP staff got off to a good start and soon acquired a good international reputation for being innovative and supportive of a multitude of urban research initiatives, workshops, and seminars, and for supporting joint initiatives with multilateral donors. Although it took a while before the aforementioned program's White Paper was published, it was a very thorough and comprehensive piece of work. Many of the initial activities of the SP aimed at multilateral donor agencies and their programs including the World Bank, UNDP, and UNCHS (the Nairobi-based UN agency for Human

Settlements). In the early 1990s, the World Bank and UNDP were themselves defining their position as regards urbanization and urban issues, as is illustrated by several policy papers published at the time (World Bank, 1991; UNDP, 1991). It was under these international conditions of developing an urban agenda and defining priorities and strategies that the SP was able to play a strategic role, especially by stressing the importance of an urban poverty focus, of local good governance, and bottom-up community participatory approaches. For example, prior to 1993, the Urban Management Program of UNDP/UNHCS did not have a specific urban poverty focus or unit. Thanks to Dutch pressure, a special urban poverty component was created, and today this is a key focal area (Moser and Holland, 1997). SP staff played a key role in strengthening the UNCHS organization, and in redirecting its focus towards the urban poor and an emphasis on community participation and community management approaches (Wils and Helmsing, 1998). SP staff played a similar role in restructuring the Municipal Development Program (MDP) implemented in many African countries: With the force of arguments and aided by financial leverage, policy change and improved performance was possible. But even while these interventions were (and still are) much appreciated internationally, they were not quite visible in the Netherlands, and it can be argued that public relations could have been better, for example in terms of disseminating information about these international activities, their achievements, and constraints. One reason for this was that SP staff, especially initially, tended to carry out most activities themselves; they rarely contracted out tasks to scientists or consultants, which might have resulted in a natural process of disseminating information about the SP and international developments, while creating allies.

When turning to bilateral activities, one of the key challenges of the SP was that it needed the support of Dutch embassies to be able to implement any bilateral program. After all, SP staff was limited to three persons, each of whom dealt with an entire continent, and they were dependent on embassy staff to initiate activities – be it from the SP budget or other sections. Support was also needed from their colleagues – especially the regional and country desks – at the Ministry in The Hague, to get any activity off the ground. In fact, this meant that many officials needed to be informed about the field of urbanization and urban poverty in the first place, and be convinced of the need for specific, concrete activities.

This was a major challenge, in a ministry that mostly dealt with rural development, agriculture, and water-related activities: It is the well-known story of trying to change the course of a super-tanker. And while all SP staff were thematic experts with an urban background, this did not apply to most other Ministry staff, many of whom were 'generalists'. According to Hoebink (1999, p. 195) many of them have a law or history degree, and only ten percent of Foreign Affairs staff had a specific thematic, development-related expertise. Concretely, the challenge was to include urban issues and policies in the annual country plans, prepared by the embassies and adjusted and approved by The Hague. This proved to be a difficult job, as recognized by the NAR (1994, p. 49). In many countries, aid remained focused on rural development; in others, current activities were categorized under a new heading. Although there were a considerable number of urban projects, it is not so clear how many were aimed at the urban poor. Mention can be made of projects carried out by Dutch institutes such as IHS, IRC and the University of Amsterdam, and small-scale projects implemented by NGOs focusing on the urban poor or strengthening local government.

SP staff then had to work very hard to convince their colleagues about the importance of the urban agenda. To some extent these efforts were successful, for example the posting of four so-called sector (later 'thematic') specialists to Dutch embassies (in Kenya, Peru, Pakistan, and Costa Rica). However, in practice these specialists also had many other duties or were more involved in issues such as small and micro enterprises and the environment, and it does not appear as though they were instrumental in changing attitudes or policies at their embassies. Even though there were (and still are) officials both in The Hague and at the embassies who have sympathy for urban issues, there were not many of these allies. They might also be overruled by their superiors, and even more so by the force of ever-changing development policies designed in The Hague. We will return to these later.

From 1990, SP staff were busy making visits to many countries with a view to identifying and formulating urban projects. Projects were started in Zambia (together with CARE), Ethiopia, and Costa Rica, but these initiatives were short lived. However, two long-term SP projects were implemented: The Bangalore Urban Poverty Alleviation Program (1993-1999), and the Santa Cruz Poverty Alleviation Program (1998-2001). The Bangalore Urban Poverty Alleviation Program (BUPP) was an urban poverty alleviation program applying empowerment approaches as a means to enhance the countervailing and claim making powers of the urban poor. But the programme also aimed to develop and test a model of sustainable, comprehensive urban poverty alleviation, by setting up a new institutional structure (Development Perspectives, 1993). The structure included a Steering Committee, a new Program Support Unit (for day-to-day program management), and new slum organizations (local-level vehicles for identifying and implementing slum activities with related guidelines, procedures and monitoring systems). The programme was successful mostly in its poverty alleviation objective, and in providing concrete physical improvements (Philips et al., 1997). The program was less successful in building sustainable and replicable institutions. But, as was anticipated, many lessons were learnt about the urban poor and poverty reduction strategies. These lessons have been extremely valuable for the Bangalore local government agencies and NGOs, for the Dutch government and its many partners which, one way or another, were involved in the program, and for other donor agencies and academics (de Wit and Krishnamurthy, 2000).

In 1998, an urban poverty alleviation program based on participatory approaches similar to those of BUPP was launched in Santa Cruz de la Sierra, Bolivia. This Dutch funded 'PAP-Santa Cruz' had the same twin objectives as BUPP: Model building and poverty alleviation. Presently available evidence (Wils, 1999) indicates that overall program progress was satisfactory, especially towards the end of the program. The most critical problem faced was the cooperation with the municipality. The municipality was slow in making the agreed funds available, and was not sufficiently active in coordinating the planning and implementation of some larger program activities in several low-income neighborhoods.

What the PAP-Santa Cruz and BUPP had in common is that they were both very participatory programs, with a key role for municipality-NGO-community partnerships. But both programs faced problems in terms of linking to or becoming firmly rooted in local poverty alleviation efforts. One reason may be that local authorities are reluctant to allow or support the type of meaningful participation the Dutch actually envision, which has elements of political empowerment, decentralization, and local-level autonomy for people to decide on funds and projects. While this is fully in line with commendable SP ideas, it could be a bridge too far for local governments in developing countries. Partly for this reason, neither program was entirely successful, and therefore did not serve their anticipated role as effective new models to be replicated elsewhere. It can be argued that the SP took a risk in putting all its eggs in just two baskets, rather than initiating a few more programs.

The Position of the Thematic Program UPA in the Ministry

The SP for Urban Poverty Alleviation had its own budget to fund a variety of activities in the field of urban issues, amounting to NLG 10 million in 1991 and increasing to about NLG 28 million in 1998 (and not, as had been anticipated, already in 1995). However, apart from these specific SP funds, other funds are being spent annually by other departments and directorates on activities linked to urban development and the urban poor, for example by the thematic departments for social welfare or the environment. Precise data are not available, but some have estimated the amounts involved at about NLG 220 million, so that altogether about NLG 250 million annually may have been spent on urban development. A useful Ministry document (MBZ, 1998) lists the many and quite diverse projects being implemented in cities, including for example projects like 'Making Cities safer from Crime', the 'Urban Management Program', and 'the Humanitarian Habitat Aid program' for people in acute crisis conditions. The Ministry supports the Dutch organisations VNG (e.g. city-twinning) and SNV (support to local governments) which carry out urban programs in developing countries, as well as the Dutch co-financing agencies (funding numerous NGOs in the South). Together they spent about NLG 50 million in urban areas (Milbert, 1999, p. 143-5; 1997 data). In 1997, Cordaid spent approximately 23 per cent of its budget in urban areas, Novib 18 per cent, Hivos 16 per cent and ICCO 5 per cent.

It can therefore be said that the Netherlands has an attractive, multifaceted program, in which the initial SP philosophy can be recognized. There is a certain emphasis on marginal groups, a focus on organization and mobilization of the poor and on improving their access to relevant institutions, on capacity building, and on institutional development. However, there are two critical problems. First, total development aid for urban poverty and development is only a very small part of all Dutch development aid funds, in stark contrast to the fact that today half of the world's poor live in cities. Secondly, it is striking that most of these funds are channeled through multilateral agencies, and that not much more money is spent directly by the SP, the Ministry, or through Dutch organizations. Doing so would obviously give a much larger guarantee that Dutch priorities and Dutch development ideals will be reflected and actually achieved. This, of course, would imply an increased Dutch capacity to formulate, implement, and monitor urban programs, but this expertise could have been built up gradually. In fact, this was one of the wishes of many individuals and organizations involved in urban development issues in the Netherlands. They felt, and still feel, that the Netherlands could have its unique approach based on valid, and by now tested, ideas and a relevant philosophy relating to urban issues (Cordaid/de Wit, 2001). They did not agree with the limited mandate given to and funds available from the SP, but would have liked to see the program grow into adulthood as a separate department or directorate , as happened to the SPs

Women & Development, and the Environment. With strong national support and probably the support from other donor agencies, the Dutch could very well have further expanded their own niche, from which to engage in urban development aid. This was exactly what happened in the first few years of the SP, but over time the program lost ground and increasingly found itself marginalized.

Ministry-Wide Policy Reform: Operation *Herijking*

As indicated, the SP gradually expanded, be it slower than expected. Initially, the staff did not always manage to spend all the funds allotted to the program, much to the displeasure of urban-focused Ministry watchers, who did not always feel that the SP strategies were very effective. In 1996, a new SP director took charge, and it obviously took time for him to make his mark on the program, which led to new accents and more delays. The number of staff was increased to four. SP staff was busy initiating new initiatives and creating awareness amongst colleagues, and managing ongoing programs. But the tide was not favorable for them. In fact, all the policy changes taking place at the Ministry since 1995 worked to their disadvantage. It started with the ambitious *Herijking* process (Policy Reform Operation), which aimed at better coordination between the Ministry of Foreign Affairs and that of Development Cooperation. It entailed an internal reorganization of both, and the delegation of development cooperation tasks to Dutch embassies. So while SP staff members were trying to create interest and obtain commitment for the urban agenda and urban issues, the Ministry and embassies were already starting deliberations as to which sectors and thematic areas could be dispensed with in the future.

The decentralization process was a very ambitious policy to delegate most development aid responsibility to program countries. The formulation and implementation of projects and programs became the sole responsibility of the embassies in Dutch Development Cooperation partner countries – within frameworks set by 'The Hague' which retained powers for program approval and program review (Hoebink, 1999, p. 197). This, again, did not create a favorable context for embassies to take on board a new sector or theme; rather, they were worried about their capacity to deal with the quite sudden increase in workload. And by the time the internal ministry reorganization and decentralization had been completed in 1998, a new minister was taking office. This led to important policy changes, which will be elaborated below, but also to seemingly never-ending reorganizations within the Ministry. The Thematic Program for Urban Poverty Alleviation was renamed the Department of Urban Development and Economics (DRU/SE), located in the Directorate of Rural and Urban Development and joined by two economists. This appears to have diluted the specific Dutch urban poverty alleviation policy mission as manifested in the 1994 White Paper. The Bangalore Urban Poverty Alleviation Program was closed in 1999, and the Santa Cruz Urban Poverty Program in 2001.

In recent years, DRU/SE staff appears to have become less visible inside and outside the Ministry, partly as a result of the decentralization operation. The tasks to formulate and implement new projects had now become the responsibility of embassies, effectively reducing many Ministry staff to the position of thematic advisors. The invisibility of urban development related staff led to increasing dissatisfaction amongst individuals and organizations in the Netherlands interested in urban development issues, who witnessed a rapidly increasing, global problem of urbanization and urban poverty. They regretted the lack of leadership of the Ministry in terms of setting an urban agenda, including an urban research agenda with related funds. They would have welcomed Dutch funded urban projects which they could help implement and monitor. Yet the SP and the later renamed urban poverty units were never very forthcoming in this respect, partly as a result of distrust and a perception that these individuals and organizations were driven by a measure of self-interest, partly due to a different vision as to the themes and approaches to apply.

A New Minister: Good Governance and the Sector Approach

Following the 1998 elections, a new government came to power and a new Labor Party minister – Mrs. Herfkens – took charge of the Ministry for Development Cooperation. A former World Bank board director, she indicated her intention to make aid effectiveness and efficiency the key objectives of her policy, while distancing herself from her predecessor (Hoebink, 1999, p. 197). She argued that, from a management point of view, the number of countries receiving Dutch aid had become too large to safeguard the quality of aid provision. But equally important is that the minister is strongly influenced by the World Bank view that aid is especially effective in countries marked by good governance (World Bank, 1998).

Accordingly, in 1998, the number of countries with which a long-term, comprehensive development cooperation relation is maintained was reduced to 21. Selection criteria for this reduction include the extent of poverty, the quality of socio-economic policy, and the quality of governance. Next, in line with her perception that aid efforts should be concentrated, and that the ownership of policy should be increased, the Minister decided to gradually start providing most bilateral aid through 'sector approaches' and to reduce the number of sectors to which aid will be given. Herewith she followed mainstream donor thinking and policy. Sector development programs are steadily gaining importance, partly as a reaction to problems experienced with the formerly dominant project approach.

Early in 1999, the Minister requested the embassies in the 21 core countries to engage in a discussion leading to the choice of up to four sectors per country. In the spirit of ownership, countries themselves were to decide on the sectors to be supported by the Dutch, and the decision-making process was to include civil society and other stakeholders. However, there is reason to believe that this decision-making process was not very thorough. The entire process was marked by considerable haste (it had to be completed in about six months). Concern was expressed as to whether this short period actually allowed for broad-based national consultation on sector choices, and the professed importance of *ownership* – especially of stakeholders like the poor and local governments. And when the embassies did announce their sector choices, it struck many that the sectors chosen were often the same as those where the Dutch had already been most active for many years (Wegelin, *et al.*, 1998). This, of course, is not entirely surprising: A sector choice may well be based on the history of a development relationship in a country, existing expertise, and the experiences of embassies. Hence, the 'established sectors' were often selected: Health, education, rural development, agriculture, and the environment.

Efforts by some urban experts and officials to get urban development recognized as a 'sector' proved unsuccessful. This is surprising and inconsistent in view of the fact that rural development was recognized as a sector, supported in as many as six of the 22 core countries. The Minister takes the position that it is not helpful to contrast urban with rural areas: They go together and are interdependent. Urban development is not seen as a sector, and specific attention will not be paid to it.[3] Sector aid will be provided to villages *and* cities, for example in case of health and education, and, at the same time, there can be support for institutional development, decentraliza-

---

3. It is interesting and ironic to note that the Netherlands itself has a special Minister for Big Cities (*Grote Steden Beleid*), in recognition of the fact that these cities have specific, unique problems which require specific, tailor-made policies and approaches, based on detailed research.

tion, participation, and capacity building for local governance (MBZ, 1999b). Only a few countries chose sectors relevant to the urban agenda; for example local governance in Tanzania and South Africa, and, in principle, participation and decentralization in Bolivia. It may be noted, however, that the Netherlands embassy in La Paz has terminated urban programs, and will focus exclusively on rural areas. This confirms the fear of many that, in theory, villages and cities are to be covered under the sector approach, but that in reality embassies will prefer to work in rural areas, where they have always worked, and have their expertise and networks.

In reaction to questions in parliament about the position of urban issues in the Ministry, the Minister agreed in 1999 to earmark NLG 10 million to be spent on urban development policy through the World Bank. However, this proved to be a one-off shot resulting from pressure, and is not indicative of any long-term policy change. The Minister maintains that no specific provisions will be made for urban development or urban poverty alleviation. This is borne out by recent developments. There has been another Ministry reorganization and the former Urban Poverty Alleviation Thematic Program – under its most recent name DRU/SE – has disappeared. On the positive side, another former SP staff member has been transferred to the Directorate of Environment, where he will be in charge of urban environmental programs in various core and non-core partner countries. This program is likely to grow.

Ministry staff itself argues that the urban agenda within the Ministry has been successfully mainstreamed: They indicate that attention is paid to urban issues across the Ministry, for example, in the Directorates of Social Welfare, Environment and of Good Governance and Human Rights. This is unconvincing. In a way the present situation is merely a return to pre-SP times. In contrast, quite a different situation exists with regard to the former SP Women & Development; it is today a department in the Social Welfare Directorate, charged with mainstreaming gender issues *and* being a nodal expert agency to promote the gender agenda and to develop and implement policy. It is however true – as already indicated – that there has been an increase of funds available for urban issues compared to pre-SP times, but the amount is not at all impressive in terms of the overall aid budget. On the positive side, the need is being perceived in the Ministry for a ministry-wide body to coordinate urban-related activities across departments, and there are plans to establish an Urban Task Force (Habitat Platform, 2001).

There is considerable disappointment, even disillusionment, amongst those groups and individuals endeavoring to get official Ministry recognition for the problems relating to urban poverty and urbanization. There was a sense of satisfaction when the SP was established and there was concern about the difficulties faced by its staff in consolidating – let alone expanding – its position, influence, and support base. There are many urban experts and staff in universities, training institutes, consultancy firms, co-financing agencies, and other NGOs presently missing an institutional location or linkage in the Ministry to address or discuss urban development issues. They continue to stress the urgent need to further mainstream urban development policy, if only as 'the urban' is not a priority sector in any partner country. Besides, they consider it important to reestablish an urban focal point in the Ministry, perceived to be essential for coordinating the efforts aimed at urban development made by Dutch and Southern organizations, as well as local governments, NGOs, and the private sector (Cordaid/Kruijssen, 2001). The arguments of these 'concerned urbanists' may be summarized as follows.

Urbanization is increasing at a rapid pace, and already about 50 per cent of all poor households worldwide live in cities. Many of them live under difficult, sometimes appalling, environmental conditions – often more so than people in rural areas. No organization professing to have poverty alleviation as its key objective can neglect these poor. By neglecting urban issues – quite in contrast to agencies like the British DFID, World Bank, UNDP, and UNCHS – the Netherlands is neglecting the development and maintenance of urban expertise, capacities, and networks of contacts, which it will no doubt sorely need in the very near future. That the Minister is channeling funds to the World Bank does not mean much; they will be hard to monitor, and have no direct consequences for the Netherlands in terms of increased capacity for projects, advisory work, and research. Urbanization is unavoidable; it is the spatial translation of global socio-economic processes of change (Wegelin et al., 1996, World Bank, 1999).

Comparing Dutch aid policy with that of another bilateral donor agency – British DFID – is interesting. The British agency has a large independent urban development aid policy, a small urban development department, and aims at implementing appropriate and innovative approaches. It has an ambitious urban research program, implemented mostly by British institutions, which develop and maintain expertise and relevant capacities (DFID, 2000a). The problems the Ministry has in linking, learning from, and using the research and other expertise of collective Dutch researchers, consultants, and NGOs are not restricted to the urban agenda alone. Hoebink (2001, p. 186) argues that the Ministry lacks expertise in terms of economic and political developments inside countries, the nature and functioning of civil society, and the impacts of interventions. Rather than blindly following multilateral agencies (such as the World Bank), the Ministry should listen to the Dutch academic world much more intensely than it has done so far.

Despite the Minister's reassuring words that sector policies such as health and education will also be implemented in cities, there is concern that embassies will tend to bypass cities, as the aforementioned case of Bolivia seems to indicate. They have little or no experience with working in complex and opaque urban contexts, and the misunderstanding may have taken root that, as urban development is not seen as a sector, no support is needed there. Besides, sector approaches tend to have centralizing tendencies. Central ministries are reluctant to channel donor funds to lower administrative levels which may be at the expense of, and undermine, the autonomy of local government: The key local administrative organization. There is a risk that sector approaches will take the form of a vertical rather than horizontal or integrated planning and implementation strategy, with the danger that the former ideal of decentralized and integrated development may be harder to effect. This is a risk already perceived by and acted upon by Danida (Nielsen, 1999; also Wit, 2000).

Conclusions: The Rise and Fall of a Dutch Urban Poverty Unit

The Netherlands is known as a reliable, committed, and often innovative donor country, spending large amounts on aid for developing and transition countries, with broad support from the Dutch population. There has always been a rural bias in its development cooperation efforts, which can be explained by Dutch history and the importance of agriculture. One could agree that way back in the 1970s and 1980s there was little reason to support urban projects as the world was largely a rural place. It becomes harder to explain why the Netherlands has not become more deeply involved in the urban problems of developing countries and why the Ministry's urban poverty unit withered away over time – one of only two thematic Ministry departments with a single poverty focus?[4] Various reasons have been offered in this article. First, the SP should have been more forceful initially, benefiting from Ministerial support, and utilizing to the extent possible existing Dutch expertise. For various reasons, including a perceived mismatch between SP needs and what Dutch experts could offer, SP staff tended to carry out much of the work themselves. It would have been better had

---

4. The other is the Department of Poverty Analysis and Policy in the Directorate of Social and Institutional Development.

program staff acted faster and made their presence felt by quickly creating a mass in terms of projects, programs, staff, and the like; this appears to have happened in the environmental SP. The Urban Poverty SP seems to have been more careful, deliberate, quality minded, spending much time on a comprehensive White Paper. Its strategies were not always seen as very effective; gradually the SP – and its successive namesakes – became less innovative and outgoing. Of course, there was also a serious capacity problem: There is only so much three persons can do.

The SP did not disappear due to disinterest on the part of the Dutch public or Dutch civil society, or to a lack of urban experts. Rather, it happened despite all that, even if civil society groups were not always united, forceful, or sufficiently active to mobilize political support to exert pressure on successive ministers, and if this support was smaller and less uniform than outside support for the other SPs. There was a ready-made national think-tank of urban experts which should have been mobilized and utilized for capacity building, policy development, and evaluation. Both SP and urban experts should have overcome some of the prevailing mistrust to allow joint action towards the common goal of effective urban poverty alleviation.

Another challenge for the SP was that it was caught up in almost continuous internal Ministry reorganizations. Obviously, the weariness about this in the Ministry was not limited to SP staff. But they were critically dependent on the willingness of other staff to take on a new theme, to get involved in a new and complex policy field, and this failed to happen: There were just not enough allies. So when the embassies were requested to select a limited number of sectors for Dutch support in 1998, it was only to be expected that more recent, weakly consolidated themes such as urban development had less chance to be selected. Now that urban issues will receive no specific policy attention anywhere, there is also no perceived need in the Ministry for urban thematic experts. The urban poverty unit has been dissolved; the few still available urban experts are working with other departments. And it does not help that only few Ministry staff have a developmental background, and that there is a neglect of the Dutch academic expertise outside the Ministry.

The number of Dutch urban experts – never a big crowd – appears to be decreasing, too. The supply is running dry, due to a lack of research, training, advisory, and policy work, or because the experts are turning to other agencies for work, resulting in a disconcerting trend for both Ministry, embassy, and civil society capacity and expertise on urban issues to decline. The experts, trainers, advisors, *and* co-financing agency staff involved in urban issues in developing countries have lost a link with the Ministry, and will not be stimulated, motivated, or paid to work in that field, as should have been the case. It also implies that the specific and very interesting Dutch urban niche slowly taking shape – with key concerns like participation, political empowerment, and income generation – is presently in cold storage.

The disappearance of a specific, urban-focused department within the Ministry will no doubt retrospectively be seen as a missed opportunity. Under present conditions, urban experts and sympathizers outside and inside the Ministry have no choice but to take a pragmatic approach starting from present opportunities. These include the recognition by the present Minister that poverty is the *raison d'être* of his ministry, which leads to the need to keep stressing the growing size but also the specific nature of urban poverty problems. Another opportunity is formed by the policies linked to the sector approach; those aimed at strengthening local governance and decentralization, and good governance issues such as empowerment, accountability, and participation. Also, the urban expert community should play a critical role in disseminating in the Netherlands information from the South on dimensions and developments regarding urban poverty, on strategies that work, and the changing context of urban poverty. Dutch politicians should also be provided with such information, so as to keep up pressure and mobilize support. These various activities should be seen as interim strategies to maintain interest in and, as much as possible, support for the urban poor. It is certain that the time will come when the Netherlands will not be able to avoid becoming officially and directly involved in urban areas, because that is where most of the world's poor will be.

References

Development Perspectives, (1993), *Participatory Urban Poverty Alleviation, a Proposal for a 'Learning by Doing' Program in Bangalore, India*, BUPP Document, Development Perspectives, Arnhem.

DfID (2000a), *Meeting the Challenge of Urban Poverty: Strategies for Achieving the International Development Targets*, Department for International Development, London.

Dijkgraaf, C. and Wit, J. de (1995), 'Participatory Approach to Urban Poverty Alleviation in Bangalore', in K. Singh and F. Steinberg (eds), *Urban India in Crisis*, pp. 219-33, New Age Publishers/HSMI, New Delhi.

Cordaid/Kruijssen, H. (2001), *Stedelijke Leefbaarheid: Absolute Voorwaarde voor Terugdringen van Armoede* (Speech Cordaid Director for a Cordaid debate on January 18).

Cordaid/de Wit, J. (2001) *Manifest voor een effectief Stedelijk Armoedebeleid*, Cordaid, Den Haag, mmv. M. Wilmink.

Goede, K. de (1994), 'Stedelijke Armoedebestrijding: Beleid Bekeken', *Derde Wereld*, Vol. 13(3), pp. 4-9.

Habitat Platform/Habitat Advies en Research Platform HARP (1998), *De Theorie en Praktijk van Concentratiesteden; een Onderzoek naar de Benadering van de Concentratiestad en de Vertaling ervan in Beleid*, Habitat Platform, Den Haag.

Habitat Platform (2001), *Proceedings and Recommendations of a Clingendael Conference on Habitat and Development Cooperation*, 17 April, Habitat Platform, Den Haag.

Hoebink, P. (1999), 'The Humanitarianisation of the Foreign Aid Program in the Netherlands', *The European Journal of Development Research*, Vol. 11: 176-202.

Hoebink, P. (2001), 'Good Governance als Voorwaarde en Doel bij enkele Europese Donoren', in *Ontwikkelingsbeleid en Goed Bestuur*, Rapporten aan de Regering, Wetenschappelijke Raad voor het Regeringsbeleid, SDU, Den Haag, pp. 163-205.

Ministerie van Buitenlandse Zaken (MBZ) (1990), *Een Wereld van Verschil: Nieuwe Kaders voor Ontwikkelingssamenwerking in de Jaren Negentig*, Tweede Kamer,No. 21813, SDU: Den Haag.

Ministerie van Buitenlandse Zaken (MBZ) (1994), *Stedelijke Armoedebestrijding*, Sector- en Themabeleidsdocumenten van Ontwikkelingssamenwerking, No. 5, Voorlichtingsdienst Ministerie van Buitenlandse Zaken, Den Haag.

Ministerie van Buitenlandse Zaken (MBZ) (1998), *Habitat, Wonen en Leven in de Stad*, Ministerie van Buitenlandse Zaken, DRU/SE, Den Haag.

Ministerie van Buitenlandse Zaken (MBZ) (1999b), *Verslag Bijeenkomst Stedelijke Ontwikkeling 31 Maart 1999*, DVL/OS, Den Haag.

Ministerie van Buitenlandse Zaken (MBZ) (2000), *De Sectorale Benadering*, Steungroep Sectorale Benadering, Den Haag.

Moser, C. and Holland, J. (1997), *Household Responses to Poverty and Vulnerability*, Urban Management Program Policy Paper, No. 24, World Bank, Washington.

Nationale Advies Raad voor Ontwikkelingssamenwerking (NAR) (1994), *Advies Ontwikkelingssamenwerking en Stedelijke Armoedebestrijding*, Ministerie van Buitenlandse Zaken, Den Haag.

Milbert, I., (1999), *What Future for Urban Development Cooperation? Assessment of Post Habitat-II Strategies*, Graduate Institute of Development Studies IUED, Geneva.

Nielsen, H. (1999), *Sector Program Support in Decentralized Government Systems- A Contextual Donor Challenge*, Danida Discussion Papers, No. 2, Danida, Copenhagen.

Oosterhout, Fon van (1996), 'De Uitdaging van Stedelijk Beheer in de Derde Wereld', *Derde Wereld*, Vol. 15(2), 199-210.

Phillips, Sue and Slater, R. (1997), *Bangalore Urban Poverty Project: Review Mission Report*, Draft Report, London.

UNCHS/HABITAT (1994), *An Urbanising World; Global Report on Human Settlements 1996*, Oxford University Press, Oxford.

UNDP (1991), *Cities, People and Poverty; Urban Development Cooperation in the 1990s*, UNDP, New York.

Wegelin, E., Wils, F. and Wit, J. de (1996), *Nederland moet Explosief Groeiende Stedelijke Armoede Bestrijden*, 1 December 1998, Dagblad Trouw.

Wils, F. et al. (1999), *Programa de Alivio a la Probreza en St. Cruz de la Sierra: Informe de Mision de Seguimiento*. Review Mission Report. Institute of Social Sciences, ISS, Den Haag.

Wils, F. and Helmsing, A.H.J. (1998), *Shadow on the Ground: The Practical Effectiveness of the Community Development Program*.

Wit, J. de and Krishnamurthy, A.N. (2000), *Lessons from the Bangalore Poverty Alleviation Program Relevant to the Bangladesh SINPA Program*, SINPA Research Reports Series, Institute for Housing and Urban Development Studies, Rotterdam.

Wit, J. de (2000), *Towards Good Governance at the Local Level: the Role of Grassroots Institutions*, ISS Working Papers, No. 325, Institute of Social Studies, The Hague.

World Bank (1991), *Urban Policy and Economic Development, An Agenda for the 1990s, a World Bank Policy Paper*, World Bank, Washington DC.

World Bank (1998), *Assessing Aid: What Works, What Doesn't and Why*, Draft Discussion Report, Policy Research Department, World Bank, Washington.

World Bank (1999), *Cities in Transition: A Strategic View of Urban and Local Government Issues*, World Bank/IBRD, Washington.

Index

accountability 158, 186, 191–192, 202, 373, 386–389, 391
Accra 142–144, 225–227, 237–239, 267, 276
affordability 227–229, 234–235, 356, 360
aid agencies 19, 217, 387, 402
alliances 170, 217, 238, 322
Argentina 82–83, 85, 90, 99–100, 334, 340
assets 4, 29, 55, 166, 172–173, 204, 213, 366–370

Bamako 267, 270–271
Bangalore 123–126, 130–135, 405, 409–410, 413, 419–421
Benin 250–255, 264, 266, 285
Bolivia 157–173, 179–187, 192–196, 324, 339
Brazil 142, 152, 187–196
brown agenda 222
budgeting, participatory 187–194
Burkina Faso 270–271, 276–279, 282–283
business associations 53, 69, 72, 80, 86, 90–94

capacity-building 377
capital, financial 32, 199, 202, 211, 214, 245, 251–259
Chennai 232–238
Chile 82–84, 90–92, 177
China 52, 317
city-hinterland 119, 314, 316–317
civil society 4, 9, 18, 146–147, 149–154, 160–164, 168, 414
cluster 32, 38, 52–59, 63–74, 87–89, 93, 95–96
clusters, survival 64–66, 74
collective action 11, 200, 206–209, 215, 217, 257
collective efficiency 70, 76–77
collective learning 51, 88, 93–96
Colombia 82–85, 88, 90–92, 178
community participation 140–142, 177, 237, 408
community-based organizations (CBOs) 10, 146, 206
connectivity 26, 290
Cordoba 82–83, 85–86, 89–90, 94, 98
Cotonou 252–255, 263

Dakar 267, 274, 276, 297
decentralisation 181, 196, 239
deconcentration 176–177, 329

delegation 176–177, 192, 412
democracy 160, 172, 181, 192–193
desakota 8, 21, 121–122, 135
development cooperation 308–309, 385, 403–419
devolution 176, 192

ecological footprint 15, 293, 316–317
ecological sustainability 222–223, 227, 233, 313–314, 316, 319, 325
economic networks 50–51, 287–288, 305–308
El Alto 161, 164–166, 168–171
empowerment 10, 141, 154, 157–158, 386
enablement 10, 200
entitlements 18, 384
environmental health 11, 148, 223, 225, 231, 237–239, 319, 359–360, 384
environmental impact 314, 321, 326
environmental management 152, 203–205, 210–213, 215–217, 326

footloose 56, 290, 292
Fordism 2, 32
foreign direct investment (FDI) 55, 313

gender 101–104, 113–117, 367, 415
Ghana 222, 266–267, 278, 299
global cities 6
globalization 247, 350
glocalisation 22
governance 1–4, 27–28, 34–35, 54, 188–189, 192–193, 201, 213–214, 307, 321–323, 325–326
governance, good 3, 27, 158, 193, 325, 378, 407–408, 413
governance, local 9, 95, 188, 192–193
grassroots organizations 112, 115–116
growth pole 37–38, 99

Habitat 188, 192, 288, 352, 405–407
Hanoi 119–120, 122, 126–136
healthy cities 139–154
Healthy Cities Program 142–143, 145, 150
hub-and-spoke district 68, 72, 74

India 72, 120, 122, 130, 132, 232–233, 321, 325
industrial district 32, 38, 51, 63–64, 67–68, 70,

73–77
informal sector 65, 101–102, 272, 295, 298, 352–354, 369
innovative milieu 84, 88–89, 96–97
inter-firm cooperation 80, 86, 90, 95
Italianate district 68, 74
Ivory Coast 266–267, 276, 278

Kenya 266–267, 297–298, 300–301, 409

Lagos 255, 265, 267, 358
learning 27, 34, 38, 50–51, 54–55, 88–89, 93, 95–99, 215
learning, organizational 95–96, 98
legitimacy 3, 201, 214, 224, 229, 236
liberalization 50–51, 73, 145, 282–283, 302, 350
Lima 101–108, 110–118, 197–213, 216–218, 342, 358
link 343
linkages 30, 45–46, 55–59, 67, 93, 208–209, 243–244, 248, 272, 287, 307, 320–321, 323, 343
livelihood 14–15, 17–18, 199–200, 243–249, 251, 262, 272, 336–337
localization 350

Madras 71, 233
  (see also Chennai)
Malaysia 56–57
Managua 12, 143, 145, 149–151, 155
Medellin 82–86, 89, 94, 96, 98
meso-institutions 8, 79, 85–87, 96–97
Mexico 58, 72, 80, 82–84, 88, 91, 178, 340
micro-enterprise 88–90, 92–93, 102, 111
micro-production 101–103, 114–117
monitoring 189, 224, 231, 236–237, 321–322, 339, 341, 409
Mossi 276

Nairobi 66, 267, 274, 284, 300, 358
neo-classical 27–28, 37–39, 44–45, 58, 79, 290
neo-liberalism 2, 177
networks, economic 49–51, 287–288, 290–292, 305–308
New Competition 73, 75, 94
Nicaragua 149–151, 177–178, 385
Nigeria 255, 265–267, 296, 298

Ouagadougou 265–267, 270, 274, 276–283
ownership 12, 141, 149–151, 153, 192, 194, 414

participation 3, 10–12, 110, 112, 115–116, 140–144, 148–149, 151–154, 157–163, 165–167, 171, 175–183, 186–190, 192–195, 206–207, 214, 219–221, 237, 339, 354–355, 361, 408, 410, 419
partnerships 7–11, 13, 18, 51, 58–59, 79, 81, 90–92, 141, 157–159, 162–163, 172–173, 198, 201–203, 214–217, 219–222, 225, 232–234, 236–238, 326, 369, 410
Peru 13, 21, 42, 52, 82–85, 99, 109, 117–118, 177–178, 203, 208–209, 216–217, 325, 340, 409
place 5–6, 14–15, 29, 43, 90, 140, 272, 287–288, 290, 293, 304, 307, 330, 334–338
popular participation 3, 12, 157, 159, 161–163, 171, 175–181, 183, 187–190, 192–193, 195, 221, 339
Porto Alegre 175, 177, 187–196
poverty 4, 9–10, 17–20, 22, 60, 64–66, 88, 91, 103, 108, 118, 145, 151, 157–161, 163–164, 198, 200, 217, 271, 347, 349–355, 366–370, 373–376, 378–379, 381, 383–387, 390, 392–411, 413–421
poverty alleviation 17, 19–20, 66, 157, 159, 163, 183, 367, 403, 406, 409–410, 413, 415–416, 418–419, 421
principal 26, 35, 39, 50, 88, 202, 207, 216, 332
private sector 6–8, 58, 81, 92, 96, 163, 176, 198, 200–201, 219–220, 223, 227–229, 323, 330, 357, 361, 363, 369
production structure 26
proximity 15, 37–38, 125, 290, 292, 300–302, 307, 362
public good 224
public health 140–141, 226, 282, 359–360, 364

Rafaela 82–83, 85–87, 89, 94, 98–99
recycling 223, 227, 232, 234, 238, 326, 358–359
regional development 3, 5–6, 9, 14–15, 17, 25, 27–28, 32, 39, 43, 55, 79–82, 85, 90–91, 93, 96–97, 122, 131, 134, 257, 306–307, 329–330, 332, 352
responsiveness 49, 95, 196, 367
rural-urban linkages 14–16, 287–288, 290, 292–293, 305–308, 310, 312, 343–345

Sahel 243–244, 250, 264, 270, 295
sanitation 148, 163, 191, 314, 322, 350, 356, 358, 360, 364–365, 384, 391, 393–394, 396–397, 399–401
Santa Cruz 194, 409–410, 413
Santiago 83, 99–100, 118
satellite district 7, 68, 70, 74
sector approach 20, 404, 413, 415, 419

Sialkot 68–69
Sinos valley 52, 60, 72
slum 19, 33, 135, 232, 352, 360, 365–366, 393, 395, 405, 409
social exclusion 2, 18–19, 21, 177, 337, 342–343, 351, 366–370
solid waste management 13–14, 16, 135, 144, 210, 217, 219, 221–222, 234, 238–239, 314, 321, 326–327, 358
space 5, 15, 17, 32–33, 37, 39, 45, 82, 128, 243–244, 278, 290–291, 293, 315, 324–326, 329–332, 334–339, 342–345
space of flows 244, 330, 335
Spearhead Program 403, 406
state, role of the 9, 58, 67, 200
structural adjustment 2, 145, 155, 177, 246, 273, 290, 311, 313, 330, 353
subcontracting 8, 39, 111, 113, 115, 117
sub-Saharan Africa 15–16, 271, 284, 288, 296–297, 299, 301, 304–306, 309
Surat Thani 53–54, 59
sustainable development 13, 16–17, 219, 221–223, 225, 238, 246, 314–315, 327, 331, 338, 342–343
sustainable livelihood 15, 17, 21, 264, 345
synergy 21–22, 217, 219–220, 239

Tanzania 143, 145–146, 155, 266–267, 271, 297–298, 301, 303, 309–311, 415
Togo 251, 255, 266, 276
training 19, 58, 85–86, 89–90, 92, 95–96, 113, 173, 182, 187, 233, 235, 305, 355, 357, 360, 392
trajectories 7, 49, 63–64, 67–68, 74–75, 244, 284
transfer mechanisms 317, 324
transition to sustainability 315, 325, 328
transnational corporations (TNCs) 1
transparency 3, 175, 191–192, 260, 378, 381, 387–388, 390–391, 399–400
trust 7, 11, 30–32, 47–49, 54, 158, 202, 215, 220, 243, 249, 257–260, 262

transportation 19, 180, 227, 229, 231–232, 234–235, 237–238, 251, 253, 321 326, 362

UNDP 21, 142–146, 155, 290, 294, 312, 351–352, 370, 407–408, 416, 420
urban development 9–11, 19, 123, 142, 152, 158, 179, 200, 205, 207, 210, 238, 270, 292, 396–400
urban fringe 8–9, 119–121, 123, 128, 131, 134, 276, 278
urban management 9–11, 142, 152–153, 219, 351–352, 394, 408, 411
urban market 253, 279
urban poverty 9, 17, 19–20, 157, 159, 163, 349, 351–352, 369–370, 373, 375, 381, 383–385, 392–393, 395–400, 403–411, 413–415, 417–420
urbanization 120–121, 128, 142, 159, 265–267, 269–271, 331–332, 336–339, 343, 349–350, 369, 403–406
Uruguay 59, 80, 178, 334, 340

Vietnam 9, 122, 126–128, 133–136
vulnerability 19, 22, 88, 157, 174, 198, 217, 351, 355, 366–370, 420

water 120–121, 144–145, 148–149, 163, 165, 169, 197–199, 204–207, 211, 225–226, 245, 273–276, 282–283, 299, 313–314, 316, 319–324, 326–327, 356–358, 360, 364–365, 376, 378, 384–387, 391, 396–400, 408
white Paper 406–407, 413, 418
World Bank 2, 18, 146, 157–158, 160, 192, 257, 265–266, 288, 299, 304, 325, 349–352, 370, 373, 375–377, 379, 391, 393–399, 407–408, 413, 415–417

Zimbabwe 266–267, 295, 300, 310–311, 388